Experiment Central

Understanding Scientific Principles Through Projects

Experiment Central

Understanding Scientific Principles Through Projects

Second Edition

VOLUME 2: CO-E

M. Rae Nelson

Kristine Krapp, editor

U·X·L

A part of Gale, Cengage Learning

Detroit • New York • San Francisco • New Haven, Conn • Waterville, Maine • London

Experiment Central
Understanding Scientific Principles Through Projects
Second Edition
M. Rae Nelson

Project Editor: Kristine Krapp

Managing Editor: Debra Kirby

Rights Acquisition and Management: Margaret Abendroth, Robyn Young

Composition: Evi Abou-El-Seoud, Mary Beth Trimper

Manufacturing: Wendy Blurton

Product Manager: Julia Furtaw

Product Design: Jennifer Wahi

Cover photographs: Images courtesy of Dreamstime, Photos.com, and iStockPhoto.

Library of Congress Cataloging-in-Publication Data

Experiment central : understanding scientific principles through projects. -- 2nd ed. / M. Rae Nelson, Kristine Krapp, editors. p. cm. --
Includes bibliographical references and index.
ISBN 978-1-4144-7613-1 (set) -- ISBN 978-1-4144-7614-8 (vol. 1) -- ISBN 978-1-4144-7615-5 (vol. 2) -- ISBN 978-1-4144-7616-2 (vol. 3) -- ISBN 978-1-4144-7617-9 (vol. 4) -- ISBN 978-1-4144-7618-6 (vol. 5) -- ISBN 978-1-4144-7619-3 (vol. 6)
1. Science--Experiments--Juvenile literature. I. Nelson, M. Rae. II. Krapp, Kristine M.

Q164.E96 2010
507.8--dc22 2009050304

Gale
27500 Drake Rd.
Farmington Hills, MI, 48331-3535

978-1-4144-7613-1 (set) 1-4144-7613-2 (set)
978-1-4144-7614-8 (vol. 1) 1-4144-7614-0 (vol. 1)
978-1-4144-7615-5 (vol. 2) 1-4144-7615-9 (vol. 2)
978-1-4144-7616-2 (vol. 3) 1-4144-7616-7 (vol. 3)
978-1-4144-7617-9 (vol. 4) 1-4144-7617-5 (vol. 4)
978-1-4144-7618-6 (vol. 5) 1-4144-7618-3 (vol. 5)
978-1-4144-7619-3 (vol. 6) 1-4144-7619-1 (vol. 6)

This title is also available as an e-book.
ISBN-13: 978-1-4144-7620-9 (set)
ISBN-10: 1-4144-7620-5 (set)
Contact your Gale sales representative for ordering information.

Printed by China Translation & Printing Services Limited, Guangdong Province, China. 1st printing. 05/2010
1 2 3 4 5 6 7 14 13 12 11 10

Table of Contents

VOLUME 1: A-CH

Reader's Guide **xxi**

Parent's and Teacher's Guide **xxv**

Experiments by Scientific Field **xxvii**

Words to Know **xxxix**

1. Acid Rain **1**

Acid Rain and Animals: How does acid rain affect brine shrimp? **5**

Acid Rain and Plants: How does acid rain affect plant growth? **9**

Acid Rain: Can acid rain harm structures? **12**

2. Adhesives **19**

Material Adhesion: How do various glues adhere to different materials? **22**

Adhesives in the Environment: Will different environmental conditions affect the properties of different adhesives? **26**

3. Air **33**

Air Density: Does warm air take up less room than cool air? **36**

Convection Currents: How can rising air cause weather changes? **39**

4. Air and Water Pollution **45**

Pollutant Bioindicators: Can lichens provide clues to an area's air pollution? **51**

Eutrophication: The effect of phosphates on water plants. **55**

5. Animal Defenses **61**

Camouflage: Does an animal's living environment relate to the color of the animal life? **63**

Ladybug Threats: How do ladybugs defend themselves when they feel threatened? **65**

6. Annual Growth **71**

Tree Growth: What can be learned from the growth patterns of trees? **74**

Lichen Growth: What can be learned from the environment by observing lichens? **79**

7. Bacteria **85**

Bacterial Growth: How do certain substances inhibit or promote bacterial growth? **90**

Bacterial Resistance: Can bacteria gain resistance to a substance after exposure? **95**

8. Biomes **103**

Building a Temperate Forest Biome **107**

Building a Desert Biome **108**

9. Bones and Muscles **113**

Bone Loss: How does the loss of calcium affect bone strength? **116**

Muscles: How does the strength of muscles affect fatigue over time? **120**

10. Caves **127**

Cave Formation: How does the acidity of a substance affect the formation of a cave? **132**

Cave Icicles: How does the mineral content of water affect the formation of stalactites and stalagmites? **135**

11. Cells **141**

Investigating Cells: What are the differences between a multicellular organism and a unicellular organism? **144**

Plant Cells: What are the cell differences between monocot and dicot plants? **145**

Yeast Cells: How do they reproduce? **147**

12. Chemical Energy **151**

Rusting: Is the chemical reaction exothermic, endothermic, or neither? **152**

Exothermic or Endothermic: Determining whether various chemical reactions are exothermic or endothermic **156**

13. Chemical Properties **163**

Slime: What happens when white glue and borax mix? **167**

Chemical Reactions: What happens when mineral oil, water, and iodine mix? **170**

Chemical Patination: Producing chemical reactions on metal **173**

14. Chemosenses **177**

Supertasters: Is there a correlation between the number of taste buds and taste perception? **180**

Smell and Taste: How does smell affect the sense of taste? **186**

15. Chlorophyll **191**

Plant Pigments: Can pigments be separated? **193**

Response to Light: Do plants grow differently in different colors of light? **197**

Budget Index **lxxxv**

Level of Difficulty Index **xcvii**

Timetable Index **cix**

General Subject Index **cxxi**

VOLUME 2: CO-E

Reader's Guide **xxi**

Parent's and Teacher's Guide **xxv**

Experiments by Scientific Field **xxvii**

Words to Know **xxxix**

16. Color **203**

Color and Flavor: How much does color affect flavor perception? **207**

Temperature and Color: What color has the highest temperature? **210**

17. Comets and Meteors **215**

Comet Nucleus: Linking a Comet's Composition to its Properties. **218**

Meteor Impact: How do the characteristics of a meteorite and its impact affect the shape of the crater? **221**

18. Composting/Landfills **229**

Living Landfill: What effect do the microorganisms in soil have on the decomposition process? **232**

Composting: Using organic material to grow plants **235**

19. Crystals **243**

Crystal Structure: Will varying shape crystals form from varying substances? **246**

Cool Crystals: How does the effect of cooling impact crystal growth? **250**

20. Density and Buoyancy **257**

Density: Can a scale of relative density predict whether one material floats on another? **260**

Buoyancy: Does water pressure affect buoyancy? **264**

21. Dissolved Oxygen **271**

Decay and Dissolved Oxygen: How does the amount of decaying matter affect the level of dissolved oxygen in water? **274**

Goldfish Breath: How does a decrease in the dissolved oxygen level affect the breathing rate of goldfish? **279**

22. DNA (Deoxyribonucleic Acid) **285**

The Stuff of Life: Isolating DNA **289**

Comparing DNA: Does the DNA from different species have the same appearance? **291**

23. Dyes **299**

Applying Dyes: How does the fiber affect the dye color? **301**

Holding the Dye: How do dye fixatives affect the colorfastness of the dye? **304**

24. Earthquakes **311**

Detecting an Earthquake: How can movement of Earth's crust be measured? **314**

Earthquake Simulation: Is the destruction greater at the epicenter? **317**

25. Eclipses **325**

Simulating Solar and Lunar Eclipses **327**

Phases of the Moon: What does each phase look like? **329**

26. Electricity **333**

Electrolytes: Do some solutions conduct electricity better than others? **335**

Batteries: Can a series of homemade electric cells form a "pile" strong enough to match the voltage of a D-cell battery? **340**

Electroplating: Using electricity to move one metal onto another metal **344**

27. Electromagnetism **349**

Magnetism: How can a magnetic field be created and detected? **351**

Electromagnetism: How can an electromagnet be created? **354**

28. Enzymes **359**

Finding the Enzyme: Which enzyme breaks down hydrogen peroxide? **362**

Tough and Tender: Does papain speed up the aging process? **365**

Stopping Enzymes: Does temperature affect enzyme action? **368**

29. Erosion **375**

Erosion: Does soil type affect the amount of water that runs off a hillside? **377**

Plants and Erosion: How do plants affect the rate of soil erosion? **381**

30. Ethnobotany **389**

Plants and Health: Which plants have anti-bacterial properties? **392**

Coiling Reeds: How does the tightness of the coil affect the ability to hold materials? **396**

Budget Index **lxxxv**

Level of Difficulty Index **xcvii**

Timetable Index **cix**

General Subject Index **cxxi**

VOLUME 3: F-K

Reader's Guide **xxi**

Parent's and Teacher's Guide **xxv**

Experiments by Scientific Field **xxvii**

Words to Know **xxxix**

31. Fish **401**

Fish Breathing: How do different fish take in oxygen? **404**

Fish Movement: How do fins and body shape affect the movement of fish? **407**

32. Flight **413**

Lift-Off: How can a glider be made to fly higher? **415**

Helicopters, Propellers, and Centripetal Force: Will it fly high? **418**

33. Flowers **423**

Self versus Cross: Will there be a difference in reproduction between self-pollinated and cross-pollinated plants of the same type? **427**

Sweet Sight: Can changing a flower's nectar and color affect the pollinators lured to the flower? **431**

34. Fluids **439**

Viscosity: How can temperature affect the viscosity of liquids? **441**

Spinning Fluids: How do different fluids behave when immersed in a spinning rod? **444**

35. Food Preservation **451**

Sweet Preservatives: How does sugar affect the preservation of fruit? **454**

Drying Foods: Does drying fruits help prevent or delay spoilage? **458**

36. Food Science **463**

Jelly and Pectin: How does acidity affect how fruit gels? **467**

Rising Foods: How much carbon dioxide do different leavening agents produce? **470**

37. Food Spoilage **477**

Preservatives: How do different substances affect the growth of mold? **481**

Spoiled Milk: How do different temperatures of liquid affect its rate of spoilage? **485**

38. Forces **491**

Newton's Laws in Action: How do water bottle rockets demonstrate Newton's laws of motion? **493**

Centripetal Action: What is the relationship between distance and force in circular motion? **501**

39. Forensic Science **507**

Fiber Evidence: How can scientific techniques be used to identify fiber? **511**

Blood Patterns: How can a blood spatter help recreate the crime? **515**

40. Fossils **521**

Making an Impression: In which soil environment does a fossil most easily form? **526**

Fossil Formation: What are the physical characteristics of an organism that make the best fossils? **530**

41. Fungi **537**

Decomposers: Food source for a common fungi **541**

Living Conditions: What is the ideal temperature for yeast growth? **544**

42. Genetics **553**

Genetic Traits: Will you share certain genetic traits more with family members than non-family members? **556**

Building a Pedigree for Taste **559**

43. Germination **565**

Effects of Temperature on Germination: What temperatures encourage and discourage germination? **566**

Comparing Germination Times: How fast can seeds grow? **570**

Seed Scarification: Does breaking the seed shell affect germination time? **573**

44. Gravity **579**

Gravity: How fast do different objects fall? **581**

Measuring Mass: How can a balance be made? **585**

45. Greenhouse Effect **589**

Creating a Greenhouse: How much will the temperature rise inside a greenhouse? **592**

Fossil Fuels: What happens when fossil fuels burn? **596**

46. Groundwater Aquifers **601**

Aquifers: How do they become polluted? **605**

Groundwater: How can it be cleaned? **609**

47. Heat **615**

Conduction: Which solid materials are the best conductors of heat? **618**

Convection: How does heat move through liquids? **622**

Heat Capacity: Which liquids have the highest heat capacity? **625**

48. Insects **631**

Ant Food: What type of foods is one type of ant attracted to? **635**

Lightning Bugs: How does the environment affect a firefly's flash? **638**

Budget Index **lxxxv**

Level of Difficulty Index **xcvii**

Timetable Index **cix**

General Subject Index **cxxi**

VOLUME 4: L-PH

Reader's Guide **xxi**

Parent's and Teacher's Guide **xxv**

Experiments by Scientific Field **xxvii**

Words to Know **xxxix**

49. Life Cycles **645**

Tadpoles: Does temperature affect the rate at which tadpoles change into frogs? **647**

Insects: How does food supply affect the growth rate of grasshoppers or crickets? **651**

50. Light Properties **659**

Looking for the Glow: Which objects glow under black light? **661**

Refraction and Defraction: Making a rainbow **664**

Refraction: How does the material affect how light travels? **666**

51. Magnetism **671**

Magnets: How do heat, cold, jarring, and rubbing affect the magnetism of a nail? **674**

Electromagnets: Does the strength of an electromagnet increase with greater current? **678**

52. Materials Science **685**

Testing Tape: Finding the properties that allow tape to support weight. **688**

Developing Renewables: Can a renewable packing material have the same qualities as a non-renewable material? **691**

53. Memory **697**

Memory Mnemonics: What techniques help in memory retention? **701**

False Memories: How can memories be influenced? **705**

54. Microorganisms **711**

Microorganisms: What is the best way to grow penicillin? **713**

Growing Microorganisms in a Petri Dish **716**

55. Mixtures and Solutions **723**

Suspensions and Solutions: Can filtration and evaporation determine whether mixtures are suspensions or solutions? **725**

Colloids: Can colloids be distinguished from suspension using the Tyndall effect? **730**

56. Mountains **735**

Mountain Plates: How does the movement of Earth's plates determine the formation of a mountain? **738**

Mountain Formations: How does the height of the mountain have an affect on desert formation? **741**

57. Nanotechnology **747**

Nanosize: How can the physical size affect a material's properties? **750**

Nanosize Substances: How can the physical size affect the rate of reaction? **753**

58. Nutrition **759**

Energizing Foods: Which foods contain carbohydrates and fats? **761**

Nutrition: Which foods contain proteins and salts? **764**

Daily Nutrition: How nutritious is my diet? **766**

59. Oceans **771**

Stratification: How does the salinity in ocean water cause it to form layers? **775**

Currents: Water behavior in density-driven currents **780**

60. Optics and Optical Illusions **787**

Optics: What is the focal length of a lens? **788**

Optical Illusions: Can the eye be fooled? **791**

61. Osmosis and Diffusion **797**

Measuring Membranes: Is a plastic bag a semipermeable membrane? **798**

Changing Concentrations: Will a bag of salt water draw in fresh water? **803**

Changing Sizes: What effect does molecule size have on osmosis **806**

62. Oxidation-Reduction **811**

Reduction: How will acid affect dirty pennies? **813**

Oxidation and Rust: How is rust produced? **817**

Oxidation Reaction: Can acid change the color of copper? **820**

63. Periodic Table **827**

Metals versus Nonmetals: Which areas of the periodic table have elements that conduct electricity? **830**

Soluble Families: How does the solubility of an element relate to where it is located on the periodic table? **835**

Active Metals: What metals give off electrons more readily than others? **838**

64. Pesticides **843**

Natural versus Synthetic: How do different types of pesticides compare against a pest? **848**

Moving through Water: How can pesticides affect nontarget plant life? **852**

65. pH **859**

Kitchen Chemistry: What is the pH of household chemicals? **861**

Chemical Titration: What is required to change a substance from an acid or a base into a neutral solution? **865**

66. Photosynthesis **871**

Photosynthesis: How does light affect plant growth? **873**

Light Intensity: How does the intensity of light affect plant growth? **877**

Budget Index **lxxxv**

Level of Difficulty Index **xcvii**

Timetable Index **cix**

General Subject Index **cxxi**

VOLUME 5: PL-SO

Reader's Guide **xxi**

Parent's and Teacher's Guide **xxv**

Experiments by Scientific Field **xxvii**

Words to Know **xxxix**

67. Plant Anatomy **883**
    - Plant Hormones: What is the affect of hormones on root and stem growth? **886**
    - Water Uptake: How do different plants differ in their water needs? **890**

68. Plants and Water **897**
    - Water Flow: How do varying solutions of water affect the amount of water a plant takes in and its turgor pressure? **900**
    - Transpiration: How do different environmental conditions affect plants' rates of transpiration? **904**

69. Polymers **911**
    - Polymer Strength: What are the tensile properties of certain polymers that make them more durable than others? **914**
    - Polymer Slime: How will adding more of a polymer change the properties of a polymer "slime"? **919**
    - Polymer Properties: How are the properties of hard plastics different? **923**

70. Potential and Kinetic Energy **929**
    - Measuring Energy: How does the height of an object affect its potential energy? **931**
    - Using Energy: Build a roller coaster **934**

71. Renewable Energy **941**
    - Capturing Wind Energy: How does the material affect the amount of wind energy harnessed? **944**
    - Hydropower: How does water pressure affect water energy? **948**

72. Rivers **955**

Weathering Erosion in Glaciers: How does a river make a trench? **957**

Stream Flow: Does the stream meander? **960**

River Flow: How does the steepness and rate of water flow affect river erosion? **962**

73. Rocks and Minerals **969**

Mineral Testing: What kind of mineral is it? **971**

Rock Classification: Is it igneous, sedimentary, or metamorphic? **975**

74. Rotation and Orbits **981**

Foucault Pendulum: How can a pendulum demonstrate the rotation of Earth? **985**

Spinning Effects: How does the speed of a rotating object affect the way centrifugal force can overcome gravity? **989**

75. Salinity **995**

Making a Hydrometer: How can salinity be measured? **997**

Density Ball: How to make a standard for measuring density **1000**

76. Scientific Method **1005**

Using the Scientific Method: What are the mystery powders? **1009**

Using the Scientific Method: Do fruit flies appear out of thin air? **1013**

77. Seashells **1019**

Shell Strength: Which shell is stronger: a clam shell or lobster shell? **1022**

Classifying Seashells **1025**

78. Separation and Identification **1031**

Chromatography: Can you identify a pen from the way its colors separate? **1034**

Identifying a Mixture: How can determining basic properties of a substance allow you to identify the substances in a mixture? **1039**

79. Simple Machines **1047**

Wheel and Axle: How can changing the size of the wheel affect the amount of work it takes to lift a load? **1051**

Lever Lifting: How does the distance from the fulcrum affect work? **1055**

The Screw: How does the distance between the threads of a screw affect the work? **1057**

80. Soil **1063**

Soil Profile: What are the different properties of the soil horizons? **1067**

Soil pH: Does the pH of soil affect plant growth? **1074**

81. Solar Energy **1081**

Capturing Solar Energy: Will seedlings grow bigger in a greenhouse? **1084**

Solar Cells: Will sunlight make a motor run? **1087**

Retaining the Sun's heat: What substance best stores heat for a solar system? **1090**

82. Sound **1095**

Wave Length: How does the length of a vibrating string affect the sound it produces? **1096**

Pitch: How does the thickness of a vibrating string affect sound? **1099**

Soundproofing: How do different materials affect sound? **1102**

Budget Index **lxxxv**

Level of Difficulty Index **xcvii**

Timetable Index **cix**

General Subject Index **cxxi**

VOLUME 6: SP-Z

Reader's Guide **xxi**

Parent's and Teacher's Guide **xxv**

Experiments by Scientific Field **xxvii**

Words to Know **xxxix**

83. Space Observation **1109**

Telescopes: How do different combinations of lenses affect the image? **1113**

Doppler Effect: How can waves measure the distance and speed of objects? **1118**

84. Stars **1123**

Tracking Stars: Where is Polaris? **1125**

Tracking the Motion of the Planets: Can a planet be followed? **1128**

85. Static Electricity **1133**

Building an Electroscope: Which objects are electrically charged? **1135**

Measuring a Charge: Does nylon or wool create a stronger static electric charge? **1139**

86. Storms **1147**

Lightning Sparks: Explore how separating charges causes an attraction between objects **1152**

Tornadoes: Making a violent vortex **1155**

Forming Hailstones: How do temperature differences affect the formation of hail? **1158**

87. Structures and Shapes **1165**

Arches and Beams: Which is strongest? **1167**

Beams and Rigidity: How does the vertical height of a beam affect its rigidity? **1170**

88. Time **1175**

Pendulums: How do the length, weight, and swing angle of a pendulum affect its oscillation time? **1180**

Water Clock: Does the amount of water in a water clock affect its accuracy? **1185**

89. Tropisms **1191**

Phototropism: Will plants follow a maze to reach light **1193**

Geotropism: Will plant roots turn toward the pull of gravity? **1197**

Heliotropism: How does the Sun affect the movement of certain plants? **1201**

90. Vegetative Propagation **1207**

Auxins: How do auxins affect plant growth? **1209**

Potatoes from Pieces: How do potatoes reproduce vegetatively? **1216**

91. Vitamins and Minerals **1223**

Vitamin C: What juices are the best sources of vitamin C? **1226**

Hard Water: Do different water sources have varying mineral content? **1231**

92. Volcanoes **1237**

Model of a Volcano: Will it blow its top? **1240**

Looking at a Seismograph: Can a volcanic eruption be detected? **1242**

93. Water Cycle **1247**

Temperature: How does temperature affect the rate of evaporation? **1248**

Surface Area: How does surface area affect the rate of evaporation? **1253**

94. Water Properties **1259**

Cohesion: Can the cohesive force of surface tension in water support an object denser than water? **1261**

Adhesion: How much weight is required to break the adhesive force between an object and water? **1264**

95. Weather **1271**

Wind: Measuring wind speed with a homemade anemometer **1273**

Clouds: Will a drop in air temperature cause a cloud to form? **1277**

96. Weather Forecasting **1283**

Dewpoint: When will dew form? **1286**

Air Pressure: How can air pressure be measured? **1289**

97. Wood **1295**

Water Absorption: How do different woods absorb water? **1298**

Wood Hardness: How does the hardness of wood relate to its building properties? **1302**

Budget Index **lxxxv**

Level of Difficulty Index **xcvii**

Timetable Index **cix**

General Subject Index **cxxi**

Reader's Guide

Experiment Central: Understanding Scientific Principles Through Projects provides in one resource a wide variety of science experiments covering nine key science curriculum fields—astronomy, biology, botany, chemistry, ecology, food science, geology, meteorology, and physics—spanning the earth sciences, life sciences, and physical sciences.

Experiment Central, 2nd edition combines, expands, and updates the original four-volume and two-volume UXL sets. This new edition includes 20 new chapters, 60 new experiments, and more than 35 enhanced experiments. Each chapter explores a scientific subject and offers experiments or projects that utilize or reinforce the topic studied. Chapters are alphabetically arranged according to scientific concept, including: Air and Water Pollution, Color, Eclipses, Forensic Science, Genetics, Magnetism, Mountains, Periodic Table, Renewable Energy, Storms and Water Cycle. Two to three experiments or projects are included in each chapter.

Entry format

Chapters are presented in a standard, easy-to-follow format. All chapters open with an explanatory overview section designed to introduce students to the scientific concept and provide the background behind a concept s discovery or important figures who helped advance the study of the field.

Each experiment is divided into eight standard sections to help students follow the experimental process clearly from beginning to end. Sections are:

- Purpose/Hypothesis
- Level of Difficulty

- Materials Needed
- Approximate Budget
- Timetable
- Step-by-Step Instructions
- Summary of Results
- Change the Variables

Chapters also include a "Design Your Own Experiment" section that allows students to apply what they have learned about a particular concept and to create their own experiments. This section is divided into:

- How to Select a Topic Relating to this Concept
- Steps in the Scientific Method
- Recording Data and Summarizing the Results
- Related Projects

Special Features

A "Words to Know" sidebar provides definitions of terms used in each chapter. A cumulative glossary collected from all the "Words to Know" sections is included in the beginning of each volume.

The "Experiments by Scientific Field" section categorizes experiments by scientific curriculum area. This section cumulates all experiments across the six-volume series.

The Parent's and Teacher's Guide recommends that a responsible adult always oversee a student's experiment and provides several safety guidelines for all students to follow.

Standard sidebars accompany experiments and projects.

- "What Are the Variables?" explains the factors that may have an impact on the outcome of a particular experiment.
- "How to Experiment Safely" clearly explains any risks involved with the experiment and how to avoid them.
- "Troubleshooter's Guide" presents problems that a student might encounter with an experiment, possible causes of the problem, and ways to remedy the problem.

Over 450 photos enhance the text; approximately 450 custom illustrations show the steps in the experiments.

Four indexes cumulate information from all the experiments in this six-volume set, including:

- Budget Index categorizes the experiments by approximate cost.
- Level of Difficulty Index lists experiments according to "easy," "moderate," or "difficult," or a combination thereof.
- Timetable Index categorizes each experiment by the amount of time needed to complete it, including setup and follow-through time.
- General Subject Index provides access to all major terms, people, places, and topics covered in the set.

Acknowledgments

The author wishes to acknowledge and thank Laurie Curtis, teacher/researcher; Cindy O'Neill, science educator; and Joyce Nelson, chemist, for their contributions to this edition as consultants.

Comments and Suggestions

We welcome your comments on *Experiment Central*. Please write: Editors, *Experiment Central*, U*X*L, 27500 Drake Rd. Farmington Hills, MI 48331-3535; call toll-free: 1-800-347-4253; or visit us at www.gale.cengage.com.

Parent's and Teacher's Guide

The experiments and projects in *Experiment Central* have been carefully constructed with issues of safety in mind, but your guidance and supervision are still required. Following the safety guidelines that accompany each experiment and project (found in the "How to Experiment Safely" sidebar box), as well as putting to work the safe practices listed below, will help your child or student avoid accidents. Oversee your child or student during experiments, and make sure he or she follows these safety guidelines:

- Always wear safety goggle is there is any possiblity of sharp objects, small particles, splashes of liquid, or gas fumes getting in someone's eyes.
- Always wear protective gloves when handling materials that could irritate the skin.
- Never leave an open flame, such as a lit candle, unattended. Never wear loose clothing around an open flame.
- Follow instructions carefully when using electrical equipment, including batteries, to avoid getting shocked.
- Be cautious when handling sharp objects or glass equipment that might break. Point scissors away from you and use them carefully.
- Always ask for help in cleaning up spills, broken glass, or other hazardous materials.
- Always use protective gloves when handling hot objects. Set them down only on a protected surface that will not be damaged by heat.

- Always wash your hands thoroughly after handling material that might contain harmful microorganisms, such as soil and pond water.
- Do not substitute materials in an experiment without asking a knowledgeable adult about possible reactions.
- Do not use or mix unidentified liquids or powders. The result might be an explosion or poisonous fumes.
- Never taste or eat any substances being used in an experiment.
- Always wear old clothing or a protective apron to avoid staining your clothes.

Experiments by Scientific Field

Chapter name in brackets, followed by experiment name. The numeral before the colon indicates volume; numbers after the colon indicate page number.

ALL SUBJECTS

[Scientific Method] Using the Scientific Method: Do fruit flies appear out of thin air? **5:1013**

[Scientific Method] Using the Scientific Method: What are the mystery powders? **5:1009**

ASTRONOMY

[Comets and Meteors] Comet Nucleus: Linking a Comet's Composition to its Properties. **2:218**

[Comets and Meteors] Meteor Impact: How do the characteristics of a meteorite and its impact affect the shape of the crater? **2:221**

[Eclipses] Phases of the Moon: What does each phase look like? **2:329**

[Eclipses] Simulating Solar and Lunar Eclipses **2:327**

[Rotation and Orbits] Foucault Pendulum: How can a pendulum demonstrate the rotation of Earth? **5:985**

[Rotation and Orbits] Spinning Effects: How does the speed of a rotating object affect the way centrifugal force can overcome gravity? **5:989**

[Space Observation] Doppler Effect: How can waves measure the distance and speed of objects? **6:1118**

[Space Observation] Telescopes: How do different combinations of lenses affect the image? **6:1113**

[Stars] Tracking Stars: Where is Polaris? **6:1125**

[Stars] Tracking the Motion of the Planets: Can a planet be followed? **6:1128**

BIOLOGY

[Animal Defenses] Camouflage: Does an animal's living environment relate to the color of the animal life? **1:63**

[Animal Defenses] Ladybug Threats: How do ladybugs defend themselves when they feel threatened? **1:65**

[Bacteria] Bacterial Growth: How do certain substances inhibit or promote bacterial growth? **1:90**

[Bacteria] Bacterial Resistance: Can bacteria gain resistance to a substance after exposure? **1:95**

[Bones and Muscles] Bone Loss: How does the loss of calcium affect bone strength? **1:116**

[Bones and Muscles] Muscles: How does the strength of muscles affect fatigue over time? **1:120**

[Cells] Investigating Cells: What are the differences between a multicellular organism and a unicellular organism? **1:141**

[Cells] Plant Cells: What are the cell differences between monocot and dicot plants? **1:145**

[Cells] Yeast Cells: How do they reproduce? **1:147**

[Chemosenses] Smell and Taste: How does smell affect the sense of taste? **1:186**

[Chemosenses] Supertasters: Is there a correlation between the number of taste buds and taste perception? **1:180**

[DNA (Deoxyribonucleic Acid)] Comparing DNA: Does the DNA from different species have the same appearance? **2:291**

[DNA (Deoxyribonucleic Acid)] The Stuff of Life: Isolating DNA **2:289**

[Enzymes] Finding the Enzyme: Which enzyme breaks down hydrogen peroxide? **2:362**

[Enzymes] Stopping Enzymes: Does temperature affect enzyme action? **2:368**

[Enzymes] Tough and Tender: Does papain speed up the aging process? **2:365**

[Fish] Fish Breathing: How do different fish take in oxygen? **3:404**

[Fish] Fish Movement: How do fins and body shape affect the movement of fish? **3:407**

[Forensic Science] Blood Patterns: How can a blood spatter help recreate the crime? **3:515**

[Forensic Science] Fiber Evidence: How can scientific techniques be used to identify fiber? **3:511**

[Fungi] Decomposers: Food source for a common fungi **3:541**

[Fungi] Living Conditions: What is the ideal temperature for yeast growth? **3:544**

[Genetics] Building a Pedigree for Taste **3:559**

[Genetics] Genetic Traits: Will you share certain genetic traits more with family members than non-family members? **3:556**

[Insects] Ant Food: What type of foods is one type of ant attracted to? **3:635**

[Insects] Lightning Bugs: How does the environment affect a firefly's flash? **3:638**

[Life Cycles] Insects: How does food supply affect the growth rate of grasshoppers or crickets? **4:651**

[Life Cycles] Tadpoles: Does temperature affect the rate at which tadpoles change into frogs? **4:647**

[Memory] False Memories: How can memories be influenced? **4:705**

[Memory] Memory Mnemonics: What techniques help in memory retention? **4:701**

[Microorganisms] Growing Microorganisms in a Petri Dish **4:716**

[Microorganisms] Microorganisms: What is the best way to grow penicillin? **4:713**

[Nutrition] Daily Nutrition: How nutritious is my diet? **4:766**

[Nutrition] Energizing Foods: Which foods contain carbohydrates and fats? **4:761**

[Nutrition] Nutrition: Which foods contain proteins and salts? **4:764**

[Osmosis and Diffusion] Changing Concentrations: Will a bag of salt water draw in fresh water? **4:803**

[Osmosis and Diffusion] Changing Sizes: What effect does molecule size have on osmosis **4:806**

[Osmosis and Diffusion] Measuring Membranes: Is a plastic bag a semipermeable membrane? **4:798**

[Seashells] Classifying Seashells **5:1025**

[Seashells] Shell Strength: Which shell is stronger: a clam shell or lobster shell? **5:1022**

BOTANY

[Annual Growth] Lichen Growth: What can be learned from the environment by observing lichens? **1:79**

[Annual Growth] Tree Growth: What can be learned from the growth patterns of trees? **1:74**

[Chlorophyll] Plant Pigments: Can pigments be separated? **1:193**

[Chlorophyll] Response to Light: Do plants grow differently in different colors of light? **1:197**

[Ethnobotany] Coiling Reeds: How does the tightness of the coil affect the ability to hold materials? **2:396**

[Ethnobotany] Plants and Health: Which plants have anti-bacterial properties? **2:392**

[Flowers] Self versus Cross: Will there be a difference in reproduction between self-pollinated and cross-pollinated plants of the same type? **3:427**

[Flowers] Sweet Sight: Can changing a flower's nectar and color affect the pollinators lured to the flower? **3:431**

[Germination] Comparing Germination Times: How fast can seeds grow? **3:570**

[Germination] Effects of Temperature on Germination: What temperatures encourage and discourage germination? **3:566**

[Germination] Seed Scarification: Does breaking the seed shell affect germination time? **3:573**

[Photosynthesis] Light Intensity: How does the intensity of light affect plant growth? **4:877**

[Photosynthesis] Photosynthesis: How does light affect plant growth? **4:873**

[Plant Anatomy] Plant Hormones: What is the affect of hormones on root and stem growth? **5:886**

[Plant Anatomy] Water Uptake: How do different plants differ in their water needs? **5:890**

[Plants and Water] Transpiration: How do different environmental conditions affect plants' rates of transpiration? **5:904**

[Plants and Water] Water Flow: How do varying solutions of water affect the amount of water a plant takes in and its turgor pressure? **5:900**

[Tropisms] Geotropism: Will plant roots turn toward the pull of gravity? **6:1197**

[Tropisms] Heliotropism: How does the Sun affect the movement of certain plants? **6:1201**

[Tropisms] Phototropism: Will plants follow a maze to reach light? **6:1193**

[Vegetative Propagation] Auxins: How do auxins affect plant growth? **6:1209**

[Vegetative Propagation] Potatoes from Pieces: How do potatoes reproduce vegetatively? **6:1216**

CHEMISTRY

[Adhesives] Adhesives in the Environment: Will different environmental conditions affect the properties of different adhesives? **1:26**

[Adhesives] Material Adhesion: How do various glues adhere to different materials? **1:22**

[Chemical Energy] Exothermic or Endothermic: Determining whether various chemical reactions are exothermic or endothermic **1:156**

[Chemical Energy] Rusting: Is the chemical reaction exothermic, endothermic, or neither? **1:152**

[Chemical Properties] Chemical Patination: Producing chemical reactions on metal **1:173**

[Chemical Properties] Chemical Reactions: What happens when mineral oil, water, and iodine mix? **1:170**

[Chemical Properties] Slime: What happens when white glue and borax mix? **1:167**

[Crystals] Cool Crystals: How does the effect of cooling impact crystal growth? **2:252**

[Crystals] Crystal Structure: Will varying shape crystals form from varying substances? **2:246**

[Dyes] Applying Dyes: How does the fiber affect the dye color? **2:301**

[Dyes] Holding the Dye: How do dye fixatives affect the colorfastness of the dye? **2:304**

[Materials Science] Developing Renewables: Can a renewable packing material have the same qualities as a non-renewable material? **4:691**

[Materials Science] Testing Tape: Finding the properties that allow tape to support weight. **4:688**

[Mixtures and Solutions] Colloids: Can colloids be distinguished from suspension using the Tyndall effect? **4:730**

[Mixtures and Solutions] Suspensions and Solutions: Can filtration and evaporation determine whether mixtures are suspensions or solutions? **4:725**

[Oxidation-Reduction] Oxidation and Rust: How is rust produced? **4:817**

[Oxidation-Reduction] Oxidation Reaction: Can acid change the color of copper? **4:820**

[Oxidation-Reduction] Reduction: How will acid affect dirty pennies? **4:813**

[Periodic Table] Active Metals: What metals give off electrons more readily than others? **4:838**

[Periodic Table] Metals versus Nonmetals: Which areas of the periodic table have elements that conduct electricity? **4:830**

[Periodic Table] Soluble Families: How does the solubility of an element relate to where it is located on the Periodic Table? **4:835**

[pH] Chemical Titration: What is required to change a substance from an acid or a base into a neutral solution? **4:865**

[pH] Kitchen Chemistry: What is the pH of household chemicals? **4:861**

[Polymers] Polymer Properties: How are the properties of hard plastics different? **5:923**

[Polymers] Polymer Slime: How will adding more of a polymer change the properties of a polymer "slime"? **5:919**

[Polymers] Polymer Strength: What are the tensile properties of certain polymers that make them more durable than others? **5:914**

[Salinity] Density Ball: How to make a standard for measuring density **5:1000**

[Salinity] Making a Hydrometer: How can salinity be measured? **5:997**

[Separation and Identification] Chromatography: Can you identify a pen from the way its colors separate? **5:1034**

[Separation and Identification] Identifying a Mixture: How can determining basic properties of a substance allow you to identify the substances in a mixture? **5:1039**

[Water Properties] Adhesion: How much weight is required to break the adhesive force between an object and water? **6:1264**

[Water Properties] Cohesion: Can the cohesive force of surface tension in water support an object denser than water? **6:1261**

ECOLOGY

[Acid Rain] Acid Rain and Animals: How does acid rain affect brine shrimp? **1:5**

[Acid Rain] Acid Rain and Plants: How does acid rain affect plant growth? **1:9**

[Acid Rain] Acid Rain: Can acid rain harm structures? **1:12**

[Air and Water Pollution] Eutrophication: The effect of phosphates on water plants. **1:55**

[Air and Water Pollution] Pollutant Bioindicators: Can lichens provide clues to an area's air pollution? **1:51**

[Biomes] Building a Desert Biome **1:108**

[Biomes] Building a Temperate Forest Biome **1:107**

[Composting/Landfills] Composting: Using organic material to grow plants **2:237**

[Composting/Landfills] Living Landfill: What effect do the microorganisms in soil have on the decomposition process? **2:232**

[Dissolved Oxygen] Decay and Dissolved Oxygen: How does the amount of decaying matter affect the level of dissolved oxygen in water? **2:274**

[Dissolved Oxygen] Goldfish Breath: How does a decrease in the dissolved oxygen level affect the breathing rate of goldfish? **2:279**

[Erosion] Erosion: Does soil type affect the amount of water that runs off a hillside? **2:377**

[Erosion] Plants and Erosion: How do plants affect the rate of soil erosion? **2:381**

[Greenhouse Effect] Creating a Greenhouse: How much will the temperature rise inside a greenhouse? **3:592**

[Greenhouse Effect] Fossil Fuels: What happens when fossil fuels burn? **3:596**

[Groundwater Aquifers] Aquifers: How do they become polluted? **3:605**

[Groundwater Aquifers] Groundwater: How can it be cleaned? **3:609**

[Pesticides] Moving through Water: How can pesticides affect nontarget plant life? **4:852**

[Pesticides] Natural versus Synthetic: How do different types of pesticides compare against a pest? **4:848**

[Renewable Energy] Capturing Wind Energy: How does the material affect the amount of wind energy harnessed? **5:944**

[Renewable Energy] Hydropower: How does water pressure affect water energy? **5:948**

[Rivers] River Flow: How does the steepness and rate of water flow affect river erosion? **5:962**

[Rivers] Stream Flow: Does the stream meander? **5:960**

[Rivers] Weathering Erosion in Glaciers: How does a river make a trench? **5:957**

[Soil] Soil pH: Does the pH of soil affect plant growth? **5:1074**

[Soil] Soil Profile: What are the different properties of the soil horizons? **5:1067**

[Solar Energy] Capturing Solar Energy: Will seedlings grow bigger in a greenhouse? **5:1084**

[Solar Energy] Retaining the Sun's heat: What substance best stores heat for a solar system? **5:1090**

[Solar Energy] Solar Cells: Will sunlight make a motor run? **5:1087**

[Water Cycle] Surface Area: How does surface area affect the rate of evaporation? **6:1253**

[Water Cycle] Temperature: How does temperature affect the rate of evaporation? **6:1248**

FOOD SCIENCE

[Food Preservation] Drying Foods: Does drying fruits help prevent or delay spoilage? **3:458**

[Food Preservation] Sweet Preservatives: How does sugar affect the preservation of fruit? **3:454**

[Food Science] Jelly and Pectin: How does acidity affect how fruit gels? **3:467**

[Food Science] Rising Foods: How much carbon dioxide do different leavening agents produce? **3:470**

[Food Spoilage] Preservatives: How do different substances affect the growth of mold? **3:481**

[Food Spoilage] Spoiled Milk: How do different temperatures of liquid affect its rate of spoilage? **3:485**

[Vitamins and Minerals] Hard Water: Do different water sources have varying mineral content? **6:1231**

[Vitamins and Minerals] Vitamin C: What juices are the best sources of vitamin C? **6:1226**

GEOLOGY

[Caves] Cave Formation: How does the acidity of a substance affect the formation of a cave? **1:132**

[Caves] Cave Icicles: How does the mineral content of water affect the formation of stalactites and stalagmites? **1:135**

[Earthquakes] Detecting an Earthquake: How can movement of Earth's crust be measured? **2:314**

[Earthquakes] Earthquake Simulation: Is the destruction greater at the epicenter? **2:317**

[Fossils] Fossil Formation: What are the physical characteristics of an organism that make the best fossils? **3:530**

[Fossils] Making an Impression: In which soil environment does a fossil most easily form? **3:526**

[Mountains] Mountain Formations: How does the height of the mountain have an affect on desert formation? **4:741**

[Mountains] Mountain Plates: How does the movement of Earth's plates determine the formation of a mountain? **4:738**

[Oceans] Currents: Water behavior in density-driven currents **4:780**

[Oceans] Stratification: How does the salinity in ocean water cause it to form layers? **4:775**

[Rocks and Minerals] Mineral Testing: What kind of mineral is it? **5:971**

[Rocks and Minerals] Rock Classification: Is it igneous, sedimentary, or metamorphic? **5:975**

[Volcanoes] Looking at a Seismograph: Can a volcanic eruption be detected? **6:1242**

[Volcanoes] Model of a Volcano: Will it blow its top? **6:1240**

METEOROLOGY

[Air] Air Density: Does warm air take up less room than cool air? **1:36**

[Air] Convection Currents: How can rising air cause weather changes? **1:39**

[Storms] Forming Hailstones: How do temperature differences affect the formation of hail? **6:1158**

[Storms] Lightning Sparks: Explore how separating charges causes an attraction between objects **6:1152**

[Storms] Tornadoes: Making a violent vortex **6:1155**

[Weather] Clouds: Will a drop in air temperature cause a cloud to form? **6:1277**

[Weather] Wind: Measuring wind speed with a homemade anemometer **6:1273**

[Weather Forecasting] Air Pressure: How can air pressure be measured? **6:1289**

[Weather Forecasting] Dewpoint: When will dew form? **6:1286**

PHYSICS

[Color] Color and Flavor: How much does color affect flavor perception? **2:207**

[Color] Temperature and Color: What color has the highest temperature? **2:210**

[Density and Buoyancy] Buoyancy: Does water pressure affect buoyancy? **2:264**

[Density and Buoyancy] Density: Can a scale of relative density predict whether one material floats on another? **2:260**

[Electricity] Batteries: Can a series of homemade electric cells form a "pile" strong enough to match the voltage of a D-cell battery? **2:340**

[Electricity] Electrolytes: Do some solutions conduct electricity better than others? **2:335**

[Electricity] Electroplating: Using electricity to move one metal onto another metal **2:344**

[Electromagnetism] Electromagnetism: How can an electromagnet be created? **2:354**

[Electromagnetism] Magnetism:How can a magnetic field be created and detected? **2:351**

[Flight] Helicopters, Propellers, and Centripetal Force: Will it fly high? **3:418**

[Flight] Lift-Off: How can a glider be made to fly higher? **3:415**

[Fluids] Spinning Fluids: How do different fluids behave when immersed in a spinning rod? **3:444**

[Fluids] Viscosity: How can temperature affect the viscosity of liquids? **3:441**

[Forces] Centripetal Action: What is the relationship between distance and force in circular motion? **3:501**

[Forces] Newton's Laws in Action: How do water bottle rockets demonstrate Newton's laws of motion? **3:493**

[Gravity] Gravity: How fast do different objects fall? **3:581**

[Gravity] Measuring Mass: How can a balance be made? **3:585**

[Heat] Conduction: Which solid materials are the best conductors of heat? **3:618**

[Heat] Convection: How does heat move through liquids? **3:622**

[Heat] Heat Capacity: Which liquids have the highest heat capacity? **3:625**

[Light Properties] Looking for the Glow: Which objects glow under black light? **4:661**

[Light Properties] Refraction and Defraction: Making a rainbow **4:664**

[Light Properties] Refraction: How does the material affect how light travels? **4:666**

[Magnetism] Electromagnets: Does the strength of an electromagnet increase with greater current? **4:678**

[Magnetism] Magnets: How do heat, cold, jarring, and rubbing affect the magnetism of a nail? **4:674**

[Nanotechnology] Nanosize Substances: How can the physical size affect the rate of reaction? **4:753**

[Nanotechnology] Nanosize: How can the physical size affect a material's properties? **4:750**

[Optics and Optical Illusions] Optical Illusions: Can the eye be fooled? **4:791**

[Optics and Optical Illusions] Optics: What is the focal length of a lens? **5:788**

[Potential and Kinetic Energy] Measuring Energy: How does the height of an object affect its potential energy? **5:931**

[Potential and Kinetic Energy] Using Energy: Build a roller coaster **5:934**

[Simple Machines] Lever Lifting: How does the distance from the fulcrum affect work? **5:1055**

[Simple Machines] The Screw: How does the distance between the threads of a screw affect the work? **5:1057**

[Simple Machines] Wheel and Axle: How can changing the size of the wheel affect the amount of work it takes to lift a load? **5:1051**

[Sound] Pitch: How does the thickness of a vibrating string affect sound? **5:1099**

[Sound] Soundproofing: How do different materials affect sound? **5:1102**

[Sound] Wave Length: How does the length of a vibrating string affect the sound it produces? **5:1096**

[Static Electricity] Building an Electroscope: Which objects are electrically charged? **6:1135**

[Static Electricity] Measuring a Charge: Does nylon or wool create a stronger static electric charge? **6:1139**

[Structures and Shapes] Arches and Beams: Which is strongest? **6:1167**

[Structures and Shapes] Beams and Rigidity: How does the vertical height of a beam affect its rigidity? **6:1170**

[Time] Pendulums: How do the length, weight, and swing angle of a pendulum affect its oscillation time? **6:1180**

[Time] Water Clock: Does the amount of water in a water clock affect its accuracy? **6:1185**

[Wood] Water Absorption: How do different woods absorb water? **6:1298**

[Wood] Wood Hardness: How does the hardness of wood relate to its building properties? **6:1302**

Words to Know

Abdomen: The third segment of an insect body.

Abscission: Barrier of special cells created at the base of leaves in autumn.

Absolute dating: The age of an object correlated to a specific fixed time, as established by some precise dating method.

Acceleration: The rate at which the velocity and/or direction of an object is changing with respect to time.

Acid: Substance that when dissolved in water is capable of reacting with a base to form salts and release hydrogen ions.

Acid rain: A form of precipitation that is significantly more acidic than neutral water, often produced as the result of industrial processes and pollution.

Acoustics: The science concerned with the production, properties, and propagation of sound waves.

Acronym: A word or phrase formed from the first letter of other words.

Active solar energy system: A solar energy system that uses pumps or fans to circulate heat captured from the Sun.

Additive: A chemical compound that is added to foods to give them some desirable quality, such as preventing them from spoiling.

Adhesion: Attraction between two different substances.

Adhesive: A substance that bonds or adheres two substances together.

Aeration: Mixing a gas, like oxygen, with a liquid, like water.

Aerobic: A process that requires oxygen.

Aerodynamics: The study of the motion of gases (particularly air) and the motion and control of objects in the air.

Agar: A nutrient rich, gelatinous substance that is used to grow bacteria.

Air: Gaseous mixture that covers Earth, composed mainly of nitrogen (about 78%) and oxygen (about 21%) with lesser amounts of argon, carbon dioxide, and other gases.

Air density: The ratio of the mass of a substance to the volume it occupies.

Air mass: A large body of air that has similar characteristics.

Air pressure: The force exerted by the weight of the atmosphere above a point on or above Earth's surface.

Alga/Algae: Single-celled or multicellular plants or plant-like organisms that contain chlorophyll, thus making their own food by photosynthesis. Algae grow mainly in water.

Alignment: Adjustment in a certain direction or orientation.

Alkali metals: The first group of elements in the periodic table, these metals have a single electron in the outermost shell.

Alkaline: Having a pH of more than 7.

Alleles: One version of the same gene.

Alloy: A mixture of two or more metals with properties different from those metals of which it is made.

Amine: An organic compound derived from ammonia.

Amino acid: One of a group of organic compounds that make up proteins.

Amnesia: Partial or total memory loss.

Amperage: A measurement of current. The common unit of measure is the ampere or amp.

Amphibians: Animals that live on land and breathe air but return to the water to reproduce.

Amplitude: The maximum displacement (difference between an original position and a later position) of the material that is vibrating. Amplitude can be thought of visually as the highest and lowest point of a wave.

Anaerobic: A process that does not require oxygen.

Anal fin: Fin on the belly of a fish, used for balance.

Anatomy: The study of the structure of living things.

Anemometer: A device that measures wind speed.

Angiosperm: A flowering plant that has its seeds produced within an ovary.

Animalcules: Life forms that Anton van Leeuwenhoek named when he first saw them under his microscope; they later became known as protozoa and bacteria.

Anther: The male reproductive organs of the plant, located on the tip of a flower's stamen.

Anthocyanin: Red pigment found in leaves, petals, stems, and other parts of a plant.

Antibiotic: A substance produced by or derived from certain fungi and other organisms, that can destroy or inhibit the growth of other microorganisms.

Antibiotic resistance: The ability of microorganisms to change so that they are not killed by antibiotics.

Antibody: A protein produced by certain cells of the body as an immune (disease-fighting) response to a specific foreign antigen.

Antigen: A substance that causes the production of an antibody when injected directly into the body.

Antioxidants: Used as a food additive, these substances can prevent food spoilage by reducing the food's exposure to air.

Aquifer: Underground layer of sand, gravel, or spongy rock that collects water.

Arch: A curved structure that spans an opening and supports a weight above the opening.

Artesian well: A well in which water is forced out under pressure.

Asexual reproduction: A reproductive process that does not involve the union of two individuals in the exchange of genetic material.

Astronomers: Scientists who study the positions, motions, and composition of stars and other objects in the sky.

Astronomy: The study of the physical properties of objects and matter outside Earth's atmosphere.

Atmosphere: Layers of air that surround Earth.

Atmospheric pressure: The pressure exerted by the atmosphere at Earth's surface due to the weight of the air.

Atom: The smallest unit of an element, made up of protons and neutrons in a central nucleus surrounded by moving electrons.

Atomic mass: Also known as atomic weight, the average mass of the atoms in an element; the number that appears under the element symbol in the periodic table.

Atomic number: The number of protons (or electrons) in an atom; the number that appears over the element symbol in the periodic table.

Atomic symbol: The one- or two-letter abbreviation for a chemical element.

Autotroph: An organism that can build all the food and produce all the energy it needs with its own resources.

Auxins: A group of plant hormones responsible for patterns of plant growth.

Axis: An imaginary straight line around which an object, like a planet, spins or turns. Earth's axis is a line that goes through the North and South Poles.

Bacteria: Single-celled microorganisms that live in soil, water, plants, and animals that play a key role in the decay of organic matter and the cycling of nutrients. Some are agents of disease.

Bacteriology: The scientific study of bacteria, their characteristics, and their activities as related to medicine, industry, and agriculture.

Barometer: An instrument for measuring atmospheric pressure, used especially in weather forecasting.

Base: Substance that when dissolved in water is capable of reacting with an acid to form salts and release hydrogen ions; has a pH of more than 7.

Base pairs: In DNA, the pairing of two nucleotides with each other: adenine (A) with thymine (T), and guanine (G) with cytosine (C).

Beam: A straight, horizontal structure that spans an opening and supports a weight above the opening.

Bedrock: Solid layer of rock lying beneath the soil and other loose material.

Beriberi: A disease caused by a deficiency of thiamine and characterized by nerve and gastrointestinal disorders.

Biochemical oxygen demand (BOD5): The amount of oxygen microorganisms use over a five-day period in 68°F (20°C) water to decay organic matter.

Biodegradable: Capable of being decomposed by biological agents.

Biological variables: Living factors such as bacteria, fungi, and animals that can affect the processes that occur in nature and in an experiment.

Bioluminescence: The chemical phenomenon in which an organism can produce its own light.

Biomass: Organic materials that are used to produce usable energy.

Biomes: Large geographical areas with specific climates and soils, as well as distinct plant and animal communities that are interdependent.

Biomimetics: The development of materials that are found in nature.

Biopesticide: Pesticide produced from substances found in nature.

Bivalve: Bivalves are characterized by shells that are divided into two parts or valves that completely enclose the mollusk like the clam or scallop.

Blanching: A cooking technique in which the food, usually vegetables and fruits, are briefly cooked in boiling water and then plunged into cold water.

Blood pattern analysis: The study of the shape, location, and pattern of blood in order to understand how it got there.

Blueshift: The shortening of the frequency of light waves toward the blue end of the visible light spectrum as they travel towards an observer; most commonly used to describe movement of stars towards Earth.

Boiling point: The temperature at which a substance changes from a liquid to a gas or vapor.

Bond: The force that holds two atoms together.

Bone joint: A place in the body where two or more bones are connected.

Bone marrow: The spongy center of many bones in which blood cells are manufactured.

Bone tissue: A group of similar cells in the bone with a common function.

Bony fish: The largest group of fish, whose skeleton is made of bone.

Boreal: Northern.

Botany: The branch of biology involving the scientific study of plant life.

Braided rivers: Wide, shallow rivers with multiple channels and pebbly islands in the middle.

Buoyancy: The tendency of a liquid to exert a lifting effect on a body immersed in it.

By-product: A secondary substance produced as the result of a physical or chemical process, in addition to the main product.

Calcium carbonate: A substance that is secreted by a mollusk to create the shell it lives in.

Calibration: To standardize or adjust a measuring instrument so its measurements are correct.

Cambium: The tissue below the bark that produces new cells, which become wood and bark.

Camouflage: Markings or coloring that help hide an animal by making it blend into the surrounding environment.

Cancellous bone: Also called spongy bone, the inner layer of a bone that has cells with large spaces in between them filled with marrow.

Canning: A method of preserving food using airtight, vacuum-sealed containers and heat processing.

Capillary action: The tendency of water to rise through a narrow tube by the force of adhesion between the water and the walls of the tube.

Caramelization: The process of heating sugars to the point at which they break down and lead to the formation of new compounds.

Carbohydrate: A compound consisting of carbon, hydrogen, and oxygen found in plants and used as a food by humans and other animals.

Carbonic acid: A weak acid that forms from the mixture of water and carbon dioxide.

Carnivore: A meat-eating organism.

Carotene: Yellow-orange pigment in plants.

Cartilage: The connective tissue that covers and protects the bones.

Cartilaginous fish: The second largest group of fish whose skeleton is made of cartilage

Cast: In paleontology, the fossil formed when a mold is later filled in by mud or mineral matter.

Catalase: An enzyme found in animal liver tissue that breaks down hydrogen peroxide into oxygen and water.

Catalyst: A compound that starts or speeds up the rate of a chemical reaction without undergoing any change in its own composition.

Caudal fin: Tail fin of a fish used for fast swimming.

Cave: Also called cavern, a hollow or natural passage under or into the ground large enough for a person to enter.

Celestial bodies: Describing planets or other objects in space.

Cell membrane: The layer that surrounds the cell, but is inside the cell wall, allowing some molecules to enter and keeping others out of the cell.

Cell theory: All living things have one or more similar cells that carry out the same functions for the living process.

Cell wall: A tough outer covering over the cell membrane of bacteria and plant cells.

Cells: The basic unit for living organisms; cells are structured to perform highly specialized functions.

Centrifugal force: The apparent force pushing a rotating body away from the center of rotation.

Centrifuge: A device that rapidly spins a solution so that the heavier components will separate from the lighter ones.

Centripetal force: Rotating force that moves towards the center or axis.

Cerebral cortex: The outer layer of the brain.

Channel: A shallow trench carved into the ground by the pressure and movement of a river.

Chemical change: The change of one or more substances into other substances.

Chemical energy: Energy stored in chemical bonds.

Chemical property: A characteristic of a substance that allows it to undergo a chemical change. Chemical properties include flammability and sensitivity to light.

Chemical reaction: Any chemical change in which at least one new substance is formed.

Chemosense: A sense stimulated by specific chemicals that cause the sensory cell to transmit a signal to the brain.

Chitin: Substance that makes up the exoskeleton of crustaceans.

Chlorophyll: A green pigment found in plants that absorbs sunlight, providing the energy used in photosynthesis, or the conversion of carbon dioxide and water to complex carbohydrates.

Chloroplasts: Small structures in plant cells that contain chlorophyll and in which the process of photosynthesis takes place.

Chromatography: A method for identifying the components of a substance based on their characteristic colors.

Chromosome: A structure of DNA found in the cell nucleus.

Cilia: Hairlike structures on olfactory receptor cells that sense odor molecules.

Circuit: The complete path of an electric current including the source of electric energy.

Circumference: The distance around a circle.

Clay: Type of soil comprising the smallest soil particles.

Cleavage: The tendency of a mineral to split along certain planes.

Climate: The average weather that a region experiences over a long period.

Coagulation: The clumping together of particles in a mixture, often because the repelling force separating them is disrupted.

Cohesion: Attraction between like substances.

Cold blooded: When an animals body temperature rises or falls to match the environment.

Collagen: A protein in bone that gives the bone elasticity.

Colloid: A mixture containing particles suspended in, but not dissolved in, a dispersing medium.

Colony: A mass of microorganisms that have been bred in a medium.

Colorfast: The ability of a material to keep its dye and not fade or change color.

Coma: Glowing cloud of gas surrounding the nucleus of a comet.

Combustion: Any chemical reaction in which heat, and usually light, is produced. It is commonly the burning of organic substances during which oxygen from the air is used to form carbon dioxide and water vapor.

Comet: An icy body orbiting in the solar system, which partially vaporizes when it nears the Sun and develops a diffuse envelope of dust and gas as well as one or more tails.

Comet head: The nucleus and the coma of a comet.

Comet nucleus: The core or center of a comet. (Plural: Comet nuclei.)

Comet tail: The most distinctive feature of comets; comets can display two basic types of tails: one gaseous and the other largely composed of dust.

Compact bone: The outer, hard layer of the bone.

Complete metamorphosis: Metamorphosis in which a larva becomes a pupa before changing into an adult form.

Composting: The process in which organic compounds break down and become dark, fertile soil called humus.

Compression: A type of force on an object where the object is pushed or squeezed from each end.

Concave: Hollowed or rounded inward, like the inside of a bowl.

Concave lens: A lens that is thinner in the middle than at the edges.

Concentration: The amount of a substance present in a given volume, such as the number of molecules in a liter.

Condensation: The process by which a gas changes into a liquid.

Conduction: The flow of heat through a solid.

Conductivity: The ability of a material to carry an electrical current.

Conductor: A substance able to carry an electrical current.

Cones: Cells in the retina that can perceive color.

Confined aquifer: An aquifer with a layer of impermeable rock above it where the water is held under pressure.

Coniferous: Refers to trees, such as pines and firs, that bear cones and have needle-like leaves that are not shed all at once.

Conservation of energy: The law of physics that states that energy can be transformed from one form to another, but can be neither created nor destroyed.

Constellations: Patterns of stars in the night sky. There are eighty-eight known constellations.

Continental drift: The theory that continents move apart slowly at a predictable rate.

Contract: To shorten, pull together.

Control experiment: A set-up that is identical to the experiment but is not affected by the variable that will be changed during the experiment.

Convection: The circulatory motion that occurs in a gas or liquid at a nonuniform temperature owing to the variation of its density and the action of gravity.

Convection current: A circular movement of a fluid in response to alternating heating and cooling.

Convex: Curved or rounded outward, like the outside of a ball.

Convex lens: A lens that is thicker in the middle than at the edges.

Coprolites: The fossilized droppings of animals.

Coriolis force: A force that makes a moving object appear to travel in a curved path over the surface of a spinning body.

Corona: The outermost atmospheric layer of the Sun.

Corrosion: An oxidation-reduction reaction in which a metal is oxidized (reacted with oxygen) and oxygen is reduced, usually in the presence of moisture.

Cotyledon: Seed leaves, which contain the stored source of food for the embryo.

Crater: An indentation caused by an object hitting the surface of a planet or moon.

Crest: The highest point reached by a wave.

Cross-pollination: The process by which pollen from one plant pollinates another plant of the same species.

Crust: The hard outer shell of Earth that floats upon the softer, denser mantle.

Crustacean: A type of arthropod characterized by hard and thick skin, and having shells that are jointed. This group includes the lobster, crab, and crayfish.

Crystal: Naturally occurring solid composed of atoms or molecules arranged in an orderly pattern that repeats at regular intervals.

Crystal faces: The flat, smooth surfaces of a crystal.

Crystal lattice: The regular and repeating pattern of the atoms in a crystal.

Cultures: Microorganisms growing in prepared nutrients.

Cumulonimbus cloud: The parent cloud of a thunderstorm; a tall, vertically developed cloud capable of producing heavy rain, high winds, and lightning.

Current: The flow of electrical charge from one point to another.

Currents: The horizontal and vertical circulation of ocean waters.

Cyanobacteria: Oxygen-producing, aquatic bacteria capable of manufacturing its own food; resembles algae.

Cycles: Occurrence of events that take place on a regular, repeating basis.

Cytology: The branch of biology concerned with the study of cells.

Cytoplasm: The semifluid substance inside a cell that surrounds the nucleus and other membrane-enclosed organelles.

Decanting: The process of separating a suspension by waiting for its heavier components to settle out and then pouring off the lighter ones.

Decibel (dB): A unit of measurement for the amplitude of sound.

Deciduous: Plants that lose their leaves during some season of the year, and then grow them back during another season.

Decompose: To break down into two or more simpler substances.

Decomposition: The breakdown of complex molecules of dead organisms into simple nutrients that can be reutilized by living organisms.

Decomposition reaction: A chemical reaction in which one substance is broken down into two or more substances.

Deficiency disease: A disease marked by a lack of an essential nutrient in the diet.

Degrade: Break down.

Dehydration: The removal of water from a material.

Denaturization: Altering an enzyme so it no longer works.

Density: The mass of a substance divided by its volume.

Density ball: A ball with the fixed standard of 1.0 gram per milliliter, which is the exact density of pure water.

Deoxyribonucleic acid (DNA): Large, complex molecules found in the nuclei of cells that carry genetic information for an organism's development; double helix. (Pronounced DEE-ox-see-rye-bo-noo-klay-ick acid)

Dependent variable: The variable in an experiment whose value depends on the value of another variable in the experiment.

Deposition: Dropping of sediments that occurs when a river loses its energy of motion.

Desert: A biome with a hot-to-cool climate and dry weather.

Desertification: Transformation of arid or semiarid productive land into desert.

Dewpoint: The point at which water vapor begins to condense.

Dicot: Plants with a pair of embryonic seeds that appear at germination.

Diffraction: The bending of light or another form of electromagnetic radiation as it passes through a tiny hole or around a sharp edge.

Diffraction grating: A device consisting of a surface into which are etched very fine, closely spaced grooves that cause different wavelengths of light to reflect or refract (bend) by different amounts.

Diffusion: Random movement of molecules that leads to a net movement of molecules from a region of high concentration to a region of low concentration.

Disinfection: Using chemicals to kill harmful organisms.

Dissolved oxygen: Oxygen molecules that have dissolved in water.

Distillation: The process of separating liquids from solids or from other liquids with different boiling points by a method of evaporation and condensation, so that each component in a mixture can be collected separately in its pure form.

DNA fingerprinting: A technique that uses DNA fragments to identify the unique DNA sequences of an individual.

DNA replication: The process by which one DNA strand unwinds and duplicates all its information, creating two new DNA strands that are identical to each other and to the original strand.

DNA (deoxyribonucleic acid): Large, complex molecules found in nuclei of cells that carry genetic information for an organism's development.

Domain: Small regions in iron that possess their own magnetic charges.

Dominant gene: A gene that passes on a certain characteristic, even when there is only one copy (allele) of the gene.

Doppler effect: The change in wavelength and frequency (number of vibrations per second) of either light or sound as the source is moving either towards or away from the observer.

Dormant: A state of inactivity in an organism.

Dorsal fin: The fin located on the back of a fish, used for balance.

Double helix: The shape taken by DNA (deoxyribonucleic acid) molecules in a nucleus.

Drought: A prolonged period of dry weather that damages crops or prevents their growth.

Dry cell: A source of electricity that uses a non-liquid electrolyte.

Dust tail: One of two types of tails a comet may have, it is composed mainly of dust and it points away from the Sun.

Dye: A colored substance that is used to give color to a material.

Dynamic equilibrium: A situation in which substances are moving into and out of cell walls at an equal rate.

Earthquake: An unpredictable event in which masses of rock suddenly shift or rupture below Earth's surface, releasing enormous amounts of energy and sending out shockwaves that sometimes cause the ground to shake dramatically.

Eclipse: A phenomenon in which the light from a celestial body is temporarily cut off by the presence of another.

Ecologists: Scientists who study the interrelationship of organisms and their environments.

Ecosystem: An ecological community, including plants, animals and microorganisms, considered together with their environment.

Efficiency: The amount of power output divided by the amount of power input. It is a measure of how well a device converts one form of power into another.

Effort: The force applied to move a load using a simple machine.

Elastomers: Any of various polymers having rubbery properties.

Electric charge repulsion: Repulsion of particles caused by a layer of negative ions surrounding each particle. The repulsion prevents coagulation and promotes the even dispersion of such particles through a mixtures.

Electrical energy: Kinetic energy resulting from the motion of electrons within any object that conducts electricity.

Electricity: A form of energy caused by the presence of electrical charges in matter.

Electrode: A material that will conduct an electrical current, usually a metal; used to carry electrons into or out of a battery.

Electrolyte: Any substance that, when dissolved in water, conducts an electric current.

Electromagnetic spectrum: The complete array of electromagnetic radiation, including radio waves (at the longest-wavelength end), microwaves, infrared radiation, visible light, ultraviolet radiation, X rays, and gamma rays (at the shortest-wavelength end).

Electromagnetism: A form of magnetic energy produced by the flow of an electric current through a metal core. Also, the study of electric and magnetic fields and their interaction with charges and currents.

Electron: A subatomic particle with a single negative electrical change that orbits the nucleus of an atom.

Electroplating: The process of coating one metal with another metal by means of an electrical current.

Electroscope: A device that determines whether an object is electrically charged.

Element: A pure substance composed of just one type of atom that cannot be broken down into anything simpler by ordinary chemical means.

Elevation: Height above sea level.

Elliptical: An orbital path which is egg-shaped or resembles an elongated circle.

Elongation: The percentage increase in length that occurs before a material breaks under tension.

Embryo: The seed of a plant, which through germination can develop into a new plant.

Embryonic: The earliest stages of development.

Endothermic reaction: A chemical reaction that absorbs heat or light energy, such as photosynthesis, the production of food by plant cells.

Energy: The ability to cause an action or to perform work.

Entomology: The study of insects.

Environmental variables: Nonliving factors such as air temperature, water, pollution, and pH that can affect processes that occur in nature and in an experiment.

Enzyme: Any of numerous complex proteins produced by living cells that act as catalysts, speeding up the rate of chemical reactions in living organisms.

Enzymology: The science of studying enzymes.

Ephemerals: Plants that lie dormant in dry soil for years until major rainstorms occur.

Epicenter: The location where the seismic waves of an earthquake first appear on the surface, usually almost directly above the focus.

Equilibrium: A balancing or canceling out of opposing forces, so that an object will remain at rest.

Erosion: The process by which topsoil is carried away by water, wind, or ice action.

Ethnobotany: The study of how cultures use plants in everyday life.

Eukaryotic: Multicellular organism whose cells contain distinct nuclei, which contain the genetic material. (Pronounced yoo-KAR-ee-ah-tic)

Euphotic zone: The upper part of the ocean where sunlight penetrates, supporting plant life, such as phytoplankton.

Eutrophication: The process by which high nutrient concentrations in a body of water eventually cause the natural wildlife to die.

Evaporation: The process by which liquid changes into a gas.

Exoskeleton: A hard outer covering on animals, which provide protection and structure.

Exothermic reaction: A chemical reaction that releases heat or light energy, such as the burning of fuel.

Experiment: A controlled observation.

Extremophiles: Bacteria that thrive in environments too harsh to support most life forms.

False memory: A memory of an event that never happened or an altered memory from what happened.

Family: A group of elements in the same column of the periodic table or in closely related columns of the table. A family of chemical compounds share similar structures and properties.

Fat: A type of lipid, or chemical compound used as a source of energy, to provide insulation and to protect organs in an animal body.

Fat-soluble vitamins: Vitamins such as A, D, E, and K that can be dissolved in the fat of plants and animals.

Fault: A crack running through rock as the result of tectonic forces.

Fault blocks: Pieces of rock from Earth's crust that press against each other and cause earthquakes when they suddenly shift or rupture from the pressure.

Fault mountain: A mountain that is formed when Earth's plates come together and cause rocks to break and move upwards.

Fermentation: A chemical reaction in which enzymes break down complex organic compounds (for example, carbohydrates and sugars) into simpler ones (for example, ethyl alcohol).

Filament: In a flower, stalk of the stamen that bears the anther.

Filtration: The mechanical separation of a liquid from the undissolved particles floating in it.

Fireball: Meteors that create an intense, bright light and, sometimes, an explosion.

First law of motion (Newton's): An object at rest or moving in a certain direction and speed will remain at rest or moving in the same motion and speed unless acted upon by a force.

Fish: Animals that live in water who have gills, fins, and are cold blooded.

Fixative: A substance that mixes with the dye to hold it to the material.

Flagella: Whiplike structures used by some organisms for movement. (Singular: flagellum.)

Flammability: The ability of a material to ignite and burn.

Flower: The reproductive part of a flowering plant.

Fluid: A substance that flows; a liquid or gas.

Fluorescence: The emission of visible light from an object when the object is bombarded with electromagnetic radiation, such as ultraviolet rays. The emission of visible light stops after the radiation source has been removed.

Focal length: The distance from the lens to the point where the light rays come together to a focus.

Focal point: The point at which rays of light converge or from which they diverge.

Focus: The point within Earth where a sudden shift or rupture occurs.

Fold mountain: A mountain that is formed when Earth's plates come together and push rocks up into folds.

Food webs: Interconnected sets of food chains, which are a sequence of organisms directly dependent on one another for food.

Force: A physical interaction (pushing or pulling) tending to change the state of motion (velocity) of an object.

Forensic science: The application of science to the law and justice system.

Fortified: The addition of nutrients, such as vitamins or minerals, to food.

Fossil: The remains, trace, or impressions of a living organism that inhabited Earth more than ten thousand years ago.

Fossil fuel: A fuel such as coal, oil, or natural gas that is formed over millions of years from the remains of plants and animals.

Fossil record: The documentation of fossils placed in relationship to one another; a key source to understand the evolution of life on Earth.

Fracture: A mineral's tendency to break into curved, rough, or jagged surfaces.

Frequency: The rate at which vibrations take place (number of times per second the motion is repeated), given in cycles per second or in hertz (Hz). Also, the number of waves that pass a given point in a given period of time.

Friction: A force that resists the motion of an object, resulting when two objects rub against one another.

Front: The area between air masses of different temperatures or densities.

Fuel cell: A device that uses hydrogen as the fuel to produce electricity and heat with water as a byproduct.

Fulcrum: The point at which a lever arm pivots.

Fungi: Kingdom of various single-celled or multicellular organisms, including mushrooms, molds, yeasts, and mildews, that do not contain chlorophyll.

Funnel cloud: A fully developed tornado vortex before it has touched the ground.

Fusion: Combining of nuclei of two or more lighter elements into one nucleus of a heavier element; the process stars use to produce energy to produce light and support themselves against their own gravity.

Galaxy: A large collection of stars and clusters of stars containing anywhere from a few million to a few trillion stars.

Gastropod: The largest group of mollusks; characterized by a single shell that is often coiled in a spiral. Snails are gastropods.

Gene: A segment of a DNA (deoxyribonucleic acid) molecule contained in the nucleus of a cell that acts as a kind of code for the production of some specific protein. Genes carry instructions for the formation, functioning, and transmission of specific traits from one generation to another.

Generator: A device that converts mechanical energy into electrical energy,

Genetic engineering: A technique that modifies the DNA of living cells in order to make them change its characteristics. Also called genetic modification.

Genetic material: Material that transfers characteristics from a parent to its offspring.

Geology: The study of the origin, history and structure of Earth.

Geothermal energy: Energy from deep within Earth.

Geotropism: The tendency of roots to bend toward Earth.

Germ theory of disease: The theory that disease is caused by microorganisms or germs, and not by spontaneous generation.

Germination: First stage in development of a plant seed.

Gibbous moon: A phase of the Moon when more than half of its surface is lighted.

Gills: Special organ located behind the head of a fish that takes in oxygen from the water.

Glacier: A large mass of ice formed from snow that has packed together and which moves slowly down a slope under its own weight.

Global warming: Warming of Earth's atmosphere as a result of an increase in the concentration of gases that store heat, such as carbon dioxide.

Glucose: A simple sugar broken down in cells to produce energy.

Gnomon: The perpendicular piece of the sundial that casts the shadow.

Golgi body: An organelles that sorts, modifies, and packages molecules.

Gravity: Force of attraction between objects, the strength of which depends on the mass of each object and the distance between them.

Greenhouse effect: The warming of Earth's atmosphere due to water vapor, carbon dioxide, and other gases in the atmosphere that trap heat radiated from Earth's surface.

Greenhouse gases: Gases that absorb infrared radiation and warm the air before the heat energy escapes into space.

Greenwich Mean Time (GMT): The time at an imaginary line that runs north and south through Greenwich, England, used as the standard for time throughout the world.

Groundwater: Water that soaks into the ground and is stored in the small spaces between the rocks and soil.

Group: A vertical column of the periodic table that contains elements possessing similar chemical characteristics.

Hardwood: Wood from angiosperm, mostly deciduous, trees.

Heartwood: The inner layers of wood that provide structure and have no living cells.

Heat: A form of energy produced by the motion of molecules that make up a substance.

Heat capacity: The measure of how well a substance stores heat.

Heat energy: The energy produced when two substances that have different temperatures are combined.

Heliotropism: The tendency of plants to turn towards the Sun throughout the day.

Herbivore: A plant-eating organism.

Hertz (Hz): The unit of measurement of frequency; a measure of the number of waves that pass a given point per second of time.

Heterogeneous: Different throughout.

Heterotrophs: Organisms that cannot make their own food and that must, therefore, obtain their food from other organisms.

High air pressure: An area where the air is cooler and more dense, and the air pressure is higher than normal.

Hippocampus: A part of the brain associated with learning and memory.

Homogenous: The same throughout.

Hormones: Chemicals produced in the cells of plants and animals that control bodily functions.

Hue: The color or shade.

Humidity: The amount of water vapor (moisture) contained in the air.

Humus: Fragrant, spongy, nutrient-rich decayed plant or animal matter.

Hydrologic cycle: Continual movement of water from the atmosphere to Earth's surface through precipitation and back to the atmosphere through evaporation and transpiration.

Hydrologists: Scientists who study water and its cycle.

Hydrology: The study of water and its cycle.

Hydrometer: An instrument that determines the specific gravity of a liquid.

Hydrophilic: A substance that is attracted to and readily mixes with water.

Hydrophobic: A substance that is repelled by and does not mix with water.

Hydropower: Energy produced from capturing moving water.

Hydrotropism: The tendency of roots to grow toward a water source.

Hypertonic solution: A solution with a higher concentration of materials than a cell immersed in the solution.

Hypha: Slender, cottony filaments making up the body of multicellular fungi. (Plural: hyphae)

Hypothesis: An idea in the form of a statement that can be tested by observation and/or experiment.

Hypotonic solution: A solution with a lower concentration of materials than a cell immersed in the solution.

Igneous rock: Rock formed from the cooling and hardening of magma.

Immiscible: Incapable of being mixed.

Imperfect flower: Flowers that have only the male reproductive organ (stamen) or the female reproductive organs (pistil).

Impermeable: Not allowing substances to pass through.

Impurities: Chemicals or other pollutants in water.

Inclined plane: A simple machine with no moving parts; a slanted surface.

Incomplete metamorphosis: Metamorphosis in which a nymph form gradually becomes an adult through molting.

Independent variable: The variable in an experiment that determines the final result of the experiment.

Indicator: Pigments that change color when they come into contact with acidic or basic solutions.

Inertia: The tendency of an object to continue in its state of motion.

Infrared radiation: Electromagnetic radiation of a wavelength shorter than radio waves but longer than visible light that takes the form of heat.

Inner core: Very dense, solid center of Earth.

Inorganic: Not containing carbon; not derived from a living organism.

Insect: A six-legged invertebrate whose body has three segments.

Insoluble: A substance that cannot be dissolved in some other substance.

Insulated wire: Electrical wire coated with a non-conducting material such as plastic.

Insulation: A material that is a poor conductor of heat or electricity.

Insulator: A material through which little or no electrical current or heat energy will flow.

Interference fringes: Bands of color that fan out around an object.

Internal skeleton: An animal that has a backbone.

Invertebrate: An animal that lacks a backbone or internal skeleton.

Ion: An atom or groups of atoms that carry an electrical charge—either positive or negative—as a result of losing or gaining one or more electrons.

Ion tail: One of two types of tails a comet may have, it is composed mainly of charged particles and it points away from the Sun.

Ionic conduction: The flow of an electrical current by the movement of charged particles, or ions.

Isobars: Continuous lines that connect areas with the same air pressure.

Isotonic solutions: Two solutions that have the same concentration of solute particles and therefore the same osmotic pressure.

Jawless fish: The smallest group of fishes, who lacks a jaw.

Kinetic energy: The energy of an object or system due to its motion.

Kingdom: One of the five classifications in the widely accepted classification system that designates all living organisms into animals, plants, fungi, protists, and monerans.

Labyrinth: A lung-like organ located above the gills that allows the fish to breathe in oxygen from the air.

Lactobacilli: A strain of bacteria.

Landfill: A method of disposing of waste materials by placing them in a depression in the ground or piling them in a mound. In a sanitary landfill, the daily deposits of waste materials are covered with a layer of soil.

Larva: Immature form (wormlike in insects; fishlike in amphibians) of an organism capable of surviving on its own. A larva does not resemble the parent and must go through metamorphosis, or change, to reach its adult stage.

Lava: Molten rock that occurs at the surface of Earth, usually through volcanic eruptions.

Lava cave: A cave formed from the flow of lava streaming over solid matter.

Leach: The movement of dissolved minerals or chemicals with water as it percolates, or oozes, downward through the soil.

Leaching: The movement of dissolved chemicals with water that is percolating, or oozing, downward through the soil.

Leavening agent: A substance used to make foods like dough and batter to rise.

Leeward: The side away from the wind or flow direction.

Lens: A piece of transparent material with two curved surfaces that bend rays of light passing through it.

Lichen: An organism composed of a fungus and a photosynthetic organism in a symbiotic relationship.

Lift: Upward force on the wings of an aircraft created by differences in air pressure on top of and underneath the wings.

Ligaments: Tough, fibrous tissue connecting bones.

Light: A form of energy that travels in waves.

Light-year: Distance light travels in one year in the vacuum of space, roughly 5.9 trillion miles (9.5 trillion kilometers).

The Local Group: A cluster of thirty galaxies, including the Milky Way, pulled together by gravity.

Long-term memory: The last category of memory in which memories are stored away and can last for years.

Low air pressure: An area where the air is warmer and less dense, and the air pressure is lower than normal.

Luminescent: Producing light through a chemical process.

Luminol: A compound used to detect blood.

Lunar eclipse: An eclipse that occurs when Earth passes between the Sun and the Moon, casting a shadow on the Moon.

Luster: A glow of reflected light; a sheen.

Machine: Any device that makes work easier by providing a mechanical advantage.

Macrominerals: Minerals needed in relatively large quantities.

Macroorganisms: Visible organisms that aid in breaking down organic matter.

Magma: Molten rock deep within Earth that consists of liquids, gases, and particles of rocks and crystals. Magma underlies areas of volcanic activity and at Earth's surface is called lava.

Magma chambers: Pools of bubbling liquid rock that are the source of energy causing volcanoes to be active.

Magma surge: A swell or rising wave of magma caused by the movement and friction of tectonic plates, which heats and melts rock, adding to the magma and its force.

Magnet: A material that attracts other like materials, especially metals.

Magnetic circuit: A series of magnetic domains aligned in the same direction.

Magnetic field: The space around an electric current or a magnet in which a magnetic force can be observed.

Magnetism: A fundamental force in nature caused by the motion of electrons in an atom.

Maillard reaction: A reaction caused by heat and sugars and resulting in foods browning and flavors.

Mammals: Animals that have a backbone, are warm blooded, have mammary glands to feed their young and have or are born with hair.

Mantle: Thick dense layer of rock that underlies Earth's crust and overlies the core; also soft tissue that is located between the shell and an animal's inner organs. The mantle produces the calcium carbonate substance that create the shell of the animal.

Manure: The waste matter of animals.

Mass: Measure of the total amount of matter in an object. Also, an object's quantity of matter as shown by its gravitational pull on another object.

Matter: Anything that has mass and takes up space.

Meandering river: A lowland river that twists and turns along its route to the sea.

Medium: A material that contains the nutrients required for a particular microorganism to grow.

Melting point: The temperature at which a substance changes from a solid to a liquid.

Memory: The process of retaining and recalling past events and experiences.

Meniscus: The curved surface of a column of liquid.

Metabolism: The process by which living organisms convert food into energy and waste products.

Metamorphic rock: Rock formed by transformation of pre-existing rock through changes in temperature and pressure.

Metamorphosis: Transformation of an immature animal into an adult.

Meteor: An object from space that becomes glowing hot when it passes into Earth's atmosphere; also called shooting star.

Meteor shower: A group of meteors that occurs when Earth's orbit intersects the orbit of a meteor stream.

Meteorites: A meteor that is large enough to survive its passage through the atmosphere and hit the ground.

Meteoroid: A piece of debris that is traveling in space.

Meteorologist: Scientist who studies the weather and the atmosphere.

Microbiology: Branch of biology dealing with microscopic forms of life.

Microclimate: A unique climate that exists only in a small, localized area.

Microorganisms: Living organisms so small that they can be seen only with the aid of a microscope.

Micropyle: Seed opening that enables water to enter easily.

Microvilli: The extension of each taste cell that pokes through the taste pore and first senses the chemicals.

Milky Way: The galaxy in which our solar system is located.

Mimicry: A characteristic in which an animal is protected against predators by resembling another, more distasteful animal.

Mineral: An inorganic substance found in nature with a definite chemical composition and structure. As a nutrient, it helps build bones and soft tissues and regulates body functions.

Mixture: A combination of two or more substances that are not chemically combined with each other and that can exist in any proportion.

Mnemonics: Techniques to improve memory.

Mold: In paleontology, the fossil formed when acidic water dissolves a shell or bone around which sand or mud has already hardened.

Molecule: The smallest particle of a substance that retains all the properties of the substance and is composed of one or more atoms.

Mollusk: An invertebrate animal usually enclosed in a shell, the largest group of shelled animals.

Molting: A process by which an animal sheds its skin or shell.

Monocot: Plants with a single embryonic leaf at germination.

Monomer: A small molecule that can be combined with itself many times over to make a large molecule, the polymer.

Moraine: Mass of boulders, stones, and other rock debris carried along and deposited by a glacier.

Mordant: A substance that fixes the dye to the material.

Mountain: A landform that stands well above its surroundings; higher than a hill.

Mucus: A thick, slippery substance that serves as a protective lubricant coating in passages of the body that communicate with the air.

Multicellular: Living things with many cells joined together.

Muscle fibers: Stacks of long, thin cells that make up muscle; there are three types of muscle fiber: skeletal, cardiac, and smooth.

Mycelium: In fungi, the mass of threadlike, branching hyphae.

Nanobots: A nanoscale robot.

Nanometer: A unit of length; this measurement is equal to one-billionth of a meter.

Nanotechnology: Technology that involves working and developing technologies on the nanometer (atomic and molecular) scale.

Nansen bottles: Self-closing containers with thermometers that draw in water at different depths.

Nebula: Bright or dark cloud, often composed of gases and dust, hovering in the space between the stars.

Nectar: A sweet liquid, found inside a flower, that attracts pollinators.

Neutralization: A chemical reaction in which the mixing of an acidic solution with a basic (alkaline) solution results in a solution that has the properties of neither an acid nor a base.

Neutron: A subatomic particle with a mass of about one atomic mass unit and no electrical charge that is found in the nucleus of an atom.

Newtonian fluid: A fluid that follows certain properties, such as the viscosity remains constant at a given temperature.

Niche: The specific location and place in the food chain that an organism occupies in its environment.

Noble gases: Also known as inert or rare gases; the elements argon, helium, krypton, neon, radon, and xenon, which are nonreactive gases and form few compounds with other elements.

Non-Newtonian fluid: A fluid whose property do not follow Newtonian properties, such as viscosity can vary based on the stress.

Nonpoint source: An unidentified source of pollution, which may actually be a number of sources.

Nucleation: The process by which crystals start growing.

Nucleotide: The basic unit of a nucleic acid. It consists of a simple sugar, a phosphate group, and a nitrogen-containing base. (Pronounced noo-KLEE-uh-tide.)

Nucleus: The central part of the cell that contains the DNA; the central core of an atom, consisting of protons and (usually) neutrons.

Nutrient: A substance needed by an organism in order for it to survive, grow, and develop.

Nutrition: The study of the food nutrients an organism needs in order to maintain well-being.

Nymph: An immature form in the life cycle of insects that go through an incomplete metamorphosis.

Objective lens: In a refracting telescope, the lens farthest away from the eye that collects the light.

Oceanographer: A person who studies the chemistry of the oceans, as well as their currents, marine life, and the ocean floor.

Oceanography: The study of the chemistry of the oceans, as well as their currents, marine life, and the ocean bed.

Olfactory: Relating to the sense of smell.

Olfactory bulb: The part of the brain that processes olfactory (smell) information.

Olfactory epithelium: The patch of mucous membrane at the top of the nasal cavity that contains the olfactory (smell) nerve cells.

Olfactory receptor cells: Nerve cells in the olfactory epithelium that detect odors and transmit the information to the brain.

Oort cloud: Region of space beyond our solar system that theoretically contains about one trillion inactive comets.

Optics: The study of the nature of light and its properties.

Orbit: The path followed by a body (such as a planet) in its travel around another body (such as the Sun).

Organelle: A membrane-enclosed structure that performs a specific function within a cell.

Organic: Containing carbon; also referring to materials that are derived from living organisms.

Oscillation: A repeated back-and-forth movement.

Osmosis: The movement of fluids and substances dissolved in liquids across a semipermeable membrane from an area of its greater concentration to an area of its lesser concentration until all substances involved reach a balance.

Outer core: A liquid core that surrounds Earth's solid inner core; made mostly of iron.

Ovary: In a plant, the base part of the pistil that bears ovules and develops into a fruit.

Ovule: Structure within the ovary that develops into a seed after fertilization.

Oxidation: A chemical reaction in which oxygen reacts with some other substance and in which ions, atoms, or molecules lose electrons.

Oxidation state: The sum of an atom's positive and negative charges.

Oxidation-reduction reaction: A chemical reaction in which one substance loses one or more electrons and the other substance gains one or more electrons.

Oxidizing agent: A chemical substance that gives up oxygen or takes on electrons from another substance.

Paleontologist: Scientist who studies the life of past geological periods as known from fossil remains.

Papain: An enzyme obtained from the fruit of the papaya used as a meat tenderizer, as a drug to clean cuts and wounds, and as a digestive aid for stomach disorders.

Papillae: The raised bumps on the tongue that contain the taste buds.

Parent material: The underlying rock from which soil forms.

Partial solar/lunar eclipse: An eclipse in which our view of the Sun/Moon is only partially blocked.

Particulate matter: Solid matter in the form of tiny particles in the atmosphere. (Pronounced par-TIK-you-let.)

Passive solar energy system: A solar energy system in which the heat of the Sun is captured, used, and stored by means of the design of a building and the materials from which it is made.

Pasteurization: The process of slow heating that kills bacteria and other microorganisms.

Peaks: The points at which the energy in a wave is maximum.

Pectin: A natural carbohydrate found in fruits and vegetables.

Pectoral fin: Pair of fins located on the side of a fish, used for steering.

Pedigree: A diagram that illustrates the pattern of inheritance of a genetic trait in a family.

Pelvic fin: Pair of fins located toward the belly of a fish, used for stability.

Pendulum: A free-swinging weight, usually consisting of a heavy object attached to the end of a long rod or string, suspended from a fixed point.

Penicillin: A mold from the fungi group of microorganisms; used as an antibiotic.

Pepsin: Digestive enzyme that breaks down protein.

Percolate: To pass through a permeable substance.

Perfect flower: Flowers that have both male and female reproductive organs.

Period: A horizontal row in the periodic table.

Periodic table: A chart organizing elements by atomic number and chemical properties into groups and periods.

Permeable: Having pores that permit a liquid or a gas to pass through.

Permineralization: A form of preservation in which mineral matter has filled in the inner and outer spaces of the cell.

Pest: Any living thing that is unwanted by humans or causes injury and disease to crops and other growth.

Pesticide: Substance used to reduce the abundance of pests.

Petal: Leafy structure of a flower just inside the sepals; they are often brightly colored and have many different shapes.

Petrifaction: Process of turning organic material into rock by the replacement of that material with minerals.

pH: A measure of the acidity or alkalinity of a solution referring to the concentration of hydrogen ions present in a liter of a given fluid. The pH scale ranges from 0 (greatest concentration of hydrogen ions and therefore most acidic) to 14 (least concentration of hydrogen ions and therefore most alkaline), with 7 representing a neutral solution, such as pure water.

Pharmacology: The science dealing with the properties, reactions, and therapeutic values of drugs.

Phases: Changes in the portion of the Moon's surface that is illuminated by light from the Sun as the Moon revolves around Earth.

Phloem: The plant tissue that carries dissolved nutrients through the plant.

Phosphorescence: The emission of visible light from an object when the object is bombarded with electromagnetic radiation, such as ultraviolet rays. The object stores part of the radiation energy and the emission of visible light continues for a period ranging from a fraction of a second to several days after the radiation source has been removed.

Photoelectric effect: The phenomenon in which light falling upon certain metals stimulates the emission of electrons and changes light into electricity.

Photosynthesis: Chemical process by which plants containing chlorophyll use sunlight to manufacture their own food by converting carbon dioxide and water to carbohydrates, releasing oxygen as a by-product.

Phototropism: The tendency of a plant to grow toward a source of light.

Photovoltaic cells: A device made of silicon that converts sunlight into electricity.

Physical change: A change in which the substance keeps its molecular identity, such as a piece of chalk that has been ground up.

Physical property: A characteristic that you can detect with your senses, such as color and shape.

Physiologist: A scientist who studies the functions and processes of living organisms.

Phytoplankton: Microscopic aquatic plants that live suspended in the water.

Pigment: A substance that displays a color because of the wavelengths of light that it reflects.

Pili: Short projections that assist bacteria in attaching to tissues.

Pistil: Female reproductive organ of flowers that is composed of the stigma, style, and ovary.

Pitch: A property of a sound, determined by its frequency; the highness or lowness of a sound.

Plant extract: The juice or liquid essence obtained from a plant by squeezing or mashing it.

Plasmolysis: Occurs in walled cells in which cytoplasm, the semifluid substance inside a cell, shrivels and the membrane pulls away from the cell wall when the vacuole loses water.

Plates: Large regions of Earth's surface, composed of the crust and uppermost mantle, which move about, forming many of Earth's major geologic surface features.

Platform: The horizontal surface of a bridge on which traffic travels.

Pnematocysts: Stinging cells.

Point source: An identified source of pollution.

Pollen: Dust-like grains or particles produced by a plant that contain male sex cells.

Pollinate: The transfer of pollen from the male reproductive organs to the female reproductive organs of plants.

Pollination: Transfer of pollen from the male reproductive organs to the female reproductive organs of plants.

Pollinator: Any animal, such as an insect or bird, that transfers the pollen from one flower to another.

Pollution: The contamination of the natural environment, usually through human activity.

Polymer: Chemical compound formed of simple molecules (known as monomers) linked with themselves many times over.

Polymerization: The bonding of two or more monomers to form a polymer.

Polyvinyl acetate: A type of polymer that is the main ingredient of white glues.

Pore: An opening or space.

Potential energy: The energy of an object or system due to its position.

Precipitation: Any form of water that falls to Earth, such as rain, snow, or sleet.

Predator: An animal that hunts another animal for food.

Preservative: An additive used to keep food from spoiling.

Primary colors: The three colors red, green, and blue; when combined evenly they produce white light and by combining varying amounts can produce the range of colors.

Prism: A piece of transparent material with a triangular cross-section. When light passes through it, it causes different colors to bend different amounts, thus separating them into a rainbow of colors.

Probe: The terminal of a voltmeter, used to connect the voltmeter to a circuit.

Producer: An organism that can manufacture its own food from nonliving materials and an external energy source, usually by photosynthesis.

Product: A compound that is formed as a result of a chemical reaction.

Prokaryote: A cell without a true nucleus, such as a bacterium.

Prominences: Masses of glowing gas, mainly hydrogen, that rise from the Sun's surface like flames.

Propeller: Radiating blades mounted on a rapidly rotating shaft, which moves aircraft forward.

Protein: A complex chemical compound consisting of many amino acids attached to each other that are essential to the structure and functioning of all living cells.

Protists: Members of the kingdom Protista, primarily single-celled organisms that are not plants or animals.

Proton: A subatomic particle with a single positive charge that is found in the nucleus of an atom.

Protozoa: Single-celled animal-like microscopic organisms that live by taking in food rather than making it by photosynthesis. They must live in the presence of water.

Pulley: A simple machine made of a cord wrapped around a wheel.

Pupa: The insect stage of development between the larva and adult in insects that go through complete metamorphosis.

Radiation: Energy transmitted in the form of electromagnetic waves or subatomic particles.

Radicule: Seed's root system.

Radio wave: Longest form of electromagnetic radiation, measuring up to 6 miles (9.6 kilometers) from peak to peak.

Radioisotope dating: A technique used to date fossils, based on the decay rate of known radioactive elements.

Radiosonde balloons: Instruments for collecting data in the atmosphere and then transmitting that data back to Earth by means of radio waves.

Radon: A radioactive gas located in the ground; invisible and odorless, radon is a health hazard when it accumulates to high levels inside homes and other structures where it is breathed.

Rain shadow: Region on the side of the mountain that receives less rainfall than the area windward of the mountain.

Rancidity: Having the condition when food has a disagreeable odor or taste from decomposing oils or fats.

Reactant: A compound present at the beginning of a chemical reaction.

Reaction: Response to an action prompted by stimulus.

Recessive gene: A gene that produces a certain characteristic only two both copies (alleles) of the gene are present.

Recycling: The use of waste materials, also known as secondary materials or recyclables, to produce new products.

Redshift: The lengthening of the frequency of light waves toward the red end of the visible light spectrum as they travel away from an observer; most commonly used to describe movement of stars away from Earth.

Reduction: A process in which a chemical substance gives off oxygen or takes on electrons.

Reed: A tall woody perennial grass that has a hollow stem.

Reflection: The bouncing of light rays in a regular pattern off the surface of an object.

Reflector telescope: A telescope that directs light from an opening at one end to a concave mirror at the far end, which reflects the light back to a smaller mirror that directs it to an eyepiece on the side of the tube.

Refraction: The bending of light rays as they pass at an angle from one transparent or clear medium into a second one of different density.

Refractor telescope: A telescope that directs light through a glass lens, which bends the light waves and brings them to a focus at an eyepiece that acts as a magnifying glass.

Relative age: The age of an object expressed in relation to another like object, such as earlier or later.

Relative density: The density of one material compared to another.

Rennin: Enzyme used in making cheese.

Resistance: A partial or complete limiting of the flow of electrical current through a material. The common unit of measure is the ohm.

Respiration: The physical process that supplies oxygen to living cells and the chemical reactions that take place inside the cells.

Resultant: A force that results from the combined action of two other forces.

Retina: The light-sensitive part of the eyeball that receives images and transmits visual impulses through the optic nerve to the brain.

Ribosome: A protein composed of two subunits that functions in protein synthesis (creation).

Rigidity: The amount an object will deflect when supporting a weight. The less it deflects for a given amount of weight, the greater its rigidity.

River: A main course of water into which many other smaller bodies of water flow.

Rock: Naturally occurring solid mixture of minerals.

Rods: Cells in the retina that are sensitive to degrees of light and movement.

Root hairs: Fine, hair-like extensions from the plant's root.

Rotate: To turn around on an axis or center.

Runoff: Water that does not soak into the ground or evaporate, but flows across the surface of the ground.

Salinity: The amount of salts dissolved in water.

Saliva: Watery mixture with chemicals that lubricates chewed food.

Sand: Granular portion of soil composed of the largest soil particles.

Sapwood: The outer wood in a tree, which is usually a lighter color.

Saturated: In referring to solutions, a solution that contains the maximum amount of solute for a given amount of solvent at a given temperature.

Saturation: The intensity of a color.

Scanning tunneling microscope: A microscope that can show images of surfaces at the atomic level by scanning a probe over a surface.

Scientific method: Collecting evidence and arriving at a conclusion under carefully controlled conditions.

Screw: A simple machine; an inclined plane wrapped around a cylinder.

Scurvy: A disease caused by a deficiency of vitamin C, which causes a weakening of connective tissue in bone and muscle.

Sea cave: A cave in sea cliffs, formed most commonly by waves eroding the rock.

Second law of motion (Newton's): The force exerted on an object is proportional to the mass of the object times the acceleration produced by the force.

Sediment: Sand, silt, clay, rock, gravel, mud, or other matter that has been transported by flowing water.

Sedimentary rock: Rock formed from compressed and solidified layers of organic or inorganic matter.

Sedimentation: A process during which gravity pulls particles out of a liquid.

Seed crystal: Small form of a crystalline structure that has all the facets of a complete new crystal contained in it.

Seedling: A small plant just starting to grow into its mature form.

Seismic belt: Boundaries where Earth's plates meet.

Seismic waves: Vibrations in rock and soil that transfer the force of an earthquake from the focus into the surrounding area.

Seismograph: A device that detects and records vibrations of the ground.

Seismology: The study and measurement of earthquakes.

Seismometer: A seismograph that measures the movement of the ground.

Self-pollination: The process in which pollen from one part of a plant fertilizes ovules on another part of the same plant.

Semipermeable membrane: A thin barrier between two solutions that permits only certain components of the solutions, usually the solvent, to pass through.

Sensory memory: Memory that the brain retains for a few seconds.

Sepal: The outermost part of a flower; typically leaflike and green.

Sexual reproduction: A reproductive process that involves the union of two individuals in the exchange of genetic material.

Shear stress: An applied force to a give area.

Shell: A region of space around the center of the atom in which electrons are located; also, a hard outer covering that protects an animal living inside.

Short-term memory: Also known as working memory, this memory was transferred here from sensory memory.

Sidereal day: The time it takes for a particular star to travel around and reach the same position in the sky; about four minutes shorter than the average solar day.

Silt: Medium-sized soil particles.

Simple machine: Any of the basic structures that provide a mechanical advantage and have no or few moving parts.

Smog: A form of air pollution produced when moisture in the air combines and reacts with the products of fossil fuel combustion. Smog is characterized by hazy skies and a tendency to cause respiratory problems among humans.

Softwood: Wood from coniferous trees, which usually remain green all year.

Soil: The upper layer of Earth that contains nutrients for plants and organisms; a mixture of mineral matter, organic matter, air, and water.

Soil horizon: An identifiable soil layer due to color, structure, and/or texture.

Soil profile: Combined soil horizons or layers.

Solar collector: A device that absorbs sunlight and collects solar heat.

Solar day: Called a day, the time between each arrival of the Sun at its highest point.

Solar eclipse: An eclipse that occurs when the Moon passes between Earth and the Sun, casting a shadow on Earth.

Solar energy: Any form of electromagnetic radiation that is emitted by the Sun.

Solubility: The tendency of a substance to dissolve in some other substance.

Soluble: A substance that can be dissolved in some other substance.

Solute: The substance that is dissolved to make a solution and exists in the least amount in a solution, for example sugar in sugar water.

Solution: A mixture of two or more substances that appears to be uniform throughout except on a molecular level.

Solvent: The major component of a solution or the liquid in which some other component is dissolved, for example water in sugar water.

Specific gravity: The ratio of the density of a substance to the density of pure water.

Specific heat capacity: The energy required to raise the temperature of 1 kilogram of the substance by 1 degree Celsius.

Speleologist: One who studies caves.

Speleology: Scientific study of caves and their plant and animal life.

Spelunkers: Also called cavers, people who explore caves for a hobby.

Spiracles: The openings on an insects side where air enters.

Spoilage: The condition when food has taken on an undesirable color, odor, or texture.

Spore: A small, usually one-celled, reproductive body that is capable of growing into a new organism.

Stalactite: Cylindrical or icicle-shaped mineral deposit projecting downward from the roof of a cave. (Pronounced sta-LACK-tite.)

Stalagmite: Cylindrical or icicle-shaped mineral deposit projecting upward from the floor of a cave. (Pronounced sta-LAG-mite.)

Stamen: Male reproductive organ of flowers that is composed of the anther and filament.

Standard: A base for comparison.

Star: A vast clump of hydrogen gas and dust that produces great energy through fusion reactions at its core.

Static electricity: A form of electricity produced by friction in which the electric charge does not flow in a current but stays in one place.

Stigma: Top part of the pistil upon which pollen lands and receives the male pollen grains during fertilization.

Stomata: Pores in the epidermis (surface) of leaves.

Storm: An extreme atmospheric disturbance, associated with strong damaging winds, and often with thunder and lightning.

Storm chasers: People who track and seek out storms, often tornadoes.

Stratification: Layers according to density; applies to fluids.

Streak: The color of the dust left when a mineral is rubbed across a rough surface.

Style: Stalk of the pistil that connects the stigma to the ovary.

Subatomic: Smaller than an atom. It usually refers to particles that make up an atom, such as protons, neutrons, and electrons.

Sublime: The process of changing a solid into a vapor without passing through the liquid phase.

Substrate: The substance on which an enzyme operates in a chemical reaction.

Succulent: Plants that live in dry environments and have water storage tissue.

Sundial: A device that uses the position of the Sun to indicate time.

Supersaturated: Solution that is more highly concentrated than is normally possible under given conditions of temperature and pressure.

Supertaster: A person who is extremely sensitive to specific tastes due to a greater number of taste buds.

Supplements: A substance intended to enhance the diet.

Surface area: The total area of the outside of an object; the area of a body of water that is exposed to the air.

Surface tension: The attractive force of molecules to each other on the surface of a liquid.

Surface water: Water in lakes, rivers, ponds, and streams.

Suspension: A temporary mixture of a solid in a gas or liquid from which the solid will eventually settle out.

Swim bladder: Located above the stomach, takes in air when the fish wants to move upwards and releases air when the fish wants to move downwards.

Symbiosis: A pattern in which two or more organisms live in close connection with each other, often to the benefit of both or all organisms.

Synthesis reaction: A chemical reaction in which two or more substances combine to form a new substance.

Synthesize: To make something artificially, in a laboratory or chemical plant, that is generally not found in nature.

Synthetic: A substance that is synthesized, or manufactured, in a laboratory; not naturally occurring.

Synthetic crystals: Artificial or manmade crystals.

Taiga: A large land biome mostly dominated by coniferous trees.

Taste buds: Groups of taste cells located on the papillae that recognize the different tastes.

Taste pore: The opening at the top of the taste bud from which chemicals reach the taste cells.

Tectonic: Relating to the forces and structures of the outer shell of Earth.

Tectonic plates: Huge flat rocks that form Earth's crust.

Telescope: A tube with lenses or mirrors that collect, transmit, and focus light.

Temperate: Mild or moderate weather conditions.

Temperature: The measure of the average energy of the molecules in a substance.

Tendon: Tough, fibrous connective tissue that attaches muscle to bone.

Tensile strength: The force needed to stretch a material until it breaks.

Terminal: A connection in an electric circuit; usually a connection on a source of electric energy such as a battery.

Terracing: A series of horizontal ridges made in a hillside to reduce erosion.

Testa: A tough outer layer that protects the embryo and endosperm of a seed from damage.

Theory of special relativity: Theory put forth by Albert Einstein that time is not absolute, but it is relative according to the speed of the observer's frame of reference.

Thermal conductivity: A number representing a material's ability to conduct heat.

Thermal energy: Kinetic energy caused by the movement of molecules due to temperature.

Thermal inversion: A region in which the warmer air lies above the colder air; can cause smog to worsen.

Thermal pollution: The discharge of heated water from industrial processes that can kill or injure water life.

Thiamine: A vitamin of the B complex that is essential to normal metabolism and nerve function.

Thigmotropism: The tendency for a plant to grow toward a surface it touches.

Third law of motion (Newton's): For every action there is an equal and opposite reaction.

Thorax: The middle segment of an insect body; the legs and wings are connected to the thorax.

Tides: The cyclic rise and fall of seawater.

Titration: A procedure in which an acid and a base are slowly mixed to achieve a neutral substance.

Topsoil: The uppermost layers of soil containing an abundant supply of decomposed organic material to supply plants with nutrients.

Tornado: A violently rotating, narrow column of air in contact with the ground and usually extending from a cumulonimbus cloud.

Total solar/lunar eclipse: An eclipse in which our view of the Sun/Moon is totally blocked.

Toxic: Poisonous.

Trace element: A chemical element present in minute quantities.

Trace minerals: Minerals needed in relatively small quantities.

Translucent: Permits the passage of light.

Transpiration: Evaporation of water in the form of water vapor from the stomata on the surfaces of leaves and stems of plants.

Troglobite: An animal that lives in a cave and is unable to live outside of one.

Troglophile: An animal that lives the majority of its life cycle in a cave but is also able to live outside of the cave.

Trogloxene: An animal that spends only part of its life cycle in a cave and returns periodically to the cave.

Tropism: The growth or movement of a plant toward or away from a stimulus.

Troposphere: The lowest layer of Earth's atmosphere, ranging to an altitude of about 9 miles (15 km) above Earth's surface.

Trough: The lowest point of a wave. (Pronounced trawf.)

Tsunami: A large wave of water caused by an underwater earthquake.

Tuber: An underground, starch-storing stem, such as a potato.

Tundra: A treeless, frozen biome with low-lying plants.

Turbine: A spinning device used to transform mechanical power from energy into electrical energy.

Turbulence: Air disturbance that affects an aircraft's flight.

Turgor pressure: The force that is exerted on a plant's cell wall by the water within the cell.

Tyndall effect: The effect achieved when colloidal particles reflect a beam of light, making it visible when shined through such a mixture.

Ultraviolet: Electromagnetic radiation (energy) of a wavelength just shorter than the violet (shortest wavelength) end of the visible light spectrum and thus with higher energy than the visible light.

Unconfined aquifer: An aquifer under a layer of permeable rock and soil.

Unicellular: Living things that have one cell. Protozoans are unicellular, for example.

Unit cell: The basic unit of the crystalline structure.

Universal law of gravity: The law of physics that defines the constancy of the force of gravity between two bodies.

Updraft: Warm, moist air that moves away from the ground.

Upwelling: The process by which lower-level, nutrient-rich waters rise upward to the ocean's surface.

Vacuole: An enclosed, space-filling sac within plant cells containing mostly water and providing structural support for the cell.

Van der Waals' force: An attractive force between two molecules based on the positive and negative side of the molecule.

Variable: Something that can affect the results of an experiment.

Vegetative propagation: A form of asexual reproduction in which plants are produced that are genetically identical to the parent.

Velocity: The rate at which the position of an object changes with time, including both the speed and the direction.

Veneer: Thin slices of wood.

Viable: The capability of developing or growing under favorable conditions.

Vibration: A regular, back-and-forth motion of molecules in the air.

Viscosity: The measure of a fluid's resistance to flow; its flowability.

Visible spectrum: The range of individual wavelengths of radiation visible to the human eye when white light is broken into its component colors as it passes through a prism or by some other means.

Vitamin: A complex organic compound found naturally in plants and animals that the body needs in small amounts for normal growth and activity.

Volatilization: The process by which a liquid changes (volatilizes) to a gas.

Volcano: A conical mountain or dome of lava, ash, and cinders that forms around a vent leading to molten rock deep within Earth.

Voltage: Also called potential difference; a measurement of the amount of electric energy stored in a mass of electric charges compared to the energy stored in some other mass of charges. The common unit of measure is the volt.

Voltmeter: An instrument for measuring the amperage, voltage, or resistance in an electrical circuit.

Volume: The amount of space occupied by a three-dimensional object; the amplitude or loudness of a sound.

Vortex: A rotating column of a fluid such as air or water.

Waste stream: The waste materials generated by the population of an area, or by a specific industrial process, and removed for disposal.

Water (hydrologic) cycle: The constant movement of water molecules on Earth as they rise into the atmosphere as water vapor, condense into droplets and fall to land or bodies of water, evaporate, and rise again.

Water clock: A device that uses the flow of water to measure time.

Water table: The level of the upper surface of groundwater.

Water vapor: Water in its gaseous state.

Water-soluble vitamins: Vitamins such as C and the B-complex vitamins that dissolve in the watery parts of plant and animal tissues.

Waterline: The highest point to which water rises on the hull of a ship. The portion of the hull below the waterline is under water.

Wave: A means of transmitting energy in which the peak energy occurs at a regular interval; the rise and fall of the ocean water.

Wavelength: The distance between the peak of a wave of light, heat, or other form of energy and the next corresponding peak.

Weather: The state of the troposphere at a particular time and place.

Weather forecasting: The scientific predictions of future weather patterns.

Weathered: Natural process that breaks down rocks and minerals at Earth's surface into simpler materials by physical (mechanical) or chemical means.

Wedge: A simple machine; a form of inclined plane.

Weight: The gravitational attraction of Earth on an object; the measure of the heaviness of an object.

Wet cell: A source of electricity that uses a liquid electrolyte.

Wetlands: Areas that are wet or covered with water for at least part of the year.

Wheel and axle: A simple machine; a larger wheel(s) fastened to a smaller cylinder, an axle, so that they turn together.

Work: The result of a force moving a mass a given distance. The greater the mass or the greater the distance, the greater the work involved.

Xanthophyll: Yellow pigment in plants.

Xerophytes: Plants that require little water to survive.

Xylem: Plant tissue consisting of elongated, thick-walled cells that transport water and mineral nutrients. (Pronounced ZY-lem.)

Yeast: A single-celled fungi that can be used to as a leavening agent.

16

Color

When we look at white light, we are seeing all the colors of the rainbow combined. Our world is filled with color. For humans, colors can add beauty, convey information, and prompt emotions. For many animals and plants, color is an essential part of their survival. What color is and how we perceive it is behind the science of color.

What is color? Color is light energy, which is a series of electromagnetic waves. The waves in visible light are a sliver of the electromagnetic spectrum. Microwaves, radio waves, and X rays are other types of waves in the electromagnetic spectrum, but the human eye cannot detect them.

White light is a combination of the colors on the electromagnetic spectrum. Each color has its own frequency and wavelength. Frequency is the number of waves that pass a point every second. The wavelength is the distance between similar points on the "wave." Red light has the longest wavelength and violet light the shortest. All the other colors fall in between.

Newton conducted many other experiments with light and color. CORBIS-BETTMANN. REPRODUCED BY PERMISSION.

Experiments with bending light It was the English scientist Isaac Newton (1642–1727), who first proved in 1666 that white light could be separated into colors. In one now-famous experiment, Newton darkened his room and made a small slit in the shutters. He placed a glass prism in front of the thin beam of light and saw a rainbow of colors. This band of colors is called a spectrum.

Newton conducted many other experiments with light and color. He demonstrated how the colors in sunlight could be separated, then

A rainbow appears because the moisture in the air or raindrops are acting as prisms. AP PHOTO/WALLA WALLA UNION-BULLETIN, JEFF HORNER.

joined again to form white light. He found that when light hits a prism, it is bent, or refracted. The wavelength of red light bends the least and the wavelength of violet light bends the most. The wavelengths cause the colors to bend and separate from one another in a certain order: red,

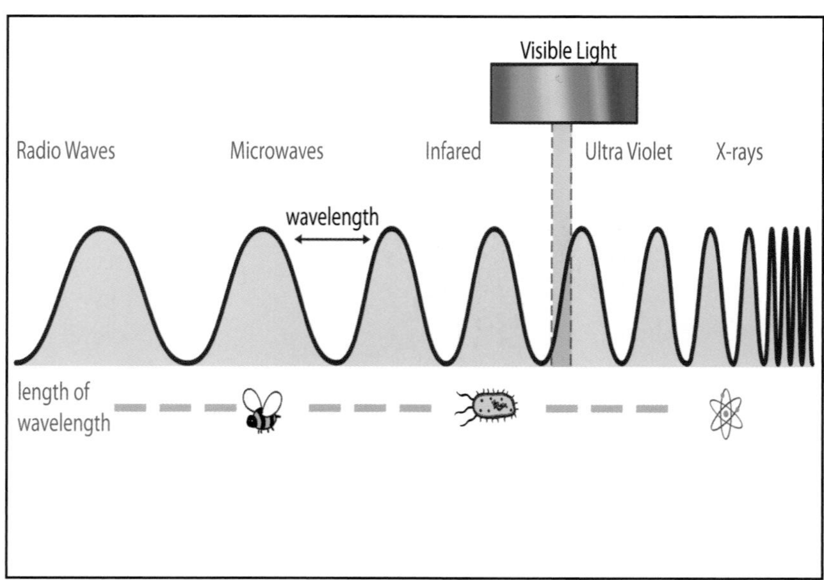

Each color has its own frequency and wavelength. ILLUSTRATION BY TEMAH NELSON.

orange, yellow, green, blue, indigo, and violet. The separation of visible light into its different colors is called dispersion. The order of light dispersion is commonly referred to by the more easily remembered name: ROY G. BIV.

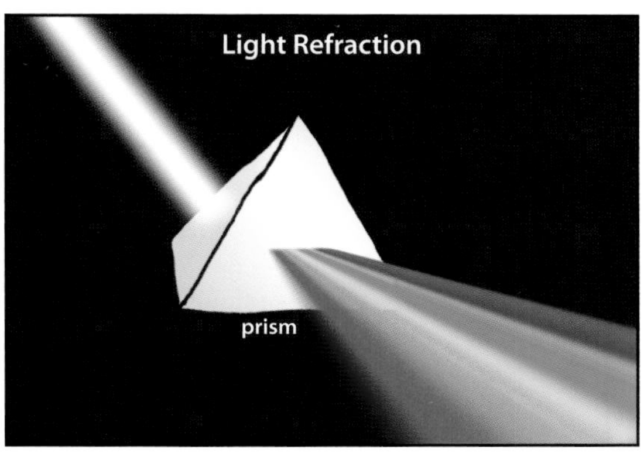

Isaac Newton first proved in 1666 that white light could be separated into colors. ILLUSTRATION BY TEMAH NELSON.

When we see a rainbow it is because the moisture in the air or raindrops is acting as a prism. The white light from the sun hits the drop and bends, dispersing into distinct colors.

In the 1800s, scientists learned that white light is actually made up of three colors: red, green and blue. These colors are referred to as primary colors. Primary colors cannot be separated into other colors. When red, green, and blue lightwaves are combined evenly they take the appearance of white light. All the other colors we perceive are mixtures of the three primary colors.

What color we see is the color that is least absorbed. An object appears blue when it absorbs all wavelengths of visible light except blue. When an object absorbs all the light wavelengths, there is no color for us to see and the object appears black. Technically, the black of night is not a color, it is the absence of us seeing any color light at all. (Pigment colors, such as paints, work by different rules than light. Mixing red, green, and blue light will produce white; blending red, green and blue paints will form a muddy black-brown.)

Rods and Cones There are two types of cells in the eye that allow us to see light: rods and cones. The rods and cones lie in the retina, a layer in the back of the eye. The cells send nerve impulses to the brain, which the brain interprets as color and images.

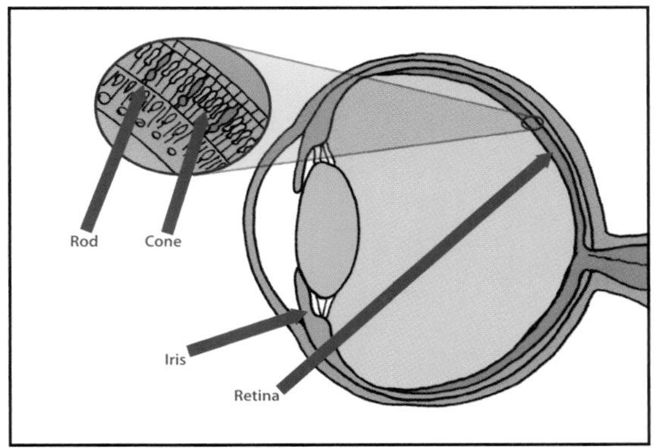

Rods and cones allow us to see light. ILLUSTRATION BY TEMAH NELSON.

Rods can detect gradations of light, movements, and shapes. In a room that is dimly lit, rods are what help us see what is in the room. People have about 120 million rods. Overall, it's the cones that allow us to see color. The eye has only about six million cones. The cones can perceive green, red, or blue but cones do not detect light that well. That's why when the room is dark we cannot see colors as well as a well-lit room.

When a person's cones do not work properly the person may be color-blind. There are

WORDS TO KNOW

Cones: Cells in the retina that can perceive color.

Electromagnetic spectrum: The complete array of electromagnetic radiation, including radio waves (at the longest-wavelength end), microwaves, infrared radiation, visible light, ultraviolet radiation, X rays, and gamma rays (at the shortest-wavelength end).

Electromagnetic waves: Waves of energy that are part of the electromagnetic spectrum.

Hue: The color or shade.

Hypothesis: An idea in the form of a statement that can be tested by observation and/or experiment.

Lens: A piece of transparent material with two curved surfaces that bend rays of light passing through it.

Nanometer: A unit of length; this measurement is equal to one-billionth of a meter.

Optics: The study of the nature of light and its properties.

Primary colors: The three colors red, green, and blue; when combined evenly they produce white light and by combining varying amounts can produce the range of colors.

Prism: A piece of transparent material with a triangular cross-section. When light passes through it, it causes different colors to bend different amounts, thus separating them into a rainbow of colors.

Refraction: The bending of light rays as they pass at an angle from one transparent or clear medium into a second one of different density.

Retina: The light-sensitive part of the eyeball that receives images and transmits visual impulses through the optic nerve to the brain.

Rods: Cells in the retina that are sensitive to degrees of light and movement.

Saturation: The intensity of a color.

different degrees and types of color-blindness, but in general, people who are color-blind can still see some color.

The most common type of color-blindness is in problems with the red/green cones. When one or more of the cones is not functioning, the brain cannot distinguish certain colors from one another. Color-blindness is an inherited trait, which means it is in the genes. It is far more common in males, affecting an estimated one out of 12 men.

How deep and how bright A red rose, apple, and sunset all may appear red, but the color of each is slightly different. A color's hue, saturation, and brightness are all aspects of color that distinguish them from one another. The hue is the color. Saturation is the intensity of the color. If grey or black is added to a red than it is less saturated and appears more mauve. A pure red is fully saturated. Brightness is the amount of light in the color.

In the following two experiment you will explore two aspects of color: how color affects perception and how heat energy relates to color.

As you conduct the following two experiments on color, consider what aspects of color you are curious about and would like to investigate further.

What Are the Variables?

Variables are anything that might affect the results of the experiment. Here are the main variables in this experiment:

- the flavor of the juice
- the ingredients in the recipe
- the temperature of the food
- the way the food is served
- information the test subjects are told about the experiment

In other words, the variables in this experiment are anything that might affect the flavor perception. If you change more than one variable, you will not be able to tell which variable had the most effect on how people perceived the flavor.

EXPERIMENT 1

Color and Flavor: How much does color affect flavor perception?

Purpose/Hypothesis People are used to specific colors relating to certain foods or flavors. A lemon is expected to be yellow, a lime green, and a strawberry red. Seeing a certain color sends signals to the brain about what the food will taste like.

In this experiment, you will investigate how color relates to the perception of flavor. If the color is different than expected, will test subjects identify the actual flavor? You can manipulate the flavor of a gelatin by using uncolored fruit juice. By adding food coloring, you can turn each gelatin a color that is different than its recognizable color.

The next step is to ask at least three people to taste the gelatin. In order to keep the experiment unbiased, do not tell the test subjects what you are testing. You will make up a series of questions, with the taste or flavor being among them. After hearing the results from the test subjects, you can observe how color affects the perception of taste.

To begin your experiment, make an educated guess about color and flavor perception. This educated guess, or prediction, is your hypothesis. A hypothesis should explain these things:

- the topic of the experiment
- the variable you will change

How to Experiment Safely

Use caution when handling the hot juice. You may want to ask an adult to help you heating the juice on the stove.

- the variable you will measure
- what you expect to happen

A hypothesis should be brief, specific, and measurable. It must be something you can test through observation. Your experiment will prove or disprove whether your hypothesis is correct. Here is one possible hypothesis for this experiment: "Test subjects will not identify the actual flavor of the colored gelatin."

In this case, the variable you will change is the flavor and the variable you will measure is people's perception of the flavor.

Level of Difficulty Moderate, due to the time involved in making the recipe and testing the subjects.

Materials Needed

- 6 envelopes of unflavored gelatin
- 3 different flavors of clear juice, all the same brand (2 cups of each juice). Apple, grape, pear, lemon, orange, and berry are some options. Clear juice is sold in some supermarkets and health food stores. It is also available from companies online.
- food coloring, colors to match the flavors
- 3 small rectangle or square pans (bread pans or 8-inch square pans work well)
- small saucepan

- glass bowl
- measuring cup
- spoons
- knife
- stove or microwave

Step 1: Measure out 1 cup of the juice, then pour into the saucepan and bring to a boil. ILLUSTRATION BY TEMAH NELSON.

Approximate Budget $10 to $20, depending upon the available juice.

Timetable Approximately four to five hours total time making and chilling the gelatin; 30 minutes testing subjects.

Step-By-Step Instructions

1. For juice 1: Pour 1 cup of the juice in the saucepan and bring to a boil.
2. While the juice heats, pour 1 cup of cold juice in a bowl and add the gelatin. As soon as the cup of juice has boiled pour it into the bowl and stir until all the gelatin is dissolved.
3. Decide what color you want the gelatin. Remember to make it a completely different color than the traditional juice. For example, if the juice is strawberry (red) you could make the color yellow to represent lemon. Add the selected food color one drop at a time into the bowl. Stir after each drop until you have a color that appears natural. Write down the color you selected for the juice.
4. Pour the colored gelatin into the bread pan.
5. Repeat the process for juice 2 and juice 3, making sure to rinse the bowl and saucepan before beginning each recipe. Remember to write down what color you have selected for each flavor juice. Only you will know!
6. Place all three pans in the refrigerator and allow to set for two to four hours. It should be firm when you jiggle the pan.
7. Cut each of the gelatins into squares and place on a plate.
8. Write down a series of questions: Is the gelatin too sweet? Is it firm enough? Does the gelatin have enough flavor? What flavor does it taste like?
9. Test each subject one at a time, apart from one another so one does not influence someone else. Tell each test subject you are testing a recipe and want his or her opinion. After the subjects taste each flavor, ask your questions.

Troubleshooter's Guide

When conducting experiments with food and people, several problems can occur. Here are two problems you may encounter, possible cause, and ways to fix the problem.

Problem: The gelatin did not taste good.

Possible cause: Depending upon the juice you purchased, you may need to add sugar or add more water. Adapt the recipe until you like the way it tastes, and make a new batch.

Problem: Everyone knew immediately the gelatins were not "natural."

Possible cause: You may have added too much food coloring to make the gelatin look unnatural. You might want to purchase and make flavored gelatins and try to match the color.

Step 7: Cut each of the gelatins into squares and place on a plate. ILLUSTRATION BY TEMAH NELSON.

What Are the Variables?

Variables are anything that might affect the results of an experiment. Here are the main variables in this experiment:

- the colors along the visible light spectrum
- the intensity of the white light being used
- the temperature of the room or outside environment
- the surface material the color light appears

In other words, the variables in this experiment are everything that might affect the temperature of the visible colors visible through the prism. If you change more than one variable, you will not be able to tell which variable had the most effect on the temperature of the colors.

10. Test at least three subjects, or until you run out of gelatin.

Summary of Results Was there one flavor more than the others that the test subjects identified correctly? How sure were the test subjects when they identified the flavor? Was there one color more than the others that the subjects could not identify? Write up a summary of your findings.

Change the Variables You can change other variables to investigate color and flavor perception. Try the experiment using different foods, such as colored candies that all actually have the same flavor. You could also change the color of the plate and place setting to measure how that affects food enjoyment or perception.

EXPERIMENT 2

Temperature and Color: What color has the highest temperature?

Purpose/Hypothesis Light energy also carries heat energy. The different colors of light energy all have unique wavelengths, and the energy of light relates to its wavelength. Along the visible spectrum (the range of wavelengths visible to the human eye) the color red has the longest wavelength and violet has the shortest.

In this experiment you will determine the temperatures of different colors of light along the visible light spectrum. Using a prism and a white light, you will separate the white light into the colors of the spectrum, much like a rainbow. You then will take temperature readings on both ends of the spectrum: the red and violet ends. The differences in the temperature readings will allow you to determine how a color's wavelength relates to heat energy. Do you think the color with the longer wavelength will have lower or higher energy than the color with the shorter wavelength?

Before you begin the experiment, make an educated guess about the outcome based on your knowledge of the visible light spectrum and the wavelengths of the different colors. This educated guess, or prediction, is your hypothesis. A hypothesis should explain these things:

- the topic of the experiment
- the variable you will change
- the variable you will measure
- what you expect to happen

How to Experiment Safely

There are no safety hazards in this experiment.

A hypothesis should be brief, specific, and measurable. It must be something you can test through observation. Your experiment will prove or disprove your hypothesis. Here is one possible hypothesis for this experiment: "The color violet will have the highest temperature reading because it has the shortest wavelength. Wavelength size decreases as the energy of the light increases."

In this case, the variable you will change is the color along the spectrum whose temperature you are measuring. The variable you will measure is the temperature of the different colors along the spectrum.

Level of Difficulty Moderate.

Materials Needed

- large prism or 2 small prisms (approximately 1 inch [2.5 centimeters] thick, available from science stores)
- flashlight
- digital thermometer
- Styrofoam, piece about 5 inches (12.7 centimeters) long, wide enough to cover the glasses (the Styrofoam holding fruit and vegetables in grocery stores or Styrofoam egg cartons work well)
- watch or timer
- 2 drinking glasses

Approximate Budget $20.

Timetable 1 hour.

Step-by-Step Instructions

1. Find a table to work on that is steady and place it against a wall. Place the flashlight on the table sideways and turn on the flashlight.

Steps 1 and 2: Place the flashlight on the table sideways and turn on the flashlight. Position the prism in front of the flashlight so that it catches light. ILLUSTRATION BY TEMAH NELSON.

Step 5: The probe senses the temperature. ILLUSTRATION BY TEMAH NELSON.

2. Position the prism in front of the flashlight so that it catches light and produces a "rainbow" on the wall behind the table. (If using two prisms, place one in front of another at a slight angle.) This can take some time. Keep moving the prisms until you get a strong, clear spectrum of color on the wall.
3. Set one drinking glass on either side of the rainbow on the table. One glass should be in the middle of the red and the other glass should be in the middle of the violet.
4. Place the Styrofoam on top of the glasses.
5. Note the temperature of the thermometer, which should be at room temperature. Carefully insert the thermometer through the Styrofoam so that it is hanging through the Styrofoam. Place its probe in line with the red color on the spectrum on the wall behind it. (The probe senses the temperature.)
6. Wait 10 minutes and note the temperature. Remove the Styrofoam with the thermometer still in it and wait for it to return to room temperature. This may take about 10 minutes.
7. Move the Styrofoam set up so that thermometer's probe is in line with the violet color on the spectrum.
8. After 10 minutes check the temperature and record.

Summary of Results Study the observations of your temperatures and decide whether your hypothesis was correct. Did you see a slight difference between the temperature of the red and violet colors? Which one had the higher temperature? What relationship does the temperature have with the wavelength of the colors? Write up a paragraph of your results. You may want to include pictures or drawings of your set-up.

Change the Variables You can vary this experiment by measuring the temperatures of other colors. You can also measure the temperatures of the non-visible spectrum, just to the left and right of the red and violet colors. What are these temperatures and how do they relate to what you know about wavelengths.

Design Your Own Experiment

How to Select a Topic Relating to this Concept

There are many aspects of the properties of color you can study. Look at the variety of colors in your home, foods, artwork, and in nature to encourage ideas. Consider if you are interested in exploring color from a physics perspective and/or from a psychological perspective.

Check the Further Readings section for this topic, and talk with a science teacher or a knowledgeable adult before finalizing your choice.

Steps in the Scientific Method To do an original experiment, you need to plan carefully and think things through. Otherwise, you might not be sure what question you are answering, what you are or should be measuring, or what your findings prove or disprove. Here are the steps in designing an experiment:

- State the purpose of—and the underlying question behind—the experiment you propose to do.
- Recognize the variables involved, and select one that will help you answer the question at hand.
- State a testable hypothesis, an educated guess about the answer to your question.
- Decide how to change the variable you selected.
- Decide how to measure your results.

Recording Data and Summarizing the Results Your experiment can be useful to others studying the same topic. When designing your experiment, develop a simple method to record your data. This method should be simple and clear enough so that others who want to do the experiment can follow it.

Your final results should be summarized and put into simple graphs, tables, and charts to display the outcome of your experiment. You might also want to have color visual displays.

Troubleshooter's Guide

Below are some problems that may occur during this project, possible causes, and ways to remedy the problems.

Problem: You could not get the prism to separate the light into a visible spectrum (rainbow).

Possible cause: The light may not be focused enough. Try to focus the light from the flashlight by magnifying it with a magnifying lens or shine the light through a small hole cut out of the bottom of a soda can. This will help to concentrate the light for the prism. You can also try using a larger prism.

Problem: There is no temperature difference between the red and violet colors.

Possible cause: The probe of the thermometer may not be directly over the light. Make sure that probe of thermometer is directly in the path of the red and violet lights as they are shining against the wall.

Related Projects Experiment 1 focused on humans and color perception. You may want to explore how animals perceive and react to color. An experiment could focus on what colors different animals can perceive and how color can affect their lives. Plants also may respond to colors in different ways. You may want to focus on saturation or hue. How can you change or measure a color's saturation, for example.

Another aspect you may want to study might be color perception or color blindness. If you choose either of these topics, experiments might be how different colors relate to certain emotions or how color-blindness is inherited. Your project does not have to be an experiment that investigates or answers a question. It can also be a model, such as Newton's original experiment with window shutters and a prism.

For More Information

"Color and Light." *Patterns in Nature.* http://acept.asu.edu/PiN/rdg/color/color.shtml (accessed on April 26, 2008). Detailed information on color and how we see.

"Color Vision and Art." *WebExhibits.* http://webexhibits.org/colorart (accessed on April 26, 2008). Information and interactives on color.

Cobb, Vicki and Josh Cobb. *Light Action! Amazing Experiments with Optics.* New York: HarperCollins, 1993. Experiments with light and color.

Davidson, Michael W. et al. "Light and Color." *Molecular Expressions.* http://micro.magnet.fsu.edu/primer/lightandcolor/index.html (accessed on April 18, 2008).

Farndon, John. *Color.* Tarrytown, NY: Marshall Cavendish, 2001. Experiments in color.

Hamilton, Gina L. *Light: Prisms, Rainbows, and Colors.* Chicago: Raintree, 2004.

Seckel, Al. *Optical Illusions: The Science of Visual Perception.* Buffalo, NY: Firefly Books, 2006. Collection of optical illusions, with information on the science of visual perception.

17

Comets and Meteors

Earth is part of a solar system that is filled with celestial objects moving about. Scientists theorize that many of these objects are materials left over from when the solar system formed—about 4.6 billion years ago. Comets and meteors are two such chunks of materials in the solar system. Every so often these objects are visible to the naked eye as brilliant streaks of light across the sky. Meteors appear regularly and are sometimes called "shooting stars"; comets show themselves with far less frequency. Astronomers look to these objects to learn more about the universe around Earth and the early history of the solar system.

Hot snowballs Comets are often referred to as dirty snowballs because of their makeup: a mixture of ice and dust. They typically move through the solar system in orbits or revolutions around the Sun ranging from a few years to several hundred thousand years.

Astronomers theorize there may be more than one trillion comets zipping about the solar system, yet spotting a comet is rare. Most comets are located on the outskirts of the solar system in a giant sphere called the Oort cloud, which surrounds the solar system. The comets in the Oort cloud can take over a million years to make a single revolution around the Sun. Occasionally one of these comets is pulled by a nearby star and gets pushed closer to the Sun. When it approaches the Sun it becomes visible to astronomers. About a dozen of these new comets are discovered every year.

A few comets have a relatively short orbit. For example Halley's Comet orbits the Sun about every 76 years. This comet is named after English astronomer Edmond Halley (1656–1742), who was the first person to work out the elliptical orbits of comets. After Halley spotted a comet in 1682, he started reading through historical records. He found that two previous comets, in 1531 and 1607, had orbital paths similar to the one he had witnessed. These three comet sightings, he concluded, were actually the same object making three appearances. Halley predicted this comet would

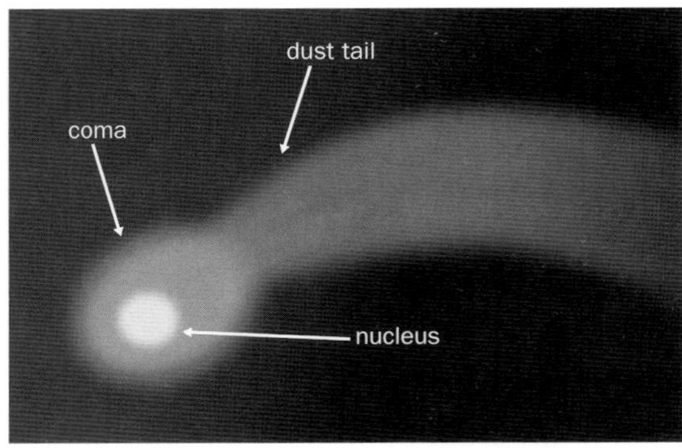

Components of a comet. GALE GROUP.

pass through again in 1758 and, although he did not live to see it, the comet appeared as predicted.

A tail's story For a short time during each orbit around the Sun, comets can become visible from Earth. When a comet approaches the Sun, it develops three basic parts: a nucleus, a coma, and a tail.

The nucleus is the dirty snowball part of the comet, made of ice and a small amount of dust and other solids. It ranges from about 1 to 10 miles (1.6–16 kilometers) across and is at the center of the comet. The nucleus and the coma make up the comet head of the comet. The coma is the blob of gas that roughly encircles the nucleus. It is the brightest part of the comet. This region is formed as the comet approaches the Sun and becomes warmer. The coma is made up of water vapor, carbon dioxide, and other gases that have sublimed from the solid nucleus. Subliming is when a material goes directly from being a solid to being a gas without becoming a liquid.

One of the most impressive sights of a comet is its tail, a long extension from the head that always points away from the Sun. Even though it does not have much mass, a comet's tail can stretch into space several million miles.

Comets often have two tails. One type of tail is a dust tail. This is made of dust leaving the nucleus. Gas and heat from the Sun push the tail backward into its long streak. The dust tail is often curved or spread out, and yellowish in appearance. Another type of tail is an ion tail. An ion tail forms when the gas particles become ionized or charged by the Sun. The molecules are pushed away from the nucleus by charged particles streaming out of the Sun. An ion tail is usually very straight and bluish.

Halley's Comet orbits the Sun about every 76 years. AP/WIDE WORLD PHOTOS

A meteor's story As a comet hurls close to the Sun and its ice melts, pieces of rock sometimes loosen. These tiny solid remnants traveling through space are called meteoroids. While the majority of meteoroids come from comets, some are fragments of planets or other celestial bodies. They are chunks of stone, metal, or a combination of the two. Wherever they originate, all meteoroids are small. Most range in size from a grain of sand to a pebble. They are the smallest known particle to orbit the Sun. They are also fast. Meteoroids are usually traveling at speeds ranging from 25,000 miles per hour (40,000 kilometers per hour) to 160,000 miles per hour (256,000 kilometers per hour).

When a speedy meteoroid tears into Earth's atmosphere, the layer of air encircling our planet, it produces a streak of light known as a shooting star, or meteor. The blaze occurs as the meteor's intense speed heats up the air around it to more than 3,000°F (1,650°C). This in turn heats up the meteor and creates a flash of light visible from the ground below. Some large meteors can produce a brilliant flash. These meteors are called fireballs and they can create an explosion that can be heard up to 30 miles (48 kilometers) away.

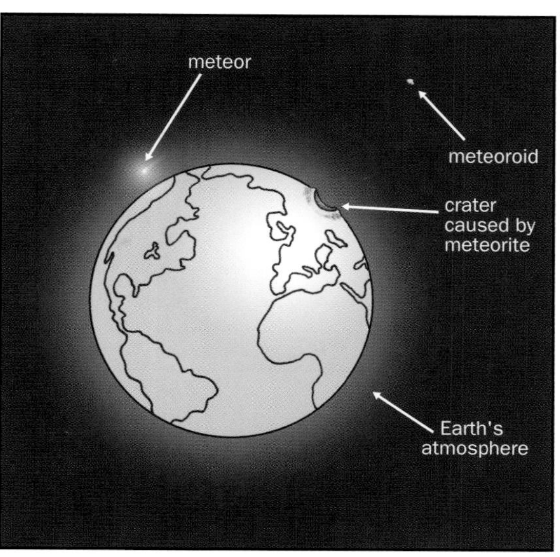

The progression of particles that break away from a comet: They first become meteoroids, then meteors, and, finally, meteorites. GALE GROUP.

While the intense heat burns up the vast majority of meteors, a small percentage make it through Earth's atmosphere. These are called meteorites. Because of their high speeds, meteorites can sometimes make huge craters when they hit the ground. A crater is a circular pit created when a celestial object crashes into a planet or other orbiting mass.

These craters are found almost everywhere in the solar system and they pocket the surface of the Moon. Scientists have found about 150 craters on Earth. One of the largest and best preserved craters on Earth is the Barringer Meteor Crater in Arizona. The Barringer formed about 50,000 years ago. It stretches nearly 1 mile (1.6 kilometers) wide and is 570 feet (174 meters) deep.

The size, speed, and angle of impact of the meteor all determine whether the crater will be simple or complex. Simple craters have a smooth, bowl shape and a raised outer rim. Complex craters have a central peak, or peaks, and a relatively shallower depth. These large craters form this shape when their initial steep wall collapses downward and inward. The explosion of the impact causes the fallen crater floor to rebound. Rock fragments blast outward, creating the central peak or peaks.

A fragment of a meteorite found in 1891 in Arizona, on display at the Monnig Meteor Gallery in Fort Worth, Texas. AP/WIDE WORLD

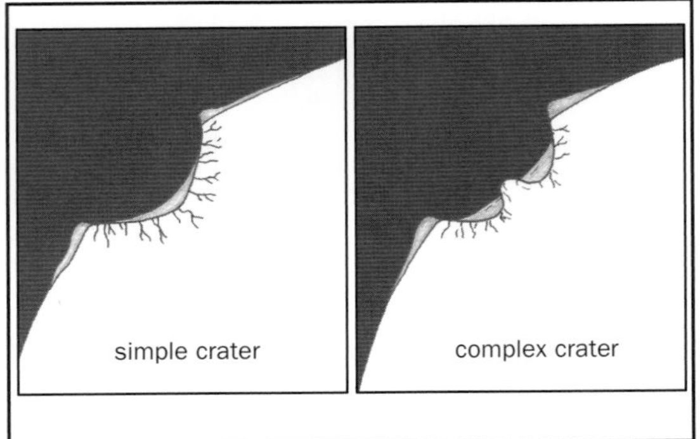

Because of their high rates of speed, meteorites can sometimes make huge craters when they hit the ground. GALE GROUP.

Showering shooting stars On any clear night, a person can probably spot some meteors. Several times every year, though, storms of meteors will fill the night sky in what is called a meteor shower.

Meteor showers occur when Earth moves through a stream of particles produced by comet leftovers. Since the orbits of comets are known, it is possible to predict many meteor showers. These showers can create a brilliant light show as they enter the atmosphere.

PROJECT 1

Comet Nucleus: Linking a Comet's Composition to its Properties.

Purpose/Hypothesis In this project, you will construct a comet* using either the same or similar ingredients that make up a real comet. Comets are composed of bits of dirt or dust, held in place by ice. The ice is a combination of water and carbon dioxide ice. Comets contain carbon-based or organic molecules and ammonia. Sodium or salt was found to be

A meteor streaks through the sky over Joshua Tree National Park in California. Stars moving through the sky are seen as a series of short lines across this 30-minute time exposure frame. AP/WIDE WORLD

WORDS TO KNOW

Coma: Glowing cloud of gas surrounding the nucleus of a comet.

Comet: An icy body orbiting in the solar system, which partially vaporizes when it nears the Sun and develops a diffuse envelope of dust and gas as well as one or more tails.

Comet head: The nucleus and the coma of a comet.

Comet nucleus: The core or center of a comet. (Plural: Comet nuclei.)

Comet tail: The most distinctive feature of comets; comets can display two basic types of tails: one gaseous and the other largely composed of dust.

Control experiment: A setup that is identical to the experiment, but is not affected by the variable that acts on the experimental group.

Crater: An indentation caused by an object hitting the surface of a planet or moon.

Dust tail: One of two types of tails a comet may have, it is composed mainly of dust and it points away from the Sun.

Fireball: Meteors that create an intense, bright light and, sometimes, an explosion.

Hypothesis: An idea in the form of a statement that can be tested by observation and/or experiment.

Ion tail: One of two types of tails a comet may have, it is composed mainly of charged particles and it points away from the Sun.

Meteor: An object from space that becomes glowing hot when it passes into Earth's atmosphere; also called shooting star.

Meteor shower: A group of meteors that occurs when Earth's orbit intersects the orbit of a meteor stream.

Meteorites: A meteor that is large enough to survive its passage through the atmosphere and hit the ground.

Meteoroid: A piece of debris that is traveling in space.

Oort cloud: Region of space beyond our solar system that theoretically contains about one trillion inactive comets.

Sublime: The process of changing a solid into a vapor without passing through the liquid phase.

Variable: Something that can affect the results of an experiment.

in the comet Hale-Bopp. Trapped gas and an uneven surface are other features of a comet.

It is these materials in the nucleus that form the brilliant head and tail when they come close to the Sun. Once you have constructed the comet, you can then observe its behavior.

*Adapted from "Making A Comet in the Classroom" by Dennis Schatz, Pacific Science Center, 1985.

How to Work Safely

Dry ice is carbon dioxide frozen at–110°F (–79°C). If you touch a piece of dry ice too long, it will freeze your skin and feel like a burn. Wear gloves when working with dry ice and do not place dry ice in your mouth. Also be careful when you pour the ammonia into the spoon to prevent it from splashing into your eyes.

Level of Difficulty Moderate (because of the number of trials and careful measurements needed).

Approximate Budget $15.

Timetable 45 minutes for initial setup; several hours observation time.

Materials Needed

- 2 cups (500 milliliters) of water
- 2 cups (500 milliliters) of dry ice, broken into pieces if possible (dry ice is available at ice companies and some butcher shops)
- 2 to 3 spoonfuls of dirt (a small dinner spoon is fine; the exact size is not important)
- 1 spoonful of ammonia
- 1 spoonful of organic material (dark or light corn syrup works, or Worcester sauce works well)
- thick gloves
- large plastic bowl
- 2 heavy-duty garbage bags
- self-sealing plastic bag
- hammer or mallet
- mixing spoon
- salt
- paper towels

Step 7: Wearing gloves, pat the meteor into a snowball shape. Keep the comet in the plastic bag when shaping. GALE GROUP.

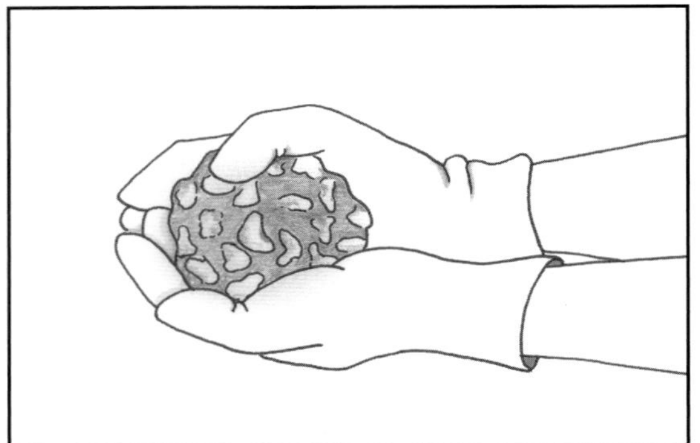

Step-by-Step Instructions

1. Cut open one garbage bag and use it to line your mixing bowl.
2. Add the water and dirt in the mixing bowl. Stir well.
3. Add a dash of ammonia
4. Add a sprinkle of salt and a spoonful of the organic material. Stir well.
5. Put on gloves and place the dry ice in the self-sealing plastic bag. Zip the bag closed and place the bag inside the second

garbage bag. Pound the dry ice with a hammer until it is crushed.

6. Add the dry ice to the ingredients in the mixing bowl and stir rapidly. Continue stirring until the mixture is slushy and almost totally frozen.
7. Lift the garbage bag with the comet out of the bowl and shape it like a snowball. Shape the plastic bag and not the snowball. Wear gloves.
8. Unwrap the comet and place it on the bag.
9. After you have observed the comet for several hours, break it apart and look at the inside.

Troubleshooter's Guide

Below is a problem that may arise during this project, a possible cause, and a way to remedy the problem.

Problem: The comet fell apart during the snowball formation.

Possible cause: You may not have broken up the dry ice into small enough bits. Try the experiment again, pounding the dry ice thoroughly.

Summary of Results Draw a picture of the comet and note how it appears. Gently blow on the comet and note your observation. After two hours have passed, note your observations of the comet and compare it to your first description. What has happened to the carbon molecules in the organic substance? Write a brief explanation of how this miniature comet relates to what occurs during a comet's orbit.

EXPERIMENT 2

Meteor Impact: How do the characteristics of a meteorite and its impact affect the shape of the crater?

Purpose/Hypothesis It was in the early 1900s that scientists first concluded a meteorite caused the formation of a crater. (Most astronomers before that time had assumed that craters were formed by volcanoes.) The first crater that scientists proved had come from a meteorite was the Barringer Meteor Crater in the Arizona desert. This gigantic depression is nearly 1 mile (1.6 kilometers) wide and 570 feet (174 meters) deep. Since that time, scientists have studied both the many craters on the Moon and the ones on Earth to study meteorite impact.

In this experiment you will investigate the factors that affect the formation of simple meteor craters. You will examine how a meteor's size, angle of impact, and speed of impact affect the crater shape. Speed in this

What Are the Variables?

Variables are anything that might affect the results of an experiment. Here are the main variables in this experiment:

- the shape of the object
- the weight of the object
- the angle of impact
- the speed of the object
- the substance the object impacts

In other words, the variables in this experiment are everything that might affect the shape of the crater. If you change more than one variable at a time, you will not be able to tell which variable changed the crater formation.

experiment is determined by the drop height. The higher the drop height, the faster the simulated meteor hits the surface.

Before you begin, make an educated guess about the outcome of this experiment based on your knowledge of meteors and craters. This educated guess, or prediction, is your hypothesis. A hypothesis should explain these things:

- the topic of the experiment
- the variable you will change
- the variable you will measure
- what you expect to happen

A hypothesis should be brief, specific, and measurable. It must be something you can test through further investigation. Your experiment will prove or disprove whether your hypothesis is correct. Here is one possible hypothesis for this experiment: "The faster and heavier the simulated meteor, the deeper and wider the crater; a meteor coming in at an angle will form an elongated crater."

In this case, the variables you will change, one at a time, are the weight of the meteor, the speed of the meteor, and the angle of impact. The variable you will measure is the depth and diameter of the crater.

Conducting a standard experiment will help you isolate each variable and measure the changes in the dependent variable. Only one variable will change between the standard experiment and each of your trials. To change only one variable at a time, it is important to always use a simulated meteor of standard weight and use a standard drop height. Then you will change one variable at a time. Your control will be a medium-weight meteor, at a vertical, 180-degree drop, and a drop height of 39 inches (1 meter).

You will complete three tests in this experiment. You will measure how the weight of a simulated meteor, the speed of the simulated meteor, and the angle of impact of the simulated meteor affect the crater's physical characteristics. For each variable you will measure the crater's depth and diameter. The diameter is the measurement across a circle. In this case, it is a point on the peak of the rim to a point on the rim on the opposite side. In actuality there are many factors affecting a meteor's crater.

For increased accuracy, you will conduct three trials of each test, then average the measurements.

Level of Difficulty Moderate (because of the number of trials and careful measurements needed).

How to Experiment Safely

There are no safety hazards in this experiment.

Materials Needed

- shallow rectangle pan or plastic container, about 12 to 18 inches (30 to 46 centimeters) long and 2 inches (5 centimeters) deep
- fine, dry sand (available at hardware stores or greenhouses)
- powder of contrasting color to sand, such as cinnamon, cocoa, or paprika
- empty shaker, such as a saltshaker
- nine small round objects of similar shape to simulate meteors: three of the same light weight, three of the same medium weight, and three of the same heavy weight (marbles, candies, or pebbles work well)
- ruler
- protractor
- string, about 4 feet (30 centimeters)
- tape
- newspapers (optional)
- cardstock, cut into thin strips about 0.125 (1/8) inches (3 millimeters) wide

Approximate Budget $10.

Timetable 1 hour.

Step-by-Step Instructions

1. Weigh each of the simulated meteors and note on a chart. Create a separate chart for mass, speed, and angle of impact. Each chart should have separate rows for the diameter and depth measurements. Make a note of the standard meteor on the chart.
2. Place newspapers under the pan or conduct the experiment outside to avoid a sandy cleanup.
3. Fill the pan about three-quarters full with sand. Shake until the sand is level.
4. With the shaker, sprinkle a light layer of the contrasting colored powder over the sand. This will help you measure the crater's shape.

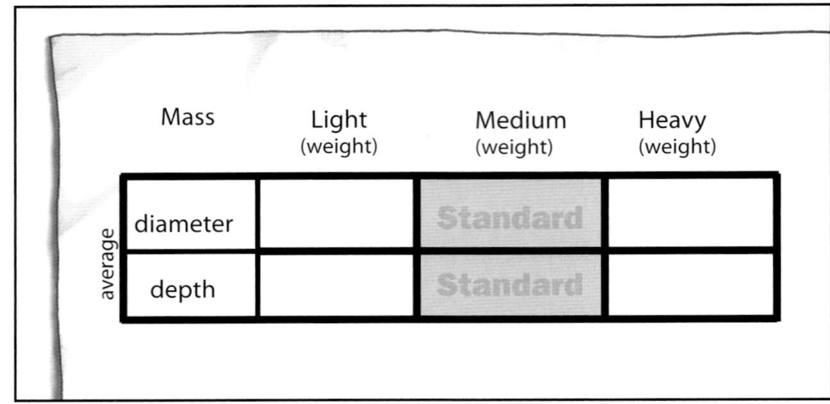

average	Mass	Light (weight)	Medium (weight)	Heavy (weight)
	diameter		Standard	
	depth		Standard	

Step 1: Example of the "Mass" data chart; one of the three charts to be created for Experiment 2. GALE GROUP.

5. Make sure the sand is level and the outer layer is even before you continue.
6. To test for the effect of size: One at a time, drop the three lightest-weight simulated meteors vertically from a height of 39 inches (1 meter) onto the surface (you may have to stand on a chair). Do not throw the object. Drop the objects so that the craters are several inches apart.
7. Measure the diameter of the resulting craters. Average the three measurements and record on a chart.
8. Measure the depth of the craters by carefully placing one of the narrow strips of paper at the bottom of the crater and marking on the paper where the paper meets the rim of the crater. Average the three measurements and record on chart.
9. Level out the sand and the contrasting-color layer.
10. To test for speed: Increase the drop heights to 79 inches (2 meters) and drop the three medium-weight simulated meteors. Again, drop them so the craters are several inches apart. Record the results. Level the sand and contrasting-color layer.
11. Using the same three medium-weight simulated meteors, decrease the drop height to 20 inches (0.5 meters). Average the measurement results and note in a chart. Level the sand and contrasting-color layer as before.

Step 6: One at a time, drop the three lightest-weight simulated meteors vertically from a height of 39 inches (1 meter) onto the surface. GALE GROUP.

12. To test for angle impact: Tie the piece of string to the midpoint of the protractor and tape the protractor to the bottom of the container. Use the string as a guide for the angle of impact.
13. Hold the string at a 75-degree angle and drop the three medium-weight meteors into the box at that angle, at the height of 39 inches (1 meter). Measure the diameter and depth of the resulting craters and record the averages on a chart. Level again.
14. Drop the three medium-weight meteors into the box at a 45-degree angle. Record the results.

Troubleshooter's Guide

Below is a problem that may arise during this experiment, a possible cause, and a way to remedy the problem.

Problem: The crater depth was too shallow to measure in some craters.

Possible cause: You may have chosen projectiles that were too light. Set aside the small and medium projectiles, and select two new sets that are heavier than whatever was the heaviest object used before. Repeat the experiment.

Summary of Results Create a graph illustrating the data in each chart. Make sure you use different colors or symbols for each of the variables in the chart and label each chart carefully.

Compare each of the variables to the standard projectile. How did the weight of the projectile affect the size of the crater? How did the angle of impact affect crater formation? For years astronomers hypothesized that objects that landed at an angle would produce an elongated-shape crater. Through experimentation scientists discovered that projectiles create round craters, independent of the angle of impact. Do your results match these findings?

Change the Variables You can vary this experiment several ways:

- Try different angles of impact
- Alter the shape of the projectiles
- Change the surface the projectile impacts
- Change the consistency of the surface

Design Your Own Experiment

How to Select a Topic Relating to this Concept Meteors and comets are amazing sights that can provide useful information about the universe. As both celestial bodies are visible to the naked eye, although comet sightings are quite rare, it may be possible to gather data on these objects through observation. Find an amateur astronomer who has observation equipment, and discuss a possible project with him or her. You may also want to investigate whether any science centers in your area have meteorite fragments that you can study.

Check the Further Readings section for predicted comet and meteor sightings, along with information gathered from previous sightings. Talk with your science teacher, along with any professional or amateur astronomers, to learn more about comets and meteors. If you do choose to observe meteors or comets during the daylight, remember to never look directly at the Sun, as it can damage your eyes.

Steps in the Scientific Method To conduct an original experiment, you need to plan carefully and think things through. Otherwise, you might not be sure what question you are answering, what you are or should be measuring, or what your findings prove or disprove.

Here are the steps in designing an experiment:

- State the purpose of—and the underlying question behind—the experiment you propose to do.
- Recognize the variables involved and select one that will help you answer the question at hand.
- State your hypothesis, an educated guess about the answer to your question.
- Decide how to change the variable you selected.
- Decide how to measure your results.

Recording Data and Summarizing the Results In any experiment you conduct, you should look for ways to clearly convey your data. You can do this by including charts and graphs for the experiments. They should be clearly labeled and easy to read. You may also want to include photographs and drawings of your experimental setup and results, which will help others visualize the steps in the experiment. You might decide to conduct an experiment that lasts several months. In this case, include pictures or drawings of the results taken at regular intervals.

If you are preparing an exhibit, you may want to display your results, such as any experimental setup you designed. If you have completed a nonexperimental project, explain clearly what your research question was and illustrate your findings.

Related Projects There are many related projects you can undertake to learn more about comets and meteors. Meteor showers occur throughout the year. Gathering data from observing meteors is one possible project. Because comet sightings are far more rare, you can create a model of an active comet orbiting the Sun, using household items to represent the objects in the solar system. Research the spatial relationships of celestial bodies in the solar system as you work on your project to ensure you have the model to scale.

You could also investigate if any craters are located in your surrounding area and, if so, set out on a field trip to examine the formation. If there are no craters in your area or you cannot visit one, you can use reference materials. You can compare how the sizes and shapes of craters relate to the meteor's composition. Why would one meteorite form a crater and another simply land on Earth? You can also conduct a research project to examine the data and theoretical information that astronomers have learned about the universe from their studies of comets and meteors.

For More Information

The Barringer Meteorite Crater. http://www.barringercrater.com (accessed on January 17, 2008). Story of the famous crater and the persistent scientist who proved a crater was caused by a meteorite, not a volcano.

Bonar, Samantha. *Comets.* New York: Franklin Watts, 1998. The makeup, orbits, and other information on comets, with illustrations.

Britt, Robert Roy. "Meteors and Meteor Showers: The Science." *Space.com.* http://www.space.com/scienceastronomy/solarsystem/meteors-ez.html (accessed on January 18, 2008). Information on meteors and meteor showers, includes animation and meteor composition.

Freudenrich, Craig C. "How Comets Work." *How Stuff Works.* http://science.howstuffworks.com/comet3.htm (accessed on January 17, 2008). Clear explanation of how comets work.

Kronk, Gary W. *Comets & Meteor Showers.* http://meteorshowersonline.com (accessed on January 18, 2008). Site on comets and meteors includes clear explanations and a calendar of times for future sightings.

"Orbits." *Near Earth Object Program.* http://neo.jpl.nasa.gov/orbits (accessed on January 18, 2008). Enter any asteroid or comet and see its orbit.

World Book's Young Scientist: Volume 1. Chicago: World Book, Inc., 1995. Well-illustrated reference with basics of space and space study.

18

Composting/Landfills

Composting is the process in which organic wastes are broken down biologically and become dark, fertile soil called humus. An ancient practice, composting probably began when the original hunter-gatherers began cultivating food and saw that crops grew better in areas where the soil contained manure, the waste matter of animals.

Agricultural composting with manure was being used in the Mesopotamia Valley in Asia as early as 13 B.C.E. Not surprisingly, Native American tribes practiced composting long ago, as did the first colonists who arrived in North America.

A smelly solution French chemist Jean Baptiste Boussingault (1802–1887) made significant contributions to agricultural chemistry by suggesting that good soil was made by the action of microorganisms, bacteria, and fungi that break down waste. Working on his farm, he applied and studied the results of organic methods of farming from 1834 to 1876.

At that time, composting used mostly animal manure or dead fish, as well as nutrient-rich muck from swampy areas. By the twentieth century, large animals such as the buffalo, whose droppings fertilized the prairie soil, were disappearing as were many of the farming communities that contributed barnyard manure to compost piles.

In 1934, Sir Albert Howard, an Englishman, developed the modern organic concept of farming. Through several years of research in Indore, India, he formulated the Indore method, a process that used three times more plant waste than manure in sandwich-like layers of green or wet material. Howard also pointed out the importance of microorganisms in the process. In 1942, J.I. Rodale began publishing *Organic Farming and Gardening.* Rodale used Howard's techniques and experimented with his own. He is considered the pioneer of organic methods of farming in the United States.

Backyard compost bins are simple to use. PETER ARNOLD INC.

Chomping microbes How does composting work? Let us begin with the basics, the organic waste. That would be vegetable scraps such as carrot tops and peelings, plus leaves, paper bags, grass clippings, tea bags, and coffee grounds. Carbon in these organic waste materials provides food for the microorganisms, starting the composting process. When these microbes chomp away and begin digesting, the carbon is burned off or oxidized, causing the composting pile to heat up. The heat kills any harmful organisms. Macroorganisms—such as earthworms, insects, mites, and grubs—continue the composting process by chewing the organic matter into smaller pieces. Through digestion and excretion, both types of organisms release important chemicals into the compost mass, which then becomes humus, a nutrient-rich soil.

The transformation is speeded up by a balanced supply of carbon and nitrogen, the oxygen required by the microorganisms, enough moisture to allow biological activity, and suitable temperatures. But it is really the diverse microorganisms that chomp away and activate the process. Without them, we would be buried in wastes.

In the United States, more garbage is generated than in any other country in the world. Materials that could be used in composting make up 20–30% of the waste stream—the waste output of any area or facility. This figure doubles in the autumn when leaves and garden clippings are added. All this waste winds up in landfills.

Landfills that raised the roof Landfills are huge depressions in the ground or equally huge mounds above ground where garbage is dumped. Like compost piles, landfills also have centuries-old beginnings. The ancient cities of the Middle East were built up over time on mounds that contained the remains of everyday life. In excavations of the ancient city of Troy, in what is now Greece, building floors were found to have layers of animal bones and artifacts that had been alternated with layers of clay. These layers piled up until it was necessary to raise roofs and rebuild doorways.

During the Bronze Age (3000–1000 B.C.E.), the city of Troy rose about 4.7 feet (1.4 meters) each century (100 years) because of these accumulations. Landfilling has also been used to extend shorelines. In New York City during the eighteenth century, shorefront roads were extended into the water by landfill that included broken dishes, old shoes, and even the rotted hulls of boats.

Macroorganisms, such as earthworms, chew organic matter into smaller pieces. PHOTO RESEARCHERS INC.

Sanitary landfills In the 1930s, solid waste materials covered with soil became known as "sanitary landfill." As with composting, a decomposition process takes place in landfills. The process has an aerobic and an anaerobic phase. Aerobic means requiring oxygen. Anaerobic means functioning without oxygen. In the aerobic phase, biodegradable solid wastes react with the landfill's oxygen to form carbon dioxide and water. The landfill temperature rises and a weak acid forms within the water, dissolving some of the minerals. Microorganisms that do not need oxygen break down wastes into hydrogen, ammonia, carbon dioxide, and inorganic acids during the anaerobic stage. Gas in the form of carbon monoxide and methane is produced in the third stage of decomposition.

In a landfill, many of the materials, such as plastic, glass, and aluminum cans, containers, and bottles, can take up to forty years or more to decompose. As a result, these materials are quickly filling the space available in landfills. That is why recycling is encouraged in most communities. In recycling, waste materials are used to produce new materials.

Dumping garbage in a landfill. CORBIS.

Americans dump slightly over half of our garbage into landfills, according to the U.S. Energy Information Administration. The remaining garbage is either recycled or burned. Landfills are not bottomless pits. Thousands of landfills have become full and closed. For example, one of the largest landfills in the world was the Fresh Kills landfill in New York State. Covering 2,200 acres, the Fresh Kills landfill officially closed in 2001. Understanding how composting and landfills work helps everyone become more aware of what happens to the garbage that is thrown away.

WORDS TO KNOW

Aerobic: A process that requires oxygen.

Anaerobic: A process that does not require oxygen.

Biodegradable: Materials that can undergo decomposition by biological variables.

Biological variables: Living factors such as bacteria, fungi, and animals that can affect the processes that occur in nature and in an experiment.

Composting: The process in which organic compounds break down and become dark, fertile soil called humus.

Control experiment: A set-up that is identical to the experiment but is not affected by the variable that will be changed during the experiment.

Decomposition: The breakdown of complex molecules of dead organisms into simple nutrients that can be reutilized by living organisms.

Environmental variables: Nonliving factors such as air temperature, water, pollution, and pH that can affect processes that occur in nature and in an experiment.

Humus: Fragrant, spongy, nutrient-rich decayed plant or animal matter.

Hypothesis: An idea in the form of a statement that can be tested by observation and/or experiment.

Landfill: A method of disposing of waste materials by placing them in a depression in the ground or piling them in a mound. In a sanitary landfill, the daily deposits of waste materials are covered with a layer of soil.

Macroorganisms: Visible organisms that aid in breaking down organic matter.

Manure: The waste matter of animals.

Microorganisms: Living organisms so small that they can be seen only with the aid of a microscope.

Organic: Any material containing carbon atoms.

pH scale: Abbreviation for potential hydrogen. The scale ranges from 0 to 14. Neutral pH is 7, such as distilled water. Acids have pH values lower than 7, such as vinegar, which has a pH of 3.3. Alkalines or bases have pH values higher than 7, such as baking soda, which has a pH of 8.2.

Recycling: The use of waste materials, also known as secondary materials or recyclables, to produce new products.

Variable: Something that can affect the results of an experiment.

Waste stream: The waste materials generated by the population of an area, or by a specific industrial process, and removed for disposal.

EXPERIMENT 1

Living Landfill: What effect do the microorganisms in soil have on the decomposition process?

Purpose/Hypothesis The purpose of this experiment is to determine what happens to common household items that are discarded and placed in a landfill. In nature, physical, chemical, and biological factors act upon our waste and work together in the process of decomposition. This experiment will determine what action organisms in the soil have on garbage. Before you begin, make an educated guess about the outcome of this experiment based on your knowledge of composting and decomposition. This educated guess, or prediction, is your hypothesis. A hypothesis should explain these things:

- the topic of the experiment
- the variable you will change
- the variable you will measure
- what you expect to happen

A hypothesis should be brief, specific, and measurable. It must be something you can test through observation. Your experiment will prove or disprove whether your hypothesis is correct. Here is one possible hypothesis for this experiment: "Household garbage covered with soil will decay faster than garbage not covered with soil."

In this case, the variable you will change is the presence or absence of soil, and the variable you will measure is the differences in condition between the garbage in the two bags after two to three months. If the garbage in the bag with soil has decayed more than the garbage in the bag without soil, you will know your hypothesis is correct.

Level of Difficulty Easy/Moderate, because of the time involved.

What Are the Variables?

Variables are anything that might affect the results of an experiment. This experiment involves both environmental variables and biological variables. Here are the main variables in this experiment:

- the presence of air—needed for living things, bacteria, fungi, etc.
- the presence and amount of water—also needed for living things, bacteria, fungi, etc.
- the temperature—warm temperatures promote biological decomposition; cold temperatures (especially freezing temperatures) can cause physical breakdown when water freezes and expands.
- the pH—extreme pH levels can stop biological activity and cause chemical breakdown. For example, strong acids and bases are corrosive and can chemically break down debris.
- the amount and types of bacteria present—these microscopic organisms in the soil consume organic matter
- the amount and types of fungi—these microscopic and macroscopic organisms also consume organic matter

In other words, the variables in this experiment are everything that might affect the amount of decomposition of the garbage. If you change more than one variable, you will not be able to tell which variable had the most effect on the decomposition.

Materials Needed

- two 1-gallon plastic bags with holes. Each bag should have approximately 20 randomly placed holes. The holes should be about 0.5 inch (1.25 centimeters) in diameter. A hole puncher or pencil can accomplish this task.
- 2 twist ties to seal bags
- 5 pairs of household garbage items (for example, 2 food containers, 2 glass bottles, 2 pieces of leftover food or bones, 2 small sticks or leaves, and 2 metal cans)

How to Experiment Safely

Always wear gloves when handling garbage. Use caution when handling sharp objects, glass, or metal.

- permanent marker
- 3 to 5 cups of soil
- plastic gloves

Approximate Budget $5 for the materials that cannot be found in your household or at school.

Timetable Three to four months for decomposition to take place.

Step-by-Step Instructions

Step 4: Completed control and test bags. GALE GROUP.

1. Prepare a sketch and written description of the materials being placed into each bag.
2. Prepare the control experiment. The control for this experiment will remove as many variables as possible from the test in order to see the results from a single variable. In one bag place one of each item and sprinkle a little water over them. Do not add soil to the control bag. Seal the bag with a twist tie.
3. Prepare the test bag. In the other bag, place one of each item. Add to the bag 3 to 5 cups of soil to cover the garbage. Sprinkle the mixture with water and seal the bag with a twist tie.

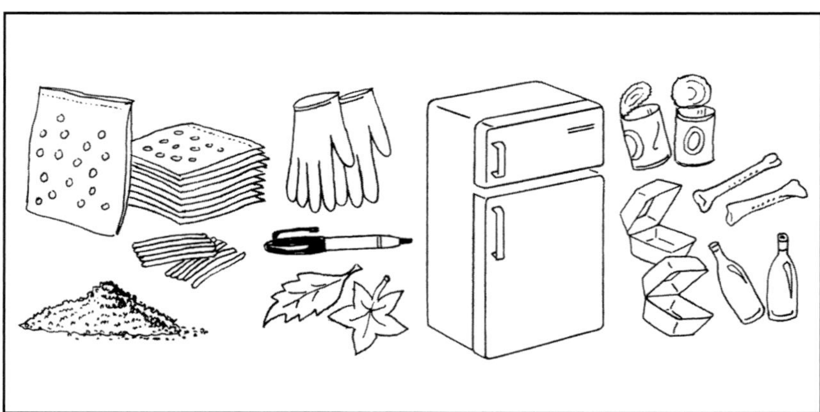
Materials needed for Experiment 1. GALE GROUP.

4. Label each bag ("control" or "test") and place both of them outside in a shady spot.
5. Open the bags every two to three weeks, sprinkle more water over the contents, and reseal the bags.
6. After three months, open the bags and pour out the contents of each onto separate pieces of newspaper. Remember to wear gloves. Record what changes have occurred to each item. Compare the differences in breakdown between the control and test bags.

Troubleshooter's Guide

Because this experiment requires living organisms to act upon waste, it is essential that the conditions in the landfill be correct. Factors such as extreme weather conditions or excessive temperatures could cause undesirable results in your experiment. If you should have problems, try the following tips: Always keep soil moist, not wet. Make sure the soil does not get too hot or cold. Temperatures between 40°F and 100°F (4°C and 38°C) are ideal. If you use black garbage bags, keep them out of the sun, because the dark color absorbs light and can overheat the soil easily.

Summary of Results When analyzing the contents of each bag, sketch the objects and write a brief description of their conditions. Look for any activity of organisms like worms or insects. If anything is smelly, slimy, or has a black stain due to bacterial action, record it in the result chart (see sample chart). Note the difference in decay between the organic waste (food) and the inorganic waste (containers).

Sample landfills results chart for Experiment 1. GALE GROUP.

	Description	Before sketch	After sketch
CONTROL ONE			
TEST ONE			
CONTROL TWO			
TEST TWO			
CONTROL THREE			
T THREE			

Change the Variables You can vary this experiment by changing the variables. For example, you can place one bag in a chilly basement or the freezer and the other bag in a warm spot outside to determine the effect of temperature. You could also add water to one bag, but not to the other, to determine the effect of water. To determine the effect of pH on decomposition, you could add an acidic material like vinegar to one bag, and add water to the other bag.

EXPERIMENT 2

Composting: Using organic material to grow plants

Purpose/Hypothesis This experiment will examine the principle of composting, the process of converting complex organic matter into the basic nutrients needed by living organisms. This experiment will utilize organic waste (household and yard waste) as nutrients for plants. It will allow you to investigate which waste products can be composted and best utilized by plants. Before you begin, make an educated guess about the outcome of the experiment based on your knowledge of composting and decomposition. This educated guess, or prediction, is your hypothesis. A hypothesis should explain these things:

- the topic of the experiment
- the variable you will change
- the variable you will measure
- what you expect to happen

A hypothesis should be brief, specific, and measurable. It must be something you can test through observation. Your experiment will prove or disprove whether your hypothesis is correct. Here is one possible hypothesis for this experiment: "Yard waste will break down faster than household waste and will provide more nutrients for plants."

In this case, the variable you will change is the type of waste used to make compost, either yard waste or household waste, and the variable you will measure is the amount of decomposition of the waste and the growth of the plants. You expect the yard waste to break down faster and produce taller plants. As a control experiment, you will grow one plant without any waste to judge the growth without compost. If the plant with yard waste compost grows taller than either of the other two plants, and the yard waste has decomposed more than the household waste, your hypothesis will be supported.

Step 2: How to fill pot #1. GALE GROUP.

Level of Difficulty Moderate, because of the time involved.

Materials Needed

- three 2-gallon (7.5-liter) potting containers (terra cotta, ceramic, or plastic) with one or more holes in the bottom for drainage
- 3 pounds (1.3 kilograms) topsoil
- 3 to 5 pounds (1.3 to 2.3 kilograms) sand
- 3 to 5 pounds. (1.3 to 2.3 kilograms) organic waste (use two types: household—table scraps, rotten vegetables, coffee grounds,

etc.—and yard waste—leaves, twigs, grass clippings, weeds, etc.)
- 3 small identical living plants (annual flowers or vegetable plants), such as sunflowers, beans, or tomatoes
- 3 stakes for markers (Popsicle sticks will work)
- plastic or rubber gloves

Approximate Budget $5 (use topsoil from your yard if available).

Timetable Two to four months.

Step-by-Step Instructions

1. Mix the topsoil and sand together to create the soil base.
2. Prepare the control experiment. Fill pot #1 with the soil base, leaving 2 inches (5 centimeters) at the top of the pot. Place one plant into the soil, covering all the roots. Water generously.
3. Prepare pot #2. Add to the soil base the household waste you collected (scraps, rotten vegetables, etc.). Mix the soil thoroughly. Place a plant into the soil, covering all the roots. Water generously.
4. Prepare pot #3. Follow the directions for pot #2 but substitute the yard waste (grass clippings, leaves, etc.) instead of household waste.
5. Put markers in the pots identifying them as "control," "household," or "yard." Place the pots in a sunny location and monitor the growth of the plants. If possible, take photographs of them at the beginning of the experiment. Water the plants when the soil feels dry. Do not allow them to dry out completely.

What Are the Variables?

Variables are anything that might affect the results of an experiment. Here are the main variables in this experiment:

- the presence of air—needed for living things, bacteria, fungi, etc.
- the presence and amount of water—also needed for living things, bacteria, fungi, etc.
- the temperature—warm temperatures promote biological decomposition; cold temperatures (especially freezing temperatures) can cause physical breakdown when water freezes and expands.
- the pH—extreme pH levels can stop biological activity and cause chemical breakdown. For example, strong acids and bases are corrosive and can chemically break down debris.
- the amount and types of bacteria present—these microscopic organisms in the soil consume organic matter
- the amount and types of fungi—these microscopic and macroscopic organisms also consume organic matter
- the type of plant—roots of plants aid in the physical breakdown of material by helping to separate materials as the roots grow through the waste

In other words, the variables in this experiment are everything that might affect the degree of decomposition and the growth rate of the plants. If you change more than one variable, you will not be able to tell which variable had the most effect on the decomposition and plant growth.

How to Experiment Safely

Wear gloves when handling waste and mixing soil.

6. Graph the weekly growth of the plants, recording the plant height, number of leaves, and root development, if visible.
7. After two to four months record the final heights and differences in the plant growth between each pot. Empty the pots and evaluate the amount of composting that occurred in the soil. Look for recognizable waste materials, record results.

Summary of Results During the experiment you will be recording the plant growth in the three pots. Ideally, the pot that is composting fastest will provide the most nutrients for its plant. It is essential to measure the height of each plant. You may also want to record which plant flowered first, how often it bloomed, and whether it produced fruit.

Change the Variables Try varying the experiment by changing the variables. You can make two identical pots with the same soil, garbage, and plants. Give one pot half as much water as the other and compare the differences in growth. You can also experiment with the pH of the waste materials. Most leaves are acidic when composted and have a low pH. Try adding 1 cup (about 0.25 liter) of garden lime (calcium carbonate) to the soil to neutralize the acidic leaves.

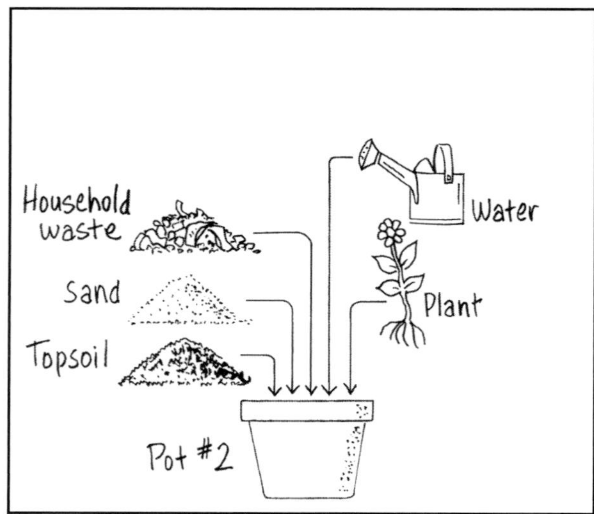

Step 3: How to fill pot #2. GALE GROUP.

Modify the Experiment You can simplify this experiment by focusing only on the soil composting and controlling which living organisms are in the soil. Worms break down organic matter. Before you add the topsoil into the pots, make sure it contains worms. If needed, add the worms carefully and divide them evenly among the three pots. Worms need moisture, air, food (organic matter), and warmth (room temperature).

First, note the condition of the waste matter before you place it in each pot. Add the topsoil (with worms). After three weeks, pour out the contents of each pot and measure the decomposition of the waste.

You can also use worms to make this experiment more challenging. Add two more pots to the experiment, so that you have five pots in total. In pots #4 and #5, duplicate the waste and process as in pots #2 and #3, except with the addition of worms. Add the same number of worms to pot #4 and pot #4. Make sure to keep all the plants moist. After several months, note the results. After the experiment is complete, carefully release the worms into a yard or other safe environment.

Troubleshooter's Guide

Because of infinite variables, such as the different kinds of organic waste that you can use in this experiment, the result can vary greatly. For instance, if you use oak leaves, which are resistant to decay and highly acidic, your experiment's results may be different than expected. If one plant dies, the experiment should be restarted from the beginning. If you notice the leaves are being eaten, try to remove the pests, but first ask for help from an adult.

Design Your Own Experiment

How to Select a Topic Relating to this Concept To create your own experiment, consider your available resources. Decide what interests you. You may want to create a compost pile of household waste and create soil for a herb garden, or find ways to reduce your consumption of non-biodegradable waste such as plastics. Although the choice is yours, you need a clear goal that will keep you motivated and interested.

	Plant height			
Week #	Control	Household	Yard	Additional Observations (use other paperas needed)

Step 7: Sample plant height data sheet. GALE GROUP.

Check the Further Readings section and talk with your science teacher or school or community media specialist to start gathering information on composting questions that interest you.

Steps in the Scientific Method To do an original experiment, you need to plan carefully and think things through. Otherwise, you might not be sure what question you are answering, what you are or should be measuring, or what your findings prove or disprove.

Here are the steps in designing an experiment:

- State the purpose of—and the underlying question behind—the experiment you propose to do.
- Recognize the variables involved, and select one that will help you answer the question at hand.
- State a testable hypothesis, an educated guess about the answer to your question.
- Decide how to change the variable you selected.
- Decide how to measure your results.

Recording Data and Summarizing the Results It is important that your experiment's results are saved for other scientists to examine and compare. You should keep a journal and record notes and measurements in it. Your experiment can then be utilized by others to answer their questions about your topic.

Related Projects When thinking about doing a project related to waste management, you need to limit your focus to one aspect of the field. For example, if you decide that recycling is your interest, choose what type of material you wish to work with. Since organic waste is smelly and metal and glass are dangerous, a good choice may be plastics. You can now begin to research ideas on how to recycle plastics. Recycling, composting, waste reduction, incineration, and conservation are all topics that can be explored and narrowed down to a concept that can lead to an interesting project.

For More Information

Appelhof, Mary. *Worms Eat My Garbage: How to Set Up & Maintain a Worm Composting System.* Kalamazoo, MI: Flower Press, 1997.

Franke, Irene, and David Brownstone. *The Green Encyclopedia.* New York: Prentice Hall, 1992. Good general reference book on environmental practices, including composting.

Leuzzi, Linda. *To the Young Environmentalist.* Stamford, CT: Franklin Watts, 1997. Interviews with respected environmentalists, including a biologist of a waste management facility.

Saunders, Tedd. *The Bottom Line of Green is Black: Strategies for Creating Profitable and Environmentally Sound Businesses.* New York: Harper and Row, 1992. Profiles of companies, such as Reader's Digest, that address landfill waste in their business practices.

U.S. Environmental Protection Agency. "Composting." http://www.epa.gov/compost/ (accessed on January 17, 2008). Explains basic composting information, regional programs, and the environmental benefits.

19

Crystals

Crystals affect your life in countless ways, from what you eat to how your computer works. Any solid matter whose particles are arranged in a regular and repeated pattern is called a crystal. The type of particle and its geometric pattern determine the properties of the crystal. Salt, sugar, and rubies are all crystals, along with many metallic elements, such as iron. Both natural rock and artificial materials are often crystalline. Our bones even contain tiny crystals of a mineral called apatite.

All crystals have flat, smooth surfaces, called faces. Some crystals, such as diamonds, are formed over millions of years, while others, such as snowflakes, are formed in a matter of hours. Crystals of the same substance have the same geometric pattern between its particles. This pattern is called a crystal lattice. In crystals the smallest possible repeating structural unit is called a unit cell. The unit cell is repeated in exactly the same neat arrangement over and over throughout the entire material.

Symbols and surgery Crystals have been a part of cultures throughout history, from ancient Egyptians to modern days. Topaz, emeralds, rubies, sapphires, and diamonds are examples of crystals long prized as gems. Their brilliance, durability, and rarity have caused people to attach superstitions and symbolism to them. Emeralds were once thought to blind snakes; amethysts to cure drunkenness; diamonds to make a soldier undefeatable; and rubies were a symbol of power.

In the 1900s, researchers began to use crystals to improve many areas of people's lives, from technology to medicine. The properties of crystals, such as hardness, conductivity, insulation, and durability, make them valuable. In modern day crystals are used in electric fuses, control circuits, industrial tools, and communication equipment. Diamonds are used in drill bits, surgery scalpels, and saw blades. The television, radio, and camera all work because of crystals. Some laser beams used in surgery and welding

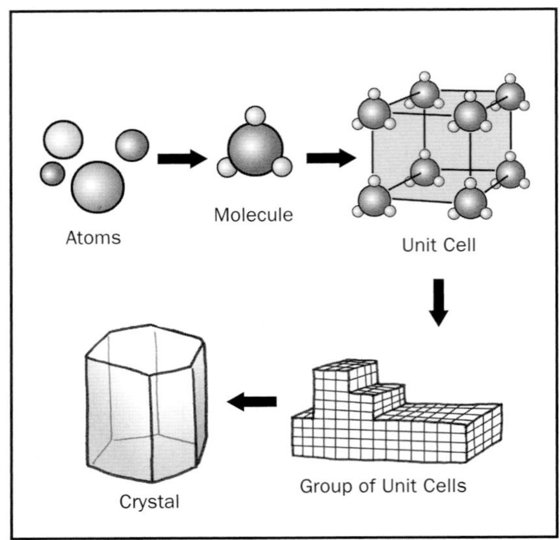

From an atom to a crystal: The smallest repeating unit in a crystal is the unit cell. GALE GROUP.

are made using crystals. Crystals are also found in watches, flat panels for computer displays, and solar-powered calculators.

Shapes and structures Crystals are made of either atoms or molecules. An atom is the smallest piece of an element that keeps the element's chemical properties. A molecule is composed of two or more atoms. It is the smallest particle of a substance that still has the properties of that substance. Inside the core of an atom are positive and negative charges.

The majority of crystals are made of ions, a charged atom or molecule. Inside the core of an atom are both positive and negative electrical charges. Atoms can either lose or gain negative charges. The charge of an atom is neutral when it has equal positive and negative charges. When an atom loses an electron it is called a positive ion and when it gains a negative charge it is called a negative ion. Most minerals and rocks are formed from ions.

The inner arrangement of the atoms or molecules, the unit cell, determines the outward shape of the crystal. Because of a crystal's geometric nature, many have strange and interesting shapes. There are seven basic crystal systems, categorized by their geometric shapes.

It is the internal structure of the crystal that determines its properties. Each atom has specific properties, yet crystals made of the same atoms can have unique properties. In graphite, the material in a pencil, carbon atoms are spaced far apart in layers. The layers are held together by weak bonds and can shift over one another. This makes graphite one of the softest minerals. On the other hand, the carbon atoms in diamond are bonded tightly to one another in closer layers. This makes a diamond a rigid and hard substance.

From televisions to wristwatches, crystals are a part of everyday life. COPYRIGHT © KELLY A. QUIN.

How a crystal reacts to electrical forces and light, its shape, hardness, color, and the rate at which it conducts heat all depend on a crystal's internal structure. Some crystals will split light, for example, causing a double image. Other crystals will bend a beam of light.

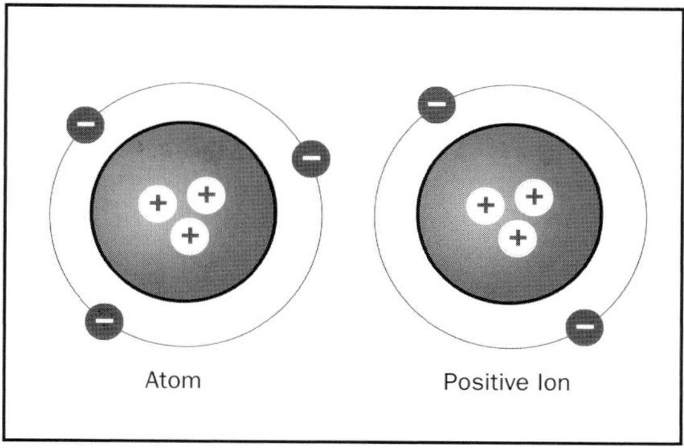

The majority of crystals are made of ions, a charged atom or molecule. GALE GROUP.

Crystal formation The size and shape of a crystal depends on how it is formed. Impurities, temperature, pressure, and the amount of space will affect what a crystal looks like. In snowflakes, for example, colder temperatures produce crystal snowflakes with sharper tips on the sides. Snowflakes that grow under warmer conditions grow more slowly, resulting in smoother shapes.

Crystals only grow large and perfect under specific conditions. Most crystals grow irregularly and sometimes it is difficult to distinguish their faces. It is rare to find a flawless crystal, which is why such perfect crystals are worth great amounts of money. While one crystal is growing it may enclose crystals of other minerals. These enclosures will appear as a visible mark in the crystal. A crystal pushed upon by some outside force can develop a twisted or bent shape.

While natural crystals can often contain flaws, artificial or synthetic crystals can be made flawless. One reason why crystals are widely used in industry and technology is that scientists learned how to synthesize artificial crystals in the laboratory, making them flawless and relatively inexpensive.

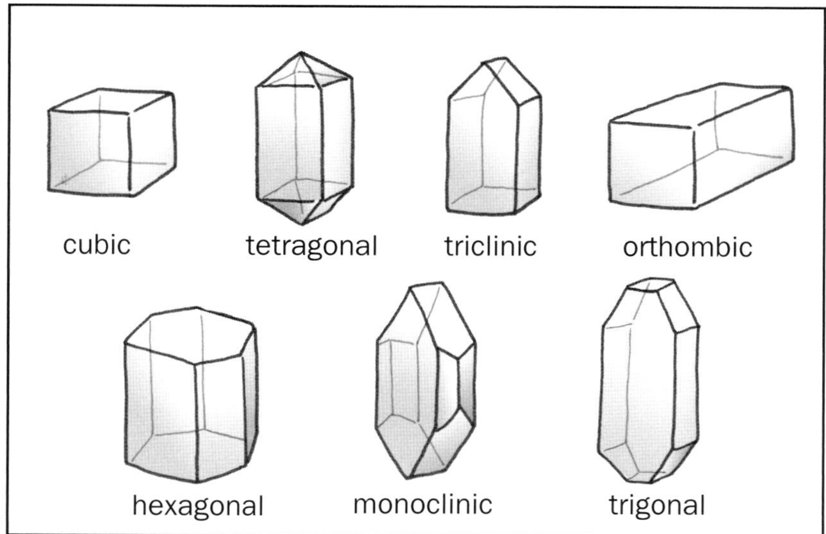

There are seven basic crystal systems, categorized by their geometric shapes. GALE GROUP.

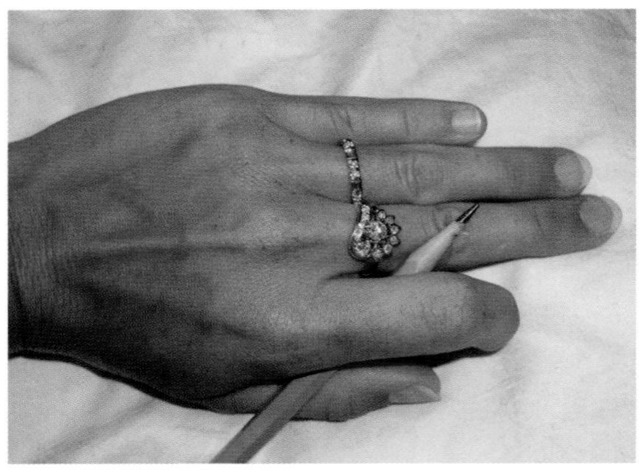

Though diamonds and graphite are comprised of carbon atoms, diamonds are rigid and hard, while the graphite used in lead pencils is soft. COPYRIGHT © KELLY A. QUIN.

Crystals start growing by a process called nucleation. Nucleation can start through the molecules themselves or through the help of solid matter already present. The nucleation process begins when the molecules in a solution, the solute molecules, have an attractive force to one another that pulls the molecules together. The more solute molecules in a solution, the greater the chance the molecules will come into contact with each other and form bonds.

When a solution contains as much dissolved solute molecules as it can hold at that temperature, it is saturated. The temperature of a solution will affect its saturation. A solution at higher temperatures will be able to dissolve more molecules than a solution at lower temperatures. If a solution is saturated at a high temperature and then cooled, it has a concentration above the saturation point. This solution is called a supersaturated solution. The molecules in a supersaturated solution are so crammed together they readily move together and can form a crystal.

The more molecules that are joined together, the stronger their attractive force. They continue to pull other molecules towards them. A small crystal that provides the attractive force to begin forming larger crystals is called a seed crystal.

EXPERIMENT 1

Crystal Structure: Will varying shape crystals form from varying substances?

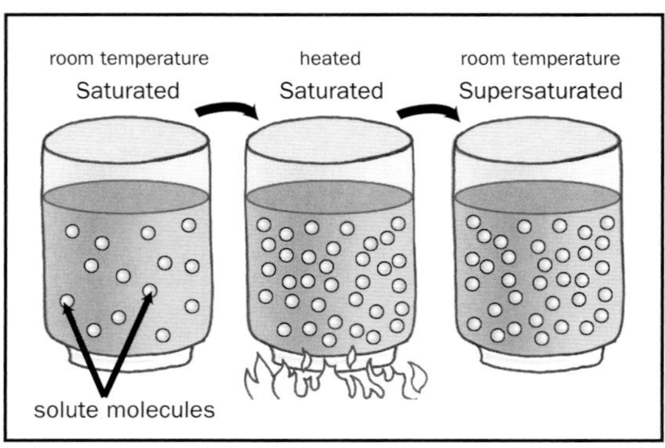

A solution at higher temperatures can dissolve more molecules than a solution at lower temperatures. GALE GROUP.

Purpose/Hypothesis Crystals come in many shapes and sizes. The substance used to make a crystal and how this substance bonds together dictates the crystal's unit cell and, thus, its shape.

In this experiment you will compare the unique crystal formations that grow from four different substances. The four crystal substances you will use are alum, Epsom salt, sugar, and salt. You will create supersaturated solutions out of the four substances and examine the crystals that form.

WORDS TO KNOW

Atom: A unit of matter, the smallest unit of an element, having all the characteristics of that element.

Control experiment: A setup that is identical to the experiment, but is not affected by the variable that acts on the experimental group.

Crystal: Naturally occurring solid composed of atoms or molecules arranged in an orderly pattern that repeats at regular intervals.

Crystal faces: The flat, smooth surfaces of a crystal.

Crystal lattice: The regular and repeating pattern of the atoms in a crystal.

Hypothesis: An idea in the form of a statement that can be tested by observation and/or experiment.

Ion: An atom or groups of atoms that carry an electrical charge—either positive or negative—as a result of losing or gaining one or more electrons.

Molecule: The smallest particle of a substance that retains all the properties of the substance and is composed of one or more atoms.

Nucleation: The process by which crystals start growing.

Saturated: In referring to solutions, a solution that contains the maximum amount of solute for a given amount of solvent at a given temperature.

Seed crystal: Small form of a crystalline structure that has all the facets of a complete new crystal contained in it.

Solute molecules: The substance that is dissolved to make a solution and exists in the least amount in a solution; for example, sugar in sugar water.

Supersaturated: Solution that is more highly concentrated than is normally possible under given conditions of temperature and pressure.

Synthetic crystals: Artificial or manmade crystals.

Unit cell: The basic unit of the crystalline structure.

Variable: Something that can affect the results of an experiment.

To begin this experiment, make an educated guess about the outcome of the experiment based on your knowledge of crystals. This educated guess, or prediction, is your hypothesis. A hypothesis should explain these things:

- the topic of the experiment
- the variable you will change
- the variable you will measure
- what you expect to happen

A hypothesis should be brief, specific, and measurable. It must be something you can test through further investigation. Your experiment will prove or disprove whether your hypothesis is correct. Here

What Are the Variables?

Variables are anything that might affect the results of an experiment. Here are the main variables in this experiment:

- the substances that make up the crystal
- the temperature of the beginning solution
- the temperature of the water
- the environment the crystal is grown in

In other words, the variables in this experiment are everything that might affect the growth of the crystals. If you change more than one variable at the same time, you will not be able to tell which variable had the most effect on the crystal's structure.

is one possible hypothesis for this experiment: "Crystals formed from different substances will develop unique shapes."

In this experiment the variable you will change will be the substance that will make up the crystal, and the variable you will measure will be the appearance of the crystal.

Level of Difficulty Moderate.

Materials Needed

- alum (small jar, found in the spice section of the grocery store)
- Epsom salt
- sugar
- salt
- water
- black saucers (or any color saucers, black construction paper, and scissors)
- hot plate or stove
- saucepan
- 4 stirring spoons
- measuring cup
- measuring spoons
- glass cup or jars
- magnifying glass (optional)
- masking tape
- marking pen

Approximate Budget $5 (most materials are common household items).

Timetable 45 minutes initial time; 30 minutes over the next week.

Step-by-Step Instructions

1. If you do not have black saucers, cut the black construction paper to fit tightly in the bottom of each saucer and place inside.
2. Make a supersaturated solution with the Epsom salt by bringing half a cup of water to the almost-boiling point, then transferring the hot water to a glass. Add 5 tablespoons Epsom salt and stir. Keep adding

Epsom salt until no more salt can be absorbed by the water. You will know this when the salt begins to fall to the bottom no matter how hard you stir.

3. Pour the solution into a saucer and label the saucer accordingly on masking tape.
4. Repeat this process with each of the other substances. Make sure to rinse the pot and use a clean spoon. For the alum, begin with 3 tablespoons; for the salt begin with 1 tablespoon, and for the sugar begin with 4 tablespoons. The sugar solution should be thick.
5. Set the saucers in a quiet place and observe them over the next week until all the liquid evaporates. When all the liquid is gone you should see crystals coating the sides and bottoms of the saucers.
6. Examine the crystals with the magnifying glass.

How to Experiment Safely

This experiment requires using very hot water to make a supersaturated solution. Ask an adult to help you when using the stove or hot plate. Do not put anything in your mouth, such as a sugar crystal, before checking with an adult.

Summary of Results Draw the results of each of the crystals and write a written description. Was your hypothesis correct? How does the Epsom salt differ from the salt? How does the salt differ from the sugar? Compare the crystal formations with the physical shape of the substance they were made from. Can you identify to which of the seven basic crystal structures the four crystals belong?

Change the Variables You can produce a variety of crystal colors and shapes by altering the substance used to form the crystal. Some substances you may have to order from a lab supply house or ask your science teacher where to get them: Potassium ferricyanide (red crystals); borax; copper acetate monohydrate (blue-green crystals); and calcium copper acetate hexahydrate (blue crystals). You can also vary the temperature of the water when making the saturated solutions and compare crystal growth.

Step 5: Set the four bowls aside in a quiet place until the liquid evaporates. GALE GROUP.

Modify the Experiment You can modify this experiment to see a crystal form under a microscope. You will first need to prepare a supersaturated solution from a crystal, such as salt. Stir several teaspoons of salt into about a half a cup of warm water until the crystals no longer dissolve. Allow the mixture to sit for several hours.

Place a drop of the solution onto a microscope slide. Set the slide under a heat lamp or in the hot sun for a few minutes so that much of the water quickly evaporates. Now place the slide under the microscope and focus. Keep observing the crystal shapes under the microscope. Can you see crystals growing? Try to observe different types of crystals and compare the shapes.

Troubleshooter's Guide

Below is a problem that may arise during this experiment, some possible causes, and some ways to remedy the problem.

Problem: No crystals grew in one or more of the solutions.

Possible cause: The solution may not have been saturated when the water was hot. You may not have stirred enough to dissolve the solids. Pour the solution back in the saucepan. Reheat the solution, adding more of the substance and stirring well after each addition until you see bits of the substance fall to the bottom.

Possible cause: The water may not have been hot enough. It should not be at the boiling point but it does need to be very hot. Pour the solution back in the saucepan. Reheat the solution, adding more of the substance and stirring well after each addition until it is saturated.

EXPERIMENT 2

Cool Crystals: How does the effect of cooling impact crystal growth?

Purpose/Hypothesis Temperature is one of the key environmental factors that affect crystal growth. This experiment examines the outcome of the same crystal-growing solution cooling at three different temperatures. You will place one jar in a cold environment while the crystals grow, the other jar will cool under room temperature conditions, and you will enclose the third jar and store it in a warm area so that it cools the slowest of the three. If the cooling is faster, the particles do not have time to form a large-scale orderly arrangement and a mass of little crystals will form instead. The size of each crystal will demonstrate how temperature impacts the growth of a crystal.

To begin this experiment, make an educated guess about the outcome of the experiment based on your knowledge of crystals, temperature, and solutions. This educated guess, or prediction, is your hypothesis. A hypothesis should explain these things:

- the topic of the experiment
- the variable you will change
- the variable you will measure
- what you expect to happen

A hypothesis should be brief, specific, and measurable. It must be something you can test through further investigation. Your experiment will prove or disprove whether your hypothesis is correct. Here is one possible hypothesis for this experiment: "The slower a supersaturated solution cools, the larger the size of the crystal."

In this experiment the variable you will change will be the cooling rate of the solution, and the variable you will measure will be the size of the crystal. If the solution that cools the quickest forms the largest crystal, you will know the above hypothesis is incorrect and you will have to reevaluate your hypothesis.

Having a control or standard crystal will help you measure the changes in the dependent variable. Only one variable will change between the control and the experimental crystals, and that is the size of the crystal. For the standard crystal, you will soak a seed crystal in plain water, which will not react with the seed crystal. At the end of the experiment you will compare the size and shape of the seed crystal with each of the other crystals.

What Are the Variables?

Variables are anything that might affect the results of an experiment. Here are the main variables in this experiment:

- the solution's rate of cooling
- the crystal-growing substance
- the surrounding air temperature
- the container the crystals are grown in
- the string the crystals are grown on

In other words, the variables in this experiment are everything that might affect the growth of the crystals. If you change more than one variable, you will not be able to tell which variable impacted crystal growth.

Level of Difficulty Moderate.

Materials Needed

- Epsom salt
- dental floss
- glass saucepan
- hot plate or stove
- saucer
- measuring cup
- measuring spoons
- 4 small glass jars
- small piece of cloth to cover glass container
- warm towel
- cold-water bath (pan with ice in cold water)
- stirring spoon
- 4 pencils (long enough to lay across the tops of the four small glass containers)
- marking pen

How to Experiment Safely

You are using very hot water in this experiment. Ask an adult to help you when using the stove or hot plate.

Approximate Budget $2 (most materials are common household items).

Timetable 20 minutes initial time; 30 minutes after several days; 20 minutes over the next two weeks.

Step-by-Step Instructions

1. To grow a seed crystal, heat a half a cup of water until it is almost at the boiling point and carefully pour it into a glass. Add 5 tablespoons of Epsom salt and stir mixture until all the salt dissolves. Continue adding Epsom salt, stirring after each addition, until the solution is completely saturated. You will know you are at the saturation point when a small amount of Epsom salt sinks to the bottom no matter how hard you stir.
2. Pour the solution into a saucer and wait at least 24 hours until small crystals have grown in the saucer. This could take two or three days. Pour out any remaining liquid and choose the four largest crystals that are roughly the same size. These are your seed crystals.
3. Cut four pieces of dental floss about 6 inches (10 centimeters) long. Take each piece and tie one end around a pencil. Cut the piece of dental floss so the other end hangs slightly above the bottom of each jar.
4. Carefully tie a seed crystal to the loose end of each piece of dental floss.
5. Heat 2 cups of water in the saucepan until it is almost boiling. Remove from heat and add 3/4 cup of Epsom salt and stir. Continue

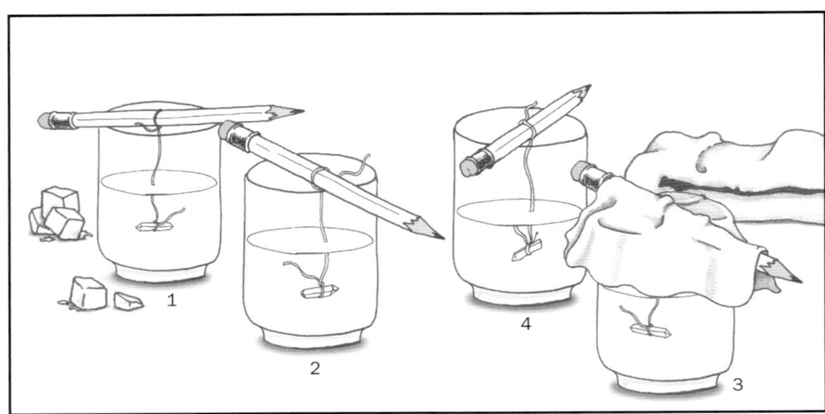

Step 6: Hang a seed crystal in each solution by laying the pencil across the jars. GALE GROUP.

to stir while you add as much Epsom salt as you can—until no more will dissolve. When the solution is saturated, set the saucepan aside to cool for two minutes. Pour equal amounts of the solution into three glass jars.

6. In the fourth glass jar pour a roughly equal amount of plain warm water. Hang a seed crystal in each solution by laying the pencil across the jars.
7. Let Jar 1 completely cool and then place it in a cold-water bath. Leave Jar 2 at room temperature. Warm a towel in a clothes dryer, wrap it around Jar 3, and drape the piece of cloth over the top of the jar before placing the jar in a warm area, like a cupboard near the stove. Leave Jar 4 at room temperature.
8. Every day place fresh ice in the cold-water bath for Jar 1, and reheat the towel for Jar 3. After about a week, compare the crystals.

Summary of Results Compare the rate of crystal growth, using the control crystal in Jar 4 as your standard. Examine if there are small crystals on the side or the bottom of the jars. Estimate the size of each crystal on the string compared to the standard, or control crystal, that was sitting in the water. Graph your results, using the percentage of growth on the y-axis and the rate of cooling on the x-axis.

Troubleshooter's Guide

Below are some problems that may arise, some possible causes, and some ways to remedy the problems.

Problem: No crystals grew in one or more of the solutions.

Possible cause: The solution may not have been saturated when the water was hot. You may not have stirred enough to dissolve the Epsom salt. Take out the seed crystal and pour the solution back into the saucepan. Reheat the solution, adding more of the Epsom salt and stirring well after each addition until you see bits of the Epsom salt fall to the bottom.

Possible cause: The water may not have been hot enough to become completely saturated. It should not be at the boiling point, but it does need to be hot. Take out the seed crystal and pour the solution back into the saucepan. Reheat the solution, adding more of the Epsom salt and stirring well after each addition until it is saturated.

Problem: The crystals are cloudy.

Possible cause: There may be impurities in the water or the jar. Examine the jar and, if it is dirty, try the experiment again with a clean jar. If the glass is clean, try repeating the experiment using distilled or purified water.

Change the Variables You can change the variables in the experiment several ways. You can alter the crystal-growing substance and repeat the experiment. You can also change the temperature of the water to make the saturated solutions. Does anything happen if the crystals are grown on a piece of yarn as opposed to dental floss?

Sugar and salt are examples of crystals that vary in size and shape. COPYRIGHT © KELLY A. QUIN.

Design Your Own Experiment

How to Select a Topic Relating to this Concept Crystals have a range of diverse physical and mechanical properties that you can explore in experiments. Explore your surroundings and make a list of all the materials made of crystals. An experiment with crystals could include exploring some of the traits crystallographers use to identify them, such as how a crystal reacts to light or its hardness.

Check the Further Readings section and talk with your science teacher or librarian to learn more about crystals. As you consider possible experiments, make sure to discuss them with your science teacher or other adult before conducting them.

Steps in the Scientific Method To do an original experiment, you need to plan carefully and think things through. Otherwise, you might not be sure what question you are answering, what you are or should be measuring, or what your findings prove or disprove.

Here are the steps in designing an experiment:

- State the purpose of—and the underlying question behind—the experiment you propose to do.
- Recognize the variables involved and select one that will help you answer the question at hand.
- State your hypothesis, an educated guess about the answer to your question.
- Decide how to change the variable you selected.
- Decide how to measure your results.

Recording Data and Summarizing the Results Your data should include charts and graphs such as the one you did for these experiments. They should be clearly labeled and easy to read. You may also want to include photographs and drawings of your experimental setup and results, which will help others visualize the steps in the experiment.

If you are preparing an exhibit, you may want to display your results, such as any experimental setup you designed. If you have completed a nonexperimental project, explain clearly what your research question was and illustrate your findings.

Related Projects Some experiments with crystals will depend on having crystals with different properties. You can examine the crystalline structures of everyday substances around you. Many rocks are crystals. You could identify the unique properties of crystalline rocks and group them according to their common properties. You could also take on a research project. You could examine what crystals are used in appliances, electronic devices, and tools, as well as what properties these crystals supply. Through interviews with professionals or library research, you could examine the work of cystallographers and determine the instruments and properties they use to identify crystals.

For More Information

Libbrecht, Kenneth G. *SnowCrystals.com.* http://www.its.caltech.edu/~atomic/snowcrystals/class/class.htm (accessed February 20, 2008). A guide to the many different crystal shapes of snowflakes.

Math Forum. http://mathforum.org/alejandre/workshops/chart.html (accessed February 20, 2008). Descriptions and links to pictures of the basic crystal systems.

Shedenhelm, W. R., and Joel E. Arem. *Discover Rocks & Minerals.* Lincolnwood, IL: Publications International, 1991. Basic facts on rocks and minerals with plenty of photographs.

Stangl, Jean. *Crystal and Crystal Gardens You Can Grow.* New York: Franklin Watts, 1990. Simple explanation of crystals with directions for growing different crystals.

Symes, R. F., and R. R. Harding. *Crystal & Gem.* New York: Alfred A. Knopf, 1991. Clear book with loads of illustrations on identifying and using various types of crystals.

20

Density and Buoyancy

What does it mean when it is said that one type of matter is more *dense* than another? What does density tell us about the nature and behavior of a substance? How does density affect the tendency of an object to float or sink in a liquid?

The density of matter is determined by the mass of a given volume of that matter. Any object at a given temperature and pressure will have a fixed volume, determined by the quantity of space it occupies and measured in cubic inches (cubic centimeters or milliliters). It also will have a fixed mass, determined by the quantity of matter contained in the substance. Mass is measured in pounds (kilograms). Density equals mass divided by volume.

The mass of different substances can vary greatly. The atoms that make up lead are tightly packed (at room temperature and pressure) and possess a large number of subatomic particles—protons, neutrons, and electrons. In contrast, the atoms that make up hydrogen gas are very loosely packed at the same temperature and pressure and possess a very small number of subatomic particles. More atoms with more subatomic particles in a given volume means higher density. Fewer atoms with fewer subatomic particles in a given volume means lower density.

A ship floats in water because of the effects of density and buoyancy. PHOTO RESEARCHERS INC.

Imagine a lifesize sculpture of a goldfish molded in solid clay. Now imagine an identical statue cast in solid lead. Both sculptures occupy the same volume, but the lead has a greater mass and is therefore denser. A third identical sculpture, this time carved from balsa wood, also occupies the same volume but contains less mass than either the clay or the lead. Balsa wood is less dense than both clay and lead.

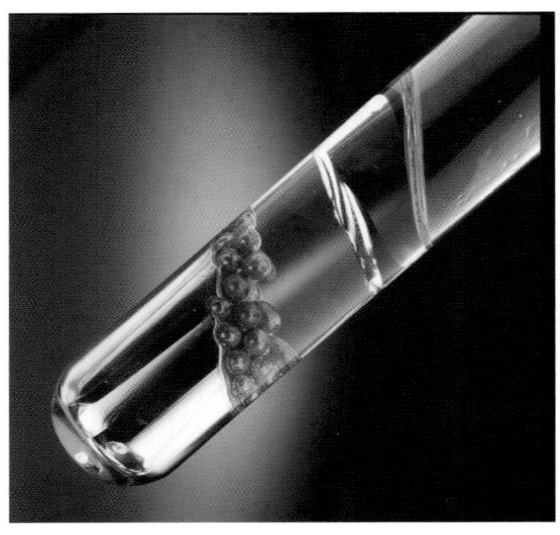

Materials placed together in a container will float or sink according to their relative density. PHOTO RESEARCHERS INC.

Density is measured on a relative scale Notice that in comparing the densities of lead, clay, and balsa wood, we have not used any units of measurement. We simply stated that balsa wood is less dense and lead is more dense compared to clay. This is called relative density.

To measure density, scientists often use a relative scale. Water is assigned a value of 1.0, and other materials are assigned numerical values greater or less than 1.0 based on their density relative to water. For example, lead has a relative density of 11.3 and balsa wood has a relative density of 0.2. Relative density compared to water is also called specific gravity.

Relative density can be observed The relative density of certain materials is easy to determine by observing the behavior of the materials when gravity acts upon them in a liquid. Substances of greater density will sink in liquids of lesser density due to the greater gravitational pull on the mass they contain. Conversely, substances of lesser density will rise. Thus, the lead goldfish will sink through water, while the balsawood goldfish will float. What about the

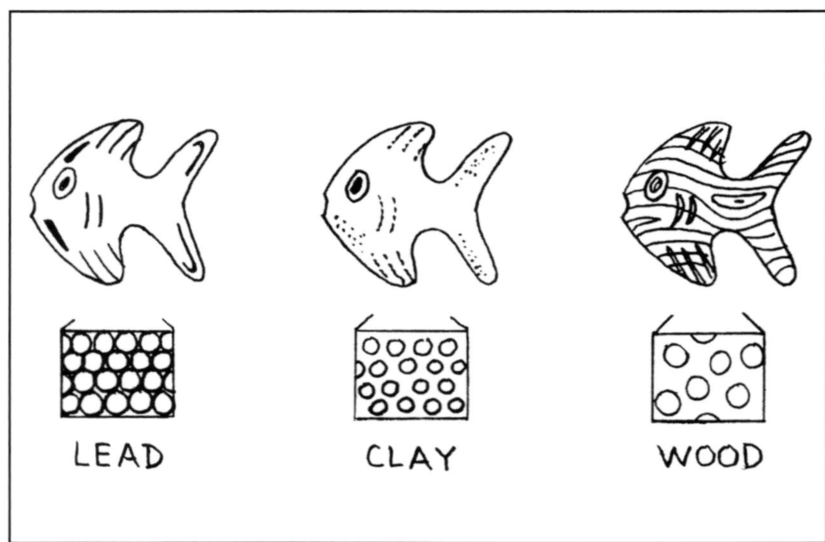

Three statues of identical shape and size have different densities depending on their mass. GALE GROUP.

clay goldfish? To predict its behavior, we would need to know its relative density.

When two immiscible liquids, such as oil and vinegar, are poured into a container, the less-dense liquid will float on top of the more-dense liquid. If a third liquid whose density falls between the first and second is poured into the container, it will form a layer between the other two liquids. A solid dropped into the container will sink through the liquids of lesser density than itself, but it will float on the layer of the liquid whose density is greater than the solid's density.

Archimedes studied the relationship between density and buoyancy. PHOTO RESEARCHERS, INC.

Look! It floats The relationship between density and buoyancy was studied in the third century B.C.E. by Archimedes, a Greek philosopher and inventor. The Archimedes Principle states that the lifting effect of a liquid on an object is equal to the weight of the liquid displaced by the object. Thus, if the object contains less mass than the mass of the displaced liquid, the object will float.

The Archimedes Principle is what makes steel ships float. If the mass of the displaced water—that is, the mass of the volume of water pushed aside by the hollow hull of the ship below the waterline—is greater than the mass of the entire ship, then the ship will float, even though steel has a relative density greater than 1.

The behavior of various materials under the effect of gravity can be observed and used to estimate their relative densities. In the first experiment, you will use such observations to create a relative density scale of your own. The experiment should ultimately help you predict the behavior of various materials, like the clay goldfish, according to their assigned density values.

The second experiment will examine the effect of increased pressure on a buoyant object containing a gas to see how changing the volume can change the buoyancy.

WORDS TO KNOW

Buoyancy: The tendency of a fluid to exert a lifting force on a body immersed in it.

Density: The mass of a substance divided by its volume.

Hypothesis: An idea phrased in the form of a statement that can be tested by observation and/or experiment.

Immiscible: Incapable of being mixed.

Mass: Measure of the total amount of matter in an object. Also, an object's quantity of matter as shown by its gravitational pull on another object.

Matter: Anything that has mass and takes up space.

Relative density: The density of one material compared to another.

Specific gravity: The density of a material compared to water.

Subatomic: Smaller than an atom. It usually refers to particles that make up an atom, such as protons, neutrons, and electrons.

Variable: Something that can affect the results of an experiment.

Volume: The amount of space occupied by a three-dimensional object.

Waterline: The highest point to which water rises on the hull of a ship. The portion of the hull below the waterline is under water.

EXPERIMENT 1

Density: Can a scale of relative density predict whether one material floats on another?

Purpose/Hypothesis In this experiment, you will first create a relative density scale for eight materials. Then you will use that information to predict whether one material will float on the other when any two of the materials are placed together in a container.

To begin the experiment, use what you know about relative density to make an educated guess about whether one material will float on the other. This educated guess, or prediction, is your hypothesis. A hypothesis should explain these things:

- the topic of the experiment
- the variable you will change
- the variable you will measure
- what you expect to happen

A hypothesis should be brief, specific, and measurable. It must be something you can test through observation. Your experiment will prove

or disprove whether your hypothesis is correct. Here is one possible hypothesis for this experiment: "A relative density scale based on the behavior of eight materials in one container will accurately predict that a material with a lower relative density will float on one with a higher relative density when the two are placed in another container."

In this case, the variables you will change are the two materials, and the variable you will measure is which material floats on the other. If the material with the lower relative density floats on the one with a higher relative density, you will know your hypothesis is correct.

What Are the Variables?

Variables are anything that could affect the results of an experiment. Here are the main variables in this experiment:

- the type and purity of the materials
- the method by which the materials are added to the container
- the order in which materials are added to the container
- the temperature at which the materials are kept
- the pressure at which the materials are kept

In other words, the variables in this experiment are everything that might affect the ability of one material to float on another. If you change more than one variable, you will not be able to tell which variable had the most effect.

Level of Difficulty Moderate.

Materials Needed

- 3 clear, narrow, glass jars with wide mouths (such as beakers or pickle jars)
- 1 probe (a knitting needle or drink stirrer will do)
- 9 disposable plastic knives
- corn oil
- motor oil (10W-30)
- maple syrup
- water, colored blue with food coloring
- lemon juice
- one 0.5-inch-diameter (1.2 centimeters) ball of clay
- one 0.5-inch-diameter (1.2 centimeters) ball of candle wax
- 1 small cork

Approximate Budget Less than $10. (Most, if not all, materials may be found in the average household.)

Timetable To be performed properly, allowing time for materials to settle and for careful observing and note taking, this experiment should take 45 to 60 minutes.

How to Experiment Safely

Before substituting other substances for those on the materials list, check with your science teacher to make sure you are not combining chemicals that will create a hazard, such as toxic fumes. Some combinations of household substances mix together easily or are the same color and therefore are not useful for this experiment. Throw away the knives and glass jars after finishing the experiment because they may be contaminated with motor oil.

Step-by-Step Instructions

1. Divide your materials into liquids and solids. Examine the liquids first and try to predict which are the most dense. Pour the five liquids into one container, beginning with the one you predict to be the most dense. Pour each liquid slowly, using a plastic knife as a guide, as illustrated. Liquids that normally do not mix may accidentally mix if they are shaken or stirred. Use a new knife for each liquid.
2. After all the liquids have been added to the container, wait for one minute to allow them to settle. Make a note of the order in which the liquids have settled, but do not assign relative density values yet. You have not yet added the solid materials, and the behavior of the solids may surprise you!
3. One by one, gently add the three solids to the container. Allow more time for them to settle. If a solid becomes coated with a liquid, its behavior may change temporarily. For example, a solid may float higher than normal if it is coated with vegetable oil. If you suspect that a solid is not behaving normally, gently poke it with the probe.
4. After you are confident that all the materials have settled to their natural levels, begin assigning relative density values. Start by identifying the layer of blue water and label that "1.0" on your relative density scale (see illustration). Then identify each material above and below the water, record it on your scale, and assign a relative density value for each. Your numerical values do not need to be exact as long as their relative values show which material is denser. For example, you could assign 0.9 to the material just above the water and 0.8 to the material just above that. Likewise you could assign 1.1 to the material just below the water, and so on.

Step 1: Pouring liquid using a knife as a guide. GALE GROUP.

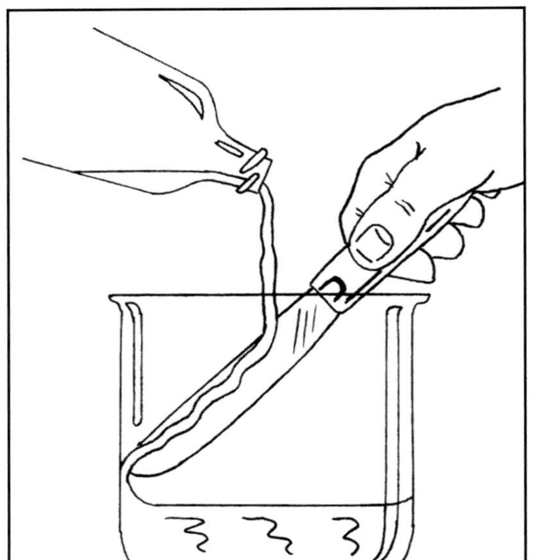

5. Select two different materials and carefully pour or place them in the second glass jar, using a new plastic knife for each liquid. (Do not pair a solid with another solid.) Record the order in which you add each material. Observe the behavior of the materials in the jar. Did your relative density scale accurately predict what would happen? If so, your hypothesis has proven correct so far.
6. Determine whether the behavior of the materials used in the previous step changes when the order of putting the materials into the jar is changed. For example, if you previously added motor oil to a jar already holding water, now reverse the order, pouring the oil in first. Use the third jar and clean knives for this test.

Summary of Results Examine your results and determine whether your hypothesis is correct. Did the observed behavior of the eight materials combined make it possible to create a useful relative scale? If any of the behaviors disagree with the scale's prediction, try to find a possible

Troubleshooter's Guide

Here are some problems that may arise during the experiment, some possible causes, and ways to remedy the problems.

Problem: Two liquids appear to mix.

Possible causes:

1. Agitation when pouring the liquid into the container may cause temporary mixing. Wait for the mixture to settle out.
2. Two of your substances are too similar in appearance, such as vegetable oil and motor oil. Replace one substance with something that is similar but provides more contrast. For example, you could use canola oil in place of vegetable oil.

Problem: The behavior of a solid in liquids is erratic: sometimes it floats, sometimes it sinks.

Possible cause: Surface tension can sometimes cause an object of greater density to float on top of a liquid of lesser density. To counteract this tension, poke the solid with the probe.

Relative Density Scale	
Material or Substance	Relative Density Value
cork	-1
water	0 (zero)
clay	1

Step 4: Sample relative density scale. GALE GROUP.

What Are the Variables?

Variables are anything that might affect the results of an experiment. Here are the main variables in this experiment:

- the rigidity or flexibility of the walls of the object
- the gas present inside the objects
- the liquid in which the objects are placed
- the pressure applied to the objects

In other words, the variables in this experiment are everything that might affect the buoyancy of the objects. If you change more than one variable, you will not be able to tell which variable had the most effect on the buoyancy.

explanation for this difference. Did you misread the layers in the first step of your experiment? Go back and double check. Write a summary of your findings.

Change the Variables You can vary this experiment in several ways. Try different liquids and solids. Compare the densities of two solids, such as clay and a piece of pencil eraser. Then create and test a combination of solids by wrapping the eraser inside a layer of clay. Be sure to check with your teacher before trying new materials to make sure they are safe when mixed!

You can also see if you get the same results when the liquids in your experiment are chilled. (Do not heat your materials.) Freeze a liquid material and see if its relative density is the same whether in liquid or solid form.

EXPERIMENT 2

Buoyancy: Does water pressure affect buoyancy?

Purpose/Hypothesis In this experiment, you will observe the effect of increased water pressure on two buoyant objects floating in a closed bottle of water. The first is a flexible drinking straw filled with air and open at one end. The second is a flexible drinking straw filled with air and sealed at both ends. Because the first straw is open at one end, an increase in pressure allows water to easily force its way into the straw. This decreases the volume of water the straw displaces and it will eventually sink. Because the second straw is sealed at both ends, the water cannot force its way inside and must actually collapse the straw to decrease the displaced volume.

To begin the experiment, use what you know about buoyancy to make an educated guess about how the straws will behave when the pressure is increased. This educated guess, or prediction, is your hypothesis. A hypothesis should explain these things:

- the topic of the experiment
- the variable you will change
- the variable you will measure
- what you expect to happen

A hypothesis should be brief, specific, and measurable. It must be something you can test through observation. Your experiment will prove or disprove whether your hypothesis is correct. Here is one possible hypothesis for this experiment: "A flexible drinking straw, filled with air and sealed at one end, will lose its buoyancy and sink at a lower pressure than one sealed at both ends."

How to Experiment Safely

Make sure the bottle's cap is secured tightly before applying pressure.

In this case, the variable you will change is the amount of pressure applied, and the variable you will measure is whether the straws sink. If the straw sealed at one end sinks at a lower pressure than the one sealed at both ends, you will know your hypothesis is correct.

Level of Difficulty Moderate.

Materials Needed

- one 1-liter transparent plastic bottle filled with water (the bottle must have flexible sides and a cap that seals)
- 2 transparent drinking straws
- modeling clay
- 1 tall drinking glass
- water

Approximate Budget Less than $5. (Most, if not all, materials may be found in the average household.)

Timetable Approximately 10 to 20 minutes.

Step-by-Step Instructions

1. Cut a 4-inch (10-centimeter) length of straw and seal one end with a lump of clay. This will be the top end of the straw. Attach a ring of clay to the straw near the open bottom end to serve as ballast to keep it upright in the water as illustrated. Fill the drinking glass with water and test the buoyancy of the first straw. Add or remove clay from the ballast until the straw floats upright in a stable manner.

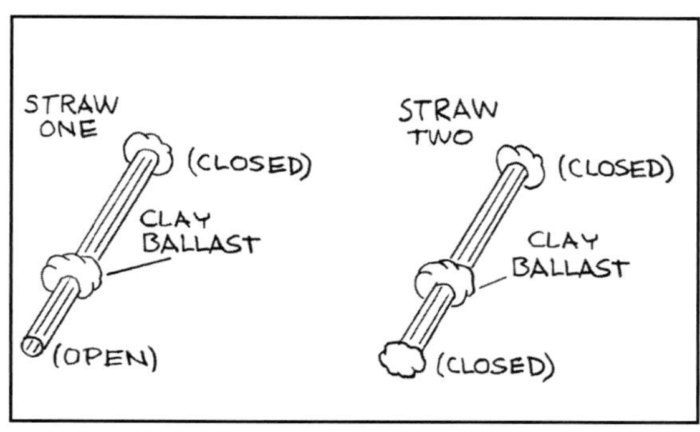

Steps 1 and 2: Set-up of straw 1 and straw 2. GALE GROUP.

2. Repeat this process with the second straw, but seal this one with clay at both ends. Check the seals by submerging the top of the straw in the drinking cup. Look for bubbles coming from the top seal. Then invert the straw and check the bottom seal.
3. Fill the bottle with water to within 1 to 2 inches (2.5 to 5.0 centimeters) of the neck. Carefully lower the two straws into the bottle with the bottom end of the straws down. Close the bottle and make sure it is sealed tightly.
4. Position the bottle on a table or counter so that one person can squeeze the bottle while another takes measurements with the ruler of the change in the bottle's width where it is squeezed. This measurement will serve as a rough gauge of the pressure applied to the water and objects inside the bottle.
5. Measure and record the approximate diameter of the bottle. Gently squeeze the bottle until its width has decreased by 0.5 inch (1.25 centimeters). Record any change that occurs in the straws (sinking, taking on water, deforming) in the appropriate column on your data chart. Repeat this process for each 0.5-inch (1.25-centimeter) change in the bottle's width. As increasing pressure is applied, the straw with the open end should sink.

narrow diameter of bottle (rough est. of pressure)	straw one (open end)	straw two (closed)
11 cm	floating at surface	floating at surface
10 cm	still floating at surface, water climbing 2 cm up into straw	still floating at surface, slight "crushing" of straw
9 cm	sinks to bottom, water 4 cm up into straw	still floating, straw "crushed" to 1/2 normal width

Note: These figures may vary depending on the size of the bottle used and the quantity of water.

Step 5: Sample recording chart. GALE GROUP.

6. Continue squeezing until the second straw sinks or until no more pressure can safely be applied to the bottle.
7. When pressure is released, the straw or straws should regain their buoyancy and return to the surface. Repeat the experiment, this time noting any changes you observe in the two straws as pressure is applied to the bottle. Watch for water rising in the unsealed straw. This is similar to a submarine flooding its ballast tanks to decrease its buoyancy and dive under water. Watch for deformation of the second straw, which should flatten as the pressure is increased.
8. Examine your results and determine whether your hypothesis is true. Repeat the experiment to double check your results. Write a summary of your findings.

Summary of Results Record your data on a chart. This chart should be as clear as possible. It will contain the information that will show whether your hypothesis is correct.

Change the Variables You can vary this experiment. Here are some possibilities. Try different numbers and lengths of straw. Compare the behavior of short straws and long straws. See if you get the same results with different liquids. Try salt water and carbonated water.

Design Your Own Experiment

How to Select a Topic Relating to this Concept Demonstrations of the properties of density and buoyancy exist in our environment in numerous forms. Everyday sights such as helium balloons floating away or a thin slick of oil on a roadside puddle show the principles we

Troubleshooter's Guide

Here are some problems that may arise during the experiment, some possible causes, and ways to solve the problem.

Problem: Neither straw sinks, even when maximum pressure is applied.

Possible causes:

1. The bottle may not be properly sealed. Check the seal. If necessary, place a small amount of clay on the threads of the bottle top to help keep a seal.
2. There is too much air in the bottle. Add water.

Problem: The first straw sinks, but the second does not.

Possible causes:

1. You are not applying enough pressure. Try having two people press on the bottle (carefully!) from either side.
2. The straws are too rigid. Use straws of less rigid plastic.
3. Your hypothesis is incorrect.

Problem: Once the straw or straws have sunk, they do not return to the surface when pressure is released.

Possible cause: The straw or straws are leaking. Check the clay seals.

Problem: The straw or straws are unstable and tend to flip over.

Possible cause: The ballast weight is not heavy enough or is not placed properly. Increase the weight or move the ballast weight farther down the straw.

have investigated in our experiments. Think of ways to vary the conditions you observe that will answer questions you have about buoyancy.

Check the Further Readings section and talk with your science teacher or school or community media specialist to start gathering information on density and buoyancy questions that may interest you. As you consider possible experiments, be sure to discuss them with your science teacher or another knowledgeable adult before trying them. Some materials or procedures might be dangerous.

Steps in the Scientific Method To do an original experiment, you need to plan carefully and think things through. Otherwise, you might not be sure which question you are answering, what you are or should be measuring, or what your findings prove or disprove.

Here are the steps in designing an experiment:

- State the purpose of—and the underlying question behind—the experiment you propose to do.
- Recognize the variables involved, and select one that will help you answer the question at hand.
- State a testable hypothesis, an educated guess about the answer to your question.
- Decide how to change the variable you selected.
- Decide how to measure your results.

Recording Data and Summarizing the Results In the experiments included here and in any experiments you develop, you can look for better ways to display your data in more accurate and interesting ways. For example, in the buoyancy experiment, try to find a better way to measure the pressure inside the bottle. Could a pressure gauge be built into the bottle's cap without altering the results?

Remember that those who view your results may not have seen the experiment performed, so you must present the information you have gathered in as clear a way as possible. Including photographs or illustrations of the steps in the experiment is a good way to show a viewer how you got from your hypothesis to your conclusion.

Related Projects Although experiments in density and buoyancy can be challenging and fun, simple demonstrations of the principles involved can also be highly informative and often can reveal surprising facts. Many aspects of density and buoyancy, such as the effect of salinity, could yield interesting experimental results.

For More Information

Gillett, Kate, ed. *The Knowledge Factory.* Brookfield, CT: Copper Beech Books, 1996. Provides some fun and enlightening observations on questions relevant to this topic, along with good ideas for projects and demonstrations.

Ray, C. Claibourne. *The New York Times Book of Science Questions and Answers.* New York: Doubleday, 1997. Addresses both everyday observations and advanced scientific concepts on a wide variety of subjects.

Wolke, Robert L. *What Einstein Didn't Know: Scientific Answers to Everyday Questions.* Secaucus, NJ: Birch Lane Press, 1997. Contains a number of interesting entries on the nature of water.

21

Dissolved Oxygen

What turns a body of water into a "dead zone" where nothing can live? One condition that can wipe out most living things in a stream, river, or lake is a low level of dissolved oxygen. The term dissolved oxygen refers to molecules of oxygen that have been dissolved in water. Some of these molecules enter the water from the surrounding air, especially if the water tumbles over falls and rapids. Other dissolved oxygen in the water is a "by-product" of photosynthesis. During photosynthesis, green plants, including those that live in the water, use the energy in sunlight to combine carbon dioxide and water to produce carbohydrates and oxygen. The oxygen is expelled by the plant and enters the water.

The level of dissolved oxygen in water can reach as high as 8 or 9 parts per million. The United States Environmental Protection Agency (EPA) considers water to be healthy if it contains at least 5 parts per million of dissolved oxygen. When the level falls below 4 parts per million, the water quality is considered to be poor. At 2 parts per million, fish become stressed and grow more slowly, and some die.

What affects the level of dissolved oxygen in water? The level of dissolved oxygen in a body of water can vary from hour to hour. The level falls as fish remove oxygen molecules from the water with their gills. The more fish in the water, the more dissolved oxygen they remove. Fish are cold-blooded, so their body systems work more slowly in cold water and speed up in warm water. The warmer the water, the more oxygen their body systems require. Plants in the water, including the tiny floating phytoplankton, also use small amounts of the dissolved oxygen for respiration (breathing).

Photosynthesis requires sunlight, so plants do not produce oxygen at night. During these dark hours, plants actually use more oxygen for respiration than they produce. That's why the level of dissolved oxygen in a body of water is lowest just before dawn, just before the Sun rises and

As more water surface is exposed to the air, more oxygen molecules enter the water. FIELDMARK PUBLICATIONS.

photosynthesis begins again. If you visit a pond or river at dawn, you might see birds picking fish out of the water. The fish are easy to catch then because they are at the surface, gulping for oxygen because the water does not provide enough for them.

Other factors also influence the level of dissolved oxygen, including the water's temperature, its salinity (salt level), and its elevation above sea level. As the water temperature decreases, the amount of dissolved oxygen increases, because gases, including oxygen, dissolve more easily in cooler water. As the level of salinity increases, the amount of dissolved oxygen decreases. Finally, bodies of water at higher elevations, such as mountain lakes, contain less dissolved oxygen than bodies of water at lower elevations. This makes sense when you remember that much of the dissolved oxygen comes from the air. The amount of oxygen in the air decreases the higher you climb on a mountain. If the air has less dissolved oxygen, the water will, too.

During hot, dry summer months, the water level in streams tends to be low, and the water often becomes stagnant. The heat and the lack of movement combine to lower dissolved oxygen levels. On the other hand, during the early spring, melting snow and cool rain keep the water temperatures low, increasing the dissolved oxygen levels. The rains lead to rushing, tumbling streams that gain more oxygen from the atmosphere. The rains also contribute the oxygen they absorbed from the atmosphere.

Another major effect on the level of dissolved oxygen in a body of water is the amount of pollutants in the water. Many pollutants, including the fertilizers that run off farm fields and home lawns, contain nutrients that help plants grow, including plants in the water. This may seem like a benefit of pollution. However, after the plants use up the nutrients in the water, they die and start to decay. The bacteria involved in the decay process use the dissolved oxygen in the water, reducing the amount of oxygen available to the fish. This process is called eutrophication. As eutrophication continues to use up the dissolved oxygen, the water can turn into a dead zone.

At high altitudes, cold temperatures raise the level of dissolved oxygen, but the higher elevation lowers it. The level of dissolved oxygen in any body of water is a complex, changing condition. PHOTO RESEARCHERS INC.

Scientists have measured the biochemical oxygen demand, the amount of oxygen required by bacteria to decay waste material. BOD_5 means the amount of oxygen that microorganisms use to decay organic matter over a five-day period in 68°F (20°C) water. The more waste in the water, the more decay that occurs, and the higher the BOD_5—the need for dissolved oxygen. For example, wastewater that has been treated has a BOD_5 of less than 30 parts per million. However, waste from a meat packing plant has a BOD_5 of 5,000 parts per million. If this meat packing waste were released into a body of water, the dissolved oxygen level in that water would drop dramatically within a few days.

How does a low level of dissolved oxygen affect the ecosystem in the water? If the level of dissolved oxygen drops for any length of time, fish that need large amounts of oxygen, such as trout and bass, go elsewhere if they can. Carp, catfish, worms, and fly larvae (the immature, wormlike stage in a fly's life cycle) can handle low oxygen levels, so they thrive. The ecosystem begins to include more organisms that can live with little or no oxygen. If the level of dissolved oxygen continues to drop, even the carp and catfish end up gasping for oxygen. The water is on its way to becoming a dead zone.

In the following two experiments, you will use a kit to measure the level of dissolved oxygen in water under several conditions. In one experiment, you will determine how the level changes as the amount of decaying matter in the water changes. In the second experiment, you will measure how the breathing rate of goldfish changes as the amount of dissolved oxygen in the water changes. Both experiments will help you better understand the concept of—and the importance of—dissolved oxygen.

A pond overrun with algae is usually not a healthy place.
PHOTO RESEARCHERS INC.

EXPERIMENT 1

Decay and Dissolved Oxygen: How does the amount of decaying matter affect the level of dissolved oxygen in water?

Purpose/Hypothesis In this experiment, you will allow different amounts of food to decay in water and measure any changes that occur in the level of dissolved oxygen.

To begin the experiment, use what you have learned about dissolved oxygen to make a guess about what will happen when the food starts to decay in the water. Will the level of dissolved oxygen in the water decrease or increase? Will the amount of change depend on the amount of decaying food? This educated guess, or prediction, is your hypothesis. A hypothesis should explain these things:

- the topic of the experiment
- the variable you will change
- the variable you will measure
- what you expect to happen

A hypothesis should be brief, specific, and measurable. It must be something you can test through observation. Your experiment will prove or disprove whether your hypothesis is correct. Here is one possible hypothesis for this experiment: "The more decaying matter in the water, the lower the level of dissolved oxygen."

WORDS TO KNOW

Biochemical oxygen demand (BOD_5): The amount of oxygen microorganisms use over a five-day period in 68°F (20°C) water to decay organic matter.

By-product: A secondary substance produced as the result of a physical or chemical process, in addition to the main product.

Control experiment: A set-up that is identical to the experiment but is not affected by the variable that will be changed during the experiment.

Dissolved oxygen: Oxygen molecules that have dissolved in water.

Elevation: Height above sea level.

Eutrophication: Natural process by which a lake or other body of water becomes enriched in dissolved nutrients, spurring aquatic plant growth.

Hypothesis: An idea in the form of a statement that can be tested by observation and/or experiment.

Photosynthesis: Chemical process by which plants containing chlorophyll use sunlight to manufacture their own food by converting carbon dioxide and water into carbohydrates, releasing oxygen as a by-product.

Phytoplankton: Microscopic aquatic plants that live suspended in the water.

Respiration: The physical process that supplies oxygen to living cells and the chemical reactions that take place inside the cells.

Salinity: The amount of salts dissolved in water.

Variable: Something that can change the results of an experiment.

In this case, the variable you will change is the presence and amount of decaying food, and the variable you will measure is the level of dissolved oxygen. As a control experiment, you will set up one container of water with no decaying food in it. That way, you can determine whether the level of dissolved oxygen changes even with no decaying food in the water. If the level of dissolved oxygen decreases with an increase in decaying food and does not change in the control container, your hypothesis is correct.

Level of Difficulty Easy/moderate.

Materials Needed

- 3 clear 0.5-gallon (1.9-liter) containers
- about 3 ounces (85 grams) of rotting fruit, such as brown apple slices or an overripe banana
- scale capable of weighing 2 ounces (57 grams)

What Are the Variables?

Variables are anything that might affect the results of an experiment. Here are the main variables in this experiment:

- the beginning levels of dissolved oxygen in each container
- the amount of decaying food in each container of water
- how much the food is decayed
- the temperature of the water in all containers
- the amount of any mixing, pouring, or splashing of the water in the containers (which would raise the dissolved oxygen level)
- the length of time the containers are allowed to sit

In other words, the variables in this experiment are everything that might affect the level of dissolved oxygen. If you change more than one variable at a time, you will not be able to determine which variable affected the results.

- dissolved oxygen test kit (kits are available from biological supply houses; one popular brand is LaMotte; see the Further Readings section for sources)
- 5 gallons (5.6 liters) water (try to obtain water that has not been treated, such as well, stream, or pond water; many water treatment plants try to reduce the level of dissolved oxygen in their water because high levels speed up corrosion in water pipes)
- wax paper
- goggles
- rubber gloves

Approximate Budget $15–$20 for the test kit and $5 for a small food scale; other materials should be available in the average household.

Timetable 15 minutes to set up; one week to observe.

Step-by-Step Instructions

1. Label the containers "1 oz.," "2 oz.," and "Control."
2. Mix your water supply thoroughly; stir the water vigorously for 5 minutes or

Dissolved Oxygen Levels

	1-oz container	2-oz container	control
Beginning of Experiment			
Day 2			
Day 3			
Day 4			
Day 5			

Step 4: Dissolved Oxygen Levels recording chart. GALE GROUP.

more if you used tap water, which tends to have a low dissolved oxygen level.

3. Nearly fill the three containers with the water.
4. Follow the directions on the water testing kit to measure the beginning level of dissolved oxygen in each container. Record the levels in a chart similar to the one illustrated. (The water in all three containers should have the same dissolved oxygen level at this point.)
5. Put wax paper on the scale and measure 1 ounce (28 grams) of rotting fruit; dump the fruit into the container marked "1 oz."
6. Measure 2 ounces (57 grams) of the same rotting fruit and dump it into the container marked "2 oz." Put no fruit in the control container.
7. Place all three containers in an area where the air temperature will remain at 70 to 72°F (21 to 22°C).
8. Every day at the same time for the next four days, use the kit to test the dissolved oxygen level in each container. Record your findings on your chart. Also note the condition of the water. Are any of the containers becoming cloudy?

How to Experiment Safely

Wear goggles and gloves to protect your eyes and skin while you test the water because you will be using chemicals that can be dangerous. You are strongly urged to have an adult help you complete the tests.

Summary of Results Study the data from your observations and decide whether your hypothesis was correct. How did the dissolved oxygen levels

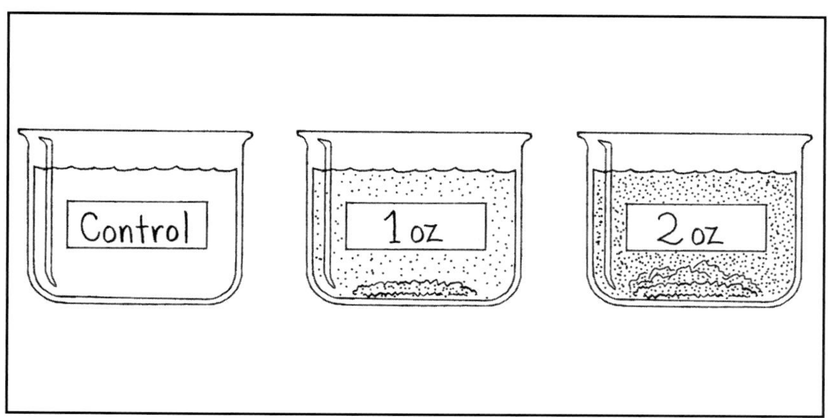

Steps 5 and 6: Set-up of control, 1 oz., and 2 oz. containers.
GALE GROUP.

Troubleshooter's Guide

Below are some problems that may arise during this experiment, some possible causes, and ways to remedy the problems.

Problem: The level of dissolved oxygen was really low in all three containers in the beginning.

Possible cause: Your water came from a source with little dissolved oxygen. Try the experiment again, but increase the beginning level of dissolved oxygen by running a tube from an aquarium pump into the water. Send bubbles of air through the water for at least 8 to 12 hours. Treat all the water so the beginning levels will be identical in all containers.

Problem: The level of dissolved oxygen dropped in all containers, including the control.

Possible cause: The water already had some decaying matter in it, especially if it was pond water. Focus on the differences in the levels of dissolved oxygen for all three containers.

Problem: The level of dissolved oxygen rose in the control container.

Possible cause: The room temperature cooled enough so that oxygen from the air entered the water. Make sure the temperature around all three containers stays at 70 to 72°F (21 to 22°C).

change in the three containers? Which container had the highest level at the end of the experiment? The lowest level? Did the level change in the control container? If so, why do you think this happened? Write a paragraph summarizing your findings and explaining whether they support your hypothesis.

Change the Variables You can vary this experiment in several ways. For example, you might try a different kind of decaying matter, such as another kind of fruit, raw meat, moldy bread, or rotting leaves. You could also increase or decrease the air temperature around all three containers to see how that affects the rate of decay and the levels of dissolved oxygen. At the end of the experiment, use aquarium pumps and tubing to bubble the same amount of air into all three containers to try to raise the level of dissolved oxygen. To change the salinity of the water, you could add different amounts of salt to two containers instead of decaying food and measure any changes in the levels of dissolved oxygen.

Modify the Experiment For a moderate to advanced version of this experiment you could measure the effect of eutrophication on both dissolved oxygen level and water life. To avoid possible harm to fish, you can use aquatic plants, which you can purchase at an aquarium or grow from seed. (Elodea and Cabomba are two popular types of aquatic plants because they are easy to grow and hearty.)

In each of the containers, you will need to first set up the proper environment for the water plants. Add the same number of plants to each container and give them several days to adjust to the new environment. Follow the experiment, adding the decaying foods to the two containers and stirring the water gently after each addition. Every day at the same time for the next several weeks note the level of dissolved oxygen and the condition of the plants.

Instead of rotting fruit, you could also add a small amount of fertilizer to each container. In this case, you can collect or purchase live plankton. Place the same amount of plankton and the same number of plants. in each of the three containers. Add different amounts of the fertilizer to container 2 and container 3. Again, measure the level of dissolved oxygen over the next several weeks and note the condition of the plants.

What Are the Variables?

Variables are anything that might affect the results of an experiment. Here are the main variables in this experiment:

- the health and size of all the goldfish
- the temperature and cleanliness of all the water
- the level of dissolved oxygen in the different containers of water

In other words, the variables in this experiment are everything that might affect the breathing rate of the fish. If you change more than one variable at a time, you will not be able to determine which change had more effect on your results.

EXPERIMENT 2

Goldfish Breath: How does a decrease in the dissolved oxygen level affect the breathing rate of goldfish?

Purpose/Hypothesis In this experiment, you will observe the breathing rate of goldfish as they swim in water with different levels of dissolved oxygen. [Note: It is recommended that you perform this experiment only if you already have access to an aquarium with four to six goldfish and only with the permission of a responsible adult. This experiment will not harm the fish as long as you limit the duration of the experiment and return the fish to the main aquarium afterwards.]

To begin the experiment, use what you know about dissolved oxygen and its effect on fish to make an educated guess about how the fishes' breathing rate will change as the level of dissolved oxygen drops. This educated guess, or prediction, is your hypothesis. A hypothesis should explain these things:

- the topic of the experiment
- the variable you will change
- the variable you will measure
- what you expect to happen

A hypothesis should be brief, specific, and measurable. It must be something you can test through observation. Your experiment will prove or

> **How to Experiment Safely**
>
> Treat the goldfish gently; avoid putting them into water that is warmer or cooler than they are used to. Limit the duration of the test to no more than 8 to 10 hours. Wear goggles and gloves to protect your eyes and skin while you test the water because you will be using chemicals that can be dangerous. You are strongly urged to have an adult help you complete the tests.

disprove whether your hypothesis is correct. Here is one possible hypothesis for this experiment: "As the dissolved oxygen level drops, the breathing rate of the goldfish will increase."

In this experiment the variable you will change is the level of dissolved oxygen, and the variable you will measure is the breathing rate of the goldfish. As a control experiment, you will observe the breathing rate of goldfish in an aquarium that has been set up for some time and in which the dissolved oxygen remains relatively constant. If the breathing rate of the control goldfish does not change, but the breathing rate of the other goldfish increases as the dissolved oxygen level drops, your hypothesis is correct.

Level of Difficulty Easy/moderate.

Materials Needed

- one 10-gallon (38-liter) or larger aquarium that has been set up for a month or longer and uses an air pump to constantly bubble air through the water (the aquarium may also include live plants, which add more dissolved oxygen to the water; other fish living in the aquarium will not affect the experiment, as long as they have been there for several weeks)
- one half-gallon (1.9-liter) container
- 4 to 6 small goldfish
- dissolved oxygen test kit (see the Further Readings section for sources)
- stopwatch
- fish net
- red and blue colored pencils
- goggles
- rubber gloves

Approximate Budget $15 to $20 for the test kit. (Ideally, you will be able to use an aquarium that is already set up at school or at home.)

Timetable 15 minutes to set up the small container; 20 minutes to check the dissolved oxygen levels and breathing rates every two hours for six hours.

Step-by-Step Instructions

1. If you have to purchase additional goldfish to conduct the experiment, place them in the aquarium and allow 24 hours for them to get used to the water. During this period, if the aquarium has a heater, turn it off and allow the water to reach air temperature. Make sure the air pump continues to work.
2. Using water from the aquarium, fill the half-gallon container.
3. Use the kit to test the dissolved oxygen level in the aquarium and in the half-gallon container. They should be the same at this point. On a graph similar to that illustrated, record the level from the aquarium in red and the level from the small container in blue.
4. Use the net to catch half of the goldfish (two or three); put them in the smaller container.
5. Use the stopwatch to measure how many times each goldfish breathes in 30 seconds. Each outward push of the gills is one breath. Average the breathing rates for the goldfish in the aquarium. Use the red

Step 3: Sample graph of dissolved oxygen levels. GALE GROUP.

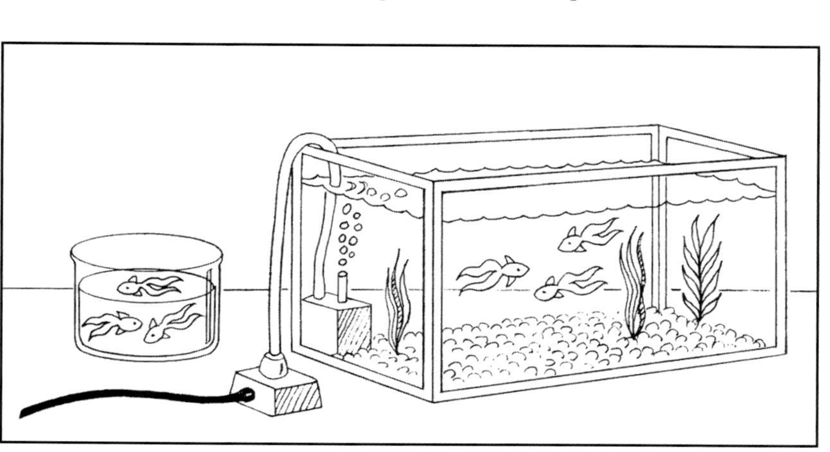

Step 4: Put 2 to 3 goldfish into smaller container. GALE GROUP.

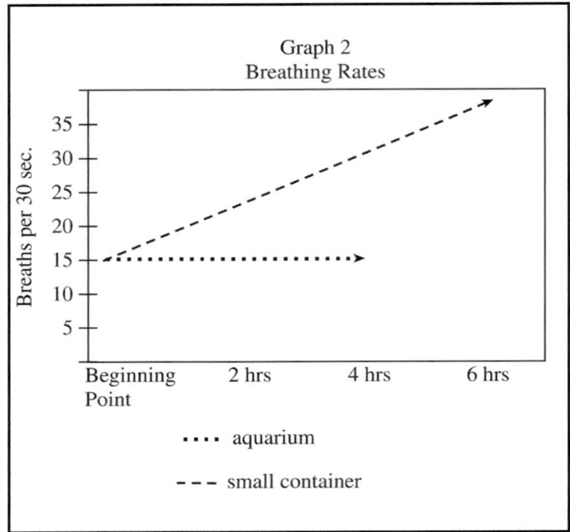

Step 5: Sample graph of goldfish breathing rates. GALE GROUP.

pencil to record the average on a graph similar to that illustrated. Then average the breathing rates for the goldfish in the small container, and use the blue pencil to record that average on the graph.

6. Wait two hours and retest the dissolved oxygen levels in both containers. Then average the breathing rates of the fish in each container. Record your findings.
7. Repeat Step 6 after four hours and after 6 hours.
8. At the end of the experiment, gently put the goldfish from the small container back into the aquarium. If you disconnected the aquarium heater, plug it back in.

Summary of Results Study the dissolved oxygen levels on the first graph. What do you notice? Did the levels change in the aquarium? Did they change in the small container? If so, why?

Now compare the breathing rates of the two groups of fish, shown on the second graph. Notice whether the breathing rates changed as the levels of dissolved oxygen changed. How did the goldfish respond to any changes in the levels of dissolved oxygen? Was your hypothesis correct? Write a paragraph summarizing your findings and explaining whether they support your hypothesis.

Change the Variables You can vary this experiment in several ways. Measure and compare any change in the breathing rates of goldfish swimming in water with and without live plants. (Disconnect any air pump so the plants are the only source of added dissolved oxygen.) Or you can bubble air through the water in the small container and measure the breathing rate of the goldfish as the level of dissolved oxygen rises.

Design Your Own Experiment

How to Select a Topic Relating to this Concept Measuring the amount of dissolved oxygen in a body of water is one of the best ways to determine the health of that water system and the environment around it. Consider the water sources near your home or school. Which ones might have high or low levels of dissolved oxygen? What might cause the high or low levels? What approaches might raise a low level? What other factors affect the health of a water system? (Examples include the pH level and the levels of ammonia, nitrates, and nitrites.)

Check the Further Readings section and talk with your science teacher or school or community media specialist to gather information on dissolved oxygen questions that interest you. As you consider possible experiments, be sure to discuss them with a knowledgeable adult before trying them. Some of the materials or procedures may be harmful to yourself or to the environment.

Troubleshooter's Guide

Below are some problems that may arise during this experiment, some possible causes, and ways to remedy the problems.

Problem: The dissolved oxygen level in the small container remained the same.

Possible cause: The fish were too small to affect the level during this time period. Try the experiment again, using bigger or more fish, putting them in a smaller container of water, or extending the time period for the testing to eight or 10 hours.

Problem: The breathing rate of the fish in the aquarium and the container dropped.

Possible cause: The water temperature might have fallen enough to slow the body processes of the goldfish. If possible, move the aquarium and small container to a warmer spot. Or leave the aquarium heater plugged in and put a heater in the small container to keep the water at the same temperature as the aquarium—a difficult feat to accomplish.

Steps in the Scientific Method To do an original experiment, you need to plan carefully and think things through. Otherwise, you might not be sure which question you are answering, what you are or should be measuring, or what your findings prove or disprove.

Here are the steps in designing an experiment:

- State the purpose of—and the underlying question behind—the experiment you propose to do.
- Recognize the variables involved, and select one that will help you answer the question at hand.
- State a testable hypothesis, an educated guess about the answer to your question.
- Decide how to change the variable you selected.
- Decide how to measure your results.

Recording Data and Summarizing the Results In your decaying food and goldfish experiments, your raw data might include charts, graphs, drawings, and photographs of the changes you observed. If you display your experiment, make clear the question you are trying to answer, the variable you changed, the variable you measured, the results, and your conclusions. Explain what materials you used, how long each step took, and other basic information.

Related Projects You can undertake a variety of projects related to dissolved oxygen and water quality in general. For example, if you have access to salt water from the ocean, you might compare its level of dissolved oxygen with that of fresh water. Or compare the level at the surface of a pond with the level at the bottom. Or compare the level of dissolved oxygen in a body of water during cool weather with the level during a heat wave. Try to determine the factors that influence these levels and whether the levels indicate pollution that is potentially harmful to the health of the organisms living in the water and the people using and drinking it.

For More Information

Carolina Biological Supply Company, 2700 York Road, Burlington, NC 27215, 1-800-334-5551. http://www.carolina.com/.

Fitzgerald, Karen. *The Story of Oxygen.* Danbury, CT: Franklin Watts, 1996. Covers the history of oxygen, its chemistry, how it works in our bodies, and its importance in our lives.

Frey Scientific, 100 Paragon Parkway, Mansfield, OH 44903, 1-800-225-FREY. http://www.freyscientific.com.

LaMotte water test kits. http://www.lamotte.com/.

Ward's Natural Science Establishment, Inc., 5100 West Henrietta Road, PO Box 92912, Rochester, NY 14692, 1-800-962-2660. http://www.wardsci.com/.

22

DNA (Deoxyribonucleic Acid)

Your hair color, a leaf's shape, a bird's wing: These diverse features all share one key inherited trait known as deoxyribonucleic acid or DNA. DNA is commonly called the building block of life, for it is the inherited substance that all characteristics build from. Passed down from generation to generation, DNA directs how an organism functions, develops, and appears. Every life form on Earth carries DNA. And unless you are an identical twin, your DNA is completely unique to you.

The findings of DNA have led to awesome advances in a wide range of fields, from medicine to crime solving. Researchers have used their knowledge of DNA to examine inherited diseases, produce medicines, study the relationships between species, and develop foods with desired characteristics. As the work to understand DNA continues, researchers hope that gaining knowledge about the molecule will help improve people's lives all over the world.

The transforming factor DNA is a large molecule inside almost every cell in the body. In humans, DNA is found in the nucleus, the brain-center of the cell. Much like a cell, a nucleus is held together by a membrane or nuclear envelope. The DNA molecule coils in the nucleus so tightly that if all of the DNA in your body were unraveled and laid end to end, it would stretch from Earth to the Moon about 6,000 times!

In the late 1800s and early 1900s, scientists were working to discover what substance played a role in heredity. From early experiments and observations researchers knew parents passed their characteristics onto their offspring. Then a 1928 experiment showed that there was some substance that transmitted infectiousness to noninfectious bacteria. This was called the "transforming factor," because it transformed the bacteria.

Scientists narrowed the possibilities of the transforming factor down to two substances: proteins or DNA. At this time, researchers knew that an organism's cells contained DNA. DNA is a simple molecule with relatively few chemical parts to it. They also knew each cell contained proteins, large molecules made of chemicals called amino acids. There are twenty amino acids that make up the hundreds of thousands of proteins in the human body. Lots of researchers argued that DNA was too simple a molecule to account for the vast diversity of life—from a weed to a human.

American scientist Oswald Avery. LIBRARY OF CONGRESS.

In 1943, American scientist Oswald Avery (1877–1955) and his colleagues conducted a groundbreaking experiment. First they took DNA from a disease-causing strain of a bacterium. Then they placed this DNA into a strain of the bacterium that did not cause disease, an inactive bacterium. They found the inactive bacterium turned into a disease-causing bacterium. Avery concluded that it was the DNA from the disease-causing strain that "transformed" the inactive form of the bacterium. Many in the scientific community were skeptical of this conclusion because they still believed DNA was too simple a substance. Then in 1952 biologists Alfred Hershey and Martha Chase conducted an experiment that conclusively proved DNA was the transforming factor, the molecule responsible for heredity.

Solving the structure The 1950s were a big decade for DNA. While many researchers were working to prove exactly what DNA did, other scientists were racing to figure out how DNA was structured. In 1953 molecular biologists James D. Watson (1928–) and Francis Crick (1916–2004) solved the puzzle of DNA's double-helix molecular structure. Their discovery is recognized as one of the most important scientific findings of the twentieth century.

Prior to Watson and Crick's discovery, researchers knew that DNA was made up of units called nucleotides. There are four types of nucleotides found in DNA, differing only in their nitrogen-containing bases: adenine (A), guanine (G), thymine (T), and cytosine (C). Each nucleotide consists of three components: a sugar deoxyribose, a phosphate group, and a nitrogen-containing base.

Watson and Crick used a type of X-ray image produced by British scientist Rosalind Franklin (1920–58) to develop their model of DNA's structure. They determined that DNA consists of long chains of repeating nucleotides, joined together and twisted around each other into a spiral shape known as a double helix. It has the appearance of a twisted ladder. The backbone of the ladder is made up of the nucleotides' sugar and phosphate molecules. The rungs of the two strands are formed by attached bases that are always complementary, A pairs with T (A-T) and G pairs C (G-C). These base pairs are held together with hydrogen bonds.

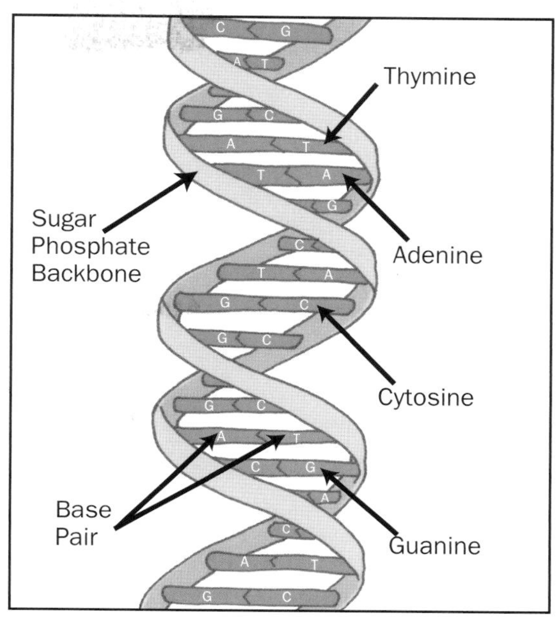

Components of a DNA strand. GALE GROUP.

Since each nucleotide always pairs with the same complementary nucleotide, this explains how DNA replicates itself. During DNA replication, the DNA helix unzips. The exposed bases match up with complementary bases of nucleotides. The nucleotides bind together to form two new strands that are identical to the strand that separated.

Sequencing the alphabet Everyone has the same four nucleotides, but it is the order of the nucleotides, the sequence, that determines DNA's instructions. Reading the sequence of the four bases, A, G, C, and T, is similar to reading the order of letters in words. Different combinations create different meanings. In some cases, just one letter out of place in a sequence can cause a person to have a completely distinct characteristic. In the disease sickle cell anemia, for example, a single base change from an A to a T changes the shape and function of red blood cells, causing blood to clog and anemia (a condition in which the blood cannot carry enough oxygen to body tissues).

Molecular biologists Francis Crick and James D. Watson were the first to map the structure of DNA. GALE GROUP.

Different species have varying amounts and sequences of DNA. Humans have about three billion base pairs in our DNA. Researchers have

WORDS TO KNOW

Amino acids: The building blocks of proteins.

Base: Substance that when dissolved in water is capable of reacting with an acid to form salts and release hydrogen ions; has a pH of more than 7.

Base pairs: In DNA, the pairing of two nucleotides with each other: adenine (A) with thymine (T), and guanine (G) with cytosine (C).

Control experiment: A setup that is identical to the experiment, but is not affected by the variable that acts on the experimental group.

Deoxyribonucleic acid (DNA): Large, complex molecules found in the nuclei of cells that carry genetic information for an organism's development; double helix. (Pronounced DEE-ox-see-rye-bo-noo-klay-ick acid)

DNA replication: The process by which one DNA strand unwinds and duplicates all its information, creating two new DNA strands that are identical to each other and to the original strand.

Double helix: The shape taken by DNA (deoxyribonucleic acid) molecules in a nucleus.

Enzyme: Any of numerous complex proteins produced by living cells that act as catalysts, speeding up the rate of chemical reactions in living organisms.

Hypothesis: An idea in the form of a statement that can be tested by observation and/or experiment.

Nucleotide: The basic unit of a nucleic acid. It consists of a simple sugar, a phosphate group, and a nitrogen-containing base. (Pronounced noo-KLEE-uh-tide.)

Protein: A complex chemical compound consisting of many amino acids attached to each other that are essential to the structure and functioning of all living cells.

Variable: Something that can affect the results of an experiment.

DNA replication: The DNA strand unwinds and complementary nucleotides bind together. GALE GROUP.

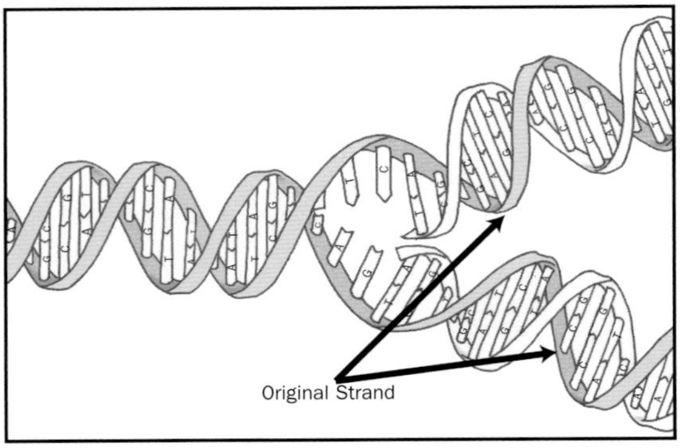

Original Strand

found no correlation between DNA length and the complexity of an organism. A species of wheat, for example, has roughly 16 billion base pairs, the fruit fly has an estimated 180 million, and a species of corn checks in at only slightly less than that of humans, at 2.5 billion.

As a general rule, the greater the similarity between DNA sequences, the more similar the organisms. In the human species, your DNA sequence is about 99.9% identical to every other person's. Your DNA sequence is even more similar to your family members. In 2003, researchers completed sequencing the entire human DNA.

PROJECT 1

The Stuff of Life: Isolating DNA

Purpose/Hypothesis DNA is present in all life. In this project, you will extract DNA to see what this molecule looks like.

DNA is twisted inside the cell nucleus. A cell's nucleus also contains proteins and other substances. To see the DNA, you will have to separate out the DNA from all the cell's other molecules. (Refer to illustration.) You will first liquefy the substance and separate the cells by blending it. Detergent or soap will break apart the cell's outer and inner membrane, in much the same way that soap loosens dirt and grease. The cell's membranes are made of a fatty substance that contain proteins. Detergent contains a substance that pulls apart the fats and proteins, freeing the DNA.

The DNA in the nucleus is wound up with proteins. To isolate the DNA from these proteins, you will use an enzyme, a protein that quickens a chemical reaction. Meat tenderizer contains enzymes that cut away the proteins. Adding alcohol will then allow you to see the DNA. DNA is not soluble in alcohol. DNA precipitates, or separates out of the solution, in alcohol, moving away from the watery part of the solution and rising towards the alcohol. Proteins and other parts of the cell will remain in the bottom watery layer.

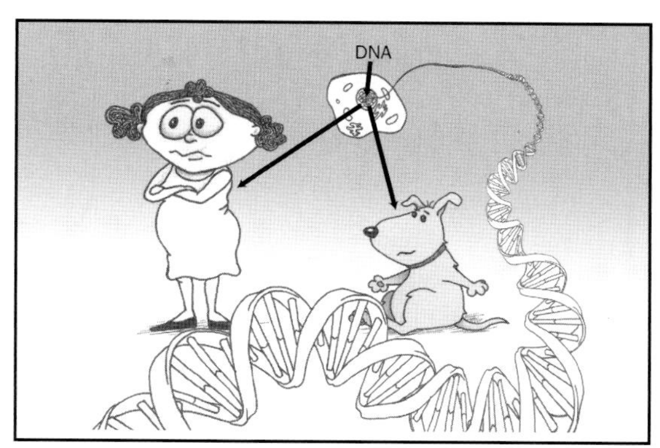

All living organisms carry DNA; its unique sequence determines individual characteristics. GALE GROUP.

Figure A. Process of DNA isolation: (1) Detergent breaks up the cell's membranes; (2) enzymes cut away the protein to (3) isolate the DNA. GALE GROUP.

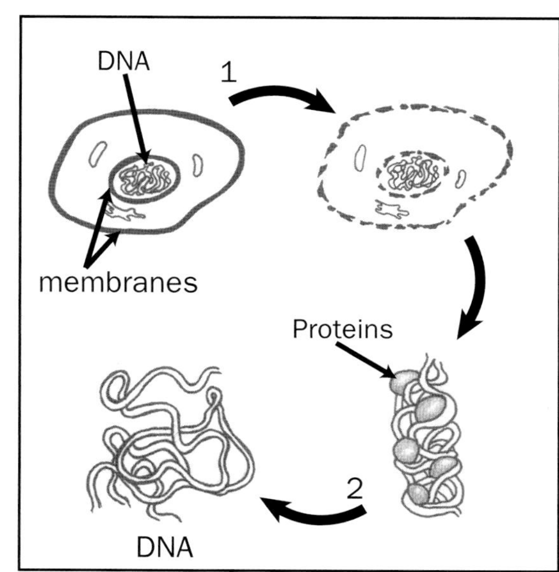

Level of Difficulty Moderate.

Materials Needed

- spinach
- knife
- salt
- coldwater
- blender
- refrigerator
- liquid soap with no conditioner
- chopstick or toothpick

How to Work Safely

Be sure to handle the knife carefully when cutting. If you get any alcohol on your hands, wash your hands immediately and make sure to keep them away from your eyes. Keep the container of alcohol away from open flames. Thoroughly wash the cup, jar, strainer, and chopstick after the experiment. Discard the mixture after you have studied and documented the results.

- strainer or cheesecloth
- cup
- small glass jar
- meat tenderizer
- 91% isopropyl alcohol (available in drug stores) or 95% ethyl alcohol (slightly preferred; available from science supply companies)

Approximate Budget $10.

Timetable 1 hour.

Step-by-Step Instructions

1. Take ½ cup of the spinach and place it in the blender. Add a large pinch of table salt and about 1/3 cup of cold water. Blend together for 10 seconds and pour the mixture into the cup.
2. Slowly pour the liquid out of the cup and into the glass jar through the cheesecloth or strainer. Fill the jar about one-quarter to one-half full.
3. Add about 2 teaspoons (10 milliliters) of liquid soap to the jar and stir slowly for five seconds.
4. Let the mixture sit for 10 minutes.
5. Add a pinch of the meat tenderizer and stir the mixture gently. Do not stir too hard.
6. Slowly pour the alcohol down the side of the glass jar (jar should be at a slight tilt) until the jar is almost full.
7. Place the jar in the refrigerator for five minutes, then remove and wait another five minutes. The DNA should have risen to the top of the glass. Use a chopstick or toothpick to extract the spinach DNA.

Step 6: Slowly pour the alcohol down the side of the glass jar (jar should be at a slight tilt) until the jar is almost full. GALE GROUP.

Summary of Results Write down what the DNA looks like. Your toothpickfull of DNA contains millions of DNA strands clumped together.

Since you were not using chemicals to extract a highly purified DNA, it also contains some proteins and other nucleic acids (ribonucleic acid or RNA) that were not separated. With the right equipment and materials in a laboratory, it is possible to extract pure DNA.

EXPERIMENT 2

Comparing DNA: Does the DNA from different species have the same appearance?

Purpose/Hypothesis The DNA molecule produces the unique characteristics for all life forms. DNA is composed of the same biochemical molecules in all species: four nucleotides and a sugar-phosphate backbone. Nucleotide sequences, which account for the distinctive characteristics, cannot be seen by the naked eye.

In this experiment you will compare if DNA appears the same in four different species. You will conduct the same DNA extraction process on each of the species and then examine its physical characteristics.

To extract DNA, you will have to separate out the DNA from all the cell's other molecules. You will first liquefy the substance and separate the cells by blending it. Detergent or soap will break apart the cell's outer and inner membrane, in much the same way that soap loosens dirt and grease. The cell's membranes are made of a fatty substance that contain proteins. Detergent contains a substance that pulls apart the fats and proteins, freeing the DNA.

The DNA in the nucleus is wound up with proteins. To isolate the DNA from these proteins, you will use an enzyme, a protein that quickens a chemical reaction. Meat tenderizer contains enzymes that cut away the proteins. Adding alcohol will then allow you to see the DNA. DNA is not soluble in alcohol. DNA precipitates or separates out of the solution in

Troubleshooter's Guide

Below are some problems that may arise during this experiment, some possible causes, and some ways to remedy the problems.

Problem: The DNA is broken into small bits. (DNA should be a long, white strand.)

Possible cause: You could have stirred too harshly when you added the enzymes or at different points throughout the experiment and broken the DNA strands. Try repeating the experiment, stirring gently every time.

Problem: You do not see any DNA. (DNA looks white and stringy.)

Possible cause: The cells may not have broken open when they were blended. Try repeating the experiment, blending the DNA until is liquidy.

Possible cause: If the soap had conditioner in it, it would not have broken open the fatty DNA cell membranes, and the DNA would not have gotten free. Make sure the soap does not have any conditioner.

Possible cause: You may not have allowed enough time for each step. Wait another 45 minutes for the DNA to rise into the alcohol layer. If you still do not see any DNA, try the experiment again, increasing the time slightly for each step.

Possible cause: You may not have had enough DNA from the source. Repeat the experiment, cutting the amount of water added to the DNA source in half before placing it in the blender.

What Are the Variables?

Variables are anything that might affect the results of an experiment. Here are the main variables in this experiment:

- the DNA source
- the type of alcohol
- the type of detergent
- the temperature of the water

In other words, the variables in this experiment are everything that might affect the appearance of the DNA. If you change more than one variable at the same time, you will not be able to tell which variable had the most effect on the DNA.

alcohol, moving away from the watery part of the solution and rising towards the alcohol. Proteins and other parts of the cell will remain in the bottom watery layer.

To begin this experiment, make an educated guess about the outcome of the experiment based on your knowledge of DNA. This educated guess, or prediction, is your hypothesis. A hypothesis should explain these things:

- the topic of the experiment
- the variable you will change
- the variable you will measure
- what you expect to happen

A hypothesis should be brief, specific, and measurable. It must be something you can test through further investigation. Your experiment will prove or disprove whether your hypothesis is correct. Here is one possible hypothesis for this experiment: "DNA will have the same physical characteristics in all the species, with each species having a unique quantity of DNA."

Variables are anything you can change in an experiment. In this case, the variable you will change will be the DNA source. The variable you will measure will be the DNA itself and the quantity of the DNA.

Level of Difficulty Difficult (this experiment is not technically difficult, but it requires careful attention to timing and each step).

Materials Needed

- four DNA sources: possible sources include banana, wheat germ, onion, kiwi, grapes, peas
- salt
- cold water
- knife
- blender
- refrigerator
- liquid soap or detergent with no conditioner
- 4 wooden sticks such as chopsticks or toothpicks
- strainer
- 4 small glass jars

- 4 cups
- marking pen
- masking tape
- meat tenderizer
- 91% isopropyl alcohol (available in drug stores) or 95% ethyl alcohol (slightly preferred; available from science supply companies)
- filter paper
- gram scale (optional)

Approximate Budget $15.

Timetable One-and-a-half hours to start; 15 minutes after a three-day waiting period.

How to Experiment Safely

Be sure to handle the knife carefully when cutting. If you get any alcohol on your hands, wash your hands immediately and make sure to keep them away from your eyes. Keep the container of alcohol away from open flames. Thoroughly wash the cup, jar, strainer, and chopstick after the experiment. Discard the mixtures after you have studied and documented the results.

Step-by-Step Instructions

1. Cut about a ½ cup of one DNA source, such as a banana, and place it in the blender. Add a large pinch of table salt and about twice as much cold water as the source. Blend together for about 10 seconds and pour into a cup.
2. Repeat the procedure with the other DNA sources.
3. Label each glass jar. Pour each mixture from the cup into its marked glass through the cheesecloth or strainer. Make sure to wash the strainer and cup between pours. Fill the jars about one-quarter to one-half full.
4. Add 2 teaspoons (10 milliliters) of liquid soap to each jar and stir slowly for five seconds.
5. Let the mixtures sit for 10 minutes.
6. Add a pinch of the meat tenderizer to each glass and stir the mixtures gently. Do not stir too hard.
7. Pour the alcohol down the sides of the glass jars until they are almost full.

Step 9: Gently extract the DNA from each substance using a toothpick or chopstick. GALE GROUP.

Troubleshooter's Guide

Below are some problems that may arise during this experiment, some possible causes, and some ways to remedy the problems.

Problem: The DNA is broken.

Possible cause: You could have stirred too harshly when you added the enzymes or at different points throughout the protocol and broken the DNA strands. Try repeating the experiment, stirring gently every time.

Problem: There was no DNA.

Possible cause: The cells may not have broken open when they were blended. Try repeating the experiment, blending the DNA until is liquidy.

Possible cause: If the soap had conditioner in it, it would not have broken open the fatty DNA cell membranes and the DNA would not have gotten free. Make sure the soap did not have any conditioner.

Possible cause: You may not have allowed enough time for each step. Wait another 45 minutes for the DNA to precipitate into the alcohol layer. If you still do not see any DNA, try the experiment again, increasing the time slightly for each step.

Possible cause: You may not have had enough DNA from the source; some DNA sources contain more water than others. Repeat the experiment, cutting the amount of water added to the DNA source in half before placing it in the blender.

8. Place the jars in the refrigerator for about five minutes and then remove them and wait another five minutes.
9. Use a chopstick or toothpick to gently extract the DNA from each substance and observe its characteristics.
10. Gently place the DNA on filter paper. (If you have a sensitive scale, weigh the filter paper.)
11. Place the filter paper aside and leave for three days or until it is completely dry. Note how much DNA each substance contained by comparing them to one another. On the scale, you can weigh the filter paper with the DNA. Subtract the weight of the filter paper from the total. Note how much the DNA from each source weighs.

Summary of Results Examine your results and determine whether your original hypothesis was correct. Did the DNA react the same way in all the sources? Did the DNA appear the same from all the species? Draw, describe, or take pictures of the DNA, both when it is freshly extracted and when it is dried. (It may be helpful to view the extracted DNA under a microscope.) Write a description of each of the species' DNA and your conclusions.

Change the Variables You can vary this experiment several ways:

- You can alter the DNA sources and observe the DNA from other plant and fruit sources. Whatever you choose, make sure the source is not too watery. Yeast, strawberries, and peas are three other good sources for this experiment.
- Using one DNA source, such as wheat germ, you can alter the type of soap or detergent.

- You can also change the amount of the soap used.
- You can change the alcohol. What happens to the DNA if you use a lesser concentration of alcohol, such as 70% rubbing alcohol?

Rice, yeast, the pufferfish (pictured), and the rat are among the organisms whose DNA sequences are known.

Design Your Own Experiment

How to Select a Topic Relating to this Concept The study of DNA is a relatively new topic of study for researchers. There are many intriguing questions and unknowns related to the topic that researchers are beginning to understand. How is the DNA of different species related? What are some ways that DNA sequences are manipulated, and how can this help treat or cure human disease?

Check the Further Readings section and talk with your science teacher or librarian to start gathering information on any questions that interest you. You could also consider visiting companies in your local area that conduct DNA research.

Steps in the Scientific Method To do an original experiment, you need to plan carefully and think things through. Otherwise, you might not be sure what question you are answering, what you are or should be measuring, or what your findings prove or disprove.

Here are the steps in designing an experiment:

- State the purpose of—and the underlying question behind—the experiment you propose to do.
- Recognize the variables involved and select one that will help you answer the question at hand.
- State your hypothesis, an educated guess about the answer to your question.
- Decide how to change the variable you selected.
- Decide how to measure your results.

Recording Data and Summarizing the Results Your data should include charts and graphs such as the one you did for these experiments. They should be clearly labeled and easy to read. As DNA is difficult to visualize, you may also want to include photographs and drawings of your experimental setup and results. This will help others visualize the steps in the experiment.

If you are preparing an exhibit, you may want to display your results, such as any experimental setup you designed. If you have completed a nonexperimental project, explain clearly what your research question was and illustrate your findings.

Related Projects Because the nucleotides or sequences of DNA are invisible to the naked eye, the majority of experiments with DNA will need special laboratory equipment. With the right equipment, you can compare the bands or fingerprints of DNA from different organisms. Called DNA fingerprinting, this is one technique that forensic scientists use to compare a suspect's DNA with the DNA found at a crime scene. Check the Resources section for companies that sell kits on DNA fingerprinting.

Using a DNA technique that combines bits of DNA from two different organisms is another possible project. Called DNA Transformation, the technique can transfer a desired trait to another organism. To perform transformation, you will need a kit, along with special equipment and adult supervision. Transformation kits are sold at many biological supply companies.

The topic of DNA also brings with it many ethical dilemmas. Transformation techniques have allowed researchers to cut-and-paste the DNA of two different species together. Should a person be forced to store his or her DNA in a computer databank if it will help solve crimes? If a DNA sequence predicts that a person may get a certain disease, does that person's insurance company have the right to know this information? You might focus on one ethical issue from differing viewpoints.

For More Information

DNA From the Beginning. http://www.dnaftb.org/dnaftb/ (accessed on March 1, 2008). An animated introduction on the basics of DNA, heredity, and genetics.

Genetics Home Reference. "What is DNA?" http://ghr.nlm.nih.gov/handbook/basics/dna (accessed on March 1, 2008). Illustrated handbook on DNA.

Groleau, Rick. "Journey into DNA." *Nova Online.* http://www.pbs.org/wgbh/nova/genome/dna.html (accessed on March 1, 2008). Interactive site on the basics of DNA and related issues.

Howard Hughes Medical Institute. *The Genes We Share with Yeast, Flies, Worms, and Mice.* http://www.hhmi.org/genesweshare (accessed on March 1, 2008). Clear report from the Howard Hughes Medical Institute.

Human Genome Project Information. http://www.ornl.gov/sci/techresources/Human_Genome/education/students.shtml (accessed on March 1, 2008). Information on the background and implications of sequencing human DNA.

Ridley, Matt. *Genome: The Autobiography of a Species in 23 Chapters.* New York: HarperColllins, 2000. Each chapter looks at one gene on a human's chromosome.

The Tech Museum of Innovation. *Understanding Genetics.* http://www.thetech.org/genetics (accessed on March 1, 2008). Online DNA exhibit includes images of cells and DNA.

23

Dyes

If you ever stained your clothing from a spilled drink, you have seen a dye at work. A dye is any substance that colors another material. Dyes are in inks, clothing, and furniture. People use them to produce a wide variety of colors in a range of materials.

A colorful world of nature In the modern day, most dyes are manufactured (synthesized) by a chemical process. But people have been using natural dyes for thousands of years. Records show that dyes were used in ancient China about 2600 B.C.E. There is evidence that ancient Egyptians used dyes for burial cloth. Dyes were used to add color to fibers, skin decorations, and writings.

The British chemist William Henry Perkin is credited with developing the first dye in the 1850s. GETTY IMAGES.

Cultures made dyes from the colors in animals, plants, and minerals. Ancient Romans and Egyptians made a purple dye from a snail. The dye was so rare and expensive to make that purple became a symbol of wealth and royalty.

People made a variety of color dyes from leaves, berries, stems, and roots. Indigo plants produced a blue, tree bark a brown, and the turmeric plant a yellow dye. The kermes insect could produce a red dye. Minerals were ground to produce reds and yellows.

Lucky dye accident The first synthetic dyes were developed in the 1800s. The person credited with developing the first dye was a British chemist named William Henry Perkin in the 1850s.

Perkin was just 18 years old when he was conducting an experiment trying to produce a drug for malaria, a deadly infectious disease. He

In some remote countries, cloth is occasionally still dyed by hand. AP PHOTO/REBECCA BLACKWELL.

was using a chemical called aniline. The experiment failed but he had produced a deep color, which he pulled out the color purple. He found that it was a deep color that did not fade. Perkins set up a factory in London and began manufacturing the color, which he named mauve. A few years later he synthesized a deep red dye.

Holding the dyes How a material dyes depends upon the composition of both the dye and the material. There are dyes for food, fabric, wood, and hair. Leather will accept a dye in a different way than a swatch (piece) of cotton.

All dyes attach to the material being dyed. Dyes for fiber, for example, form a strong bond with the fiber. Hair dyes attach to the hair strand. Synthetic dyes have compounds in them that "fix" the dye to the fabric. Natural dyes often need a fixative agent, called a mordant. A mordant reacts with the dye and fiber to bind the dye to the material. Mordants generally contain metal, such as iron and aluminum.

There are thousands of unique dye colors manufactured today. Dyes have become a part of everyday life, from the clothes we wear to the paints

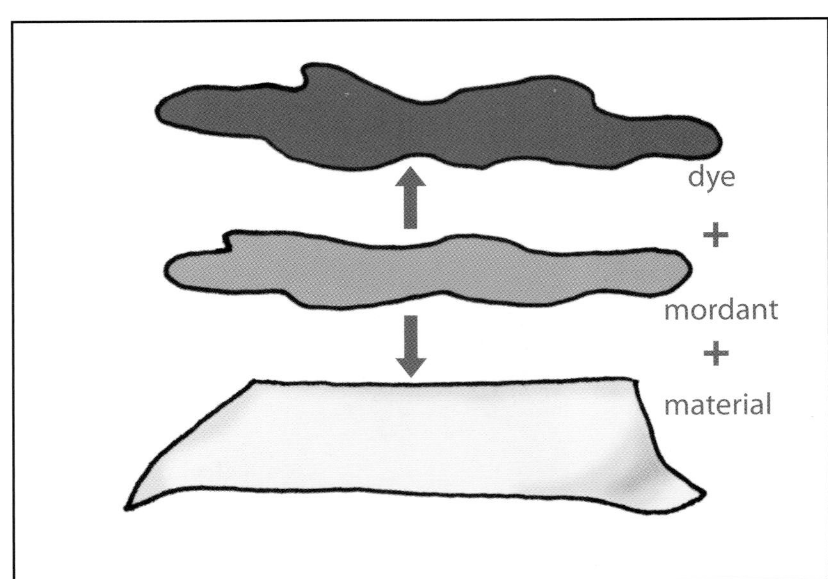

A mordant reacts with the dye and fiber to bind the dye to the material. ILLUSTRATION BY TEMAH NELSON.

WORDS TO KNOW

Control experiment: A setup that is identical to the experiment, but is not affected by the variable that acts on the experimental group.

Colorfast: The ability of a material to keep its dye and not fade or change color.

Dye: A colored substance that is used to give color to a material.

Fixative: A substance that mixes with the dye to hold it to the material.

Hypothesis: An idea in the form of a statement that can be tested by observation and/or experiment.

Mordant: A substance that fixes the dye to the material.

Synthetic: Something that is made artificially, in a laboratory or chemical plant, but is generally not found in nature.

Variable: Something that can affect the results of an experiment.

on the walls. They have also become a part of research and technological developments. In the medical and biological fields, dyes are used to color pills and identify tissues or other biological structures.

There are many applications for dyes. In the following two experiment, you will investigate how dyes affect different materials and how a dye stays in the material.

EXPERIMENT 1

Applying Dyes: How does the fiber affect the dye color?

Purpose/Hypothesis In this experiment, you will observe the role of the material in dyeing. How a dye colors depends upon the fiber it is coloring. Using a natural dye, you will experiment with both natural and synthetic (man-made) fibers. Natural fibers include cotton, wool, and silk. Natural fibers include fibers from animals, such as wool, and fibers from plants, such as cotton. Synthetic fibers include polyester, nylon and rayon. By making your own natural dye and applying it to different fabrics, you will be able to determine how dyes affect each type of fiber.

What Are the Variables?

Variables are anything that might affect the results of an experiment. Here are the main variables in this experiment:

- the cleanliness of the fabric
- the type of fabric
- the color of the fabric
- the type of dye
- the time dyed

In other words, the variables in this experiment are anything that might affect how the fabric dyes. If you change more than one variable, you will not be able to tell which variable had the most effect on the fabric color.

How to Experiment Safely

Be careful and ask an adult for help when working with boiling water. This can be a messy experiment. Make sure an adult knows that the wooden utensil and other materials you work could be dyed slightly, and wear appropriate clothing. Carefully dispose of the dye bath when you are finished.

To begin the experiment, use what you know about fibers and dyes to make an educated guess about how the dyes will affect the different fabrics. This educated guess, or prediction, is your hypothesis. A hypothesis should explain these things:

- the topic of the experiment
- the variable you will change
- the variable you will measure
- what you expect to happen

A hypothesis should be brief, specific, and measurable. It must be something you can test through observation. Your experiment will prove or disprove whether your hypothesis is correct. Here is one possible hypothesis for this experiment: "Natural fibers, such as cotton and wool, will accept natural dyes the best."

In this case, the variable you will change is the fabric, and the variable you will measure is the color.

Level of Difficulty Easy/moderate (due to the time involved).

Materials Needed

- 2 to 3 fresh beets for the dye (other dye sources that work well include purple cabbage, coffee grounds, and onion skins)
- metal pot
- colander
- scissors
- wooden stirring stick that can pick up dye
- plastic plate, which will pick up dye
- knife
- paper towels
- container or pot that can get slightly dyed
- 4 to 5 different types of white fabric pieces, about 5 x 5 inches, including cotton, wool, polyester, linen, and silk

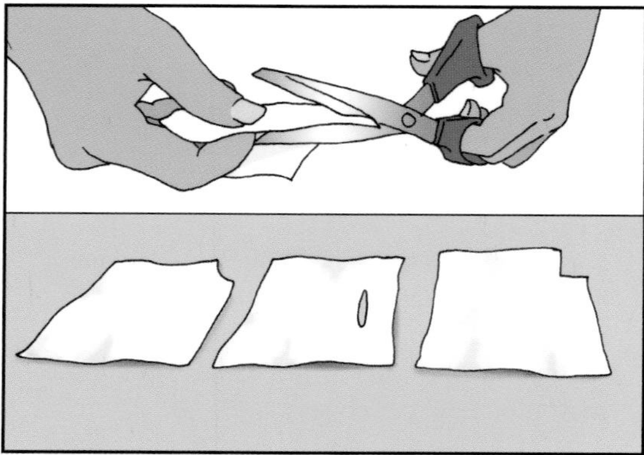

Step 1: Use the scissors to cut each piece in a way that will help you distinguish it from other pieces. ILLUSTRATION BY TEMAH NELSON.

Approximate Budget Less than $5. (The fabric can be taken from old clothes or fabric stores may give samples away.)

Timetable Approximately one hour and 30 minutes to prepare dye, eight hours to three days total time.

Step 3: Empty the hot beet-water into the colander. ILLUSTRATION BY TEMAH NELSON.

Step-by-Step Instructions

1. Wash all the fabric pieces by machine or by hand to make sure they are clean. Use the scissors to cut each piece in a way that will help you distinguish it from other pieces. You may want to cut the corner from the polyester, for example, and make the cotton piece a triangle. One can have nothing cut. Write down the identification for each type of fabric.
2. Cut up the beets and place them in the pot. Pour enough water in the pot to cover all the beets and bring to a simmer. Allow the beets to simmer for about an hour. Use the wooden spoon to stir occasionally.
3. Set the container under the colander in a sink or outside, and carefully empty the hot beet-water into the colander. The container holds your dye.
4. Place the fabric swatches into the container. Use the wooden stirrer to move the pieces around. Set aside overnight.
5. Use the wooden utensil to look at the fabric. You may want to leave the fabric in for several more hours or days to absorb more of the dye. When you are ready to take the fabric out of the dye, take the pieces out in a sink or outside. Hold each pieces out under clear water and roll it in paper towels. Set the material pieces on the plate and allow to dry.

Step 5: Use the wooden utensil to look at the fabric. ILLUSTRATION BY TEMAH NELSON.

Summary of Results Match the identification with the type of fabric. How did each fabric dye compared to one another? Was there one type of material that dyed the brightest? Write up a

Troubleshooter's Guide

There should not be any significant problems with this experiment. If one of the types of material is clean and does not accept the dye, that may be the material. You could leave all the fabrics in the dye for a longer amount of time to make sure.

paragraph of your results; you may want to take pictures.

Change the Variables You can vary this experiment. Here are some possibilities. Try different dye sources, such as flowers, onion skins, or bark. You could use a synthetic, store-bought dye and compare the color to the natural dye. Try blends of two types of fiber while also dyeing 100% pieces of each blend, to determine which of the types of fibers accepts dye more than the other.

EXPERIMENT 2

Holding the Dye: How do dye fixatives affect the colorfastness of the dye?

Purpose/Hypothesis Adding a fixative to the dyeing process helps ensure that the dye color will stay attached to the material. Dyes can fade over time from washing. Exposure to sunlight and air can also cause a color to fade. Mordants are used to help fix natural dyes. The mordant, a metal-based substance, attaches to the fiber and the dye binds to the mordant. Synthetic dyes can bond directly to the fiber.

In this experiment, you can test the colorfastness of a synthetic dye, a natural dye without a mordant, and a natural dye with a mordant. The mordant you will use is alum (aluminum sulfate). After dying the same type of material in each of the three dye baths, you can test for colorfastness by repeatedly washing the materials with soap. By comparing each of the materials against an unwashed piece you can judge how the material held onto the dye relative to the other washed materials.

To begin the experiment, use what you know about dyes and colorfastness to make an educated guess about how each material will fix the dye. This educated guess, or prediction, is your hypothesis. A hypothesis should explain these things:

- the topic of the experiment
- the variable you will change
- the variable you will measure
- what you expect to happen

A hypothesis should be brief, specific, and measurable. It must be something you can test through observation. Your experiment will prove

or disprove whether your hypothesis is correct. Here is one possible hypothesis for this experiment: "The natural dye with the mordant will retain the dye color more than the synthetic or natural dye alone."

In this case, the variable you will change will be the dye fixative. The variable you will measure will be how much each material retains its color relative to one another. If the material with the natural dye and mordant retains its color the best, you will know your hypothesis is correct.

Setting up a control will help you isolate one variable. For the control, you will only dye the material. For the experiment, you will compare the experimental material against the control to judge the colorfastness.

What Are the Variables?

Variables are anything that might affect the results of an experiment. Here are the main variables in this experiment:

- the type of material
- the color of the material
- the amount of soap
- the type of pan used
- the amount of times the material is washed

In other words, the variables in this experiment are everything that might affect the amount of dye color the material retains. If you change more than one variable, you will not be able to tell which variable had the most effect on the colorfastness.

Level of Difficulty Moderate, because of the time and care involved.

Materials Needed

- purple cabbage or 3 to 4 fresh red beets
- synthetic fabric dye, red dye if you are using beets and purple if you are using cabbage (available at drug or fabric stores)
- stainless steel pot
- 3 plastic container (which may get dyed)
- scissors
- 6 squares of white wool, about 5 to 6 inches (13–15 cm) square
- stove
- alum (available in grocery stores)
- measuring spoons and cup
- liquid soap
- strainer
- plastic plates
- 2 to 3 wooden sticks or spoons
- paper towels
- glass jar with cover (a mayonnaise jar works well)

Approximate Budget $8.

How to Experiment Safely

Be careful and ask an adult for help when working with boiling water. This can be a messy experiment. You may want to work outside whenever possible. Make sure an adult knows that the wooden utensil and other materials you work may get dyed, and wear appropriate clothing. Carefully dispose of the dye bath when you are finished.

Timetable Approximately two hours to prepare dye and carry out experiment, three to four days total time, depending upon how long the material takes to dry.

Step-by-Step Instructions

1. Wash the pieces of wool by machine or by hand to make sure they are clean.
2. Use the scissors to cut the pieces in three ways to help you identify which pair will be in each dye bath. You can cut a diagonal off the corner off two pieces; cut a square in the corner of two more pieces, and cut a small triangle in the middle of one side of two more pieces. It does not matter what you cut, as long as there are three sets of two pieces that are identifiable. Assign each identification marking to one of the dye baths and write it down.
3. Bring three cups of water to a boil and reduce to a simmer. Add about a quarter teaspoon alum and stir. Wet the two pieces assigned to the mordant/natural dye bath and place in the hot water.
4. Simmer for about an hour and turn off the stove. Allow the material to sit overnight in the alum water.
5. Before you are about to die, remove the two pieces from the alum water and place on a plate. Wet the remaining four pieces of wool.
6. For the natural dye: Cut up the beets or cabbage and place them in the pot. Pour enough water in the pot to cover the food and simmer for about 30 minutes or until the water is a color you like. Use the wooden spoon to stir occasionally.
7. While the natural dye is simmering, follow the directions on the package. Make sure you use a container that does not matter if it gets dyed.
8. When the cabbage or beets has finished simmering, place a plastic container under the strainer in a sink or outside, and carefully empty the hot beet-water into the colander. The container holds your dye.

Step 2: Use scissors to cut the pieces in three ways to help you identify each pair. ILLUSTRATION BY TEMAH NELSON.

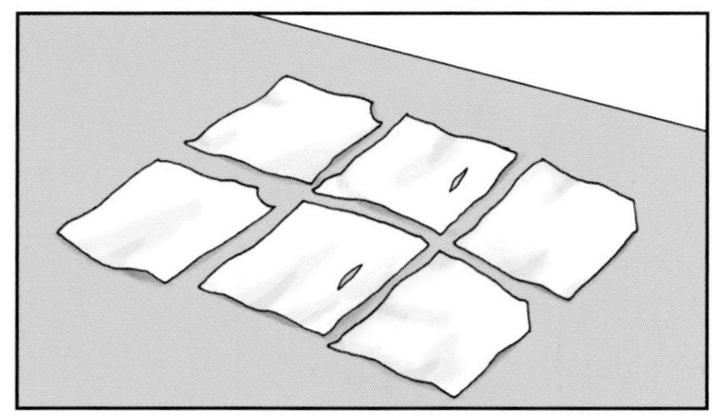

9. Place the four wet fabric swatches assigned to the natural dye bath into the container. Use the wooden stirrer to move the pieces around. Set aside overnight.
10. Place the two wet fabric swatches assigned to the synthetic dye into the synthetic dye bath. Use a wooden stirrer to move the pieces around. Set aside as directed or until you like the color.
11. When all the squares are dyed, set them on a paper towel and roll the paper towel until the material is damp. Hang them over a plate in the sink or outside and allow to dry. Set one of each pair aside.
12. Fill the glass jar with warm water and add a few drops of soap. Place one of each pair of the dyed wool pieces into the jar. Cover and shake for at least ten seconds.
13. Rinse the wool squares under running water and allow to dry.
14. Repeat the washing and drying process two more times.

Step 3: Wet the two pieces assigned to the mordant/natural dye bath and place in the hot water. ILLUSTRATION BY TEMAH NELSON.

Step 12: Cover and shake with the dyed wool for at least ten seconds. ILLUSTRATION BY TEMAH NELSON.

Summary of Results Compare the control wool pieces to the washed wool. How does each compare to its non-washed partner? Is there one dye that washed out completely? Did the mordant help fix the dye? Match the identification with the assigned dye bath. Was your hypothesis correct? Write up a paragraph of your results; you may want to take pictures or attach swatches.

Change the Variables One variable you can change to further explore colorfastness is pH. The pH is a measure of how acidic a solution is. Depending upon the material, a low or high pH can affect how the dye bonds and fixes to the material. You can also change the material or type of dye. You can compare different brands of purchased dyes or different types of natural dyes.

Design Your Own Experiment

How to Select a Topic Relating to this Concept Are you interested in experimenting with how to make dye, change dye colors, or remove dyes? Perhaps you would like to learn more about the chemistry behind how a dye attaches to a fabric. Have you ever wondered why some dyes dissolve in water and others only dissolve in oil?

Check the Further Readings section and talk with your science teacher to gather information about dye questions that interest you. You may also want to explore the museums in your area for special exhibits on color or dyes.

Steps in the Scientific Method To conduct an original experiment, you need to plan carefully and think things through. Otherwise you may not be sure what question you are answering, what you are or should be measuring, or what your findings prove or disprove.

Here are the steps in designing an experiment:

- State the purpose of—and the underlying question behind—the experiment you propose to do.
- Recognize the variables involved, and select one that will help you answer the question at hand.
- State a testable hypothesis, an educated guess about the answer to your question.
- Decide how to change the variable you selected.
- Decide how to measure your results.

Recording Data and Summarizing the Results Your data should include charts, graphs or some type of visual representation. They should be clearly labeled and easy to read. You may also want to include samples, photos, or colored drawings of your experimental set-up and results.

If you are preparing an exhibit, display the materials you dyed or dyes themselves to help explain what you did and what you discovered. Observers could even test them out the dyes for themselves. If you have completed a nonexperimental project, you will want to explain clearly what your research question was and illustrate your findings.

Related Projects There are many possible experiments relating to dyes. You could investigate how dyes are removed or the chemistry behind dye removal. You could further investigate why some clothes retain their dye and others lose their color in the wash. There are many different types of dyes developed for different materials. You could explore how a wood dye is different from a fabric dye or hair dye. Why does bleach remove some dyes? Look around you for objects or materials that are dyed and consider what questions you can investigate.

For More Information

"Dyeing to Find Out: Extracting Nature's Colors." *Kids Gardening.* http://www.kidsgardening.com/growingideas/projects/may03/pg1.html (accessed on April 24, 2008). Information and how techniques how to use plant materials to dye.

Gardner, Robert. *Science Projects about Chemistry.* Hillside, NJ: Enslow Publishers, 1994. Focuses on experiments in causing and analyzing chemical reactions.

Van Cleave, Janice. *A+ Projects in Chemistry.* New York: Wiley, 1993. Outlines many experiments and includes information about the scientific method.

24

Earthquakes

According to the ancient Greeks, earthquakes occurred when the god Atlas shifted the weight of the world from one shoulder to the other. Other cultures believed that earthquakes were a sign of punishment. We now know that earthquakes are the shaking or trembling of the earth caused by underground shock waves or vibrations. Believe it or not, over a million earthquakes take place each year. Sometimes the trembling and shaking is gentle and hardly noticeable. Other times the motion is much more violent, causing cracks in the surface of the earth.

There's a whole lot of shaking going on Huge blocks of rocks called plates make up Earth's outer shell, or crust. These plates fit together like a cracked egg shell. The plates push and pull on each other constantly. Sometimes this pressure causes a fault, or a break in the rocks. Large pieces of these rocks, called fault blocks, can overlap. Pressure pushes on the rocks for centuries, finally causing them to rupture and snap in one big surge, resulting in a major earthquake.

Like a chain reaction, force from the movement of the rocks results in vibrations of the surrounding ground. These vibrations, or seismic waves, (pronounced SIZE-mic; relating to earthquakes) travel away from the break. Strong shaking from these waves lasts from 30 to 60 seconds and can cause buildings and highways to collapse.

Earthquakes can actually be beneficial. The constant shifting and upheaval of Earth's crust builds mountains and highlands. The planet would be flat without them.

Developing a theory On November 1, 1755, the port of Lisbon, Portugal, was hit by a terrible earthquake. More than 60,000 people died. The day of the earthquake was a religious holiday, and many of those killed were crushed in churches. Because earthquakes were thought to be a punishment from God, it did not make sense that one would take place on a holy day. People also asked why innocent children would be

Dr. Charles F. Richter developed the Richter Scale, which measures earthquake magnitude. AP/WIDE WORLD PHOTOS.

punished? Soon after the earthquake, some people started to look for scientific reasons. The Marquez de Pombal, a Portugese nobleman, asked Lisbon's surviving priests to fill out questionnaires documenting information about the earthquake. The questionnaires included questions about the time and the direction of the earthquake shock.

In 1760, John Michell, an English physicist, came up with an interesting theory. He reasoned that if you could record the underground shock waves and the points at which the waves stopped, you could determine the point of origin, or epicenter, of an earthquake. Epicenters existed deep in the rocks beneath the sea, he said. His theories, which were fairly accurate, were the start of seismology, the science of earthquakes and their origins.

Measuring an earthquake In the first century, Chang Heng—a Chinese astronomer, mathematician, and writer—invented the earliest earthquake recorder. This device measured the occurrence and direction of an earthquake's

In the famous Lisbon, Portugal, earthquake of 1755, residents were killed by toppling buildings, fires, and high waves. CORBIS/BETTMANN.

WORDS TO KNOW

Earthquake: An unpredictable event in which masses of rock suddenly shift or rupture below Earth's surface, releasing enormous amounts of energy and sending out shockwaves that sometimes cause the ground to shake dramatically.

Epicenter: The location where the seismic waves of an earthquake first appear on the surface, usually almost directly above the focus.

Fault: A crack running through rock as the result of tectonic forces.

Fault blocks: Pieces of rock from Earth's crust that press against each other and cause earthquakes when they suddenly shift or rupture from the pressure.

Focus: The point within Earth where a sudden shift or rupture occurs.

Hypothesis: An idea in the form of a statement that can be tested by observation and experiment.

Plates: Huge blocks of rocks that make up Earth's outer shell and fit together like a cracked egg.

Seismic waves: Vibrations in rock and soil that transfer the force of an earthquake from the focus into the surrounding area.

Seismograph: A device that detects and records vibrations of the ground.

Seismology: The study and measurement of earthquakes.

Tectonic: Relating to the forces and structures of the outer shell of Earth.

Tsunami: A large wave of water caused by an underwater earthquake.

Variable: Something that can affect the results of an experiment.

motion. Italian physicist Luigi Palmieri has been credited with inventing the first seismograph in 1855. Seismographs detect and record earthquake waves. To pinpoint how dangerous an earthquake was, American seismologist Charles F. Richter (1900–1985) began measuring the peaks and valleys of these waves in the 1930s. He came up with a mathematical formula, known as the Richter (pronounced RIK-ter) Scale, which measures earthquake magnitude on a scale from 1 to 10. The Richter Scale also measures how much energy is released in an earthquake. Increasing one whole number on the Richter Scale, from 5.0 to 6.0 for example, represents an increase of 10 times the magnitude and about 60 times the energy.

Earth is a dynamic and changing planet. Conducting experiments will help you understand how earthquakes are part of the changes that are taking place.

What Are the Variables?

Variables are anything that might affect the results of an experiment. Here are the main variables in this experiment:

- the amount of simulated earthquake disturbance
- the distance of the disturbance from the seismograph
- the surface on which you place your seismograph

In other words, the variables in this experiment are everything that might affect the amount of disturbance recorded on your seismograph. If you change more than one variable, you will not be able to tell which variable had the most effect on the seismograph recordings.

EXPERIMENT 1

Detecting an Earthquake: How can movement of Earth's crust be measured?

Purpose/Hypothesis In this experiment, you will construct a simple seismograph and simulate the forces that cause an earthquake. Your seismograph is a simple model, but you will see if it can detect vibrational activity in your house or building.

You probably have an educated guess about the outcome of this experiment based on what you already know about earthquakes. This educated guess, or prediction, is your hypothesis. A hypothesis should explain these things:

- the topic of the experiment
- the variable you will change
- the variable you will measure
- what you expect to happen

A hypothesis should be brief, specific, and measurable. It must be something you can test through observation. Your experiment will prove or disprove whether your hypothesis is correct. Here is one possible hypothesis for this experiment: "By simulating an earthquake with various types of disturbances, you will detect and record various types of vibrational activity on your seismograph."

In this case, the variable you will change is the amount of simulated earthquake disturbance, and the variable you will measure is the amount of displacement recorded on your seismograph. If a greater simulated disturbance results in a greater displacement on your seismograph, you will know your hypothesis is correct.

Level of Difficulty Moderate. (The design of your seismograph is easy, but you may need someone to hold some pieces while you attach them. Also, you will need help from friends in creating vibrations.)

Materials Needed

- 1 or 2 helpers
- cardboard box about 12 inches × 12 inches (30 centimeters × 30 centimeters) with an opening on top

- scissors
- ruler
- adding machine tape
- string
- pencil (or dowel)
- 5-ounce (about 148-milliliter) paper cup
- masking tape
- black marking pen
- small rocks or marbles
- modeling clay

How to Experiment Safely

Use caution when handling scissors and cutting cardboard. Be careful when simulating an earthquake so you do not damage items in the room or hurt yourself or others.

Approximate Budget $3.

Timetable One hour.

Step-by-Step Instructions

1. Turn the box on its side so the opening is facing outward.
2. Cut a 2-inch (5-centimeter) circle in the center of the top side of the box.
3. Cut two ½-inch × 4-inch (1.25-centimeter × 10-centimeter) slots in the box. The first slot should be in the center of the bottom, near the front opening. The second slot should be in the back center near the bottom. See the illustration.
4. Thread the adding machine tape through the slots, so the leading edge comes out the front slot.
5. Cut two 24-inch (61-centimeter) lengths of string.
6. Use the point of a pencil to poke two holes below the rim of the cup opposite each other.
7. Tie one string onto each hole in the cup.
8. Bring the free ends of the string through the 2-inch (5-centimeter) circle in the top side of the box.
9. Tape or tie the ends of the string to the pencil and lay the pencil across the hole.
10. Push the marking pen through the bottom of the cup, tip down.

Steps 2 to 4: Initial set-up of seismograph box. GALE GROUP.

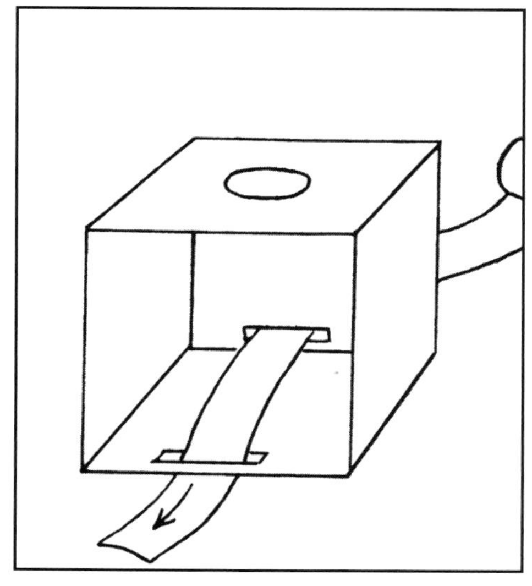

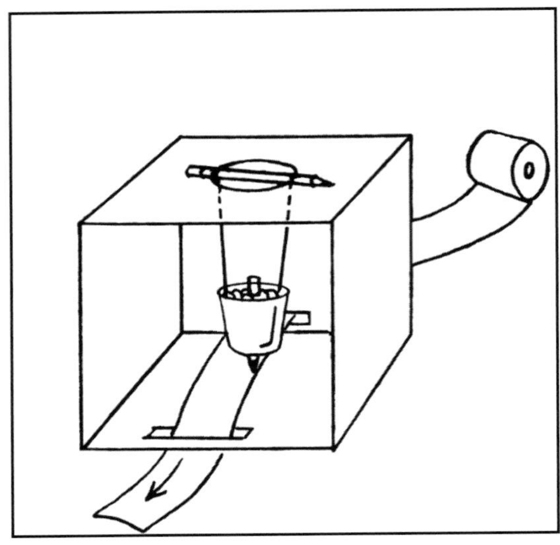

Steps 7 to 12: Completion of seismograph box. GALE GROUP.

11. Fill the cup with the rocks or marbles.
12. Adjust the height of the cup/pen/rock device so the marker tip just touches the adding machine tape. (You can adjust the string on the pencil, then fix the pencil in place using the modeling clay and masking tape.)
13. Test the device by pulling the adding machine tape forward with one hand and shaking the box gently with the other and observe the markings left on the paper.
14. Perform a seismic test indoors. Place your seismograph on the floor in the middle of the room. Have several of your friends walk, skip, jog, and run around in the room in a circle, always keeping the same distance away from the seismograph. While they are moving about, record the seismic waves, or seismic activity, by slowly pulling the adding machine tape through the instrument (see illustration).
15. Label the tape with the location and activities.

Summary of Results Compare your tapes. Do they show greater movement when the activity was more vigorous? In other words, does your seismograph accurately detect and record seismic activity?

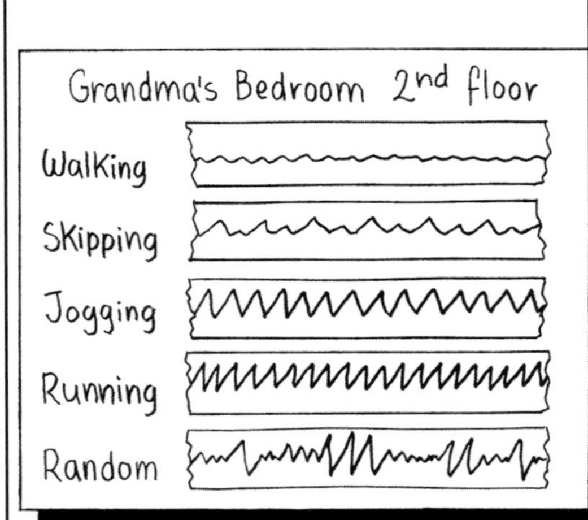

Steps 14 and 15: Sample recording sheets of seismic results from walking, skipping, jogging, running. GALE GROUP.

Change the Variables You can change one of the variables and repeat this experiment. For example, you can have your friends move closer or farther away from the seismograph to determine how the recordings vary. You can also place the seismograph on a shaky table, like an old card table, to see if this amplifies the disturbances.

Be sure to change only one variable at a time. Otherwise, you will not be able to determine which variable affected the results.

EXPERIMENT 2

Earthquake Simulation: Is the destruction greater at the epicenter?

Purpose/Hypothesis In this experiment, you will create a simulated city and suburbs with buildings and houses. By locating different types of structures at various distances from the epicenter, you will determine the destructive power of an earthquake.

You probably have an educated guess about the outcome of this experiment based on what you already know about earthquakes. This educated guess, or prediction, is your hypothesis. A hypothesis should explain these things:

- the topic of the experiment
- the variable you will change
- the variable you will measure
- what you expect to happen

A hypothesis should be brief, specific, and measurable. It must be something you can test through observation. Your experiment will prove or disprove whether your hypothesis is correct. Here is one possible hypothesis for this experiment: "Greater destruction occurs at the epicenter than at the outer limits of an earthquake."

In this case, the variable you will change is the distance from the simulated earthquake disturbance, and the variable you will measure is the amount of visible destruction of the structures in your simulated city and suburbs. If there is more destruction near the epicenter, you will know your hypothesis is correct.

Troubleshooter's Guide

Experiments do not always work out as planned. Below are some problems that may arise during this experiment, some possible causes, and ways to remedy the problems.

Problem: Nothing is being recorded on the adding machine tape.

Possible cause: The pen is not touching the tape. Adjust the height of the marker pen. Gently shake the box and pull the tape until a mark appears.

Problem: The adding machine tape does not move easily through the slots.

Possible cause: The slots are too small. Enlarge the slots to allow the tape to move freely.

Problem: The model works during the test, but when your friends run or jump, nothing happens.

Possible cause: The friends are not making strong enough vibrations. Have them jump up and down. If that doesn't work, have them move closer to the siesmograph.

Level of Difficulty Easy/moderate.

Materials Needed

- cardboard sheet, 24 inches × 24 inches (60 centimeters ×60 centimeters)
- 8 sheets of 8-½-inch × 11-inch (22 centimeter ×28 centimeter) paper

What Are the Variables?

Variables are anything that might affect the results of an experiment. Here are the main variables in this experiment:

- the size of the balloon, hence the amount of the simulated earthquake disturbance
- the positions of the buildings in the simulated city and suburb areas
- the height of the buildings
- the type of building construction
- the surface on which the buildings are constructed

In other words, the variables in this experiment are everything that might affect the amount of destruction. If you change more than one variable, you will not be able to tell which variable had the most effect on the seismograph recordings.

- marking pen
- 30 sugar cubes
- 8–10 spherical balloons
- adhesive tape
- 4 coffee cans
- ruler
- drawing compass
- safety pin

Approximate Budget $3 for balloons and sugar cubes.

Timetable 1 hour or less.

Step-by-Step Instructions

1. Using tape, connect the edges of four sheets of paper to form a large rectangle—two sheets wide by two sheets long.
2. In the center of the rectangle, where the four corners join together, draw a small bullseye with the compass. Adjust the compass so the first circle has a 1-inch (2.5-centimeter) radius around the center of the bullseye. Continue to draw circles so that each is 1 inch (2.5 centimeters) bigger in radius than the circle inside it. Mark the center of the bullseye X; this will be the epicenter. Label the paper "City."
3. Using the above illustration as a guide, randomly place ten sugar cubes on your City bullseye pattern. These represent city dwellings of three stories. Outline these cubes on the paper with your marking pen, and write 3, for three stories, in the center of the outlines.
4. Repeat steps 1 and 2 with the remaining pieces of paper, only this time label the paper "Suburb."
5. Randomly place ten sugar cubes on your Suburb bullseye pattern. Outline these cubes with your marking pen and mark 1 in the center of the outlines. These represent a rural or suburban area that has one-story homes.
6. Place the four coffee cans in a square pattern about 24 inches (61 centimeters) from each other.
7. Place the cardboard sheet on top of the coffee cans.

8. Blow up two balloons. Make them full, but small enough to fit under the cardboard sheet. Tape one to the center of the underside of the cardboard.
9. Place the City bullseye pattern on the cardboard. Try to position the epicenter mark directly over the spot where the balloon is taped.
10. Stack three sugar cubes on top of each other over each outline.
11. Using your safety pin, carefully pop the balloon.
12. Using a marking pen and ruler, mark and measure the new positions of the cubes with dotted lines.
13. Remove the broken balloon. Tape the second balloon under the center of the cardboard sheet and repeat steps 9 through 12 for the

How to Experiment Safely

Use caution when blowing up and handling balloons. Ask an adult to help. Place the safety pin in fabric or cardboard when it is not being used. Discard the sugar cubes after you have used them.

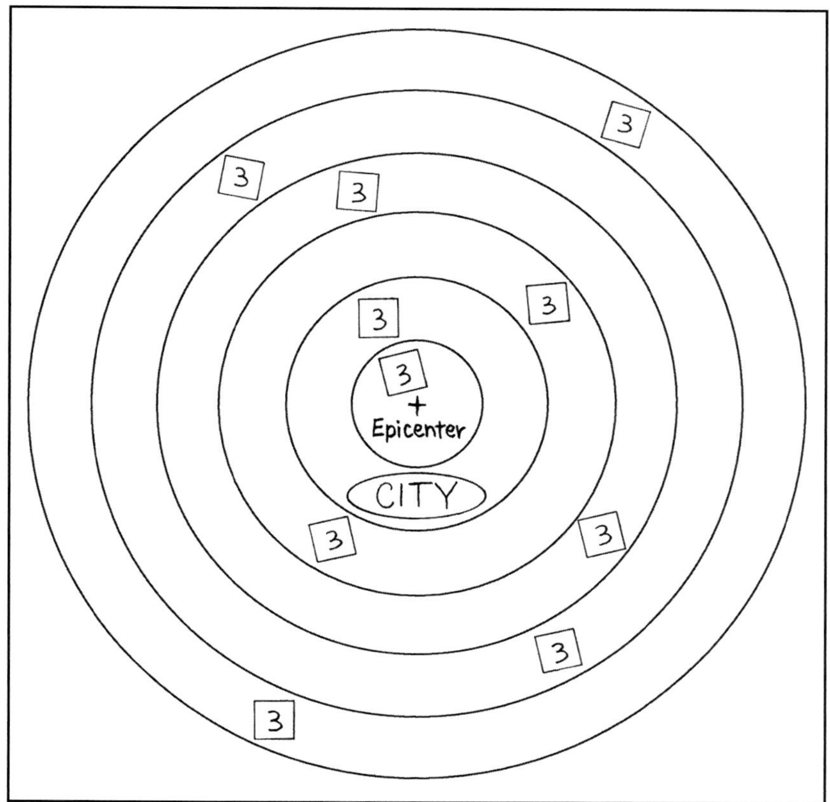

Step 3: "City" bullseye with ten outlines marked 3 and an X at the epicenter. GALE GROUP.

Troubleshooter's Guide

Your experiment may not have worked out as planned. Below is a problem that may arise during this experiment, a possible cause, and a way to solve the problem.

Problem: My balloon is not creating much damage.

Possible cause: The cardboard may be too thick and is absorbing the jolt. Try a thinner piece of cardboard. Also make sure the balloon is firmly attached to the cardboard.

Suburb bullseye pattern. This time, place only one sugar cube over each outline.

Summary of Results Compare the destruction on your two bullseye patterns. How did the simulated city compare to the suburb? Write up your results and describe the differences. Did your hypothesis hold true? Was the destruction near the epicenter greater in both cases?

Change the Variables You can change the variables and repeat the experiment. For example, you can change the thickness of the cardboard to determine if the destruction increases or decreases. You can also change the height of the buildings. One interesting experiment might be to pick one of the three-story building outlines near the epicenter and place four stacks of three sugar cubes centered on the outline and arranged in a tight square so the stacks are touching. You can then compare the amount of damage of this type of building construction with a single three-story stack. Does a wider and broader base increase or decrease the amount of destruction?

Remember to change only one variable at a time or you will not be able to determine which variable affected the results.

Steps 6 to 9: Set-up of simulated earthquake using City bullseye pattern. GALE GROUP.

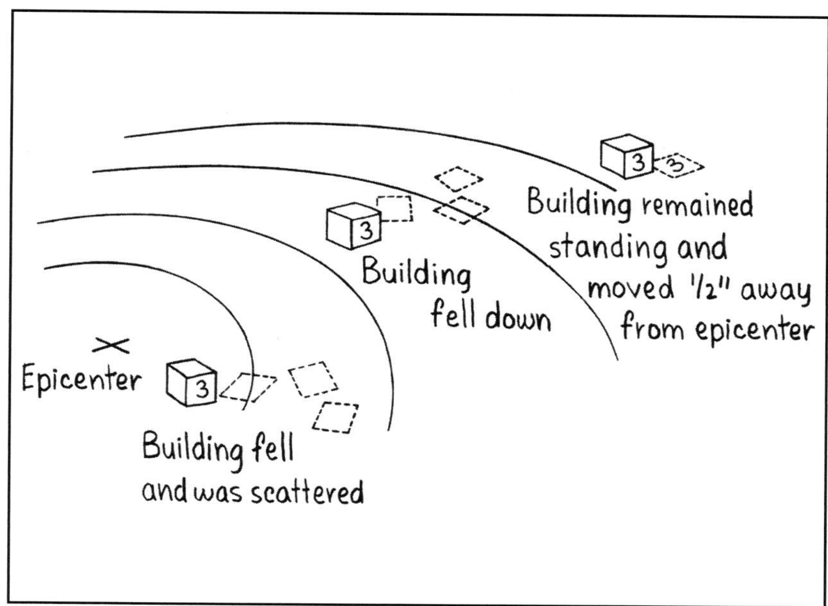

Step 12: Record seismic movement from simulated earthquake. GALE GROUP.

Modify the Experiment For a more advanced version of this experiment, you can examine earthquake-resistant structures. As you conduct the experiment, make a note of what structures (sugar cubes) were affected by the earthquake and the properties of each structure. For example, how many stories were the structures that fell as opposed to those that did not move. What shape were the affected and non-affected structures?

In Experiment 2, all the structures were made of the same material (sugar cubes). Some materials are relatively brittle (easily broken). Examples of brittle materials include brick and stone. Building materials that have some elasticity are more likely to move with the quake rather than break. Wood is an example of a relatively elastic material. The foundation of a structure also plays an important role in its stability during an earthquake.

In order to determine the properties of an earthquake-resistant structure, experiment with altering the buildings' foundation and material. For example, how would the quake affect a building made of rubber or clay compared to stone? Make sure to change only one variable at a time and keep track of your data.

View of the San Andreas Fault in California. U.S. GEOLOGICAL SURVEY.

Design Your Own Experiment

How to Select a Topic Relating to this Concept Earth is dynamic and changing. Earthquakes, volcanoes, and tidal waves called tsunamis (pronounced SUE-nahm-ease; large waves of water caused by underwater earthquakes) are disastrous forces of nature that demonstrate Earth's motion. If you are fascinated with the power of these natural disasters, you can explore topics relating to earth science.

Major earthquakes are always reported in newspapers. You can look up major earthquakes in your local library. Newspaper accounts cover details such as seismic activity and the severity of the earthquake. One of the more recent ones in the United States took place in 1989 in San Francisco. Another took place in Turkey in 1999.

Steps in the Scientific Method To do an original experiment, you need to plan carefully and think things through. Otherwise, you might not be sure what question you are answering, what you are or should be measuring, or what your findings prove or disprove. Here are the steps in designing an experiment:

- State the purpose of—and the underlying question behind—the experiment you propose to do.
- Recognize the variables involved, and select one that will help you answer the question at hand.
- State a testable hypothesis, an educated guess about the answer to your question.
- Decide how to change the variable you selected.
- Decide how to measure your results.

Recording Data and Summarizing the Results Your experiment can be useful to others studying the same topic. When designing your experiment, develop a simple method to record your data. This method should be simple and clear enough so that others who want to do the experiment can follow it.

Your final results should be summarized and put into simple graphs, tables, and charts to display the outcome of your experiment.

Related Projects Building an actual model of a city, town, or region that can be affected by a simulated earthquake is another way to understand the dynamics of a real earthquake.

For More Information

Bolt, Bruce A. *Earthquakes and Geological Discovery.* New York: Scientific American Library, 1997. Offers geological facts and photos about earthquakes.

Rubin, Ken. *Volcano & Earthquakes.* New York: Simon & Schuster Books for Young Readers, 2007.

Smith, Bruce, and David McKay. *Geology Projects For Young Scientists.* New York: Franklin Watts, 1992. Describes earthquake experiments and the geological background of why earthquakes occur.

U.S. Geological Survey. *Earthquakes.* http://www.usgs.gov/science/science.php?term=304 (accessed on January 8, 2008).

25

Eclipses

Imagine living in ancient times. You stroll down a dirt road leading to a favorite temple. It is a nice day, but without warning, the sky starts to get dark. The Sun looks strange and, gradually, something huge blocks it out, although a bright ring can be seen around its edge.

We now know that this phenomenon is a solar eclipse. An eclipse occurs when one celestial body passes in front of another, partly or completely cutting off our view of it. Today, we would get advance information through newspapers and magazines or by news reports on television or radio if a major eclipse was expected. To most ancient people, who had no explanations for the darkness, an eclipse was terrifying.

Close encounters in the sky In the eighth century B.C.E., Babylonian scholars began systematically observing and writing down celestial phenomena, as they studied astronomy. These scholars watched the motion of the planets and noticed that sometimes two planets came close together. Sometimes the Moon passed in front of the Sun. Sometimes Earth's shadow fell on the Moon. After studying these phenomena for many years, they identified certain experiences as occurring in cycles. They also developed mathematical formulas involving time and distances that helped them to predict eclipses.

The Moon completely blocks out our view of the Sun during a solar eclipse. PHOTO RESEARCHERS INC.

Thales of Miletus (624–546 B.C.E.) was a Greek philosopher who may have learned astronomical methods from the Babylonian scholars. Thales accurately predicted a solar eclipse on May 28, 585 B.C.E.—probably the earliest, most public eclipse prediction. The term *eclipse* comes from the Greek words meaning "to leave out," because when one occurred, either the Sun or the Moon was "left out." In fact, the theory that Earth was a sphere began getting attention

Red light waves from the Sun cause the Moon to turn a reddish color during a lunar eclipse. PHOTO RESEARCHERS INC.

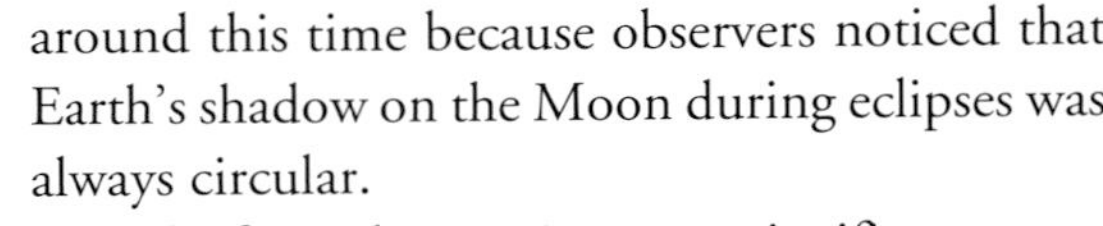

around this time because observers noticed that Earth's shadow on the Moon during eclipses was always circular.

The first eclipse to interest a significant number of astronomers took place on April 22, 1715. The shadow of the eclipse fell across Great Britain and parts of Europe. English astronomer Edmond Halley (1656–1742) plotted its path and prepared maps enabling many to watch its course.

Celestial line-up The two most commonly known eclipses are solar and lunar. Earth revolves around the Sun. The Moon revolves around Earth. The Moon takes a month to complete a revolution; Earth takes a year. Sometimes these three bodies end up in a straight line and cause an eclipse.

Two conditions have to be met for a total solar eclipse—one in which our view of the Sun is completely blocked. The Sun, Moon, and Earth must lie in a perfectly straight line, and the Moon must be a certain distance from Earth to cover the Sun. When these conditions are met, the Moon totally blocks our view of the Sun for a period of about seven minutes. If the Moon is too far away from Earth, or if it is not exactly aligned between Earth and the Sun, it will only partially block the Sun, causing a partial solar eclipse.

For a total lunar eclipse, the Sun, Earth, and Moon must lie in a perfectly straight line. Did you catch the difference? In this case, Earth is in the middle, not the Moon. Earth's shadow across the Moon is what causes the darkness. Lunar eclipses can happen only during a full Moon, when Earth's dark side faces the Moon's bright side. In this position, Earth casts a shadow, causing the Moon to darken.

Celestial fireworks The bright ring you might see around the Sun during a solar eclipse is the corona, the Sun's outermost layer, which appears to be a pearly color. The red plumes that shoot out around this ring are called prominences.

In 1869, British astronomer Joseph Norman Lockyer became the first person to observe solar prominences in the daytime. PHOTO RESEARCHERS INC.

WORDS TO KNOW

Astronomy: The study of the physical properties of objects and matter outside Earth's atmosphere.

Celestial bodies: Describing planets or other objects in space.

Corona: The outermost atmospheric layer of the Sun.

Cycles: Occurrence of events that take place on a regular, repeating basis.

Eclipse: A phenomenon in which the light from a celestial body is temporarily cut off by the presence of another.

Gibbous moon: A phase of the Moon when more than half of its surface is lighted.

Hypothesis: An idea in the form of a statement that can be tested by observation and/or experiment.

Lunar eclipse: An eclipse that occurs when Earth passes between the Sun and the Moon, casting a shadow on the Moon.

Partial solar/lunar eclipse: An eclipse in which our view of the Sun/Moon is only partially blocked.

Phases: Changes in the portion of the Moon's surface that is illuminated by light from the Sun as the Moon revolves around Earth.

Prominences: Masses of glowing gas, mainly hydrogen, that rise from the Sun's surface like flames.

Solar eclipse: An eclipse that occurs when the Moon passes between Earth and the Sun, casting a shadow on Earth.

Total solar/lunar eclipse: An eclipse in which our view of the Sun/Moon is totally blocked.

Variable: Something that can affect the results of an experiment.

Like fireworks, these streams of glowing gas shoot out from the Sun and extend many miles into space. No wonder ancient people were terrified. Lunar eclipses have a colorful side also. They can make the Moon turn red. This reddish color is actually an accumulation of light waves from the Sun.

By constructing models that simulate eclipses, we can better understand the extraordinary processes that cause them.

How to Experiment Safely

Use caution when handling the lamp. Do not touch or move it until it has cooled for at least five minutes.

PROJECT 1

Simulating Solar and Lunar Eclipses

Purpose/Hypothesis This project will create a model that demonstrates a solar and lunar eclipse. By adjusting the alignment and distances of the model Sun, Moon, and Earth, you should be able to demonstrate both partial and total eclipses.

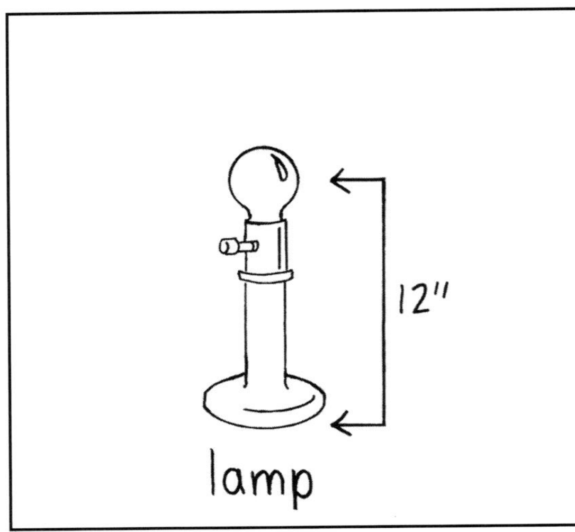

Lamp without shade and measured distance of 12 inches. GALE GROUP.

Level of Difficulty Easy/moderate. (The assembly and principles are not difficult, but it takes patience to adjust the objects to get the desired effect.)

Materials Needed

- 2 Styrofoam balls, one ball 2 inches (5 centimeters) and one 0.5 inch (1.25 centimeters) in diameter
- two 4-inch (10-centimeter) Styrofoam squares
- small table lamp (measuring 12 inches in height) with no lamp shade and a 40-watt bulb
- 2 wooden dowels (as long as the height of the lamp from its base to the middle of the bulb)
- ruler

Step 5: Solar eclipse set-up. GALE GROUP.

Approximate Budget $3 for the Styrofoam pieces and the dowels.

Timetable Less than one hour.

Step-by-Step Instructions

1. Poke each dowel into the center of a Styrofoam square.
2. Place the small Styrofoam ball, representing the Moon, onto one dowel.
3. Place the large Styrofoam ball, representing Earth, onto the other dowel.
4. Place the lamp on a sturdy table and plug it in. Turn it on.
5. Here is the challenge! Place the Sun (lamp), Earth (large ball), and Moon (small ball) on a flat surface in perfect alignment to

create a solar and lunar eclipse. Follow the diagrams illustrated.

Summary of Results Make a diagram of your experiment, measuring and marking the distances and height of the experiment parts for others to see and try. Through the shadows you created with the lamp, were you able to create full eclipses or only partial eclipses?

PROJECT 2

Phases of the Moon: What does each phase look like?

Purpose/Hypothesis In this project, you will create models of the changes in the illuminated Moon surface as the Moon revolves around Earth. These changes are called phases. You will create diagrams called sun prints representing these Moon phases.

Level of Difficulty Easy/moderate.

Materials Needed

- 8 sheets of dark blue construction paper, 8½ x 11 inches (21.5 x 28 centimeters)
- 8 sheets of black construction paper, 8½ x 11 inches (21.5 x 28 centimeters)
- adhesive tape
- marker
- 30 x 30-inch (75 x 75-centimeter) board
- sunny day
- scissors
- drawing compass

Approximate Budget $5 for paper supplies.

Timetable Approximately 1 hour to set up the model and a whole day for the sun prints to mature.

Troubleshooter's Guide

Here is a problem that may arise during this project, a possible cause, and a way to remedy the problem.

Problem: You cannot get the shadow to cover the entire object to create the "eclipse."

Possible cause: Your alignment may be off. Make sure you line up the objects on the same level.

Step 5: Lunar eclipse set-up. GALE GROUP.

How to Experiment Safely

Use caution with the compass and scissors.

Step-by-Step Instructions

1. Use the compass to draw a 7-inch (18-centimeter) diameter circle on eight sheets of blue construction paper.
2. Draw an 8-inch (20-centimeter) diameter circle on eight sheets of black construction paper.
3. Cut out the circles.
4. Tape eight blue circles onto the board in a circle.
5. Mark the board as shown in the diagram illustrated above.
6. Place the black circles over the blue circles to show: new Moon; crescent Moon; first-quarter Moon; gibbous Moon; full Moon; gibbous Moon; third-quarter Moon; crescent Moon.
7. Leave the board in a sunny location for at least 8 hours.
8. Take the black paper off after 8 hours and examine the results.
9. Highlight the lightened areas or boundaries with the marker.

Note: the darker blue areas that were covered are the shaded part of the Moon we cannot see.

Illustration of the Moon's revolution around Earth. GALE GROUP.

Summary of Results Label the board and write a brief description for each Moon phase, that is, how it was caused and what it looks like.

Design Your Own Experiment

How to Select a Topic Relating to this Concept Astronomy is a fascinating field of study, with topics such as meteor/meteorites, telescopes, space travel, and stars. Read your local paper to find out about upcoming events in the sky. Then research who saw the phenomena first and when and how theories developed.

Check the Further Readings section and talk with your science teacher or school or community media specialist to start gathering information on eclipse questions that interest you.

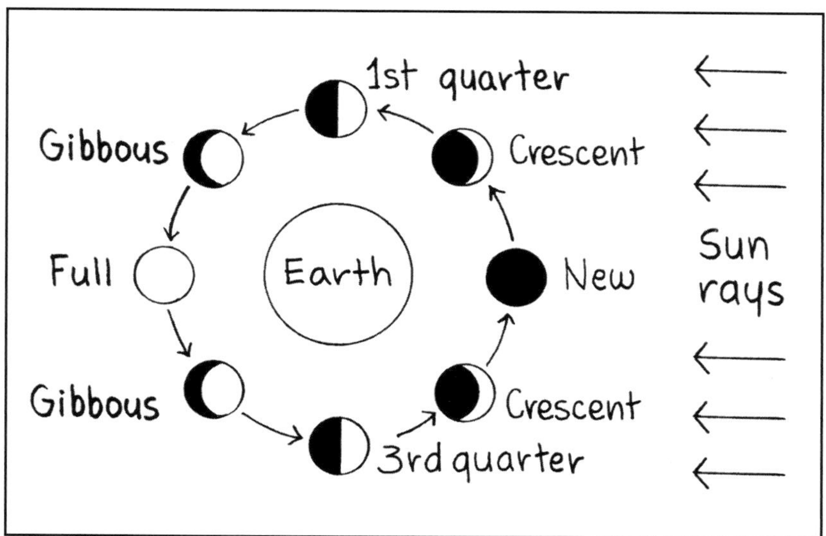

Step 5: Set-up for recording phases of the moon. GALE GROUP.

Steps in the Scientific Method To do an original experiment, you need to plan carefully and think things through. Otherwise, you might not be sure what question you are answering, what you are or should be measuring, or what your findings prove or disprove.

Here are the steps in designing an experiment:

- State the purpose of—and the underlying question behind—the experiment you propose to do.
- Recognize the variables involved, and select one that will help you answer the question at hand.
- State a testable hypothesis, an educated guess about the answer to your question.
- Decide how to change the variable you selected.
- Decide how to measure your results.

Recording Data and Summarizing the Results When performing an experiment, it is important to keep your data organized in tables. Your information needs to be analyzed and presented

Steps 6 to 8: Completed sun prints. GALE GROUP.

Troubleshooter's Guide

Here is a problem that may arise during this project, a possible cause, and a way to remedy the problem.

Problem: The sun prints are not forming.

Possible cause: They have not had enough time. Give the sun prints two days, for eight hours each day, in full sunlight.

in a visual manner. Graphs, drawings, or pictures of events are great tools for displaying your data.

Related Projects Creating models like these are always fun and interesting. However, creating a mini-instrument, such as a telescope with lenses and cardboard, might be useful. Ask a teacher or your parents for help.

For More Information

Aronson, Billy. *Eclipses: Nature's Blackouts.* New York: Franklin Watts, 1996. Explains what causes eclipses of the Sun and Moon and describes how they have been viewed and studied at different times in history.

National Aeronautics and Space Administration. *NASA Eclipse Home Page.* http://sunearth.gsfc.nasa.gov/eclipse/transit/transit.html (accessed on January 11, 2008).

26

Electricity

We know that electricity will flow through certain objects and not others. We are told that it is dangerous to plug in an ungrounded electrical device while standing in water because the electricity may flow through our bodies and the water to the ground, giving us a shock. But how, exactly, does water conduct electricity? Do all liquids conduct electricity equally well? And how have we made this property useful in our everyday lives?

How electricity flows through metals Most of the electricity we use every day is conducted from its source through metal wires to the appliances we use. Most metals, such as copper, conduct electricity well because they possess a great number of free electrons. An electron is an extremely small particle with a single electrical charge that orbits the nucleus of an atom. Materials with few or no free electrons do not conduct electricity and are called insulators. They are commonly used to coat the wiring we use, allowing the electric current to flow safely and efficiently through the wire.

The flow of electrons in an electric current was the focus of many experiments done by the French scientist André-Marie Ampere (1775–1836). Ampere developed the system we now use for measuring this electron flow. The common electrical unit of measurement of current, the ampere or amp, is named for him.

How electricity flows through liquids Electricity can flow through liquids by the process of ionic conduction, the movement of ions (charged particles) within the liquid.

Substances that conduct electricity when they are dissolved in water are called electrolytes. When a positive electrode and a negative electrode (such as wires attached to the terminals of a battery) are placed in an electrolytic solution, ions transport free electrons between the two electrodes, bridging the gap and allowing the flow of electricity.

André-Marie Ampere studied electrical current. PHOTO RESEARCHERS INC.

In the first experiment, you will determine whether certain substances are electrolytes. Using a voltmeter, you will test various solutions and liquids and compare them to find which conducts electricity the best. When the two probes (positive and negative) of the voltmeter are placed in a liquid, the meter will indicate how much current (from the battery inside the meter) is passing between the probes. A strong electrolyte will conduct more current, and a weak electrolyte will conduct less. Acids in water, such as lemon juice, make good electrolytes because they contribute many hydrogen ions. Other solutions, such as organic compounds that contain sugar and starch, contribute few or no hydrogen ions and do not conduct electricity well.

Electrolytes and ionic conduction make batteries work The batteries used to power watches, flashlights, and cars all rely on electrolytes to function. The first battery was developed by the Italian scientist Alessandro Volta (1745–1827), who also invented and gave his name to the measurement of the force of a current, called voltage. Volta discovered that a weak electric current is created when two different metals (he used copper and zinc) are pressed together, separated only by a thin layer of electrolyte-soaked fabric. The electrolyte between the metals carries free electrons from one to the other, creating an electric current. Combining a number of these "cells" in a series increases the force of the current, forming a useful battery.

Today's common household batteries, called dry cell batteries, use the same principle. One metal serves as a positive electrode, another metal serves as a negative electrode, and a dry electrolyte "paste" allows ionic conduction between the two. The batteries found in most cars are wet cell batteries, which use a liquid electrolyte to allow conduction.

In the second experiment, you will construct a single battery cell using two different metals and a lemon as an electrolyte. (Lemons contain citric acid.) After finding the voltage of that single cell, you will estimate how many lemons would be necessary in series to equal the voltage of a single D-cell battery. Finally, you will test your estimate and your hypothesis by constructing a multi-cell battery or "pile" and comparing its voltage to that of a D-cell battery.

The third project explores one of electricity's applications: electroplating. Electroplating is a commonly used process of coating ("plating") one metal onto another metal. Jewelry and silverware are electroplated to make them look more appealing, car parts are electroplated to protect them from rusting and keep them shiny.

Alessandro Volta studied electrolytes and electrical current. PHOTO RESEARCHERS INC.

EXPERIMENT 1

Electrolytes: Do some solutions conduct electricity better than others?

Purpose/Hypothesis Using a voltmeter, we can determine how well different substances act as electrolytes by measuring their resistance when they are dissolved in water. The lower the resistance, the more conductive the electrolyte. In this experiment, you will predict whether certain substances are electrolytes. Before you begin,

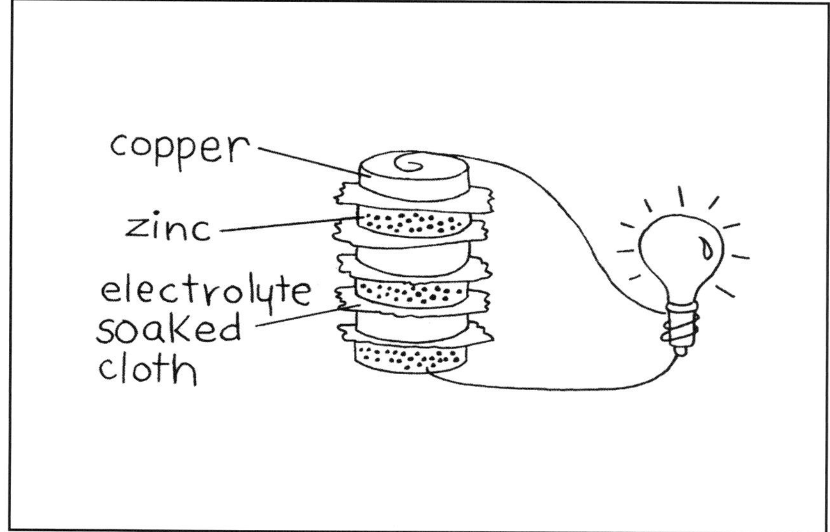

By combining different metals and a strong electrolyte, Alessandro Volta was able to create an electric current in a "Volta Pile," illustrated. GALE GROUP.

WORDS TO KNOW

Amperage: A measurement of current. The common unit of measure is the ampere or amp.

Circuit: The complete path of an electric current including the source of electric energy.

Current: The flow of electrical charge from one point to another.

Dry cell: A source of electricity that uses a non-liquid electrolyte.

Electrode: A material that will conduct an electrical current, usually a metal; used to carry electrons into or out of a battery.

Electrolyte: Any substance that, when dissolved in water, conducts an electric current.

Electron: A subatomic particle that orbits the nucleus of an atom. It has a single electrical charge.

Electroplating: The process of coating one metal with another metal by means of an electrical current.

Hypothesis: An idea in the form of a statement that can be tested by observation and/or experiment.

Ion: An atom or groups of atoms that carry an electrical charge—either positive or negative—as the result of losing or gaining one or more electrons.

Ionic conduction: The flow of an electrical current by the movement of charged particles, or ions.

Insulator: A material through which little or no electrical current will flow.

Probe: The terminal of a voltmeter, used to connect the voltmeter to a circuit.

Resistance: A partial or complete limiting of the flow of electrical current through a material. The common unit of measure is the ohm.

Variable: Something that can affect the results of an experiment.

Voltage: Also called potential difference; a measurement of the amount of electric energy stored in a mass of electric charges compared to the energy stored in some other mass of charges. The common unit of measure is the volt.

Voltmeter: An instrument for measuring the amperage, voltage, or resistance in an electrical circuit.

Wet cell: A source of electricity that uses a liquid electrolyte.

make an educated guess about the outcome of this experiment based on your knowledge of electricity and conductivity. This educated guess, or prediction, is your hypothesis. A hypothesis should explain these things:

- the topic of the experiment
- the variable you will change
- the variable you will measure
- what you expect to happen

A hypothesis should be brief, specific, and measurable. It must be something you can test through observation. Your experiment will prove

or disprove whether your hypothesis is correct. Here is one possible hypothesis for this experiment: "Acids and other substances that contribute hydrogen ions make better electrolytes than organic compounds such as sugars and starches."

In this case, the variable you will change is the material you use as an electrolyte, and the variable you will measure is the resistance of the solution. You expect acids, such as vinegar and lemon juice, will have lower resistance than sugars and starches and are therefore better electrolytes.

What Are the Variables?

Variables are anything that might affect the results of an experiment. Here are the main variables in this experiment:

- the substances being tested for conductivity
- the concentration of the solutions
- the distance between the probes placed in the solutions

In other words, the variables in this experiment are everything that might affect conductivity. If you change more than one variable, you will not be able to tell which variable had the most effect on conductivity.

Level of Difficulty Moderate.

Materials Needed

- 6 wide-mouth glass jars
- distilled water
- salt
- sugar
- cornstarch
- vinegar
- lemon juice
- adhesive labels or strips of masking tape
- voltmeter (most electronics supply stores carry these)
- measuring spoons
- stirrer

Approximate Budget $30. (An inexpensive, analog voltmeter will suffice. Try to borrow one from school to reduce costs.)

Timetable Less than 1 hour.

Step-by-Step Instructions

1. Pour 0.5 cup (0.125 liter) of distilled water in a jar. Add 1 tablespoon of salt and stir.

A voltmeter is used to measure the flow of current in a circuit. PHOTO RESEARCHERS INC.

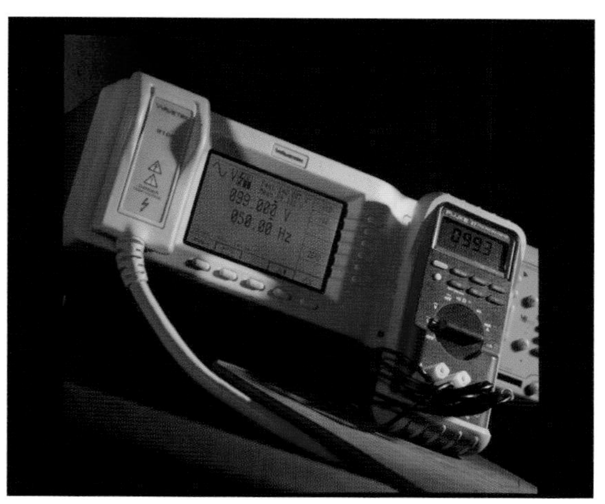

How to Experiment Safely

The battery in the voltmeter (usually one AA-cell) will provide all the voltage you will need for this experiment. Do not try to add batteries to the experiment, and NEVER experiment with household current or car batteries. Both are dangerous and potentially life-threatening. If you choose to test other substances for conductivity, check with your science teacher to make sure you are not testing materials that will create a hazard (such as flammable liquids).

2. Label the jar with the name of the substance on an adhesive label or strip of masking tape.
3. Rinse your measuring spoon and stirrer thoroughly in distilled water and repeat steps 1 and 2, using the sugar in a second jar, and the cornstarch in a third jar.
4. Pour 0.5 cup (0.125 liter) of lemon juice into the fourth jar and 0.5 cup of vinegar into the fifth jar. The sixth jar will contain only 0.5 cup (0.125 liter) of distilled water. Remember to label each jar, and rinse your measuring spoons and stirrers in distilled water after each mixture is prepared.
5. Place the glass jars so that the labels are visible. (Your set-up should look like the illustration.)
6. Set your voltmeter to measure resistance. Resistance is the measure of how much a circuit reduces the flow of electricity. With the probes touching, the voltmeter should read zero because there is no resistance, and all of the current is getting through. When you

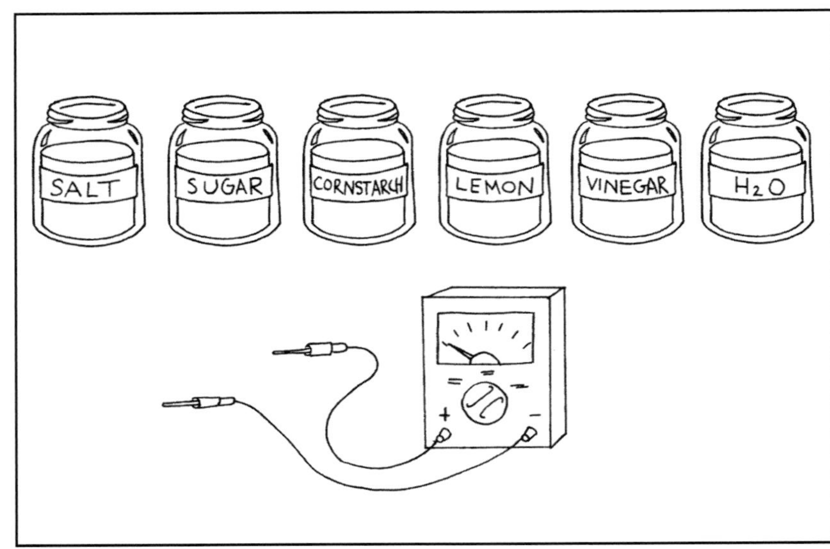

Steps 1 to 5: Electrolyte set-up. GALE GROUP.

separate the probes, the meter goes to the other end of the scale and reads "infinity" because none of the current is getting through. To test something for measurable resistance, wet your fingertip and place the probes on it, just barely separated. The meter reading should shift slightly away from infinite resistance because a small current is flowing across your fingertip. If you are unsure how to set your voltmeter for resistance or which scale indicates resistance, check the meter's instruction manual.

7. When testing the various substances, you must be sure that the voltmeter probes do not touch and that they remain at the same distance from each other for each test. (Otherwise you are adding another variable to your experiment.) Tape the probes together as illustrated. If necessary, place a ball of tape between the probe grips. Do not tape the metal part of the probes! The distance between the probe tips should be about 0.5 inch (1.25 centimeter).
8. Dip the electrodes into the first solution and observe the resistance reading on the voltmeter. Record your data, rinse the probes with distilled water, and repeat this step with each jar.

Troubleshooter's Guide

This experiment requires careful attention when setting up your solutions and preparing the probes. Failing to wash a measuring spoon or allowing the probes to touch will alter your results. Here is a problem that may arise during the experiment, some possible causes, and some ways to remedy the problem.

Problem: The voltmeter is giving inconsistent readings or no readings.

Possible causes:

1. The voltmeter is not set properly to measure resistance. Check the instruction manual.
2. Your probe tips are too close to each other. Separate them and try again.
3. You have tape connecting the metal sections of the meter's probes.
4. The probe connections to the voltmeter are loose. Press the connections firmly into the voltmeter.

Summary of Results Compare your data from the six different tests. Determine which of the substances are electrolytes and which are not. Rank them from strongest to weakest.

Check your findings against the predictions you made in your hypothesis. Which substances did you accurately predict would be electrolytes? Which substances did not behave as you expected?

Step 7: Probe tip set-up. GALE GROUP.

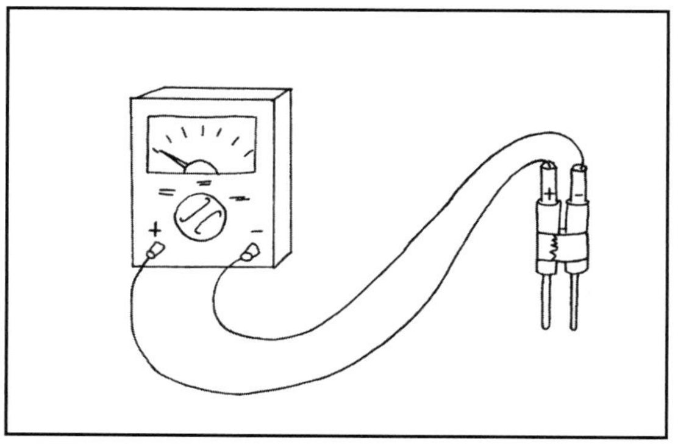

What Are the Variables?

Variables are anything that might affect the results of an experiment. Here are the main variables in this experiment:

- the type of electrolyte used
- the metals used as electrodes
- the type and gauge (diameter) of wire used
- the number of cells placed in series

In other words, the variables in this experiment are everything that might affect the output voltage of your multiple-cell battery. If you change more than one variable, you will not be able to tell which variable had the most effect on the voltage.

Change the Variables Think about the other variables you might change to investigate electrolytes. How would combining two electrolytes affect the results? Would lowering or raising the temperature of a solution affect conductivity? Remember to check with your science teacher before heating or mixing substances. Does adding more of an electrolyte to a solution increase the conductivity? A number of interesting follow-up experiments can be performed using the same materials and methods.

EXPERIMENT 2

Batteries: Can a series of homemade electric cells form a "pile" strong enough to match the voltage of a D-cell battery?

Purpose/Hypothesis In this experiment, you will construct a cell from copper and zinc electrodes and a lemon. The lemon contains citric acid, which is a weak electrolyte. After measuring the voltage of that one cell, you will add more cells to the pile to attempt to match the voltage of a D-cell battery. Before you begin, make an educated guess about the outcome of this experiment based on your knowledge of batteries. This educated guess, or prediction, is your hypothesis. A hypothesis should explain these things:

- the topic of the experiment
- the variable you will change
- the variable you will measure
- what you expect to happen

A hypothesis should be brief, specific, and measurable. It must be something you can test through observation. Your experiment will prove or disprove whether your hypothesis is correct. Here is one possible hypothesis for this experiment: "A multicell battery constructed of zinc, copper, and lemons can equal the voltage output of a D-cell battery."

In this case, the variable you will change is the number of cells you place in series, and the variable you will measure is the output voltage. You expect that it is possible to equal the output voltage of a D-cell battery.

How to Experiment Safely

Do not change the number or type of battery used in this experiment without first consulting your science teacher. NEVER experiment with household current or car batteries! Both are dangerous and potentially life-threatening.

Level of Difficulty Easy/moderate.

Materials Needed

- 10 lemons
- 10 copper nails (available at most hardware stores)
- 10 small zinc or zinc-plated nails or screws (available at most hardware stores)
- 10 feet (3 meters) of small diameter insulated copper wire
- fresh D-cell battery
- small flashlight bulb
- voltmeter with alligator-clip probes

Approximate Budget $30. (An inexpensive analog voltmeter will suffice. Try to borrow one from school to reduce costs.)

Timetable About 20 minutes.

Step-by-Step Instructions

1. Cut one 6-inch (15-centimeter) length of wire and strip the insulation off both ends.
2. Wind one end of the wire securely around a copper nail and push the copper nail into a lemon.
3. Cut a second 6-inch (15-centimeter) length of wire, strip the insulation of both ends, and wind one end around a zinc nail.
4. Roll and squeeze the lemons to loosen the juices. Push the zinc nail into the lemon about 1 inch (2.5 centimeters) from the copper nail. Be sure the two nails are not touching, either outside or inside the

Step 4: A lemon cell. GALE GROUP.

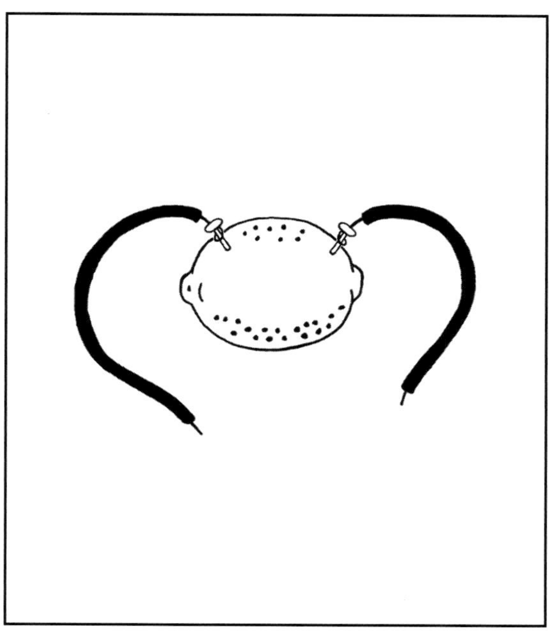

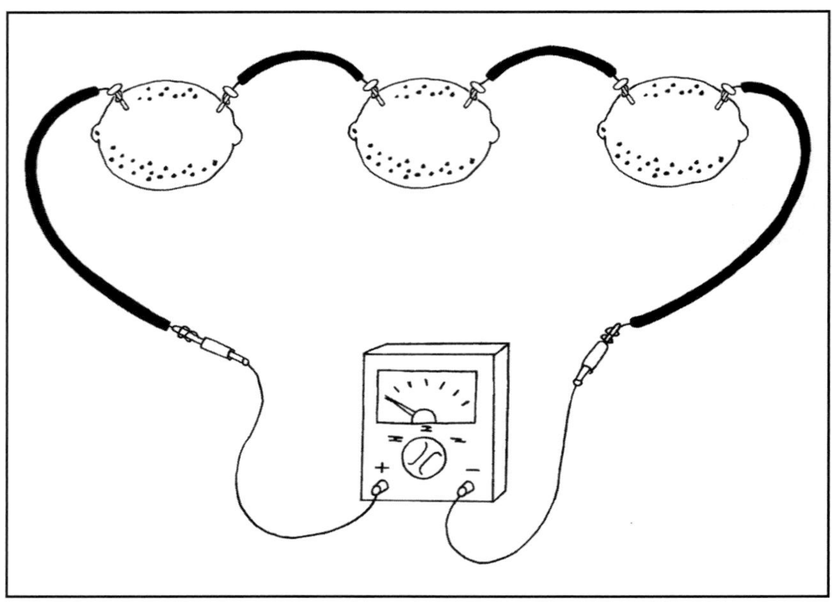

Step 8: Lemon multicell battery. GALE GROUP.

lemon, and avoid wetting the wire with lemon juice. Your cell should look like the illustration.

5. Set the voltmeter to measure direct current (DC) voltage. Connect the voltmeter to your cell by attaching one of the meter's alligator clips to each of the two loose wire ends. Observe and make note of the voltage of your cell.
6. Disconnect the voltmeter and use it to test the voltage of your D-cell battery by touching the probes to the positive and negative terminals of the cell. Make note of the voltage.
7. Calculate the minimum number of homemade lemon cells that would be needed to match the voltage of the D-cell battery. Do not be surprised if it is more lemons than you expected. That is one reason we do not power our flashlights with lemons!
8. Build as many lemon cells as needed and connect them in a series, as illustrated.

Steps 8 and 9: Sample voltage chart. GALE GROUP.

Voltage Chart

Number of lemons	Total voltage output	Powers flaslight?
1		
2		
3		
4		
5		
6		
7		
8		
9		
10		

Check the total voltage output of the "pile" after each lemon is added and make a note of the measurement on your data chart (see illustration). Remember the lemons must be connected properly, positive terminal (copper) to negative terminal (zinc). Your multicell battery should look something like the illustration.

9. After your battery is complete, test its voltage by touching the meter's probes to the loose wire ends. Because some current can be lost due to resistance in the wires and connections, you may need to add another lemon or two to match the D-cell's voltage. After your battery is powerful enough, connect the loose wire ends to the flashlight bulb—one wire to the bottom of the metal base and one to the side of the base. If your voltage reading is correct, it should light with the same intensity as when connected to the D-cell.
10. Examine your results and determine whether your hypothesis is true. If it is, you might connect both the lemon battery and the D-cell to flashlight bulbs to demonstrate the proof of your findings.

Summary of Results Write a summary of your findings. Your data from Steps 8 and 9 should be recorded on a chart. This chart should contain the information that will show whether your hypothesis is correct. You can increase the clarity of your results by converting the data into graph form.

Change the Variables Think about the other variables you might change to investigate other questions about electrolytes and batteries. Can you increase the output of a lemon cell by using

Troubleshooter's Guide

This experiment involves a number of electrical connections that may need to be checked and rechecked to ensure that they are not loose. When you are doing experiments in electricity, the results can easily be affected by inexact assembly of your circuit. Many hobby stores carry some simple tools, such as battery holders, that will make experiments easier and more visually impressive. Here are some problems that may arise during your experiment, some possible causes, and some ways to remedy the problems.

Problem: The first lemon cell shows no voltage on the voltmeter.

Possible causes:

1. The voltmeter may be calibrated incorrectly. Check it by testing the D-cell. (Its voltage is printed on the battery case.)
2. The electrodes are placed too far apart or are touching. Remove and check the electrodes.
3. A connection is loose. Check all your connections and secure them with electrical tape if necessary.

Problem: The lemon cells connected together do not increase the total voltage as expected.

Possible causes:

1. Resistance in the wires is reducing voltage output. Shorten the length of the wires. Check that the bare wire ends are tightly wrapped around the nails.
2. The electrodes are placed too far apart or are inserted incorrectly. Check your electrodes.
3. Your hypothesis is incorrect. Your materials may not be sufficient to generate the voltage required. Consider what changes you could make to the electrodes and the electrolyte.

How to Experiment Safely

Have an adult helper assist you with connecting the alligator clips to the 6-volt battery. Make sure the negative and positive wires do not touch one another.

different metals? Would lemon juice in a glass jar work more efficiently than an actual lemon? How much current could you produce with a Volta pile instead of a lemon cell? (A simple Volta pile can be constructed using nickels, pennies, and an electrolyte-soaked paper towel.) After you know how to make a cell and measure its output, you can construct a number of interesting experiments comparing their output.

PROJECT 3

Electroplating: Using electricity to move one metal onto another metal

Purpose/Hypothesis In this project, you will use electroplating to coat a layer of copper onto a quarter. (A quarter is a mixture of copper and nickel.) Electroplating needs an electric current. You can generate an electric current using a battery, wires, and an electrolyte solution.

The metal that will be coated, the quarter, is attached to the negative terminal of the battery. The copper is attached to the positive battery terminal. Both metals are placed in the solution. The electrolyte solution contains vinegar, which helps dissolve the copper. It also contains salt, which contains a positive charge and is attracted to the negatively-charged quarter. The electrical current will move the particles of the copper through the solution and plate them onto the quarter.

Step 3: Attach the strip of copper to the alligator clip that is attached to the positive terminal. ILLUSTRATION BY TEMAH NELSON.

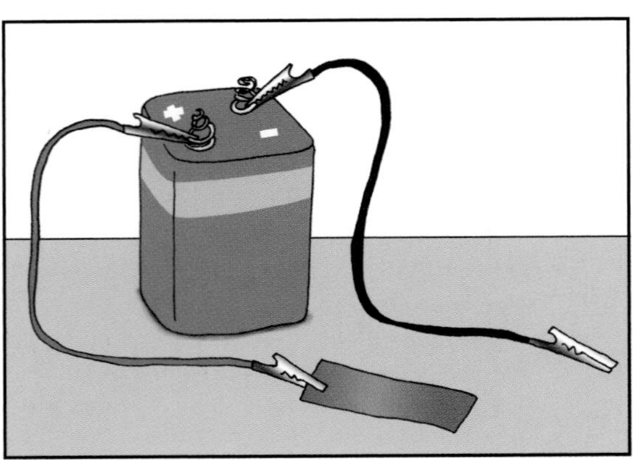

Level of Difficulty Moderate.

Materials Needed

- 1 6-volt battery (available from hardware stores)
- 2 alligator clips
- thin strip of copper, about 1 by 3 inches, such as copper flashing or sheets (available from hardware or craft stores)
- tin snips or scissors to cut copper if needed
- 1quarter
- small plastic container

- dishwashing soap
- 1 cup of white vinegar
- a pinch of Epsom salt

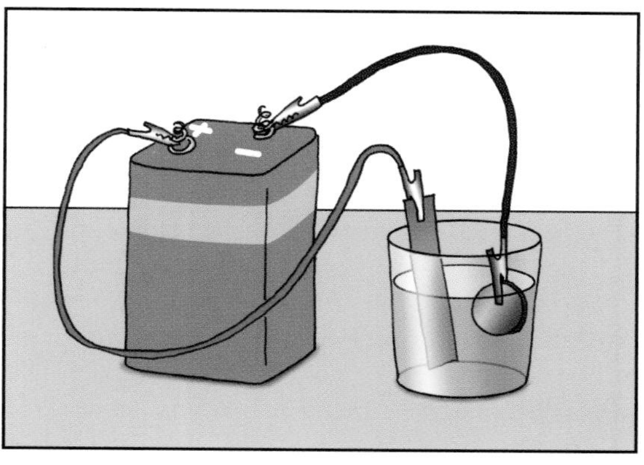

Step 5: Place the copper strip and the quarter into the cup with vinegar solution. ILLUSTRATION BY TEMAH NELSON.

Approximate Budget $15.

Timetable 1 hour and 15 minutes.

Step-by-Step Instructions

1. In a small plastic container stir together 1 cup of vinegar and a pinch of salt until the salt is dissolved.
2. Attach one alligator clip to the positive battery terminal and one alligator clip to the negative side. Keep the clips separated from one another.
3. Attach the strip of copper to the alligator clip that is attached to the positive terminal. (You may need to use snips to cut the piece of copper into a strip that will fit in the cup.) Only some of the copper needs to be immersed in the solution.
4. Wash the quarter with dishwashing soap, rinse, and dry. Attach the quarter to the alligator clip attached to the negative terminal.
5. Continuing to keep both clips separate, place the copper strip and the quarter into the cup with vinegar solution, making sure that they do not touch one another. The solution does not need to cover all the copper.
6. Observe and record the changes to the quarter, the copper and the vinegar solution over the course of an hour. Disconnect the clips from the battery and remove the metals from the solution.

Step 6: Disconnect the clips from the battery and remove the metals from the solution. ILLUSTRATION BY TEMAH NELSON.

Summary of Results Take another clean quarter and compare it to the electroplated quarter. How did the quarter and copper change over the course of an hour? Try to scrape the copper plating off of the quarter. Does the copper come off? What color is the electrolyte solution? Write a summary of your findings. You may want to include drawings of the metals.

Troubleshooter's Guide

This experiment involves several electrical connections that may need to be checked and rechecked to ensure that they are not loose. When you are doing experiments in electricity, the results can easily be affected by loose connections in a circuit. Here are some problems that may arise during your experiment, some possible causes, and some ways to remedy the problems.

Problem: The quarter does not change color

Possible causes:

1. The alligator clips may not be properly attached to the battery, check to make sure they are secure and repeat the experiment.
2. The quarter may be attached to the positive terminal on the battery, make sure that it is attached to the negative terminal.

Problem: The quarter has a black residue on it.

Possible cause: The black residue could be an indicator of too much salt in the solution. Make sure there is just a pinch of salt in the vinegar solution, and try the experiment again.

Design Your Own Experiment

How to Select a Topic Relating to this Concept Our everyday lives rely heavily upon batteries and electricity. Other aspects of this topic you might find valuable for exploration are rechargeable cells, photovoltaic cells, and the relationship between electrolytes and our bodies' functions.

Check the Further Readings section and talk with your science teacher or school or community media specialist to start gathering information on electricity questions that interest you. Electricity and electric currents can be dangerous. Before you conduct an electricity experiment or project, always check with an adult.

Steps in the Scientific Method To do an original experiment, you need to plan carefully and think things through. Otherwise, you might not be sure what question you are answering, what you are or should be measuring, or what your findings prove or disprove.

Here are the steps in designing an experiment:

- State the purpose of—and the underlying question behind—the experiment you propose to do.
- Recognize the variables involved, and select one that will help you answer the question at hand.
- State a testable hypothesis, an educated guess about the answer to your question.
- Decide how to change the variable you selected.
- Decide how to measure your results.

Recording Data and Summarizing the Results In the experiments included here and in any experiments you develop, you can look for ways to make your data displays more accurate and interesting. For example, in the lemon experiment, try displaying the data from your chart in graph form.

Remember that those who view your results may not have seen the experiment performed, so you must present the information you have gathered in as clear a way as possible. Including photographs or illustrations of the steps in the experiment is a good way to show a viewer how you got from your hypothesis to your conclusion.

Related Projects Simple variations on the experiments and project in this section can prove valuable and informative. Some solids, for example, will act as electrolytes when melted. Find out which. Will an electrolytic solution work as efficiently when it is chilled in an ice bath? Figure out why or why not.

For More Information

Andrew Rader Studios. "Electricity and Magnetism." *Rader's Physics4kids.com.* http://www.physics4kids.com/files/elec_intro.html (accessed on February 9, 2008). Basic information on electricity and magnetism.

Energy Information Administration. "Electricity: A Secondary Energy Source." *Energy Kid's Page.* http://www.eia.doe.gov/kids/energyfacts/sources/electricity.html (accessed on February 12, 2008). Explanation of electricity includes information on static electricity.

Macaulay, David, and Neil Ardley. *The New Way Things Work.* Boston: Houghton Mifflin, 1998. Detailed description of how machines work, including those that use electricity and magnetism.

McKeever, Susan, ed. *The DK Science Encyclopedia.* New York: DK Publishing, Inc., 1993. Contains informative entries on current, batteries, and circuits, as well as a number of good ideas for projects and demonstrations.

Ray, C. Claibourne. *The New York Times Book of Science Questions and Answers.* New York: Doubleday, 1997. Addresses both everyday observations and advanced scientific concepts on a wide variety of subjects.

27

Electromagnetism

Electromagnetism is the energy produced by an electric current moving through a metal core. To understand electromagnetism, you need to understand the basics of electricity.

What is electricity? Electricity is produced by the movement of electrons. Atoms usually have a balanced or neutral electrical charge, with an equal number of electrons (with a negative charge) and protons (with a positive charge). However, some electrons can be removed from atoms, creating an imbalance. The atoms that lost electrons become positively charged, while the atoms that received electrons become negatively charged.

When the charge between two objects is unbalanced, the extra electrons on the negatively charged object are drawn toward the positively charged object in order to balance the charges again. This movement of electrons is electricity.

How can electricity create a magnet? Objects with like charges (positive-positive or negative-negative) repel or push each other away,

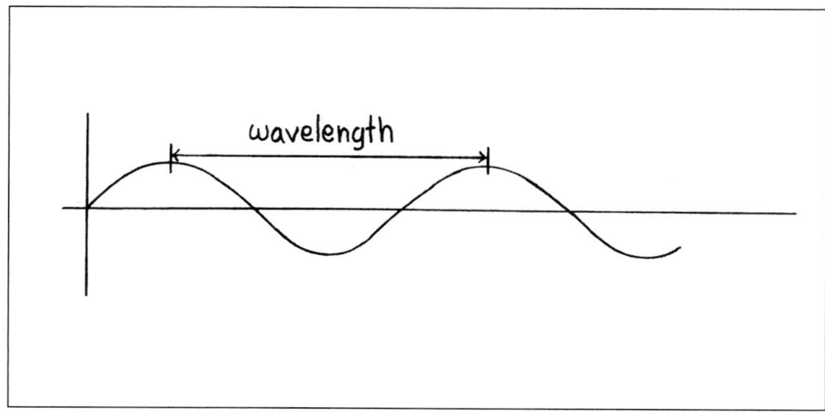

The electromagnetic wavelength is the distance between the wave's highest points, or peaks. GALE GROUP.

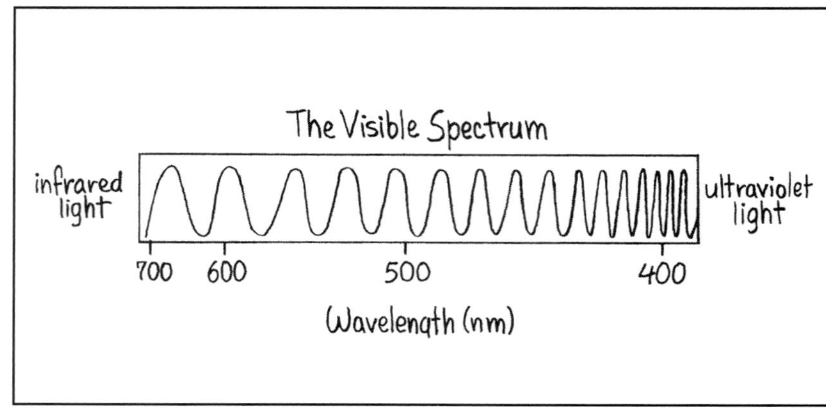

The electromagnetic spectrum. GALE GROUP.

while objects with opposite charges (positive-negative) attract each other. A magnetic field can be produced by using electric charges to create attracting or repelling forces. For example, scientists discovered that when a wire is coiled around a piece of iron, and electric current flows through the wire, the iron becomes magnetized—an electromagnet.

Electromagnetic waves are everywhere When the force of a magnetic field alternates direction, first attracting and then repelling, it produces an electromagnetic wave that radiates away from the source. A wave of any kind can be described by two numbers: its wavelength and its frequency. The wavelength is the distance between the wave's highest points, or peaks. The frequency is the number of those peaks that pass any point every second. Like other kinds of waves, electromagnetic waves carry energy at different frequencies, from very low (such as radio waves) to very high (such as gamma rays). X-rays, microwaves, and visible light are all kinds of electromagnetic radiation. The electromagnetic spectrum contains all these frequencies.

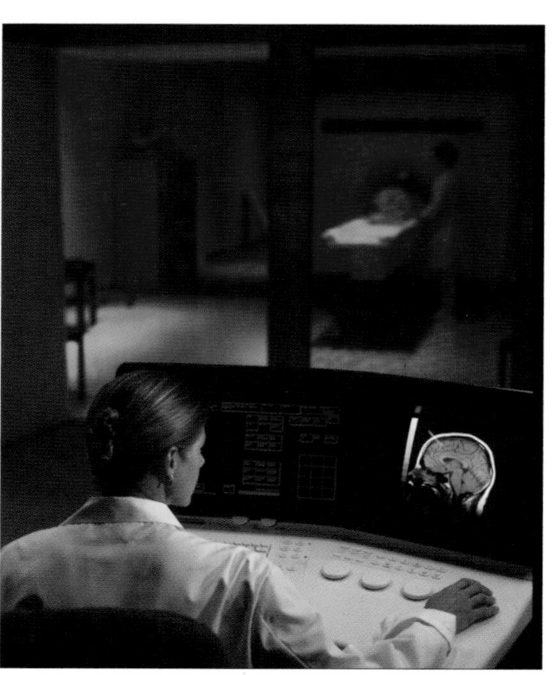

A magnetic resonance imaging (MRI) machine uses electricity and magnetism to create clear pictures of internal organs. PHOTO RESEARCHERS INC.

The study of electromagnetism is the study of the relationship between electricity and magnetism. The principles behind electromagnetism are used in electric motors and generators, televisions, diagnosis of illnesses, and in many other parts of our lives.

WORDS TO KNOW

Atom: The smallest unit of an element, made up of protons and neutrons in a central nucleus surrounded by moving electrons.

Control experiment: A set-up that is identical to the experiment but is not affected by the variable that will be changed during the experiment.

Electricity: A form of energy caused by the presence of electrical charges in matter.

Electromagnetic spectrum: The complete array of electromagnetic radiation, including radio waves (at the longest-wavelength end), microwaves, infrared radiation, visible light, ultraviolet radiation, X rays, and gamma rays (at the shortest-wavelength end).

Electron: A subatomic particle with a single negative electrical change that orbits the nucleus of an atom.

Electromagnetism: A form of magnetic energy produced by the flow of an electric current through a metal core.

Frequency: The number of times a wave peak passes a given point every second.

Hypothesis: An idea in the form of a statement that can be tested by observation and/or experiment.

Magnet: A material that attracts other like materials, especially metals.

Magnetic field: An area around a magnet where magnetic forces act.

Peaks: The points at which the energy in a wave is maximum.

Proton: A subatomic particle with a single negative electrical change that is found in the nucleus of an atom.

Radiation: Energy transmitted in the form of electromagnetic waves or subatomic particles.

Wave: A means of transmitting energy in which the peak energy occurs at a regular interval.

Wavelength: The distance between the peak of a wave of light, heat, or other form of energy and the next corresponding peak.

Variable: Something that can affect the results of an experiment.

Exploring with magnets and electricity can be fascinating. Do you have questions about electromagnetism? You might be able to answer them by performing the following experiments.

EXPERIMENT 1

Magnetism: How can a magnetic field be created and detected?

Purpose/Hypothesis In this experiment, you will demonstrate the relationship between electricity and magnetism and create and detect magnetic fields. Magnetic fields are all around us and are easy to create. Before you begin, make an educated guess about the outcome of this experiment based

What Are the Variables?

Variables are anything that might affect the results of an experiment. Here are the main variables in this experiment:

- the direction of the wire
- the magnetization of the needle
- the direction of the current

In other words, the variables in this experiment are everything that might affect the movement of the needle. If you change more than one variable, you will not be able to tell which variable had the most effect on the movement of the needle.

on your knowledge of electricity and magnetism. This educated guess, or prediction, is your hypothesis. A hypothesis should explain these things:

- the topic of the experiment
- the variable you will change
- the variable you will measure
- what you expect to happen

A hypothesis should be brief, specific, and measurable. It must be something you can test through observation. Your experiment will prove or disprove whether your hypothesis is correct. Here is one possible hypothesis for this experiment: "A magnetized needle will point perpendicularly through a charged wire, showing where the magnetic field produced by the wire lies."

In this case, the variable you will change will be the magnetism of the needle, and the variable you will measure will be the movement of the needle. You expect the needle to be perpendicular to the wire.

Setting up a control experiment will help you isolate one variable. Only one variable will change between the control and the experimental condition, and that will be the magnetization of the needle. For the control, you will not magnetize the needle. Then you will be able to compare the movement of a magnetized and unmagnetized needle. If only the magnetized needle points perpendicular to the wire, your hypothesis will be supported.

How to Experiment Safely

Any time you are experimenting with electricity, follow the directions exactly. The levels of electricity here are very low and cannot really hurt you, but electricity can always give you a shock if you are not extremely careful. Handle only wires covered with insulation, keep water away from the experiment, and keep your hands dry as you work. Do not use a vehicle battery. It is much too powerful and can cause a serious shock, or may even explode.

Level of Difficulty Moderate.

Materials Needed

- approximately 8 feet (2.4 meters) of 18-to 24-gauge insulated wire
- 2 metal sewing needles
- thread
- permanent magnet
- 6-volt lantern battery
- tape
- paper
- scissors

Approximate Budget $20.

Timetable 2 hours.

Step-by-Step Instructions

1. Magnetize the needle: Rub one side of the permanent magnet against the needle at least 30 times, always in the same direction.
2. Cut the paper into the shape of an arrow and stick the magnetized needle into the arrow lengthwise as illustrated.
3. Tape the thread to the top edge of the arrow.
4. Make a loop of wire about 3 inches (7.5 centimeters) in diameter. Continue to wrap the wire around this original loop, making a coil of five loops. Leave a length of wire free at either end.
5. Use the thread to tie the wire loops together tightly.
6. Then tie your paper arrow to the top of the loop. It should hang freely in the center of the loop.
7. Attach one end of the wire to each terminal of your battery—one to the positive terminal and one to the negative terminal.
8. Carefully observe the paper arrow.
9. Move the wire loop in different directions and watch what happens to the arrow.
10. Repeat the procedure with the other needle, but without magnetizing it. What do you observe?

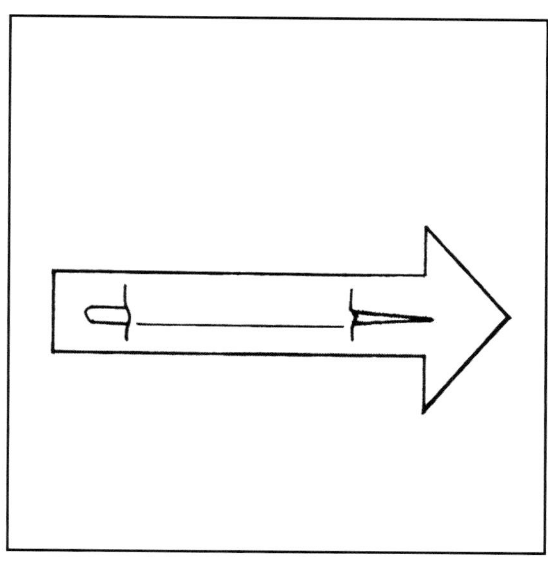

Step 2: Cut paper into the shape of an arrow and stick the magnetized needle into the arrow lengthwise. GALE GROUP.

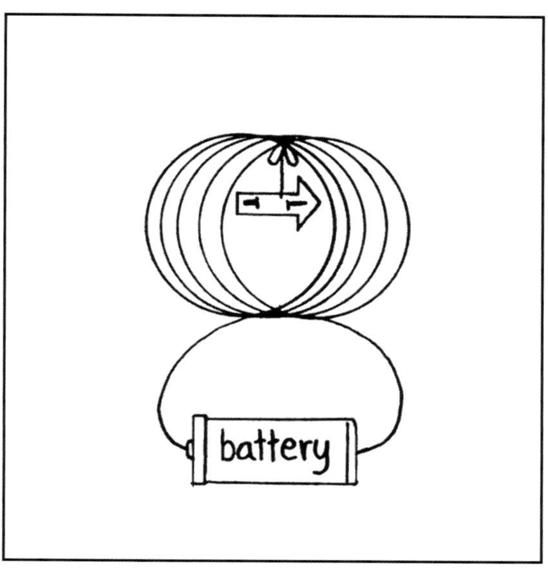

Steps 4 to 7: Wire loop set-up. GALE GROUP.

Summary of Results Record your observations. Where did the arrow point? What does that tell you about the location of the magnetic field produced by the electric current flowing through your wire loops? Was your hypothesis correct?

Change the Variables You can vary this experiment in several ways. Try reversing the direction

Troubleshooter's Guide

Here is a problem that may arise during this experiment, some possible causes, and ways to remedy the problem.

Problem: The arrow is not affected when the wire loop is attached to the battery.

Possible causes:

1. The wires are not tightly connected to the battery. Check your connections and try again.
2. Your needle is not magnetized well enough. Pull it out of the arrow and rub your magnet across it a number of times. Be sure to rub it in only one direction with only one pole of the magnet.
3. You do not have enough loops of wire. Try looping some more wire around your original loop.
4. Your battery is dead. Replace it and try again.

of the electric current by attaching the wires to the opposite terminals. Where does the arrow point now? You should find that the direction of the magnetic field depends on the direction of the electric current. You can also use different kinds of batteries with different voltages. See what effects they have on your magnetized needle, if any. Warning! Do not use a vehicle battery.

EXPERIMENT 2

Electromagnetism: How can an electromagnet be created?

Purpose/Hypothesis Electric currents create magnetic fields. When you increase the strength of the current, you increase the strength of the magnetic field. In this experiment, you will demonstrate this by building an electromagnet and observing the movement of electric charges. Before you begin, make an educated guess about the outcome of this experiment based on your knowledge of electricity and magnetism. This educated guess, or prediction, is your hypothesis. A hypothesis should explain these things:

- the topic of the experiment
- the variable you will change

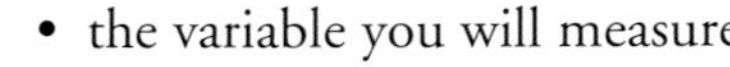

- the variable you will measure
- what you expect to happen

A hypothesis should be brief, specific, and measurable. It must be something you can test through observation. Your experiment will prove or disprove whether your hypothesis is correct. Here is one possible hypothesis for this experiment: "The more wire you wrap around a nail attached to a battery, the stronger the nail's magnetism and the more objects it can pick up."

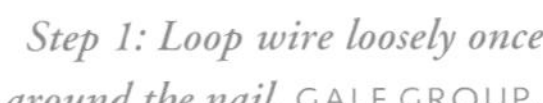

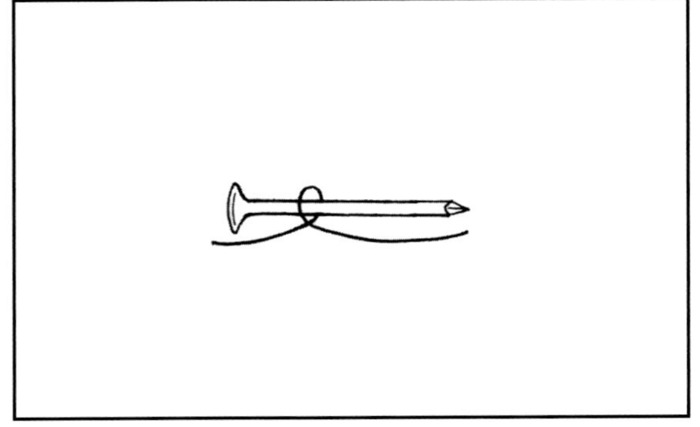

Step 1: Loop wire loosely once around the nail. GALE GROUP.

In this case, the variable you will change is the amount of wire wrapped around the nail, and the variable you will measure will be the number of objects it will pick up. You expect that by adding turns of wire you will be able to pick up more objects.

Level of Difficulty Easy.

Materials Needed

- several feet (about 1 meter) of insulated wire
- 6-volt lantern battery
- large nail or bolt
- permanent magnet
- supply of metal paper clips

Approximate Budget $20.

Timetable Two hours to build and test.

Step-by-Step Instructions

1. As your control experiment, loop the wire loosely once around the nail.
2. Attach either end of the large wire loop to the battery's terminals.
3. Place a pile of paper clips on the table.
4. Touch the nail to the paper clips. Record how many it picks up on a data sheet similar to the one illustrated.
5. Remove the nail and wire from the battery. Beginning at one end of the nail, wrap several tight loops around it, all in the same direction. Record the number of loops you wrap.
6. Again attach the end of the wire to the battery terminal. Touch the nail to the paper clips, and record how many stick to it.

What Are the Variables?

Variables are anything that might affect the results of an experiment. Here are the main variables in this experiment:

- the strength of the magnet
- the number of wire coils around nail
- the size of the nail
- the weight of the objects

In other words, the variables in this experiment are everything that might affect the number of objects that the electromagnet can pick up. If you change more than one variable, you will not be able to tell which variable had the most effect on the strength of the magnet.

Only one variable will change between the control experiment and the experimental condition, and that is the number of wire coils around the nail. The control will have only one wire coil.

You will count how many paper clips your magnet is able to pick up as you add coils. If increasing the number of coils increases the number of objects it can pick up, your hypothesis was supported.

How to Experiment Safely

As with any project dealing with electricity, be extremely careful with wires and batteries. Keep everything away from water and keep your hands clean and dry. Do not use a vehicle battery. It is much too powerful and can cause a serious shock or may even explode.

Troubleshooter's Guide

Below is a problem that may arise during this experiment, some possible causes, and ways to remedy the problem.

Problem: The electromagnet will not pick up any paper clips.

Possible causes:

1. The wire connections are not tight enough on the battery terminals. Check them and tighten.
2. You do not have enough loops around your nail. Try adding more in the same direction.
3. Your paper clips are too big for the strength of the magnet. Try using smaller paper clips or thumbtacks.
4. Your nail or bolt is dirty or not made of iron or steel. Try a different nail or bolt.

7. Wrap more wire loops in the same direction. Attach the wire to the battery again and try picking up clips.
8. Repeat several times with more loops every time. Keep recording how many loops you wrap around the nail and how many clips it picks up.

Summary of Results Study the results on your data sheet. Did more loops create a stronger magnetic field? How could you tell? Was your hypothesis correct? Summarize what you have discovered.

Change the Variables You can vary this experiment. For example, try using a different kind of material for your magnet, such as wood or plastic. What happens? What can you conclude? Or try a much larger or smaller metal object as a magnet. What is the effect on the number of objects that the magnet can pick up?

Data Sheet

# of coils	# of clips picked up
0	—
1	—
2	—
3	—

Step 4: Data sheet for Experiment 2. GALE GROUP.

You can also change the wire. Try thinner or thicker wire. What effect does that have on your magnetic field?

Try using different kinds of batteries, with smaller and larger voltages. What is your hypothesis about what will happen to the magnetic field? Warning! Do not use a vehicle battery.

Finally, you can experiment with different objects to pick up, smaller, larger, or made of different materials. What do you predict will happen?

Design Your Own Experiment

How to Select a Topic Relating to this Concept Are you interested in further exploring kinds of magnets, magnetic fields, and their relation to electric currents? Perhaps you would like to build your own electric motor, investigate static electricity, or explore how electromagnetism is used in generating electricity, computer memory, television images, and many other facets of electrical engineering.

Check the Further Readings section and talk with your science teacher or school or community media specialist to start gathering information on electromagnetism questions that interest you.

Steps in the Scientific Method To do an original experiment, you need to plan carefully and think things through. Otherwise you may not be sure what question you are answering, what you are or should be measuring, or what your findings prove or disprove.

Here are the steps in designing an experiment:

- State the purpose of—and the underlying question behind—the experiment you propose to do.
- Recognize the variables involved, and select one that will help you answer the question at hand.
- State a testable hypothesis, an educated guess about the answer to your question.
- Decide how to change the variable you selected.
- Decide how to measure your results.

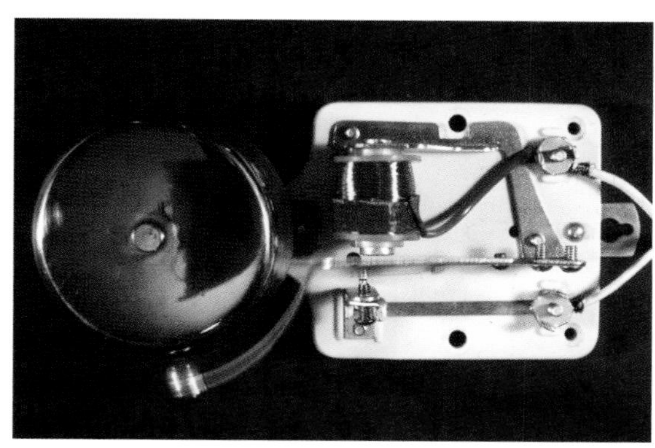

The electromagnet in this electric bell generates a current that activates the bell. PETER ARNOLD INC.

Recording Data and Summarizing the Results Your data should include charts, such as the one you did for these experiments. They should be

We depend on electric motors, which depend on electromagnetism. PETER ARNOLD INC.

clearly labeled and easy to read. You may also want to include photos, graphs, or drawings of your experimental set-up and results.

If you are preparing an exhibit, display the devices you create to help explain what you did and what you discovered. Observers could even test your magnets. If you have done a nonexperimental project, explain clearly what your research question was and illustrate your findings.

Related Projects In addition to experimental projects, you could build motors and large magnets that produce currents to light up a lamp or run an appliance. Or you could investigate the many uses of electromagnetism, especially the field of medicine. There are many possibilities!

For More Information

Andrew Rader Studios. "Moving Electrons." *Rader's Physics4kids.com.* http://www.physics4kids.com/files/elec_intro.html (accessed on January 13, 2008).

Steve, Parker. *Electricity and Magnetism.* Milwaukee, WI: Gareth Stevens Publishing, 2007.

Tomecek, Stephen M. *Electromagnetism, and How It Works.*New York: Chelsea House, 2007.

Whalley, Margaret. *Electricity and Magnetism.* Chicago: World Book, 1997. Introduces basic principles of electricity and magnetism through experiments and activities.

Wood, Robert, and Bill Wright. *Electricity and Magnetism Fundamentals: Funtastic Science Activities for Kids.* Philadelphia: Chelsea House Publishing, 1998. Through several different activities the relationship between electricity and magnetism is demonstrated.

28

Enzymes

You could not run a race or digest food without enzymes. Actually, you could not grow up without enzymes working in your body. Present in all living things, enzymes are catalysts, that is, little chemical spark plugs that activate some 1,000 to 2,000 reactions in each cell. Enzymes control the way our bodies work. They help other life forms function as well. For example, the silkworm cannot break out of its cocoon without enzymes.

A hunk of meat, a hawk, and a discovery Rene Antoine de Reaumur was a French scientist who wanted to know how food was digested. In 1750, he tried a unique experiment. Tying a very tiny metal cage containing a small piece of meat on a long string, he taught his pet hawk to swallow the cage. The string hung out of the bird's mouth, and de Reaumur very carefully pulled out the cage after 15 minutes without injuring the animal. The meat did not look the same. Its color was gone and it looked puffy and soft. He tried the experiment two more times, leaving the cage inside longer. The meat was totally soft after one hour, and after three it looked like lumpy soup. De Reaumur did not know he had witnessed the work of enzymes, but his experiments gave other scientists the first clue about their existence and function.

What's in a name? The word enzyme comes from two Greek words meaning "in yeast." German scientist Willy Kuhne came up with the term in 1876. Kuhne noticed that the yeast used to make bread acted as a catalyst, producing a chemical reaction. Once added to the dough in the bread-making process, yeast splits into sugar molecules. They, in turn, produce alcohol and carbon dioxide. Carbon dioxide gas bubbles trapped in the dough cause it to rise. Kuhne reasoned that yeast was a catalyst for this new chemical compound, so he used the word enzyme to describe other catalysts.

Based on the work of de Reaumur and others, Kuhne understood that digestive juices were also catalysts, because they caused a reaction that broke food down into a simpler form. Catalyst is actually a Swedish word that means "to break down."

Pepsin was the first enzyme prepared from animal tissue. Extracted from the lining of the stomach, it aids digestion. Pepsin is actually a Greek word meaning "to digest." Later it was discovered that enzymes could work outside the living cell, which made them more useful to scientists.

As simple as a lock and key There are thousands of different enzymes in each cell. Each enzyme is responsible for a single reaction within the cell, and the process works like a lock and key. As the key, each enzyme has a specific shape. It targets a specific substrate, the substance on which the enzyme does its work. This substrate, which matches the shape and size of the enzyme, is the lock. Each enzyme can only work with one substrate or, at most, a small number of chemically related substrates. After the substrate and enzyme come together, a new compound is activated and formed. The study of how an enzyme behaves is called enzymology.

Enzymes in yeast help make beer. CORBIS.

Yeast is the catalyst that caused this bread to rise. CORBIS CORPORATION.

Enzyme industry By-products of animals slaughtered for meat provide animal enzymes, but no animal is raised just for enzymes. Rennin, an enzyme in the stomach lining of slaughtered calves, is used to make cheese. Plants provide other enzymes. Papain, an enzyme from the fruit of the papaya tree, helps digestion. It also tenderizes meat and is used as an antibacterial cleaner for bad wounds. Enzymes are also chemically produced in factories.

Remember the yeast Kuhne observed? Yeast has an enzyme that not only helps to make bread but also activates the process of making beer and wine. The yeast is grown in large tanks. When it

WORDS TO KNOW

Catalase: An enzyme found in animal liver tissue that breaks down hydrogen peroxide into oxygen and water.

Catalyst: A compound that starts or speeds up the rate of a chemical reaction without undergoing any change in its own composition.

Control experiment: A set-up that is identical to the experiment but is not affected by the variable that affects the experimental group.

Decomposition: The breakdown of complex molecules into simple molecules.

Denaturization: Altering an enzyme so it no longer works.

Enzymes: Any of numerous complex proteins produced by living cells that act as catalysts.

Enzymology: The science of studying enzymes.

Hypothesis: An idea in the form of a statement that can be tested by observation and/or experiment.

Papain: An enzyme obtained from the fruit of the papaya used as a meat tenderizer, as a drug to clean cuts and wounds, and as a digestive aid for stomach disorders.

Pepsin: Digestive enzyme that breaks down protein.

Protein: A complex substance consisting of a long chain of molecules linked together. It is produced and used by living cells to perform various functions.

Reaction: Response to an action prompted by stimulus.

Rennin: Enzyme used in making cheese.

Substrate: The substance on which an enzyme operates in a chemical reaction.

Variable: Anything that might affect the results of an experiment.

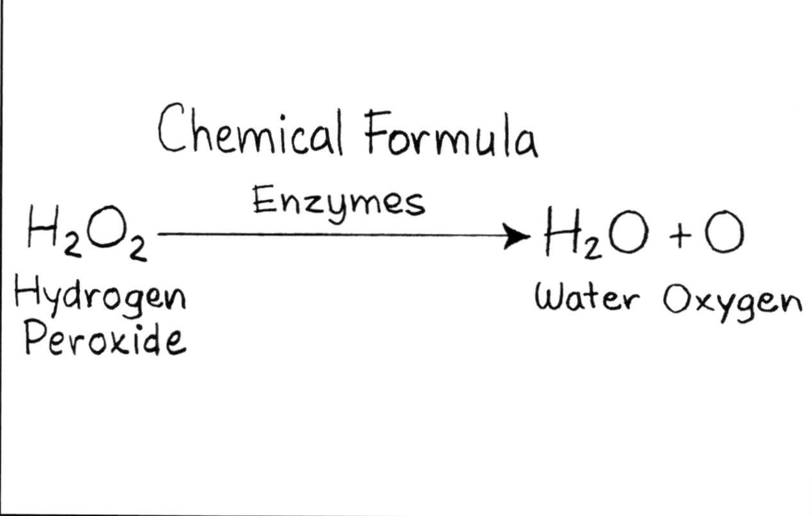

Chemical formula showing hydrogen peroxide broken down by enzymes into water and oxygen. GALE GROUP.

What Are the Variables?

Variables are anything that might affect the results of an experiment. Here are the main variables in this experiment:

- Tissue freshness—use only fresh, raw materials, nothing cooked or frozen.
- Tissue temperature—all materials should be at room temperature.
- Tissue quantity—this experiment will tell you how much plant and animal tissue is to be used and how to process it.

In other words, the variables in this experiment are everything that might affect the chemical reaction of the materials with the hydrogen peroxide. If you change more than one variable, you will not be able to tell which variable had the most effect on the chemical reaction. Alterations may change the rate of the reaction or result in the denaturization of the enzymes.

starts producing enzymes, they are removed. Other enzymes produced by bacteria are used in some laundry products to help break down stains.

Life processes cannot function without enzymes. Conducting experiments will help you become familiar with these important molecules.

EXPERIMENT 1

Finding the Enzyme: Which enzyme breaks down hydrogen peroxide?

Purpose/Hypothesis Without enzymes, many chemical reactions do not take place. In this experiment you will identify the presence of an enzyme in liver tissue, known as catalase, that breaks down highly reactive hydrogen peroxide into harmless water and oxygen. This is an important chemical reaction that takes place inside the body. Catalase prevents the potentially destructive oxidation effects of any hydrogen peroxide that may be generated in the body as the result of various other chemical reactions.

To begin this experiment, use what you know about enzymes to make an educated guess about how the enzymes in liver tissue will affect hydrogen peroxide. This educated guess, or prediction, is your hypothesis. A hypothesis should explain these things:

- the topic of the experiment
- the variable you will change
- the variable you will measure
- what you expect to happen

A hypothesis should be brief, specific, and measurable. It must be something you can test through observation. Your experiment will prove or disprove whether your hypothesis is correct. Here is one possible hypothesis for this experiment: "Animal liver tissue contains the enzyme that breaks down hydrogen peroxide."

In this case, the variable you will change is the material being tested, liver in one cup and potato in another cup, and the variable you will measure is the presence of oxygen bubbles. Your cup filled with water will serve as a control experiment to allow you to observe any oxygen bubbles that might be produced without the presence of hydrogen peroxide. If the liver sample reacts with hydrogen peroxide and produces oxygen bubbles and the water sample does not, you will know your hypothesis is correct.

How to Experiment Safely

Wear goggles when handling hydrogen peroxide. If you accidentally get some on your skin, wash it off quickly. Also be careful not to get it near your eyes, ears, nose, or mouth. You will be handling raw meat, so you must carefully wash all surfaces before and after the experiment. Do not eat the meat after the experiment.

Level of Difficulty Easy/moderate.

Materials Needed

- 1 small piece of liver—fresh, never frozen or cooked
- 1 potato—fresh, never frozen or cooked
- hydrogen peroxide
- 4 clear cups—plastic or glass
- knife
- spoon or lab spatula
- water
- goggles
- labels

	with water	with hydrogen peroxide
Liver		
Potato		

Sample recording chart for Experiment 1. GALE GROUP.

Troubleshooter's Guide

Here is a problem that may arise during this experiment, a possible cause, and a way to remedy the problem.

Problem: Nothing happened in any of the cups.

Possible cause: The materials may be too old. Check the freshness of the tissue samples as well as of the hydrogen peroxide. Hydrogen peroxide needs to be stored in a dark bottle and capped at all times.

Approximate Budget Less than $10 for hydrogen peroxide, potato, and liver.

Timetable Approximately 20 minutes.

Step-by-Step Instructions

1. Cut a 0.5-inch (1.25-centimeter) cube of liver and smash it into a paste using a spoon. Place it in a cup.
2. Smash another 0.5-inch (1.25-centimeter) cube of liver into a paste. Place it into a separate cup. (Don't forget to clean the spoon.)
3. Cut a 0.5-inch (1.25-centimeter) cube of potato and smash it. Place it in a separate cup.
4. Smash another 0.5-inch (1.25-centimeter) cube of potato and place it in the last cup.
5. Label the cups:
   a. Cup 1: Liver and water
   b. Cup 2: Liver and hydrogen peroxide
   c. Cup 3: Potato and water
   d. Cup 4: Potato and hydrogen peroxide

Steps 5 to 7: Set-up of control and test cups. GALE GROUP.

6. Fill cups 1 and 3 halfway with water. These will serve as your control experiment.
7. Fill cups 2 and 4 halfway with hydrogen peroxide. These will test which material has the enzyme.
8. Observe what takes place. If the enzyme for the breakdown of hydrogen peroxide is present, oxygen will form bubbles. When hydrogen peroxide breaks down, it separates into water and oxygen.
9. Record your results.

Summary of Results Make a chart like the one illustrated to show what you observed. Determine which tissue has the enzymes that cause the breakdown of the hydrogen peroxide into water and oxygen. Was it the tissue you predicted in your hypothesis?

Change the Variables You can change the variables and conduct a similar experiment. For example, place the pieces of liver and potato in the refrigerator to see if temperature affects the action of the enzyme.

What Are the Variables?

Variables are anything that might affect the results of an experiment. Here are the main variables in this experiment:

- the kind of meat—only beef from a steak or filet should be used.
- the type of tenderizer or enzyme—use the natural tenderizer extracted from the papaya fruit.
- the amount of tenderizer used.
- the temperature—the control and experimental meat must both be aged in the refrigerator.
- the amount of time the tenderizer is in place on the beef.

In other words, the variables in this experiment are everything that might affect the degree of decomposition of the beef. If you change more than one variable, you will not be able to tell which variable had the most effect on the decomposition process.

EXPERIMENT 2

Tough and Tender: Does papain speed up the aging process?

Purpose/Hypothesis This experiment deals with the aging process of beef. The older or more aged meat is, the softer the meat tends to be. This is a natural process of decomposition, the breakdown of organic matter. Beef can take weeks to become tender, but a natural tenderizer called papain can speed up the process. Papain is an enzyme extracted from the papaya fruit.

To begin the experiment, use what you know about enzymes to make an educated guess about how papain will affect the aging process of beef. This educated guess, or prediction, is your hypothesis. A hypothesis should explain these things:

- the topic of the experiment
- the variable you will change

How to Experiment Safely

In this experiment you will handle raw meat, so you must carefully wash all surfaces before and after the experiment. Do not eat the meat after the experiment. Be careful not to get meat tenderizer in your eyes.

- the variable you will measure
- what you expect to happen

A hypothesis should be brief, specific, and measurable. It must be something you can test through observation. Your experiment will prove or disprove whether you hypothesis is correct. Here is one possible hypothesis for this experiment: "Beef will age faster if it is sprinkled with papain."

In this case, the variable you will change is whether papain tenderizer is used on the beef, and the variable you will measure is the appearance of the meat after 24 hours. If the meat with the tenderizer is more decomposed, you will know your hypothesis is correct.

Level of Difficulty Easy/moderate.

Materials Needed

- beef from a steak or filet—8 to 10 ounces (230 to 250 grams) is sufficient
- Adolph's All Natural Tenderizer, a natural tenderizer made from papaya
- 2 plastic storage containers with lids

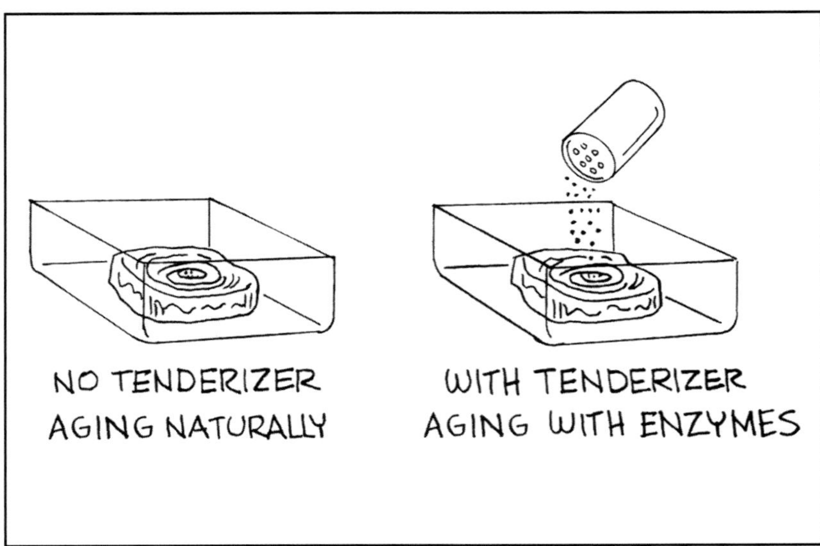

Step 2: Sprinkle about ½ teaspoon of meat tenderizer on one steak, leaving the other to age naturally. GALE GROUP.

- measuring spoons
- toothpicks
- slides
- microscope
- stain (optional—congo red or methalene blue)

Note: Do not add any additional solutions to the meat. For example, vinegar may stop the enzyme process.

Step 5: After the storage period, use a clean toothpick to scratch the surface of the meat without the tenderizer. GALE GROUP.

Approximate Budget About $15. (Price of beef will vary. You can borrow a microscope from a friend or use one in school.)

Timetable About 24 hours—10 minutes to set up the experiment and 30 minutes to view the results; the rest is storage time in the refrigerator.

Step-By-Step Instructions

1. In two plastic containers, place equal amounts of beef steak.
2. Sprinkle about ½ teaspoon of meat tenderizer on one steak.
3. Seal both containers and mark the lid of the container with the tenderized steak "Tenderizer."
4. Place both containers in the refrigerator and leave for 24 hours.
5. After the storage period, use a clean toothpick to scratch the surface of the meat without the tenderizer.

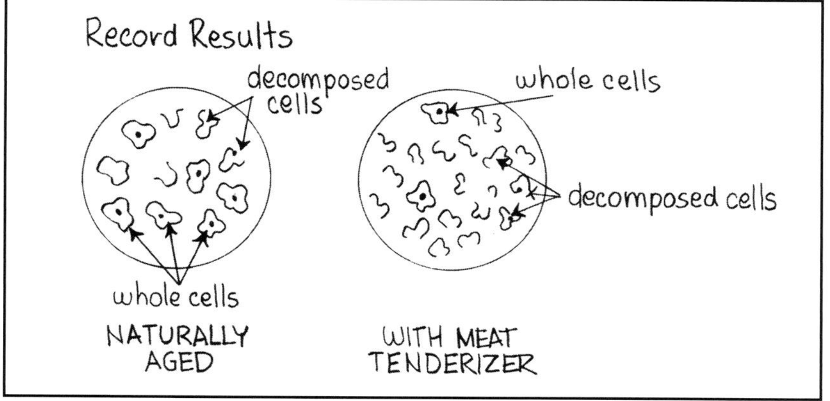

Step 7: Slide views of naturally aged and tenderized meat cells. GALE GROUP.

6. Wipe the toothpick onto a clean slide. (Add one drop of stain if you wish.)
7. View the slide under the microscope at 40 to 70 medium power. Record your results.
8. Repeat Steps 5 to 7 for the piece of meat with the tenderizer.

Troubleshooter's Guide

Here is a problem that may arise during this experiment, a possible cause, and a way to remedy the problem.

Problem: You cannot see a difference in decomposition.

Possible cause: Decomposition is not obvious at this point. Stain the cells. Cells that have not experienced decomposition have a nuclei inside. When decomposition takes place, the cell membrane is broken and the nucleus is released.

Summary of Results Reflect on your hypothesis. The goal was to cause an increase in decomposition of meat (speed up the aging process to make the meat tender). Was your hypothesis correct? This should be evident in large amounts of decayed cells. Is it true? Did more cells decay with tenderized meat? Write a summary of your findings.

Change the Variables You can change the variables and conduct similar experiments. For example, you can vary the amount of tenderizer used to see if that changes the degree of decomposition. You can also change the amount of time for the experiment to 36 or 48 hours.

EXPERIMENT 3

Stopping Enzymes: Does temperature affect enzyme action?

Purpose/Hypothesis Enzymes are a type of protein. And, like all proteins, enzymes function best at certain temperatures. If the temperature is too low or too high, the enzyme's structure can change and it will not be able to activate a reaction.

In this experiment, you will explore how temperature affects the activity of one particular enzyme. The enzyme you will use is bromelain, which is found in pineapple. Bromelain breaks down proteins. The protein you will use is gelatin. Gelatin is a form of protein called collagen that is found in our bones.

As you prepare the gelatin, you will add bromelain-rich pineapple juice, prepared at different temperatures. You will heat the bromelain and freeze the bromelain. Adding small items to the gelatin, such as peas, will help you measure the activity of the enzyme. You can determine if the

How to Experiment Safely

This experiment involves heating pineapple juice over a stove or hot plate. Have an adult present when heating the juice. Also, if the pineapple is purchased whole, have an adult cut the pineapple into chunks.

bromelain is active by measuring if the gelatin sets. If the gelatin remains in a liquid or partial liquid form, the proteins were broken apart and the food items will not sit firmly in the gelatin.

To begin the experiment, use what you know about enzymes to make an educated guess about how temperature will affect the activity of bromelain. This educated guess, or prediction, is your hypothesis. A hypothesis should explain these things:

- the topic of the experiment
- the variable you will change
- the variable you will measure
- what you expect to happen

A hypothesis should be brief, specific, and measurable. It must be something you can test through observation. Your experiment will prove or disprove whether you hypothesis is correct. Here is one possible hypothesis for this experiment: "Heating bromelain will cause it be inactive and allow the gelatin to set."

In this case, the variable you will change is the temperature the bromelain is prepared, and the variable you will measure is the appearance of the gelatin and placement of the added items. If the gelatin mixed with the heated bromelain becomes firm, then you will know your hypothesis is correct.

What Are the Variables?

Variables are anything that might affect the results of an experiment. Here are the main variables in this experiment:

- the kind of gelatin
- the amount of gelatin used
- the bromelain—use the bromelain from the same pineapple
- the amount of pineapple juice used
- the amount of time the gelatin is allowed to set

In other words, the variables in this experiment are everything that might affect the degree to which the gelatin sets. If you change more than one variable, you will not be able to tell which variable had the most effect on the gelling.

You will need two controls in this experiment. The first control is the gelatin by itself so that you can observe that it sets firmly. The second control is the gelatin mixed with pineapple juice that is prepared at room temperature. The pineapple juice gelatin will allow you to observe how temperature affects the bromelain in the experimental trials. If the heated pineapple juice sets similar to the gelatin without pineapple juice, than you will know your hypothesis is correct.

Level of Difficulty Moderate.

Materials Needed

- pineapple with skin removed and sealed in its juice; or 1 fresh pineapple (do not use canned or frozen pineapple)
- 4 glasses (they can be plastic)
- 3 small containers for the pineapple juice
- gelatin; enough to make 2 cups
- measuring cups and spoons
- marking tape and pen

Step 2: squeeze 4 tablespoons of pineapple juice into a small container. ILLUSTRATION BY TEMAH NELSON.

- hot plate or stove
- small pan
- 5 tablespoons of small, light food items, such as peas, corn, rice, blueberries or dried cranberries
- mixing spoon
- tablespoon
- freezer or cold water bath (ice cubs and a bowl)

Approximate Budget About $8, assuming all household items are available.

Timetable About two hours—six hours (including waiting time) to prepare and analyze the experiment; the rest is waiting time while the gelatin sets.

Step-By-Step Instructions

1. Label the four glasses: "Gelatin Control," "Gelatin Bromelain Control," "Hot Bromelain," "Cold Bromelain,"
2. Pour or squeeze 4 tablespoons of pineapple juice into a small container, label the container "Cold Bromelain."and place in the freezer. You could also place the container in a cold water bath (a container filled with ice cubes and cold water). Allow the juice to freeze for an hour.
3. While the bromelain is freezing, squeeze or pour 5 tablespoons of pineapple juice in a small pan and simmer for at least three minutes. You will need 4 tablespoons of pineapple juice after it has simmered. After three minutes, set the pan aside.
4. After one hour, take the juice out of the freezer and allow to come to room temperature.
5. While you are waiting, prepare 2 cups of the gelatin.

Step 9: In the glass labeled "Hot Bromelain," add 4 tablespoons of the pineapple juice that was heated. ILLUSTRATION BY TEMAH NELSON.

Step 14: When the control gelatin is firm, remove all the glasses from the refrigerator. Gently shake each of the glasses and note the results. ILLUSTRATION BY TEMAH NELSON.

6. Pour a half cup of gelatin into each of the four glasses. Remove 2 tablespoons of the gelatin from each of the glasses.
7. In the glass labeled "Gelatin Bromelain Control," mix in 4 tablespoons of room temperature pineapple juice. This is one of your controls.
8. In the glass labeled "Gelatin Control," mix in 4 tablespoons of water. This is your second control.
9. In the glass labeled "Hot Bromelain," add 4 tablespoons of the pineapple juice that was heated. Make sure to use a clean spoon.
10. In the glass labeled "Cold Bromelain," stir in the pineapple juice that was cooled.
11. Set all the containers in the refrigerator and check on them in about 30 minutes.
12. While the gelatin is in the refrigerator, prepare the food item you want to add. Make sure it is clean and dry. If you are adding blueberries, for example, they should be thawed and patted dry with a paper towel.
13. When the control gelatin, labeled "Gelatin," is thickened, add 1 tablespoon of the blueberries or whatever item you choose to all four of the gelatin glasses. Return them to the refrigerator and wait about another two hours.
14. When the control gelatin is firm, remove all the glasses from the refrigerator. Gently shake each of the glasses and note the results.

Summary of Results Shake each of the gelatin glasses gently. Is the gelatin that contained the heated bromelain less firm than the control gelatin

Troubleshooter's Guide

Here is a problem that may arise during this experiment, a possible cause, and a way to remedy the problem.

Problem: All of the gelatins became firm.

Possible cause: The pineapple you used may have been treated at some point, which may have deactivated the bromelain. Try the experiment again, and make sure to use fresh pineapple.

Problem: None of the gelatins became firm.

Possible cause: The time the gelatin takes to set depends on the temperature in the refrigerator. You may not have allowed enough time for the gelatins to set. Repeat the experiment, doubling the time in the refrigerator.

Possible cause: The gelatin you purchased may not be good. Buy another package of gelatin and repeat the experiment.

without bromelain? Was your hypothesis correct? Did freezing the bromelain make any difference? Look at where the blueberries (or whatever item you used) is sitting in the gelatin, compared to the control gelatins. Are they set in the gelatin or did more of them sink towards the bottom of the glass? In the gelatin made without bromelain, the blueberries should be firmly set in the gelatin. Which control do each of the two trials resemble more closely? You can draw your results and write a summary of your findings.

Change the Variables There are several ways that you can change the variables in this experiment. You can try to stop the enzyme activity by altering the acidity (the pH) of the enzyme. You can also change the amount of time the pineapple juice is heated or cooled. What happens if you heat and cool the juice multiple times? You can also try altering the enzyme or source of the enzyme. Bromelain is the main ingredient in many meat tenderizers. Laundry detergents contain different enzymes.

Design Your Own Experiment

How to Select A Topic Relating to this Concept Enzymes and the chemical reactions they produce are all around you. If you can identify one reaction, you have a start. Once you discover a chemical reaction, find out what is taking place. For example, the solid food you eat is turned into other substances by enzymes. What exactly are those enzymes? What do they do?

Check the Further Readings section and talk with your science teacher or school or community media specialist to start gathering information on enzyme questions that interest you. As you consider possible experiments, be sure to discuss them with your science teacher or another knowledgeable adult before trying them. Some of the materials or processes might be dangerous.

Steps in the Scientific Method To do an original experiment, you need to plan carefully and think things through. Otherwise, you might not be sure what question you are answering, what you are or should be measuring, or what your findings prove or disprove.

Here are the steps in designing an experiment:

- State the purpose of—and the underlying question behind—the experiment you propose to do.
- Recognize the variables involved, and select one that will help you answer the question at hand.
- State a testable hypothesis, an educated guess about the answer to your question.
- Decide how to change the variable you selected.
- Decide how to measure your results.

Recording Data and Summarizing the Results Photos, illustrations, and graphs are great visuals. Make clear the beginning question, the variable you changed, the variable you measured, the results, and your conclusion. Label everything clearly and show how it fits together.

Related Projects Try changing the conditions of the enzyme reactions. For example, add vinegar to the hydrogen peroxide. Or cook the liver and potato before testing.

For More Information

Brain, Marshall. "How Cells Work." *HowStuffWorks.* http://science.howstuffworks.com/cell2.htm (accessed on February 16, 2008). Explanation of how enzymes work in cells.

The Dorling Kindersley Science Encyclopedia. New York: Dorling Kindersley, Inc., 1993. Contains several well-illustrated chapters such as "Catalysts," "Digestion," and "Chemistry of the Body" that discuss enzymes.

Dr. Saul's Biology in Motion. *Enzyme Characteristics.* http://biologyinmotion.com/minilec/wrench. html (accessed on February 16, 2008). Brief explanation with interactive graphic of enzymes.

Lopez, D. A. *Enzymes: The Fountain of Life.* Neville Press, 1994. Provides examples of how enzymes make our bodies work.

29

Erosion

Soil erosion is the process by which topsoil is carried away by water, wind, or ice. Different types of soil have different abilities to absorb water, and so, are affected by erosion in varying degrees. Bare soil and soil on steep slopes are especially vulnerable to erosion.

Is erosion a new problem? Throughout history, people have been affected by soil erosion due to natural conditions, as well as erosion caused by their own actions. As long ago as 4500 B.C.E,, the Sumerians cleared land to grow food. They irrigated the land by building canals in the fertile valley where the Tigris and Euphrates rivers meet (in present-day Iraq). During the time of the Babylonian culture, which followed the Sumerians in about 1800 B.C.E., the people continued to dig canals. The rivers became muddy, and deposits of silt, medium-sized soil particles, settled in the irrigation canals and clogged them. The people had to carry silt out of the canals in baskets to keep the water flowing.

Over time, the people began to neglect the canals. As silt filled the valley, the land could support fewer and fewer people. About 700 years ago, the Babylonian canals were finally destroyed by the invasion of the Mongols, and the land returned to desert.

During the Dust Bowl, winds blew away as much as 3 to 4 inches (8 to 10 centimeters) of topsoil, ruining farmland. PHOTO RESEARCHERS INC.

Is erosion a problem in the United States? Not long ago, in the 1930s, North American prairies suffered from extreme wind erosion. During a period of high rainfall, large expanses of land were plowed to grow wheat. This period was followed by years of drought. The exposed soil of the fields was blown away in hot, dry wind storms. The blowing soil of the Dust Bowl, as it was called, blackened the skies, ruined crops, and left farm fields bare and unproductive.

WORDS TO KNOW

Control experiment: A set-up that is identical to the experiment but is not affected by the variable that affects the experimental group. Results from the control experiment are compared to results from the actual experiment.

Drought: A prolonged period of dry weather that damages crops or prevents their growth.

Ecosystem: An ecological community, including plants, animals, and microorganisms, considered together with their environment.

Erosion: The process by which topsoil is carried away by water, wind, or ice action.

Hypothesis: An idea in the form of a statement that can be tested by observation and/or experiment.

Inorganic: Not made of or coming from living things.

Organic: Made of or coming from living things.

Runoff: Water in excess of what can be absorbed by the ground.

Silt: Medium-sized soil particles.

Terracing: A series of horizontal ridges made in a hillside to reduce erosion.

Topsoil: The uppermost layers of soil containing an abundant supply of decomposed organic material to supply plants with nutrients.

Variable: Something that can affect the results of an experiment.

Today we often hear about erosion. Satellite images show red earth spilling into the ocean off the coast of the island of Madagascar. Here, and in many other places where people clear tropical forests and grow crops on hillsides, extremely high rates of erosion carry away massive quantities of topsoil.

On hillsides that no longer have tree roots to hold topsoil in place, rain easily carries the soil into the ocean. LIAISON AGENCY.

It is important to understand why erosion occurs and how humans both cause it and are affected by it. Erosion is something that concerns everyone. Erosion affects the places where we live and our sources of food and water. It also affects our recreation areas—trails, beaches, lakes, and rivers.

What kind of questions do you have about erosion? You'll have an opportunity to explore the erosion process in the following experiments. You will also think about designing your own experiments to learn more about this natural phenomenon and how it can have a huge impact on our lives.

EXPERIMENT 1

Erosion: Does soil type affect the amount of water that runs off a hillside?

Purpose/Hypothesis In this experiment, you will find out how the type of soil affects how much erosion can occur. Soil is a mixture of inorganic materials (rocks, sand, silt, or clay) and organic materials (decomposing leaves and organisms). The ratio of these components to each other determines the kind of soil and its texture. In turn, the texture of soil determines how well the soil can support plants and withstand erosion. Before you begin, make an educated guess about the outcome of this experiment based on your knowledge of soils and erosion. This educated guess, or prediction, is your hypothesis. A hypothesis should explain these things:

- the topic of the experiment
- the variable you will change
- the variable you will measure
- what you expect to happen

A hypothesis should be brief, specific, and measurable. It must be something you can test through observation. Your experiment will prove or disprove your hypothesis. Here is one possible hypothesis for this experiment: "The looser and coarser the texture of the soil, the less runoff and erosion will occur."

In this case, the variable you will change will be the texture of the soil, and the variables you will measure are the amount of water that runs off and the amount of soil it carries with it, judged by the color of the runoff water. You expect the looser and coarser soils to have less water runoff and less soil erosion.

Setting up a control experiment will help you isolate one variable. Only one variable will change between the control and the experimental soil pans, and that variable is the kind of soil used. For the control, you will

What Are the Variables?

Variables are anything that might affect the results of an experiment. Here are the main variables in this experiment:

- the kind of soil used
- the slope of the soil
- the rate at which you pour water on the slope

In other words, the variables in this experiment are everything that might affect the amount of water and soil that run off. If you change more than one variable, you will not be able to tell which variable had the most effect on the runoff and erosion.

How to Experiment Safely

Wash your hands carefully after you handle soil, especially if you are using soil from outdoors. Be careful when digging to avoid broken glass or other trash in the soil.

use potting soil. For your experimental soil pans, you will use sand, clay, and neighborhood soil.

You will measure the amount of water that runs off your soil pans and how much erosion occurs. If the looser- and coarser-textured soils have less runoff, your hypothesis is correct.

Level of Difficulty Moderate, because of materials needed.

Materials Needed

- 2 to 3 pounds (1 to 1.5 kilograms) of purchased potting soil
- 2 to 3 pounds (1 to 1.5 kilograms) sand
- 2 to 3 pounds (1 to 1.5 kilograms) clay
- 2 to 3 pounds (1 to 1.5 kilograms) neighborhood soil
- 4 shallow pans. Cookie sheets with 0.5 to 1.0 inch (1.25 to 2.5 centimeters) high edges work well.
- 4 glass jars, approximately 24 fluid ounces (680 milliliters)
- scrap lumber
- a sprinkler can or hose nozzle with mist setting
- water
- measuring cup
- labels
- outdoor area to conduct experiment, since it may be messy
- a baking dish, approximately 9 × 13 × 2 inches (23 × 33 × 5 centimeters)
- magnifying glass (optional)

Steps 3 to 6: Set-up of soil "hillside." GALE GROUP.

Approximate Budget $10 if soils must be purchased.

Timetable 2 to 3 hours.

Step-by-Step Instructions

1. First, examine your soils. You may want to look at their particles with a magnifying glass. On your chart (see illustration) record your soils in the order of their textures,

Steps 8 to 10: Labeled jars containing different types of soil run-off. GALE GROUP.

from coarse to fine. If you cannot see separate particles, then the texture is very fine.

2. Place your shallow pans in a row and place a different kind of soil in each one. Fill each pan evenly up to its edges all around.

Soil type	Amount of water used	Amount of water collected	Water color
1.			
2.			
3.			
4.			

Recording chart for Experiment 1. GALE GROUP.

Troubleshooter's Guide

Experiments do not always work out as planned. Even so, figuring out what went wrong can definitely be a learning experience. Here are some problems that may arise during this experiment, some possible causes, and some ways to remedy the problems.

Problem: Soil is sliding down the pans.

Possible cause: The incline of your pans is too steep. Try lowering the support on which you are resting your pans.

Problem: No water is running off.

Possible cause: You are not using enough water for the amounts and kinds of soil you are using. Use more water, but be sure you use the same amount for all of your trials.

Problem: All the runoff water is clear.

Possible cause: Your soils are packed very tightly so no soil comes off with the water. Try stirring your soils a bit in their pans. But remember, even if the water is clear, it could still be carrying away nutrients instead of bringing those nutrients to plants that need them.

3. Prop one end of your potting soil pan on a board to simulate a hill. The exact slope is not important, but you must use the same slope for each pan.
4. Place the bottom end of the pan so it is resting in the baking dish.
5. Measure 3 cups of water into your sprinkler can.
6. Sprinkle the water over your "hillside," mostly from the top edge, and watch what happens.
7. After the can is empty, wait 5 minutes.
8. Pour the water from the baking dish pan into a glass jar. Look at its color and measure how much you have collected. The darker the water, the more soil has run off.
9. Label the jar with the type of soil.
10. Repeat the procedure for sand, clay, and neighborhood soil.

Summary of Results Record your results on a chart like the one illustrated.

Compare the amounts and colors of water in each jar. The darker the water, the more soil has run off in it. What have you discovered? Did coarser soils have less runoff? Was your hypothesis correct? Fill in your chart carefully and summarize what you found.

Change the Variables You can vary this experiment by changing the variables. For example, use soils from different areas of your neighborhood (near a stream, a park, a baseball diamond) or buy different kinds of potting soils from a plant-supply store. Or try mixing your soils. Just record how much of each kind you use in each mixture. You can also try propping up your plants at different slopes, such as 30 degrees, 45 degrees, 60 degrees, and so on. Using the same kind of soil and different slopes, run several more trials. What happens? How does slope affect erosion?

EXPERIMENT 2

Plants and Erosion: How do plants affect the rate of soil erosion?

Purpose/Hypothesis Soil is an important part of an ecosystem. An ecosystem is a community of plants, animals, and microorganisms considered together with their environment. Because soil is the foundation for life on Earth, erosion can be a serious problem for the living beings that depend upon it—including humans.

In this experiment, you will explore how the rate of soil erosion is affected by plants growing on the soil. Plant cover—either growing plants or fallen leaves and branches—protects soil from erosion by slowing down flowing water or absorbing the impact of rain drops. Roots of trees and other plants help to prevent erosion by holding the soil in place. Roots absorb water and provide stability to the soil. Before you begin, make an educated guess about the outcome of this experiment based on your knowledge of soils, plants, and erosion. This educated guess, or prediction, is your hypothesis. A hypothesis should explain these things:

- the topic of the experiment
- the variable you will change
- the variable you will measure
- what you expect to happen

A hypothesis should be brief, specific, and measurable. It must be something you can test through observation. Your experiment will prove or disprove whether your hypothesis is correct. Here is one possible hypothesis for this experiment: "Less soil will erode from a hillside with plant cover (a layer of leaves or growing grass) than from a hillside with no plant cover."

In this case, the variable you will change is the amount of plant cover, and the variables you will measure are the amount of water that runs off and the color of the soil that runs off. You expect the looser and coarser soils to have less water runoff and soil erosion.

Setting up a control experiment will help you isolate one variable. Only one variable will change between the control and the experimental

What Are the Variables?

Variables are anything that might affect the results of an experiment. Here are the main variables in this experiment:

- the kind of soil used
- the slope of the soil
- the rate at which you pour water on the slope

In other words, the variables in this experiment are everything that might affect the amount of water and soil that run off. If you change more than one variable, you will not be able to tell which variable had the most effect on the runoff and erosion.

How to Experiment Safely

Be careful when collecting fallen leaves or grass clippings, as broken glass or other trash might be in the leaves or grass. Wash your hands thoroughly afterward. If you collect soil from your neighborhood rather than using potting soil, use caution when collecting and handling the soil. Do not dig soil where you do not have permission to do so.

trays, and that variable is the presence or absence of growing plants or plant cover. For the control, you will use potting soil without any vegetation. For your experimental trays, you will use grass and leaf litter (leaves and/or grass clippings).

You will measure how much erosion occurs in each of the trays by measuring water that runs off and comparing the color of the water. If the experimental trays show less erosion than the control tray, then your hypothesis was correct.

Level of Difficulty Moderate, because of materials and time required.

Materials Needed

- 2 to 3 pounds (1 to 1.5 kilograms) purchased potting soil
- 1 to 2 pounds (0.5 to 1.0 kilograms) small gravel
- leaf litter (fallen leaves, twigs, and grass clippings)
- grass seed
- 3 shallow pans or trays (plant trays from a garden shop are designed to allow drainage; you may wish to use glass casserole dishes that allow you to observe the roots; otherwise, cookie sheets with edges will work.)
- 4 glass jars, approximately 24 fluid ounces (680 milliliters)
- a sprinkler can or hose nozzle with mist setting
- water

Step 2: Set-up of Tray 1, Tray 2, and Tray 3 and their contents. GALE GROUP.

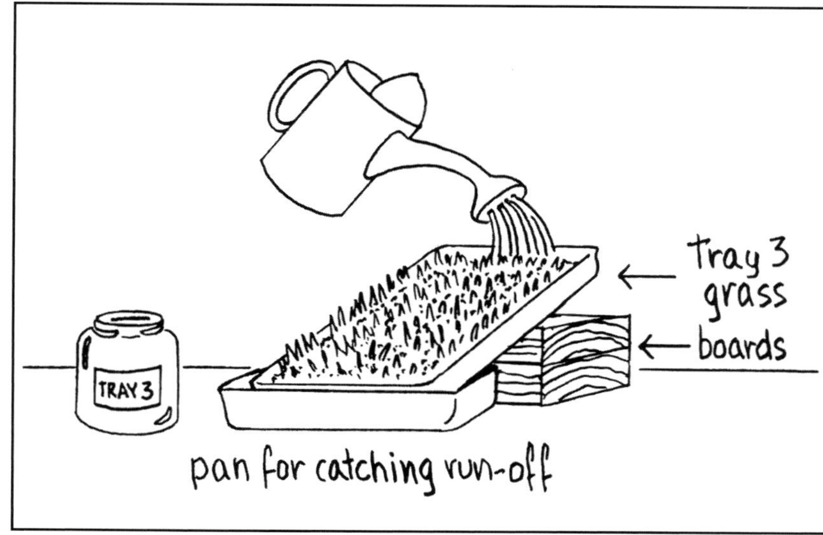

Steps 5 to 8: Set-up of erosion "hillside." GALE GROUP.

- labels
- measuring cup
- board or scrap lumber
- an area with adequate light for growing grass
- an outside area or other place for conducting the experiment, which may be messy
- a baking dish, approximately 9 × 13 × 2 inches (23 × 33 × 5 centimeters) or a dish pan to collect water that runs off

Approximate Budget $10 if soil and plant trays are purchased.

Timetable Approximately two weeks.

Step-by-Step Instructions

1. Prepare three trays by putting an equal amount of potting soil in each tray. If you are using pans or cookie sheets, spread a layer of gravel on the bottom of the pan before adding the soil. This will allow for drainage since you will be watering all three pans while the grass is growing.
2. Set Tray 1 aside. In Tray 2, cover the soil with a layer of leaves and grass clippings. In Tray 3, sprinkle grass seed on the top of the soil.

3. Place the three trays in a place where they are level and have similar light and temperature conditions. (The temperature must be above 50°F (10°C) for the grass to grow.)
4. Use the sprinkling can to give each tray the same amount of water. Continue watering all three trays approximately every 3 days until the grass in Tray 3 is about 0.5 inches (1.25 centimeters) tall. This may take one week or longer. You may have to adjust your watering schedule depending on how fast the soil dries. Check the soil daily to see if it looks and feels moist.
5. When the grass has grown, you are ready to do the erosion test. Prop the end of Tray 1 (soil only) on a board to simulate a hill. The exact slope is not important, but you must use the same slope for each tray.
6. Place the bottom end of the tray so it is resting in the baking dish or dish pan.
7. Measure 3 cups of water into the sprinkler can.
8. Sprinkle the water over your "hillside," mostly from the top edge, and watch what happens.
9. When the can is empty, wait five minutes.
10. Pour the water from the baking pan into a glass jar. Look at its color and measure how much you have collected.
11. Label your jar (Tray 1: soil only).

Tray	Description	Water color	Water (run-off) volume in tablespoons or oz.
1	soil		
2	leaf litter		
3	grass		

Recording chart for Experiment 2. GALE GROUP.

12. Repeat procedure for Tray 2 (soil with leaf litter) and Tray 3 (soil with grass). Be sure to label each jar so you can compare the quantity and color of the water.

Summary of Results Record your results on a chart like the one illustrated.

When you have finished, compare the amounts and colors of water in each jar. The darker the water, the more soil has run off. What have you discovered? Did the trays with leaf litter and grass have less runoff than the control tray? Did the tray with grass have less runoff than the tray with leaf litter? Was your hypothesis correct? Fill in your chart carefully and summarize what you found.

Change the Variables You can vary this experiment by changing the variables. There are several possibilities. For example, you could cover the trays of soil with different amounts of leaf litter and compare the effect on erosion. When there is more leaf litter, is there less erosion?

You could also try growing other types of plants. For instance, what is the difference in the amount of runoff from a tray with bean plants versus a tray with grass? You might want to combine several types of plants. Some plants have extensive root systems, while other plants have broad leaves. Which characteristic seems to make a greater difference in preventing erosion?

Another way to change the variables is to prop a tray at an angle and try terracing the soil (forming "steps" with the soil). If you plant grass on terraced soil, how does the amount of runoff compare with the amount from a tray of grass that was grown on one level?

Modify the Experiment The effects of erosion can cause harm both to the soil itself and surrounding areas. Erosion can lead to nutrient loss in the

Troubleshooter's Guide

Below are some problems that may arise during this experiment, some possible causes, and some ways to remedy the problems.

Problem: The grass did not grow.

Possible cause: Perhaps there was too much or too little light or water, or the temperature was too cold or too hot. Adjust these conditions and plant some more grass seed. If this fails, try another kind of seed.

Problem: Soil is sliding down the trays when they are inclined.

Possible cause: The incline of your trays is too steep. Try lowering the support on which you are resting your trays.

Problem: No water is running off.

Possible cause: You are not using enough water for the amounts and kind of soil you are using. Use more water, but be sure you use the same amount for all of your trials.

Problem: All the water is the same color.

Possible cause: The grass and leaf cover are not thick enough to show a difference from the control tray. Add more leaf litter to Tray 2 and try again. Add more grass seed to Tray 3 and continue watering all three trays until the grass grows more thickly. Then try the erosion test again.

Many organisms live in the soil and are threatened by erosion.
PHOTO RESEARCHERS INC.

soil. It can also lead to the spread of potential pollutants, such as fertilizers in runoff entering lakes. For a more advanced experiment, you can test how erosion may affect substances in the soil and waters.

Purchase a soil test kit and fertilizer at a home gardening store. Some of the soil quality measures will most likely be nitrogen, phosphorus, and pH. Make sure the fertilizer you purchase contains phosphates and other substances that the soil test measures. Following the directions, add fertilizer to all the trays. Test each tray's soil for each measure, including the pH. Follow the steps in the experiment.

When you have completed the experiment, check both the runoff and each of the soils again. Note the results. Were there some substances that leached (were removed) more than others? If you want to continue to grow the grass after repeated runoffs, do you think that would alter the growth? Conduct some research and determine what the affect would be if the runoff was to enter lakes, streams, and oceans.

Design Your Own Experiment

How to Select a Topic Relating to this Concept If you are interested in erosion or its effects, you can create many fascinating experiments. For example, you could study the effects on erosion of different kinds of plants growing in the soil. How about the difference between the size or age of plants? Or the number of plants growing in one place?

Or perhaps you are interested in the effects of human development (building) on erosion. What are the effects of concrete or pavement? What are the effects of deforestation or drainage of wetlands?

Erosion can also be caused by wind or ice. What would happen if you blew a fan over different kinds of soils?

Check the Further Readings section and talk with your science teacher or school or community media specialist to start gathering information on erosion questions that interest you. You may also want to find out if there is an Agricultural Research Station or Cooperative Extension Office near you. If so, they can tell you about local erosion problems and projects.

Steps in the Scientific Method To do an original experiment, you need to plan carefully and think things through. Otherwise you might not be sure what question you are answering, what you are or should be measuring, or what your findings prove or disprove.

Here are the steps in designing an experiment:

- State the purpose of—and the underlying question behind—the experiment you propose to do.
- Recognize the variables involved, and select one that will help you answer the question at hand.
- State a testable hypothesis, an educated guess about the answer to your question.
- Decide how to change the variable you selected.
- Decide how to measure your results.

Recording Data and Summarizing the Results Your data should include charts, such as the one you did for these experiments. They should be clearly labeled and easy to read. You may also want to include photos, graphs, or drawings of your experimental setup and results.

If you are preparing an exhibit, you may want to bring in some of your actual results, such as jars of water or soil clearly labeled with their origins. If you have done a nonexperimental project, you will want to explain clearly what your research question was and provide illustrations of your findings.

Related Projects You can design projects that are similar to these experiments, involving trials and charts of data to summarize your results. You could also prepare a model that demonstrates a point you are interested in with regard to erosion or its effects. Or you could do an investigation into agricultural or building considerations that include erosion. You could do a research project on the environmental and ecological effects of erosion and present your findings in a poster or booklet. The possibilities are numerous.

For More Information

Environmental Defense Fund Worldwide. http://www.environmentaldefense.org/home.cfm Current news relating to many environmental issues, including erosion.

Giono, Jean. *The Man Who Planted Trees.* White River Junction, VT.: Chelsea Green Publishing Company, 1985. Story about a man who single-handedly transformed his environment by planting trees over time.

Temperate Forests. New York: Habitat Ecology Learning Program, Wildlife Conservation Society, 1995. Provides activities for learning more about trees and forests and humans' impact on them.

30

Ethnobotany

Ethnobotany is the study of how cultures use plants in their everyday lives. "Ethno" refers to cultures and "botany" refers to plants. Since the beginning of civilization, cultures have used plants in numerous ways, including for food, medicine, clothing, dyes, decoration, religious ceremonies, tools, and shelter.

An ethnobotanist studies and often lives with cultures to fully understand how and why people incorporate native plants in their lives. An ethnobotanist is usually a botanist or biologist who has had additional training. Ethnobotanists can focus on one or more of the following specialties: archaeology, chemistry, linguistics (study of language), anthropology, ecology (study of how living things interact with one another), or pharmacology (study of medicines).

Plants as medicine Throughout history, cultures have used plants as a source of medicine. Dating back over 5,000 years, the Sumerians describe using the plants laurel, caraway, and thyme for medicinal uses. The Chinese have long used herbs in healing practices. The first known Chinese herb book dates back from 2700 B.C.E. This book lists 365 plants and their uses.

The Egyptians were known to bury their pharaohs with medicinal plants believing the plants would be useful to the deceased in the afterlife. The Egyptians used garlic, mint, coriander, and other herbs for medicinal purposes. Ancient Greeks and Romans also used plants for healing. In the first century, the Greek surgeon Dioscorides published a catalog of 600 plants in the Mediterranean. This illustrated book provided information on the medicinal use of the plant, how and when it was gathered, and whether it was poisonous or edible. This was one of the first books of its kind.

During the Middle Ages and into the seventeenth century, plants continued to be widely used as a form of medicine. Herbal medicine books were published and translated into different languages. However, in the nineteenth century, with the rapid advances related to chemistry and

*The foxglove plant (*Digitalis purpurea*) is the source of the cardiac medicine Digoxin.* AP PHOTO/DR. SCOTT M. LIEBERMAN.

other sciences, plants began to lose their importance in the world of medicine. Chemically synthesized (manufactured) drugs began to replace plants as a source of medicine in industrialized countries.

In the late twentieth century there was a shift back to the appreciation of plants and their contributions to medicine. One way that people select plants that may fight human disease is to look at how plants protect themselves against disease and pests. Researchers look at those plants and then isolate and study the disease-fighting compounds plants produce.

Many commonly used drugs are derived from plants, such as heart medications and aspirin. Pharmaceutical companies are increasingly interested in the development of new drugs whose origins are from plants. The rainforests and jungles of South America are an area of special interest due to their diverse and abundant plant life.

The World Health Organization (WHO) estimates that 80% of the world's population uses plant-based medicine for part of their healthcare. In non-industrialized societies the use of plant-based medicines in treating illnesses is universal. It is estimated that 25% of new drugs that are developed in the United States have their origins in plants. Given these statistics, the destruction of the rainforests and the loss of potential medicinal plants is of increasing concern.

Plants as a part of life All cultures use plants for tools. A basket is a kind of tool. Think about baskets that you have in your home and consider what they are made of. Ancient cultures, Native American cultures, and people today all used or use baskets to hold items in their home. Native Americans used baskets to hold grain, water, plant materials and even their babies. They also used baskets in ceremonial rituals.

Reeds and grasses are common plant materials used in basket making. The Pomo used shells and bird feathers to decorate their baskets for use during ceremonies. Today, we use baskets to hold foods, magazines,

WORDS TO KNOW

Agar: A nutrient rich, gelatinous substance that is used to grow bacteria.

Bacteria: Microscopic single celled organisms that reproduce quickly.

Botany: The study of plants.

Control experiment: A setup that is identical to the experiment, but is not affected by the variable that acts on the experimental group.

Ethnobotany: The study of how cultures use plants in everyday life.

Hypothesis: An idea in the form of a statement that can be tested by observation and/or experiment.

Plant extract: The juice or liquid essence obtained from a plant by squeezing or mashing it.

Reed: A tall woody perennial grass that has a hollow stem.

Synthetic: Something that is made artificially, in a laboratory or chemical plant, but is generally not found in nature.

Variable: Something that can change the results of an experiment.

and laundry. We also use baskets for decorations in our homes and on our doors.

People have used all parts of plants to make weapons for hunting. Spears, blow darts and fishing lines were made from reeds and grasses. Shelters were made from plants: straw, grasses, and large palm leaves are just a few of the materials that were used. Plants were used in religious ceremonies. Dyes derived from plants were used to adorn the bodies of native people during special ceremonies. Often the wrappings used in the basket were dyed in various colors to form unique patterns. The containers used in such ceremonies were often made from plants and leaves.

The importance of ethnobotany The relationship between cultures and plants is complex and diverse. Throughout time people have used plants for food, shelter, clothing, medicine, tools, and religious ceremonies. Ethnobotany helps us understand the nature and importance of our relationship to the plant world. If we want to preserve our natural world from deforestation and development this understanding is vital.

In the experiments that follow you will use plants in two different ways. In Experiment 1, you will test the antibacterial properties of three common plants. In Experiment 2, you will make discs out of reeds in the same way that Native Americans made baskets and test their ability to hold water.

What Are the Variables?

Variables are anything that might affect the results of an experiment. Here are the main variables in this experiment:

- the concentration of plant extract
- the temperature from the heat lamp
- time the bacteria is allowed to grow
- the amount of bacteria
- the type of bacteria

In other words, the variables in this experiment are everything that might affect the growth of bacteria on the agar plates. If you change more than one variable, you will not be able to tell which variable had the most affect on bacterial growth.

EXPERIMENT 1

Plants and Health: Which plants have anti-bacterial properties?

Purpose/Hypothesis Historically and in the modern day, people use plants to prevent and fight diseases, such as harmful bacteria. In this experiment you will measure the antibacterial properties of different plants. You will use a non-harmful type of bacteria, taken from your mouth, and place it on agar. Agar is a gel that supplies bacteria with food and a growth environment.

You will then place paper discs saturated with three different plant extracts: garlic, onion, and thyme. Garlic, onion, and thyme are all well known for their use in cooking but they have also been used for their medicinal properties. People have used garlic to fight off bacterial infections. Onion and thyme have a history of being used to heal skin infections and wounds. By measuring which plant extract has the least amount of bacteria growth around it, you can determine the antibacterial properties of each plant.

People have used all parts of plants to make weapons for hunting, and shelters were also made from plants. ILLUSTRATION BY TEMAH NELSON.

Before you begin, make an educated guess about the outcome of this experiment based on your knowledge of plants and ethnobotany. This educated guess, or prediction, is your hypothesis. A hypothesis should explain these things:

- the topic of the experiment
- the variable you will change
- the variable you will measure
- what you expect to happen

A hypothesis should be brief, specific, and measurable. It must be something you can test through observation. Your experiment will prove or disprove whether your hypothesis is correct. Here is one possible hypothesis for this experiment: "Garlic is known to have antibacterial properties and therefore will inhibit the growth of bacteria on the agar plates."

In this case, the variable you will change is the type of plant extract placed onto the agar plate, and the variable you will measure is the amount of bacteria growth around the paper disc soaked in plant extracts. If the garlic has the least amount of bacteria growth around the paper disc, you will know your hypothesis is correct.

How to Experiment Safely

When growing any kind of bacteria, make sure to keep all surfaces and materials that come in contact with the bacteria clean. When bacteria are disposed of after the experiment, use bleach to disinfect the Petri dish and place the dish in the trash. Be careful when cutting with the knife and handling the hot water.

Setting up a control experiment will help you isolate one variable. Only one variable will change between the control and the experimental discs, and that variable is the solution you use to immerse the disc. For the control, you will use sugar water. For your experimental discs, you are using sugar-water plus a plant extract.

Level of Difficulty Moderate (this experiment requires careful attention to cleanliness).

Materials Needed

- agar (obtained at health food store or online science store)
- 2 sterilized Petri dishes (available online at science stores)
- cotton swabs
- 1 teaspoon powdered sugar
- 1 teaspoon water
- coffee filter
- hole punch
- 1 small yellow onion
- 1 clove of garlic
- several leaves of thyme
- marker
- spoons (optional)
- garlic press (optional)
- mortar and pestle (optional)
- knife
- small cup
- tweezers
- heat lamp with 125 watt bulb

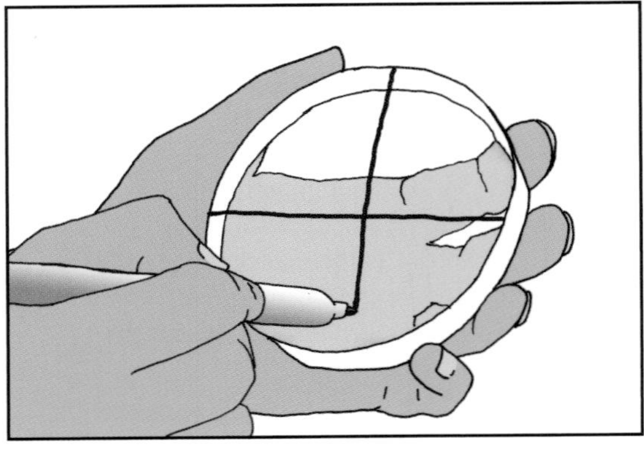

Step 1: Use the marker on the outside bottom to divide the Petri dish in quarters. ILLUSTRATION BY TEMAH NELSON.

Approximate Budget $15 to $20 (try to obtain the Petri dishes from your school).

Timetable Approximately one hour working time; three days total time.

Step-by-Step Instructions

1. If needed, prepare agar according to directions on the agar bottle or packet.
2. Flip the Petri dish so the bottom is facing up. Use the marker on the outside bottom to divide the Petri dish in quarters. At the edge of the Petri dish, mark each quarter: "O;" (for onion) "G;" (for garlic) "T;" (for thyme) and "C" (for control).
3. Pour the agar into the plate and cover. Let the agar sit until it is hardened (approximately four to five hours). Once hardened, turn the dish upside down to prevent condensation on the agar. Place the dish in the refrigerator until you are ready to use it. You may consider preparing two or more agar dishes at a time in case you want to repeat this experiment.
4. Use the hole punch to punch four circles out of the coffee filter. Do not touch the paper discs with your hands.
5. In a cup, mix 1 teaspoon of powdered sugar into 1 teaspoon of water.
6. Drop the solution onto one of the discs until the disc is completely covered in the sugar-water solution. This is your control. Set aside.
7. Swipe the inside of your cheek with the cotton swab to gather bacteria. Swirl the swab into the sugar solution, stirring it around.
8. Pour the sugar solution with the bacteria onto the agar plate, making sure the solution covers the entire plate.
9. Use the tweezers to place the control disc in the middle of the Control quarter of the agar plate. Clean off the tweezers by placing them in a cup of hot water and shaking them off until dry.
10. To prepare the onion disc: Hold the disc with the tweezers. Slice the onion in half and squeeze a drop of onion juice onto one disc. Make sure the disc is completely

Step 9: Use the tweezers to place the control disc in the middle of the Control quarter of the agar plate. ILLUSTRATION BY TEMAH NELSON.

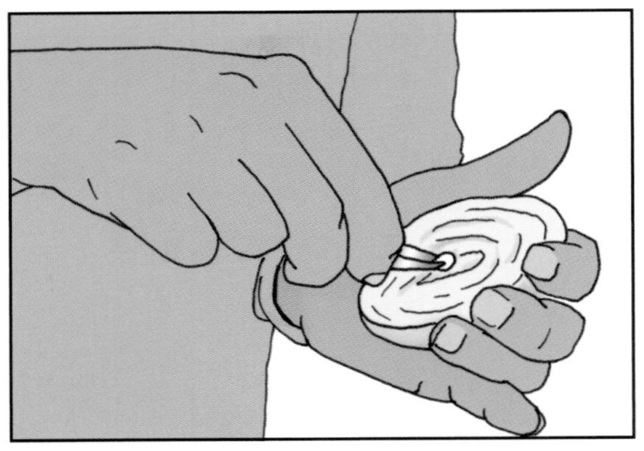

covered in juice. Using the tweezers, place this disc onto the onion quarter of the agar plate. Again, clean off the tweezers in hot water.

11. To prepare the garlic disc: Cut the garlic clove. If you have a garlic press, squeeze a clove until there is enough juice to cover a fresh paper disc. You can also press the garlic with a spoon. Use tweezers to hold and place the disc on the garlic quarter of the agar plate. Clean the tweezers.
12. To prepare the thyme disc: Hold the disc with the tweezers. The thyme leaves can be crushed with a spoon on a cutting board or with a mortar and pestle. You need just enough extract of the plant to wet the paper disc. With the tweezers, place the disc on the thyme quadrant.
13. Cover the agar plate and place it under the heat lamp. Make observations on bacterial growth every eight hours for two to three days. If possible, count the colonies (groups) of bacteria in each quadrant.

Step 13: Cover the agar plate and place it under the heat lamp. ILLUSTRATION BY TEMAH NELSON.

Summary of Results Draw or sketch the bacterial growth around each disc. After observing the bacterial growth over two to three days, what did you observe? Is there less bacteria growth around all the plant extract discs when compared to the control disc? Was your hypothesis correct? Write up a paragraph summarizing your results.

Change the Variables You can change the variables and repeat this experiment. For example, you can use different plant extracts. Research different plants and try ones that have antibacterial properties. You can also grow different bacteria. Our homes are filled with bacteria on doorknobs, toilet seats, and countertops. Take swabs from these places or others and see if they will grow on the agar plates. Temperature is another variable you can change. Will certain extracts prevent bacterial growth only in certain temperatures?

When you conduct further experiments, remember to change only one variable at a time or you will not be able to tell which variable affected the results.

Troubleshooter's Guide

Here are some problems that may arise during this experiment, possible causes, and ways to remedy the problems.

Problem: There was no bacteria growth on the agar plate.

Possible cause: Bacteria grows well under warm conditions; check the temperature of your heat lamp. A 125 watt heat lamp is approximately, 82 degrees Fahrenheit (28 degrees Celsius). If the wattage was not high enough, replace and repeat the experiment. You can also allow the bacteria to grow for several more days.

Possible cause: There may not have been enough bacteria collected on your cotton swab taken from your mouth. Try experiment again on a new agar plate and make sure you get a generous swab of bacteria from inside your cheek. Repeat the experiment.

Problem: The bacteria grew the same around the discs with plant extracts as the control.

Possible cause: The concentration of plant extracts was too weak. Your plants may have been too old. Try the experiment again using a fresh garlic, onion, or thyme.

EXPERIMENT 2

Coiling Reeds: How does the tightness of the coil affect the ability to hold materials?

Purpose/Hypothesis Baskets are made out of plant materials such as reeds, grasses, pine needles, and willow branches. Native Americans became quite skilled at making baskets from plant materials that were available to them. The Pomo (a Native American tribe from California) were known as one of the best basket makers. They used local grasses and wrapped and coiled them into baskets. Many reeds and grasses first need to be soaked in water to make them pliable. Through a weaving or coiling process, the reeds are then made into baskets to hold a variety of objects, such as grains, vegetables, and water.

In this experiment you will make two discs out of reeds using a coiling process. One of the discs will be a looser weave than the second disc. You can then measure how the tightness of the coiling process affects the ability of the reeds to contain different materials. You will see if the coils will hold small objects, such as rice, and water.

Before you begin, make an educated guess about the outcome of this experiment based on your knowledge of baskets and plants. This educated guess, or prediction, is your hypothesis. A hypothesis should explain these things:

- the topic of the experiment
- the variable you will change
- the variable you will measure
- what you expect to happen

A hypothesis should be brief, specific, and measurable. It must be something you can test through observation. Your experiment will prove or disprove whether your hypothesis is correct. Here is one possible hypothesis for this experiment: "The disc that is more tightly coiled will hold small objects such as rice but not water."

In this case, the variable you will change is the tightness of the coil, and the variable you will measure is what substances the disc holds.

What Are the Variables?

Variables are anything that might affect the results of an experiment. Here are the main variables in this experiment:

- the type of reed
- the diameter of the coil
- the amount of substance placed on the disc
- where the substance is poured on the disc

In other words, the variables in this experiment are everything that might affect how the coil holds the materials. If you change more than one variable, you will not be able to tell which variable had the most effect on the ability of the coil to hold materials.

Level of Difficulty Moderate.

Materials Needed

- reeds or cane (available at basket making stores or online)
- embroidery needle
- raffia 1–2 ounces (28–57 grams) (available from craft stores)
- dried beans or other similar size item, such as dried fruits
- rice
- small bowl
- teaspoons
- damp towel

Approximate Budget $15

Timetable 2 hours

How to Experiment Safely

Embroidery needles are sharp. Be careful when sewing through the reeds.

Step-By-Step Instructions

1. Separate the raffia into individual strands. Briefly dip the strands in warm water and keep them in a damp towel. You will use the raffia to wrap around the reeds, and it is easier to work with when it is slightly damp.
2. Gather a bunch of reeds together that are approximately as big as your little finger (1 centimeter). The reeds should be pliable and easily bent without breaking. If this is not the case you may try soaking the reeds in warm water for about two hours or longer until the reed is pliable.
3. Thread a strand of raffia through the embroidery needle. Make sure you use only a single strand of raffia.

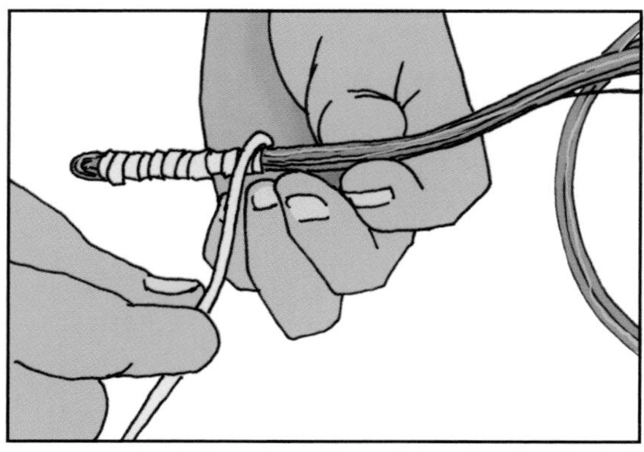

Step 4: Starting at one end, begin to wrap the raffia around the bundle of reeds until you have covered approximately two inches of the reeds. ILLUSTRATION BY TEMAH NELSON.

4. Starting at one end, begin to wrap the raffia around the bundle of reeds until you have covered approximately 2 inches (5 centimeters) of the reeds.
5. Bend the 2 inches (5 centimeters) of raffia-covered reeds in half so the two lengths meet each other. With the raffia-threaded needle, thread the raffia through both sides of the raffia-covered reeds to connect the two sides. You have just started your coiling process.
6. Continue wrapping the reeds with raffia while coiling the reeds around themselves. Every inch you will need to sew the reeds together with the raffia. Continue this process until you have a disc approximately 3–4 inches (7.5–10 centimeters) wide.
7. Continue this same process in making a second disc, except this time sew the reeds together every half an inch. Try to coil, wrap and sew this disc as tightly as possible. Stop when the second disc is the same size as the first disc, approximately 3 to 4 inches (7.5–10 centimeters) wide. If possible, bend them both into a bowl shape.
8. Hold the first coiled disc above the bowl and place two tablespoon of rice in the center of the disc. Shake the disc back and forth gently, trying not to have any rice spill off the sides.
9. Measure how much rice fell into the bowl and note the results.
10. Empty the bowl and repeat this same process with the second, tightly-coiled disc. Note how much rice dropped into the bowl.
11. Repeat Steps 8–10 for dried beans (or other small object) and water, making sure to empty the bowl both times.

Step 5: Bend the 2 inches (5 centimeters) of raffia covered reeds in half so the two lengths meet each other. ILLUSTRATION BY TEMAH NELSON.

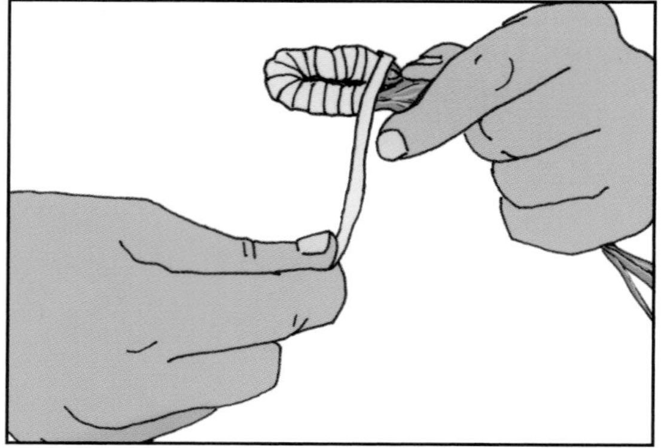

Summary of Results Look at the data for each of the discs. Is the second disc tight enough to hold water or other small objects? For what purposes could you use both discs? If the second disc does not hold water, think about ways you could change the coil to make it hold water.

Consider other plant parts that may help make the coil contain small objects or a liquid.

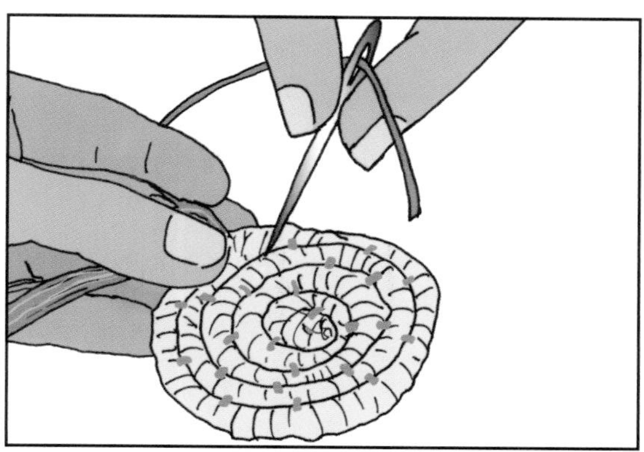

Step 6: Continue wrapping the reeds with raffia while coiling the reeds around themselves. ILLUSTRATION BY TEMAH NELSON.

Design Your Own Experiment

How to Select a Topic Relating to this Concept Many cultures use a wide variety of plant materials to make containers, baskets, and tools. Research the indigenous plants where you live and make baskets from the materials in your own backyard. Coiling is just one technique used in basket making, weaving is another. Pine needles and willow branches are just some materials that are commonly found in basket making.

Check the Further Readings section and talk with your science teacher or school or community media specialist to start gathering information on ethnobotany questions that interest you. As you consider possible experiments and projects, be sure to discuss them with your science teacher or another knowledgeable adult before trying them. Some of them might be dangerous.

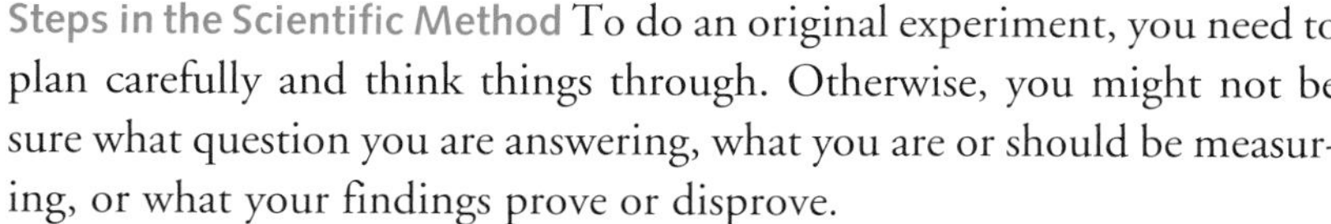

Steps in the Scientific Method To do an original experiment, you need to plan carefully and think things through. Otherwise, you might not be sure what question you are answering, what you are or should be measuring, or what your findings prove or disprove.

Here are the steps in designing an experiment:

- State the purpose of—and the underlying question behind—the experiment you propose to do.
- Recognize the variables involved, and select one that will help you answer the question at hand.
- State a testable hypothesis, an educated guess about the answer to your question.
- Decide how to change the variable you selected.
- Decide how to measure your results.

Step 8: Hold the first coiled disc above the bowl and place two tablespoon of rice in the center of the disc. ILLUSTRATION BY TEMAH NELSON.

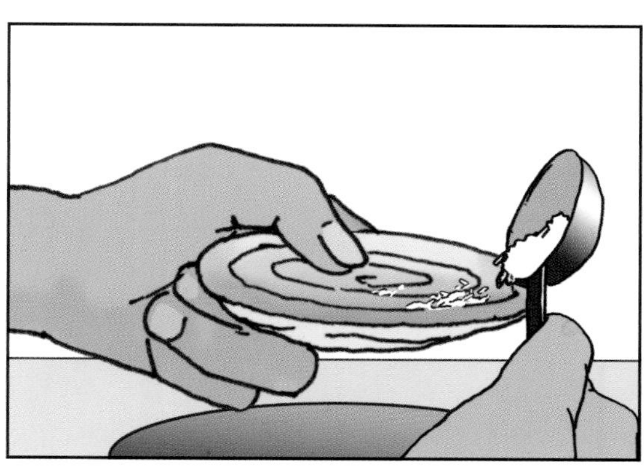

Troubleshooter's Guide

Here is a problem that may arise during this project, a possible cause, and a way to remedy it.

Problem: The reeds did not bend easily, perhaps even broke in half.

Possible cause: The reeds should be pliable and easily bent without breaking. If this is not the case you may try soaking the reeds in warm water for a couple of hours or longer until you achieve a pliable reed.

Problem: The coils both have large holes and don't hold anything.

Possible cause: Making baskets and coiling reeds takes practice. Initially, your first few discs may be loose and have holes between the stitching. Keep trying. As you gain more skill and are able to tightly coil and sew the reeds together you will begin to form a tighter disc.

Recording Data and Summarizing the Results Record your data on the bacteria experiment and the disc coiling experiment. You could draw or photograph your results. After the data is collected and analyzed, your final responsibility is to make a conclusion based on your experiment and decide whether your hypothesis was true.

Related Projects These experiments have focused on two ways that people use plants: plants as medicine and plants as containers. Plants are used in many other ways. You could research how cultures use plants in religious ceremonies or as decorations on their clothes or in their homes. When you discover what plants are used for, you can experiment using different types of plants. For example, you could examine which plants make the strongest or deepest dyes. Plants are also used to create musical instruments. You could examine how reeds or other plant materials can make different sounds.

For More Information

"ACT for Kids!" *Amazon Conservation Team.* http://www.ethnobotany.org/kids/index.html (accessed April 17, 2008). Information and activities related to Amazon rainforest.

Bernstein, Bonnie. *Native American Crafts Workshop.* California: Pittman Learning, 1982. Craft projects for children based on Native American traditions.

Buhner, Stephen. *Herbal Antibiotics.* Vermont: Storey Books, 1999. Examines the natural alternatives for trating drug-resistant bacteria.

Budget Index

Chapter name in brackets, followed by experiment name. The numeral before the colon indicates volume; numbers after the colon indicate page number.

LESS THAN $5

[Air] Air Density: Does warm air take up less room than cool air? **1:36**

[Animal Defenses] Camouflage: Does an animal's living environment relate to the color of the animal life? **1:63**

[Annual Growth] Tree Growth: What can be learned from the growth patterns of trees? **1:74**

[Bones and Muscles] Muscles: How does the strength of muscles affect fatigue over time? **1:120**

[Chemical Properties] Slime: What happens when white glue and borax mix? **1:167**

[Crystals] Cool Crystals: How does the effect of cooling impact crystal growth? **2:252**

[Density and Buoyancy] Buoyancy: Does water pressure affect buoyancy? **2:264**

[Dyes] Applying Dyes: How does the fiber affect the dye color? **2:301**

[Earthquakes] Detecting an Earthquake: How can movement of Earth's crust be measured? **2:314**

[Earthquakes] Earthquake Simulation: Is the destruction greater at the epicenter? **2:317**

[Eclipses] Simulating Solar and Lunar Eclipses **2:327**

[Flight] Helicopters, Propellers, and Centripetal Force: Will it fly high? **3:418**

[Food Spoilage] Spoiled Milk: How do different temperatures of liquid affect its rate of spoilage? **3:485**

[Forces] Centripetal Action: What is the relationship between distance and force in circular motion? **3:501**

[Fungi] Decomposers: Food source for a common fungi **3:541**

[Genetics] Building a Pedigree for Taste **3:559**

[Germination] Comparing Germination Times: How fast can seeds grow? **3:570**

[Gravity] Gravity: How fast do different objects fall? **3:581**

[Gravity] Measuring Mass: How can a balance be made? **3:585**

[Greenhouse Effect] Fossil Fuels: What happens when fossil fuels burn? **3:596**

[Heat] Conduction: Which solid materials are the best conductors of heat? **3:618**

[Heat] Convection: How does heat move through liquids? **3:622**

[Insects] Lightning Bugs: How does the environment affect a firefly's flash? **3:638**

[Memory] False Memories: How can memories be influenced? **4:705**

[Memory] Memory Mnemonics: What techniques help in memory retention? **4:701**

[Microorganisms] Microorganisms: What is the best way to grow penicillin? **4:713**

[Nutrition] Daily Nutrition: How nutritious is my diet? **4:766**

[Nutrition] Energizing Foods: Which foods contain carbohydrates and fats? **4:761**

[Oceans] Currents: Water behavior in density-driven currents **4:780**

[Optics and Optical Illusions] Optical Illusions: Can the eye be fooled? **4:791**

[Osmosis and Diffusion] Changing Concentrations: Will a bag of salt water draw in fresh water? **4:803**

[Oxidation-Reduction] Reduction: How will acid affect dirty pennies? **4:813**

[pH] Kitchen Chemistry: What is the pH of household chemicals? **4:861**

[Potential and Kinetic Energy] Measuring Energy: How does the height of an object affect its potential energy? **5:931**

[Rocks and Minerals] Rock Classification: Is it igneous, sedimentary, or metamorphic? **5:975**

[Scientific Method] Using the Scientific Method: Do fruit flies appear out of thin air? **5:1013**

[Simple Machines] Lever Lifting: How does the distance from the fulcrum affect work? **5:1055**

[Simple Machines] Wheel and Axle: How can changing the size of the wheel affect the amount of work it takes to lift a load? **5:1051**

[Space Observation] Doppler Effect: How can waves measure the distance and speed of objects? **6:1118**

[Stars] Tracking the Motion of the Planets: Can a planet be followed? **6:1128**

[Static Electricity] Building an Electroscope: Which objects are electrically charged? **6:1135**

[Static Electricity] Measuring a Charge: Does nylon or wool create a stronger static electric charge? **6:1139**

[Storms] Lightning Sparks: Explore how separating charges causes an attraction between objects **6:1152**

[Tropisms] Phototropism: Will plants follow a maze to reach light? **6:1193**

[Volcanoes] Looking at a Seismograph: Can a volcanic eruption be detected? **6:1242**

[Water Cycle] Surface Area: How does surface area affect the rate of evaporation? **6:1253**

[Weather] Clouds: Will a drop in air temperature cause a cloud to form? **6:1277**

[Weather] Wind: Measuring wind speed with a homemade anemometer **6:1273**

[Weather Forecasting] Air Pressure: How can air pressure be measured? **6:1289**

[Weather Forecasting] Dewpoint: When will dew form? **6:1286**

[Wood] Water Absorption: How do different woods absorb water? **6:1298**

[Wood] Wood Hardness: How does the hardness of wood relate to its building properties? **6:1302**

$5–$10

[Acid Rain] Acid Rain and Animals: How does acid rain affect brine shrimp? **1:5**

[Acid Rain] Acid Rain and Plants: How does acid rain affect plant growth? **1:9**

[Acid Rain] Acid Rain: Can acid rain harm structures? **1:12**

[Adhesives] Adhesives in the Environment: Will different environmental conditions affect the properties of different adhesives? **1:26**

[Adhesives] Material Adhesion: How do various glues adhere to different materials? **1:22**

[Air] Convection Currents: How can rising air cause weather changes? **1:39**

[Air and Water Pollution] Eutrophication: The effect of phosphates on water plants. **1:55**

[Air and Water Pollution] Pollutant Bioindicators: Can lichens provide clues to an area's air pollution? **1:51**

[Annual Growth] Lichen Growth: What can be learned from the environment by observing lichens? **1:79**

[Bones and Muscles] Bone Loss: How does the loss of calcium affect bone strength? **1:116**

[Caves] Cave Formation: How does the acidity of a substance affect the formation of a cave? **1:132**

[Caves] Cave Icicles: How does the mineral content of water affect the formation of stalactites and stalagmites? **1:135**

[Cells] Investigating Cells: What are the differences between a multicellular organism and a unicellular organism? **1:141**

[Cells] Plant Cells: What are the cell differences between monocot and dicot plants? **1:145**

[Cells] Yeast Cells: How do they reproduce? **1:147**

[Chemical Energy] Rusting: Is the chemical reaction exothermic, endothermic, or neither? **1:152**

[Chemosenses] Smell and Taste: How does smell affect the sense of taste? **1:186**

[Chemosenses] Supertasters: Is there a correlation between the number of taste buds and taste perception? **1:180**

[Chlorophyll] Plant Pigments: Can pigments be separated? **1:193**

[Comets and Meteors] Meteor Impact: How do the characteristics of a meteorite and its impact affect the shape of the crater? **2:221**

[Composting/Landfills] Composting: Using organic material to grow plants **2:237**

[Composting/Landfills] Living Landfill: What effect do the microorganisms in soil have on the decomposition process? **2:232**

[Crystals] Crystal Structure: Will varying shape crystals form from varying substances? **2:246**

[Density and Buoyancy] Density: Can a scale of relative density predict whether one material floats on another? **2:260**

[DNA (Deoxyribonucleic Acid)] The Stuff of Life: Isolating DNA **2:289**

[Dyes] Holding the Dye: How do dye fixatives affect the color-fastness of the dye? **2:304**

[Eclipses] Phases of the Moon: What does each phase look like? **2:329**

[Enzymes] Finding the Enzyme: Which enzyme breaks down hydrogen peroxide? **2:362**

[Enzymes] Stopping Enzymes: Does temperature affect enzyme action? **2:368**

[Erosion] Erosion: Does soil type affect the amount of water that runs off a hillside? **2:377**

[Erosion] Plants and Erosion: How do plants affect the rate of soil erosion? **2:381**

[Flight] Lift-Off: How can a glider be made to fly higher? **3:415**

[Flowers] Sweet Sight: Can changing a flower's nectar and color affect the pollinators lured to the flower? **3:431**

[Fluids] Spinning Fluids: How do different fluids behave when immersed in a spinning rod? **3:444**

[Fluids] Viscosity: How can temperature affect the viscosity of liquids? **3:441**

[Food Preservation] Drying Foods: Does drying fruits help prevent or delay spoilage? **3:458**

[Food Preservation] Sweet Preservatives: How does sugar affect the preservation of fruit? **3:454**

[Food Science] Jelly and Pectin: How does acidity affect how fruit gels? **3:463**

[Food Science] Rising Foods: How much carbon dioxide do different leavening agents produce? **3:470**

[Food Spoilage] Preservatives: How do different substances affect the growth of mold? **3:481**

[Forensic Science] Blood Patterns: How can a blood spatter help recreate the crime? **3:515**

[Fossils] Fossil Formation: What are the physical characteristics of an organism that make the best fossils? **3:530**

[Fossils] Making an Impression: In which soil environment does a fossil most easily form? **3:526**

[Fungi] Living Conditions: What is the ideal temperature for yeast growth? **3:544**

[Genetics] Genetic Traits: Will you share certain genetic traits more with family members than non-family members? **3:556**

[Germination] Effects of Temperature on Germination: What temperatures encourage and discourage germination? **3:566**

[Germination] Seed Scarification: Does breaking the seed shell affect germination time? **3:573**

[Greenhouse Effect] Creating a Greenhouse: How much will the temperature rise inside a greenhouse? **3:592**

[Groundwater Aquifers] Groundwater: How can it be cleaned? **3:609**

[Insects] Ant Food: What type of foods is one type of ant attracted to? **3:635**

[Magnetism] Electromagnets: Does the strength of an electromagnet increase with greater current? **4:678**

[Magnetism] Magnets: How do heat, cold, jarring, and rubbing affect the magnetism of a nail? **4:674**

[Materials Science] Developing Renewables: Can a renewable packing material have the same qualities as a non-renewable material? **4:691**

[Materials Science] Testing Tape: Finding the properties that allow tape to support weight. **4:688**

[Microorganisms] Growing Microorganisms in a Petri Dish **4:716**

[Mountains] Mountain Formations: How does the height of the mountain have an affect on desert formation? **4:741**

[Mountains] Mountain Plates: How does the movement of Earth's plates determine the formation of a mountain? **4:738**

[Nanotechnology] Nanosize Substances: How can the physical size affect the rate of reaction? **4:753**

[Nanotechnology] Nanosize: How can the physical size affect a material's properties? **4:750**

[Oceans] Stratification: How does the salinity in ocean water cause it to form layers? **4:775**

[Osmosis and Diffusion] Changing Sizes: What effect does molecule size have on osmosis **4:806**

[Osmosis and Diffusion] Measuring Membranes: Is a plastic bag a semipermeable membrane? **4:798**

[Oxidation-Reduction] Oxidation and Rust: How is rust produced? **4:817**

[Oxidation-Reduction] Oxidation Reaction: Can acid change the color of copper? **4:820**

[Periodic Table] Active Metals: What metals give off electrons more readily than others? **4:838**

[Pesticides] Moving through Water: How can pesticides affect nontarget plant life? **4:852**

[pH] Chemical Titration: What is required to change a substance from an acid or a base into a neutral solution? **4:865**

[Photosynthesis] Photosynthesis: How does light affect plant growth? **4:873**

[Plants and Water] Water Flow: How do varying solutions of water affect the amount of water a plant takes in and its turgor pressure? **5:900**

[Polymers] Polymer Properties: How are the properties of hard plastics different? **5:923**

[Polymers] Polymer Slime: How will adding more of a polymer change the properties of a polymer "slime"? **5:919**

[Polymers] Polymer Strength: What are the tensile properties of certain polymers that make them more durable than others? **5:914**

[Renewable Energy] Hydropower: How does water pressure affect water energy? **5:948**

[Rivers] River Flow: How does the steepness and rate of water flow affect river erosion? **5:962**

[Rivers] Stream Flow: Does the stream meander? **5:960**

[Rocks and Minerals] Mineral Testing: What kind of mineral is it? **5:971**

[Rotation and Orbits] Foucault Pendulum: How can a pendulum demonstrate the rotation of Earth? **5:985**

[Rotation and Orbits] Spinning Effects: How does the speed of a rotating object affect the way centrifugal force can overcome gravity? **5:989**

[Salinity] Density Ball: How to make a standard for measuring density **5:1000**

[Salinity] Making a Hydrometer: How can salinity be measured? **5:997**

[Scientific Method] Using the Scientific Method: What are the mystery powders? **5:1009**

[Separation and Identification] Chromatography: Can you identify a pen from the way its colors separate? **5:1034**

[Simple Machines] The Screw: How does the distance between the threads of a screw affect the work? **5:1037**

[Soil] Soil pH: Does the pH of soil affect plant growth? **5:1074**

[Sound] Pitch: How does the thickness of a vibrating string affect sound? **5:1099**

[Sound] Soundproofing: How do different materials affect sound? **5:1102**

[Sound] Wave Length: How does the length of a vibrating string affect the sound it produces? **5:1096**

[Storms] Tornadoes: Making a violent vortex **6:1155**

[Time] Pendulums: How do the length, weight, and swing angle of a pendulum affect its oscillation time? **6:1180**

[Time] Water Clock: Does the amount of water in a water clock affect its accuracy? **6:1185**

[Tropisms] Heliotropism: How does the Sun affect the movement of certain plants? **6:1201**

[Vegetative Propagation] Auxins: How do auxins affect plant growth? **6:1209**

[Vegetative Propagation] Potatoes from Pieces: How do potatoes reproduce vegetatively? **6:1216**

[Vitamins and Minerals] Hard Water: Do different water sources have varying mineral content? **6:1231**

[Vitamins and Minerals] Vitamin C: What juices are the best sources of Vitamin C? **6:1226**

[Water Cycle] Temperature: How does temperature affect the rate of evaporation? **2:1248**

[Water Properties] Cohesion: Can the cohesive force of surface tension in water support an object denser than water? **6:1261**

$11–$15

[Animal Defenses] Ladybug Threats: How do ladybugs defend themselves when they feel threatened? **1:65**

[Chemical Properties] Chemical Patination: Producing chemical reactions on metal **1:173**

[Chemical Properties] Chemical Reactions: What happens when mineral oil, water, and iodine mix? **1:170**

[Comets and Meteors] Comet Nucleus: Linking a Comet's Composition to its Properties. **2:218**

[DNA (Deoxyribonucleic Acid)] Comparing DNA: Does the DNA from different species have the same appearance? **2:291**

[Electricity] Batteries: Can a series of homemade electric cells form a "pile" strong enough to match the voltage of a D-cell battery? **2:340**

[Electricity] Electroplating: Using electricity to move one metal onto another metal **2:344**

[Enzymes] Tough and Tender: Does papain speed up the aging process? **2:365**

[Ethnobotany] Coiling Reeds: How does the tightness of the coil affect the ability to hold materials? **2:396**

[Groundwater Aquifers] Aquifers: How do they become polluted? **3:605**

[Heat] Heat Capacity: Which liquids have the highest heat capacity? **3:625**

[Light Properties] Refraction: How does the material affect how light travels? **4:666**

[Mixtures and Solutions] Colloids: Can colloids be distinguished from suspension using the Tyndall effect? **4:730**

[Mixtures and Solutions] Suspensions and Solutions: Can filtration and evaporation determine whether mixtures are suspensions or solutions? **4:725**

[Periodic Table] Soluble Families: How does the solubility of an element relate to where it is located on the Periodic Table? **4:835**

[Pesticides] Natural versus Synthetic: How do different types of pesticides compare against a pest? **4:848**

[Plant Anatomy] Plant Hormones: What is the affect of hormones on root and stem growth? **5:886**

[Plants and Water] Transpiration: How do different environmental conditions affect plants' rates of transpiration? **5:904**

[Renewable Energy] Capturing Wind Energy: How does the material affect the amount of wind energy harnessed? **5:944**

[Rivers] Weathering Erosion in Glaciers: How does a river make a trench? **5:957**

[Seashells] Classifying Seashells **5:1025**

[Seashells] Shell Strength: Which shell is stronger: a clam shell or lobster shell? **5:1022**

[Separation and Identification] Identifying a Mixture: How can determining basic properties of a substance allow you to identify the substances in a mixture? **5:1039**

[Solar Energy] Retaining the Sun's heat: What substance best stores heat for a solar system? **5:1090**

[Space Observation] Telescopes: How do different combinations of lenses affect the image? **6:1113**

[Storms] Forming Hailstones: How do temperature differences affect the formation of hail? **6:1158**

[Structures and Shapes] Arches and Beams: Which is strongest? **6:1167**

[Structures and Shapes] Beams and Rigidity: How does the vertical height of a beam affect its rigidity? **6:1170**

[Volcanoes] Model of a Volcano: Will it blow its top? **6:1240**

[Water Properties] Adhesion: How much weight is required to break the adhesive force between an object and water? **6:1264**

$16–$20

[Bacteria] Bacterial Resistance: Can bacteria gain resistance to a substance after exposure? **1:95**

[Color] Color and Flavor: How much does color affect flavor perception? **1:207**

[Color] Temperature and Color: What color has the highest temperature? **1:210**

[Dissolved Oxygen] Goldfish Breath: How does a decrease in the dissolved oxygen level affect the breathing rate of goldfish? **2:279**

[Electromagnetism] Electromagnetism: How can an electromagnet be created? **2:354**

[Electromagnetism] Magnetism:How can a magnetic field be created and detected? **2:351**

[Ethnobotany] Plants and Health: Which plants have antibacterial properties? **2:392**

[Flowers] Self versus Cross: Will there be a difference in reproduction between self-pollinated and cross-pollinated plants of the same type? **3:427**

[Forces] Newton's Laws in Action: How do water bottle rockets demonstrate Newton's laws of motion? **3:493**

[Forensic Science] Fiber Evidence: How can scientific techniques be used to identify fiber? **3:511**

[Nutrition] Nutrition: Which foods contain proteins and salts? **4:764**

[Optics and Optical Illusions] Optics: What is the focal length of a lens? **4:788**

[Periodic Table] Metals versus Nonmetals: Which areas of the periodic table have elements that conduct electricity? **4:830**

[Photosynthesis] Light Intensity: How does the intensity of light affect plant growth? **4:877**

[Plant Anatomy] Water Uptake: How do different plants differ in their water needs? **5:890**

[Potential and Kinetic Energy] Using Energy: Build a roller coaster **5:934**

[Soil] Soil Profile: What are the different properties of the soil horizons? **5:1067**

[Stars] Tracking Stars: Where is Polaris? **6:1125**

[Tropisms] Geotropism: Will plant roots turn toward the pull of gravity? **5:1197**

$21–$25

[Bacteria] Bacterial Growth: How do certain substances inhibit or promote bacterial growth? **1:90**

[Biomes] Building a Desert Biome **1:108**

[Biomes] Building a Temperate Forest Biome **1:107**

[Chemical Energy] Exothermic or Endothermic: Determining whether various chemical reactions are exothermic or endothermic **1:156**

[Dissolved Oxygen] Decay and Dissolved Oxygen: How does the amount of decaying matter affect the level of dissolved oxygen in water? **2:274**

[Fish] Fish Breathing: How do different fish take in oxygen? **3:404**

[Fish] Fish Movement: How do fins and body shape affect the movement of fish? **3:407**

[Light Properties] Looking for the Glow: Which objects glow under black light? **4:661**

[Solar Energy] Capturing Solar Energy: Will seedlings grow bigger in a greenhouse? **5:1084**

[Solar Energy] Solar Cells: Will sunlight make a motor run? **5:1087**

$26–$30

[Electricity] Electrolytes: Do some solutions conduct electricity better than others? **2:335**

[Life Cycles] Insects: How does food supply affect the growth rate of grasshoppers or crickets? **4:651**

[Life Cycles] Tadpoles: Does temperature affect the rate at which tadpoles change into frogs? **4:647**

[Light Properties] Refraction and Defraction: Making a rainbow **4:664**

$31–$35

[Chlorophyll] Response to Light: Do plants grow differently in different colors of light? **1:197**

Level of Difficulty Index

Chapter name in brackets, followed by experiment name. The numeral before the colon indicates volume; numbers after the colon indicate page number.

EASY

Easy means that the average student should easily be able to complete the tasks outlined in the project/experiment, and that the time spent on the project is not overly restrictive.

[Air] Air Density: Does warm air take up less room than cool air? **1:36**

[Air and Water Pollution] Eutrophication: The effect of phosphates on water plants. **1:55**

[Bones and Muscles] Muscles: How does the strength of muscles affect fatigue over time? **1:120**

[Chemosenses] Smell and Taste: How does smell affect the sense of taste? **1:186**

[Electromagnetism] Electromagnetism: How can an electromagnet be created? **2:354**

[Flight] Helicopters, Propellers, and Centripetal Force: Will it fly high? **3:418**

[Flight] Lift-Off: How can a glider be made to fly higher? **3:415**

[Fungi] Decomposers: Food source for a common fungi **3:541**

[Nanotechnology] Nanosize Substances: How can the physical size affect the rate of reaction? **4:753**

[Nutrition] Energizing Foods: Which foods contain carbohydrates and fats? **4:761**

[Oceans] Currents: Water behavior in density-driven currents **4:780**

[Osmosis and Diffusion] Changing Concentrations: Will a bag of salt water draw in fresh water? **4:803**

[Potential and Kinetic Energy] Measuring Energy: How does the height of an object affect its potential energy? **5:931**

[Rivers] River Flow: How does the steepness and rate of water flow affect river erosion? **5:962**

[Rivers] Stream Flow: Does the stream meander? **5:960**

[Rotation and Orbits] Spinning Effects: How does the speed of a rotating object affect the way centrifugal force can overcome gravity? **5:989**

[Simple Machines] Lever Lifting: How does the distance from the fulcrum affect work? **5:1055**

[Sound] Pitch: How does the thickness of a vibrating string affect sound? **5:1099**

[Sound] Wave Length: How does the length of a vibrating string affect the sound it produces? **5:1096**

[Space Observation] Doppler Effect: How can waves measure the distance and speed of objects? **6:1118**

[Storms] Lightning Sparks: Explore how separating charges causes an attraction between objects **6:1152**

[Storms] Tornadoes: Making a violent vortex **6:1155**

[Volcanoes] Looking at a Seismograph: Can a volcanic eruption be detected? **6:1242**

[Water Cycle] Surface Area: How does surface area affect the rate of evaporation? **6:1253**

[Water Cycle] Temperature: How does temperature affect the rate of evaporation? **6:1248**

[Weather Forecasting] Air Pressure: How can air pressure be measured? **6:1289**

[Weather Forecasting] Dewpoint: When will dew form? **6:1286**

EASY/MODERATE

Easy/Moderate means that the average student should have little trouble completing the tasks outlined in the project/experiment, and that the time spent on the project is not overly restrictive.

[Air] Convection Currents: How can rising air cause weather changes? **1:39**

[Bones and Muscles] Bone Loss: How does the loss of calcium affect bone strength? **1:116**

[Caves] Cave Formation: How does the acidity of a substance affect the formation of a cave? **1:132**

[Chemical Properties] Slime: What happens when white glue and borax mix? **1:167**

[Chemosenses] Supertasters: Is there a correlation between the number of taste buds and taste perception? **1:180**

[Composting/Landfills] Living Landfill: What effect do the micro-organisms in soil have on the decomposition process? **2:232**

[Dissolved Oxygen] Decay and Dissolved Oxygen: How does the amount of decaying matter affect the level of dissolved oxygen in water? **2:274**

[Dissolved Oxygen] Goldfish Breath: How does a decrease in the dissolved oxygen level affect the breathing rate of goldfish? **2:279**

[Dyes] Applying Dyes: How does the fiber affect the dye color? **2:301**

[Earthquakes] Earthquake Simulation: Is the destruction greater at the epicenter? **2:317**

[Eclipses] Phases of the Moon: What does each phase look like? **2:329**

[Eclipses] Simulating Solar and Lunar Eclipses **2:327**

[Enzymes] Finding the Enzyme: Which enzyme breaks down hydrogen peroxide? **2:362**

[Enzymes] Tough and Tender: Does papain speed up the aging process? **2:365**

[Fluids] Spinning Fluids: How do different fluids behave when immersed in a spinning rod? **3:444**

[Food Spoilage] Spoiled Milk: How do different temperatures of liquid affect its rate of spoilage? **3:485**

[Forces] Centripetal Action: What is the relationship between distance and force in circular motion? **3:501**

[Fossils] Making an Impression: In which soil environment does a fossil most easily form? **3:526**

[Genetics] Building a Pedigree for Taste **3:559**

[Genetics] Genetic Traits: Will you share certain genetic traits more with family members than non-family members? **3:556**

[Germination] Comparing Germination Times: How fast can seeds grow? **3:570**

[Germination] Effects of Temperature on Germination: What temperatures encourage and discourage germination? **3:566**

[Greenhouse Effect] Creating a Greenhouse: How much will the temperature rise inside a greenhouse? **3:592**

[Heat] Convection: How does heat move through liquids? **3:622**

[Light Properties] Looking for the Glow: Which objects glow under black light? **4:661**

[Light Properties] Refraction and Defraction: Making a rainbow **4:664**

[Magnetism] Electromagnets: Does the strength of an electromagnet increase with greater current? **4:678**

[Magnetism] Magnets: How do heat, cold, jarring, and rubbing affect the magnetism of a nail? **4:674**

[Materials Science] Testing Tape: Finding the properties that allow tape to support weight. **4:688**

[Memory] False Memories: How can memories be influenced? **4:705**

[Microorganisms] Microorganisms: What is the best way to grow penicillin? **4:713**

[Mountains] Mountain Formations: How does the height of the mountain have an affect on desert formation? **4:741**

[Mountains] Mountain Plates: How does the movement of Earth's plates determine the formation of a mountain? **4:738**

[Nanotechnology] Nanosize: How can the physical size affect a material's properties? **4:750**

[Oceans] Stratification: How does the salinity in ocean water cause it to form layers? **4:775**

[Oxidation-Reduction] Oxidation and Rust: How is rust produced? **4:817**

[Periodic Table] Soluble Families: How does the solubility of an element relate to where it is located on the Periodic Table? **4:835**

[Pesticides] Moving through Water: How can pesticides affect nontarget plant life? **4:852**

[Plants and Water] Water Flow: How do varying solutions of water affect the amount of water a plant takes in and its turgor pressure? **5:900**

[Scientific Method] Using the Scientific Method: Do fruit flies appear out of thin air? **5:1013**

[Scientific Method] Using the Scientific Method: What are the mystery powders? **5:1009**

[Seashells] Classifying Seashells **5:1025**

[Seashells] Shell Strength: Which shell is stronger: a clam shell or lobster shell? **5:1022**

[Simple Machines] Wheel and Axle: How can changing the size of the wheel affect the amount of work it takes to lift a load? **5:1051**

[Solar Energy] Capturing Solar Energy: Will seedlings grow bigger in a greenhouse? **5:1084**

[Solar Energy] Solar Cells: Will sunlight make a motor run? **5:1087**

[Static Electricity] Building an Electroscope: Which objects are electrically charged? **6:1135**

[Static Electricity] Measuring a Charge: Does nylon or wool create a stronger static electric charge? **6:1139**

[Structures and Shapes] Arches and Beams: Which is strongest? **6:1167**

[Time] Pendulums: How do the length, weight, and swing angle of a pendulum affect its oscillation time? **6:1180**

[Tropisms] Heliotropism: How does the Sun affect the movement of certain plants? **6:1201**

[Vitamins and Minerals] Hard Water: Do different water sources have varying mineral content? **6:1231**

[Water Properties] Adhesion: How much weight is required to break the adhesive force between an object and water? **6:1264**

[Water Properties] Cohesion: Can the cohesive force of surface tension in water support an object denser than water? **6:1261**

[Weather] Clouds: Will a drop in air temperature cause a cloud to form? **6:1277**

[Weather] Wind: Measuring wind speed with a homemade anemometer **6:1273**

MODERATE

Moderate means that the average student should find tasks outlined in the project/experiment challenging but not difficult, and that the time spent on the project/experiment may be more extensive.

[Acid Rain] Acid Rain and Animals: How does acid rain affect brine shrimp? **1:5**

[Acid Rain] Acid Rain and Plants: How does acid rain affect plant growth? **1:9**

[Acid Rain] Acid Rain: Can acid rain harm structures? **1:12**

[Adhesives] Adhesives in the Environment: Will different environmental conditions affect the properties of different adhesives? **1:26**

[Adhesives] Material Adhesion: How do various glues adhere to different materials? **1:22**

[Air and Water Pollution] Pollutant Bioindicators: Can lichens provide clues to an area's air pollution? **1:51**

[Animal Defenses] Camouflage: Does an animal's living environment relate to the color of the animal life? **1:63**

[Animal Defenses] Ladybug Threats: How do ladybugs defend themselves when they feel threatened? **1:65**

[Annual Growth] Lichen Growth: What can be learned from the environment by observing lichens? **1:79**

[Annual Growth] Tree Growth: What can be learned from the growth patterns of trees? **1:74**

[Biomes] Building a Temperate Forest Biome **1:107**

[Caves] Cave Icicles: How does the mineral content of water affect the formation of stalactites and stalagmites? **1:135**

[Chemical Energy] Exothermic or Endothermic: Determining whether various chemical reactions are exothermic or endothermic **1:156**

[Chemical Energy] Rusting: Is the chemical reaction exothermic, endothermic, or neither? **1:152**

[Chemical Properties] Chemical Patination: Producing chemical reactions on metal **1:173**

[Chemical Properties] Chemical Reactions: What happens when mineral oil, water, and iodine mix? **1:170**

[Chlorophyll] Plant Pigments: Can pigments be separated? **1:193**

[Chlorophyll] Response to Light: Do plants grow differently in different colors of light? **1:197**

[Color] Color and Flavor: How much does color affect flavor perception? **2:207**

[Color] Temperature and Color: What color has the highest temperature? **2:210**

[Comets and Meteors] Comet Nucleus: Linking a Comet's Composition to its Properties. **2:218**

[Comets and Meteors] Meteor Impact: How do the characteristics of a meteorite and its impact affect the shape of the crater? **2:221**

[Composting/Landfills] Composting: Using organic material to grow plants **2:237**

[Crystals] Cool Crystals: How does the effect of cooling impact crystal growth? **2:252**

[Crystals] Crystal Structure: Will varying shape crystals form from varying substances? **2:246**

[Density and Buoyancy] Buoyancy: Does water pressure affect buoyancy? **2:264**

[Density and Buoyancy] Density: Can a scale of relative density predict whether one material floats on another? **2:260**

[DNA (Deoxyribonucleic Acid)] The Stuff of Life: Isolating DNA **2:289**

[Dyes] Holding the Dye: How do dye fixatives affect the color-fastness of the dye? **2:304**

[Earthquakes] Detecting an Earthquake: How can movement of Earth's crust be measured? **2:314**

[Electricity] Batteries: Can a series of homemade electric cells form a "pile" strong enough to match the voltage of a D-cell battery? **2:340**

[Electricity] Electrolytes: Do some solutions conduct electricity better than others? **2:335**

[Electricity] Electroplating: Using electricity to move one metal onto another metal **2:344**

[Electromagnetism] Magnetism:How can a magnetic field be created and detected? **2:351**

[Enzymes] Stopping Enzymes: Does temperature affect enzyme action? **2:368**

[Erosion] Erosion: Does soil type affect the amount of water that runs off a hillside? **2:377**

[Erosion] Plants and Erosion: How do plants affect the rate of soil erosion? **2:381**

[Ethnobotany] Coiling Reeds: How does the tightness of the coil affect the ability to hold materials? **2:396**

[Ethnobotany] Plants and Health: Which plants have anti-bacterial properties? **2:392**

[Fish] Fish Breathing: How do different fish take in oxygen? **3:404**

[Fish] Fish Movement: How do fins and body shape affect the movement of fish? **3:407**

[Flowers] Self versus Cross: Will there be a difference in reproduction between self-pollinated and cross-pollinated plants of the same type? **3:427**

[Fluids] Viscosity: How can temperature affect the viscosity of liquids? **3:441**

[Food Preservation] Drying Foods: Does drying fruits help prevent or delay spoilage? **3:458**

[Food Preservation] Sweet Preservatives: How does sugar affect the preservation of fruit? **3:454**

[Food Science] Jelly and Pectin: How does acidity affect how fruit gels? **3:467**

[Food Science] Rising Foods: How much carbon dioxide do different leavening agents produce? **3:470**

[Food Spoilage] Preservatives: How do different substances affect the growth of mold? **3:481**

[Forensic Science] Blood Patterns: How can a blood spatter help recreate the crime? **3:515**

[Fossils] Fossil Formation: What are the physical characteristics of an organism that make the best fossils? **3:530**

[Fungi] Living Conditions: What is the ideal temperature for yeast growth? **3:544**

[Germination] Seed Scarification: Does breaking the seed shell affect germination time? **3:573**

[Gravity] Gravity: How fast do different objects fall? **3:581**

[Gravity] Measuring Mass: How can a balance be made? **3:585**

[Greenhouse Effect] Fossil Fuels: What happens when fossil fuels burn? **3:596**

[Groundwater Aquifers] Aquifers: How do they become polluted? **3:605**

[Groundwater Aquifers] Groundwater: How can it be cleaned? **3:609**

[Insects] Ant Food: What type of foods is one type of ant attracted to? **3:635**

[Insects] Lightning Bugs: How does the environment affect a firefly's flash? **3:638**

[Light Properties] Refraction: How does the material affect how light travels? **4:666**

[Materials Science] Developing Renewables: Can a renewable packing material have the same qualities as a non-renewable material? **4:691**

[Microorganisms] Growing Microorganisms in a Petri Dish **4:716**

[Mixtures and Solutions] Colloids: Can colloids be distinguished from suspension using the Tyndall effect? **4:730**

[Mixtures and Solutions] Suspensions and Solutions: Can filtration and evaporation determine whether mixtures are suspensions or solutions? **4:725**

[Nutrition] Nutrition: Which foods contain proteins and salts? **4:764**

[Optics and Optical Illusions] Optics: What is the focal length of a lens? **4:788**

[Osmosis and Diffusion] Changing Sizes: What effect does molecule size have on osmosis **4:806**

[Osmosis and Diffusion] Measuring Membranes: Is a plastic bag a semipermeable membrane? **4:798**

[Oxidation-Reduction] Oxidation Reaction: Can acid change the color of copper? **4:820**

[Oxidation-Reduction] Reduction: How will acid affect dirty pennies? **4:813**

[Periodic Table] Active Metals: What metals give off electrons more readily than others? **4:838**

[Periodic Table] Metals versus Nonmetals: Which areas of the periodic table have elements that conduct electricity? **4:830**

[Pesticides] Natural versus Synthetic: How do different types of pesticides compare against a pest? **4:848**

[Photosynthesis] Light Intensity: How does the intensity of light affect plant growth? **4:877**

[Photosynthesis] Photosynthesis: How does light affect plant growth? **4:873**

[Plant Anatomy] Plant Hormones: What is the affect of hormones on root and stem growth? **5:886**

[Plants and Water] Transpiration: How do different environmental conditions affect plants' rates of transpiration? **5:904**

[Polymers] Polymer Properties: How are the properties of hard plastics different? **5:923**

[Polymers] Polymer Slime: How will adding more of a polymer change the properties of a polymer "slime"? **5:919**

[Potential and Kinetic Energy] Using Energy: Build a roller coaster **5:934**

[Renewable Energy] Capturing Wind Energy: How does the material affect the amount of wind energy harnessed? **5:944**

[Renewable Energy] Hydropower: How does water pressure affect water energy? **5:948**

[Rivers] Weathering Erosion in Glaciers: How does a river make a trench? **5:957**

[Rocks and Minerals] Rock Classification: Is it igneous, sedimentary, or metamorphic? **5:975**

[Salinity] Density Ball: How to make a standard for measuring density **5:1000**

[Separation and Identification] Identifying a Mixture: How can determining basic properties of a substance allow you to identify the substances in a mixture? **5:1039**

[Simple Machines] The Screw: How does the distance between the threads of a screw affect the work? **5:1057**

[Soil] Soil pH: Does the pH of soil affect plant growth? **5:1074**

[Sound] Soundproofing: How do different materials affect sound? **5:1102**

[Space Observation] Telescopes: How do different combinations of lenses affect the image? **6:1113**

[Stars] Tracking Stars: Where is Polaris? **6:1125**

[Stars] Tracking the Motion of the Planets: Can a planet be followed? **6:1128**

[Storms] Forming Hailstones: How do temperature differences affect the formation of hail? **6:1158**

[Structures and Shapes] Beams and Rigidity: How does the vertical height of a beam affect its rigidity? **6:1170**

[Time] Water Clock: Does the amount of water in a water clock affect its accuracy? **6:1185**

[Tropisms] Geotropism: Will plant roots turn toward the pull of gravity? **6:1197**

[Tropisms] Phototropism: Will plants follow a maze to reach light? **6:1193**

[Vegetative Propagation] Auxins: How do auxins affect plant growth? **6:1209**

[Vegetative Propagation] Potatoes from Pieces: How do potatoes reproduce vegetatively? **6:1216**

[Vitamins and Minerals] Vitamin C: What juices are the best sources of vitamin C? **6:1226**

[Volcanoes] Model of a Volcano: Will it blow its top? **6:1240**

[Wood] Water Absorption: How do different woods absorb water? **6:1298**

[Wood] Wood Hardness: How does the hardness of wood relate to its building properties? **6:1302**

MODERATE/DIFFICULT

Moderate/Difficult means that the average student should find tasks outlined in the project/experiment challenging, and that the time spent on the project/experiment may be more extensive.

[Bacteria] Bacterial Growth: How do certain substances inhibit or promote bacterial growth? **1:90**

[Biomes] Building a Desert Biome **1:108**

[Cells] Investigating Cells: What are the differences between a multicellular organism and a unicellular organism? **1:141**

[Cells] Plant Cells: What are the cell differences between monocot and dicot plants? **1:145**

[Cells] Yeast Cells: How do they reproduce? **1:147**

[Flowers] Sweet Sight: Can changing a flower's nectar and color affect the pollinators lured to the flower? **3:431**

[Heat] Conduction: Which solid materials are the best conductors of heat? **3:618**

[Heat] Heat Capacity: Which liquids have the highest heat capacity? **3:625**

[Memory] Memory Mnemonics: What techniques help in memory retention? **4:701**

[Nutrition] Daily Nutrition: How nutritious is my diet? **4:766**

[Plant Anatomy] Water Uptake: How do different plants differ in their water needs? **6:390**

[Rocks and Minerals] Mineral Testing: What kind of mineral is it? **6:971**

[Rotation and Orbits] Foucault Pendulum: How can a pendulum demonstrate the rotation of Earth? **6:985**

[Salinity] Making a Hydrometer: How can salinity be measured? **6:997**

[Separation and Identification] Chromatography: Can you identify a pen from the way its colors separate? **6:1034**

[Solar Energy] Retaining the Sun's heat: What substance best stores heat for a solar system? **6:1090**

DIFFICULT

Difficult means that the average student wil probably find the tasks outlined in the project/experiment mentally and/or physically challenging, and that the time spent on the project/experiment may be more extensive.

[Bacteria] Bacterial Resistance: Can bacteria gain resistance to a substance after exposure? **1:95**

[DNA (Deoxyribonucleic Acid)] Comparing DNA: Does the DNA from different species have the same appearance? **2:291**

[Forces] Newton's Laws in Action: How do water bottle rockets demonstrate Newton's laws of motion? **3:493**

[Forensic Science] Fiber Evidence: How can scientific techniques be used to identify fiber? **3:511**

[Life Cycles] Insects: How does food supply affect the growth rate of grasshoppers or crickets? **4:651**

[Life Cycles] Tadpoles: Does temperature affect the rate at which tadpoles change into frogs? **4:647**

[Optics and Optical Illusions] Optical Illusions: Can the eye be fooled? **4:791**

[pH] Chemical Titration: What is required to change a substance from an acid or a base into a neutral solution? **4:865**

[pH] Kitchen Chemistry: What is the pH of household chemicals? **4:861**

[Polymers] Polymer Strength: What are the tensile properties of certain polymers that make them more durable than others? **5:914**

[Soil] Soil Profile: What are the different properties of the soil horizons? **5:1067**

Timetable Index

Chapter name in brackets, followed by experiment name. The numeral before the colon indicates volume; numbers after the colon indicate page number.

LESS THAN 15 MINUTES

[Greenhouse Effect] Fossil Fuels: What happens when fossil fuels burn? **4:596**

15 TO 20 MINUTES

[Air] Air Density: Does warm air take up less room than cool air? **1:36**

[Air] Convection Currents: How can rising air cause weather changes? **1:39**

[Chemosenses] Smell and Taste: How does smell affect the sense of taste? **1:186**

[Density and Buoyancy] Buoyancy: Does water pressure affect buoyancy? **2:264**

[Enzymes] Finding the Enzyme: Which enzyme breaks down hydrogen peroxide? **2:362**

[Flight] Helicopters, Propellers, and Centripetal Force: Will it fly high? **3:148**

[Fluids] Spinning Fluids: How do different fluids behave when immersed in a spinning rod? **3:444**

[Heat] Convection: How does heat move through liquids? **3:622**

[Light Properties] Looking for the Glow: Which objects glow under black light? **4:661**

[Magnetism] Electromagnets: Does the strength of an electromagnet increase with greater current? **4:678**

[Nanotechnology] Nanosize Substances: How can the physical size affect the rate of reaction? **4:753**

[Rocks and Minerals] Mineral Testing: What kind of mineral is it? **5:971**

[Rotation and Orbits] Spinning Effects: How does the speed of a rotating object affect the way centrifugal force can overcome gravity? **5:989**

[Simple Machines] Lever Lifting: How does the distance from the fulcrum affect work? **5:1055**

[Simple Machines] The Screw: How does the distance between the threads of a screw affect the work? **5:1057**

[Simple Machines] Wheel and Axle: How can changing the size of the wheel affect the amount of work it takes to lift a load? **5:1051**

[Space Observation] Doppler Effect: How can waves measure the distance and speed of objects? **6:1118**

[Static Electricity] Measuring a Charge: Does nylon or wool create a stronger static electric charge? **6:1139**

[Volcanoes] Looking at a Seismograph: Can a volcanic eruption be detected? **6:1242**

[Water Properties] Cohesion: Can the cohesive force of surface tension in water support an object denser than water? **6:1261**

[Weather] Wind: Measuring wind speed with a homemade anemometer **6:1273**

30 TO 45 MINUTES

[Annual Growth] Tree Growth: What can be learned from the growth patterns of trees? **1:74**

[Caves] Cave Formation: How does the acidity of a substance affect the formation of a cave? **1:132**

[Chemical Energy] Rusting: Is the chemical reaction exothermic, endothermic, or neither? **1:152**

[Flight] Lift-Off: How can a glider be made to fly higher? **3:415**

[Food Science] Rising Foods: How much carbon dioxide do different leavening agents produce? **3:470**

[Forces] Centripetal Action: What is the relationship between distance and force in circular motion? **3:501**

[Gravity] Gravity: How fast do different objects fall? **3:581**

[Gravity] Measuring Mass: How can a balance be made? **3:585**

[Heat] Conduction: Which solid materials are the best conductors of heat? **3:618**

[Light Properties] Refraction and Defraction: Making a rainbow **4:664**

[Light Properties] Refraction: How does the material affect how light travels? **4:666**

[Magnetism] Magnets: How do heat, cold, jarring, and rubbing affect the magnetism of a nail? **4:674**

[Materials Science] Testing Tape: Finding the properties that allow tape to support weight. **4:688**

[Memory] False Memories: How can memories be influenced? **4:705**

[Mountains] Mountain Plates: How does the movement of Earth's plates determine the formation of a mountain? **4:738**

[Periodic Table] Soluble Families: How does the solubility of an element relate to where it is located on the Periodic Table? **4:835**

[Rivers] Stream Flow: Does the stream meander? **5:960**

[Salinity] Density Ball: How to make a standard for measuring density **5:1000**

[Scientific Method] Using the Scientific Method: What are the mystery powders? **5:1009**

[Solar Energy] Capturing Solar Energy: Will seedlings grow bigger in a greenhouse? **5:1084**

[Solar Energy] Solar Cells: Will sunlight make a motor run? **5:1087**

[Sound] Soundproofing: How do different materials affect sound? **5:1102**

[Static Electricity] Building an Electroscope: Which objects are electrically charged? **6:1135**

[Storms] Forming Hailstones: How do temperature differences affect the formation of hail? **6:1158**

[Storms] Lightning Sparks: Explore how separating charges causes an attraction between objects **6:1152**

[Storms] Tornadoes: Making a violent vortex **6:1155**

[Structures and Shapes] Arches and Beams: Which is strongest? **6:1167**

[Structures and Shapes] Beams and Rigidity: How does the vertical height of a beam affect its rigidity? **6:1170**

[Time] Pendulums: How do the length, weight, and swing angle of a pendulum affect its oscillation time? **6:1180**

[Time] Water Clock: Does the amount of water in a water clock affect its accuracy? **6:1185**

[Vitamins and Minerals] Hard Water: Do different water sources have varying mineral content? **6:1231**

[Wood] Wood Hardness: How does the hardness of wood relate to its building properties? **6:1302**

1 HOUR

[Animal Defenses] Ladybug Threats: How do ladybugs defend themselves when they feel threatened? **1:65**

[Bones and Muscles] Muscles: How does the strength of muscles affect fatigue over time? **1:120**

[Cells] Investigating Cells: What are the differences between a multicellular organism and a unicellular organism? **1:141**

[Cells] Plant Cells: What are the cell differences between monocot and dicot plants? **1:145**

[Cells] Yeast Cells: How do they reproduce? **1:147**

[Chemical Energy] Exothermic or Endothermic: Determining whether various chemical reactions are exothermic or endothermic **1:156**

[Chemical Properties] Slime: What happens when white glue and borax mix? **1:167**

[Chemosenses] Supertasters: Is there a correlation between the number of taste buds and taste perception? **1:180**

[Color] Temperature and Color: What color has the highest temperature? **2:210**

[Comets and Meteors] Meteor Impact: How do the characteristics of a meteorite and its impact affect the shape of the crater? **2:221**

[Density and Buoyancy] Density: Can a scale of relative density predict whether one material floats on another? **2:260**

[DNA (Deoxyribonucleic Acid)] The Stuff of Life: Isolating DNA **2:289**

[Earthquakes] Detecting an Earthquake: How can movement of Earth's crust be measured? **2:314**

[Earthquakes] Earthquake Simulation: Is the destruction greater at the epicenter? **2:317**

[Eclipses] Simulating Solar and Lunar Eclipses **2:327**

[Electricity] Batteries: Can a series of homemade electric cells form a "pile" strong enough to match the voltage of a D-cell battery? **2:340**

[Electricity] Electrolytes: Do some solutions conduct electricity better than others? **2:335**

[Electricity] Electroplating: Using electricity to move one metal onto another metal **2:344**

[Fish] Fish Breathing: How do different fish take in oxygen? **3:404**

[Forensic Science] Blood Patterns: How can a blood spatter help recreate the crime? **3:515**

[Fossils] Fossil Formation: What are the physical characteristics of an organism that make the best fossils? **3:530**

[Insects] Ant Food: What type of foods is one type of ant attracted to? **3:635**

[Materials Science] Developing Renewables: Can a renewable packing material have the same qualities as a non-renewable material? **4:691**

[Mixtures and Solutions] Colloids: Can colloids be distinguished from suspension using the Tyndall effect? **4:730**

[Mixtures and Solutions] Suspensions and Solutions: Can filtration and evaporation determine whether mixtures are suspensions or solutions? **4:725**

[Mountains] Mountain Formations: How does the height of the mountain have an affect on desert formation? **4:741**

[Nutrition] Energizing Foods: Which foods contain carbohydrates and fats? **4:761**

[Nutrition] Nutrition: Which foods contain proteins and salts? **4:764**

[Oceans] Currents: Water behavior in density-driven currents **4:780**

[Periodic Table] Metals versus Nonmetals: Which areas of the periodic table have elements that conduct electricity? **4:830**

[pH] Chemical Titration: What is required to change a substance from an acid or a base into a neutral solution? **4:865**

[pH] Kitchen Chemistry: What is the pH of household chemicals? **4:861**

[Polymers] Polymer Properties: How are the properties of hard plastics different? **5:923**

[Polymers] Polymer Slime: How will adding more of a polymer change the properties of a polymer "slime"? **5:919**

[Polymers] Polymer Strength: What are the tensile properties of certain polymers that make them more durable than others? **5:914**

[Potential and Kinetic Energy] Measuring Energy: How does the height of an object affect its potential energy? **5:931**

[Renewable Energy] Capturing Wind Energy: How does the material affect the amount of wind energy harnessed? **5:944**

[Rocks and Minerals] Rock Classification: Is it igneous, sedimentary, or metamorphic? **5:975**

[Rotation and Orbits] Foucault Pendulum: How can a pendulum demonstrate the rotation of Earth? **5:985**

[Salinity] Making a Hydrometer: How can salinity be measured? **5:997**

[Sound] Pitch: How does the thickness of a vibrating string affect sound? **5:1099**

[Sound] Wave Length: How does the length of a vibrating string affect the sound it produces? **5:1096**

[Space Observation] Telescopes: How do different combinations of lenses affect the image? **6:1113**

[Vitamins and Minerals] Vitamin C: What juices are the best sources of vitamin C? **6:1226**

[Weather] Clouds: Will a drop in air temperature cause a cloud to form? **6:1277**

2 HOURS

[Chlorophyll] Plant Pigments: Can pigments be separated? **1:193**

[Electromagnetism] Electromagnetism: How can an electromagnet be created? **2:354**

[Electromagnetism] Magnetism:How can a magnetic field be created and detected? **2:351**

[Ethnobotany] Coiling Reeds: How does the tightness of the coil affect the ability to hold materials? **2:396**

[Fluids] Viscosity: How can temperature affect the viscosity of liquids? **3:441**

[Food Science] Jelly and Pectin: How does acidity affect how fruit gels? **3:467**

[Forces] Newton's Laws in Action: How do water bottle rockets demonstrate Newton's laws of motion? **3:493**

[Forensic Science] Fiber Evidence: How can scientific techniques be used to identify fiber? **3:511**

[Groundwater Aquifers] Aquifers: How do they become polluted? **3:605**

[Groundwater Aquifers] Groundwater: How can it be cleaned? **3:609**

[Heat] Heat Capacity: Which liquids have the highest heat capacity? **3:625**

[Oceans] Stratification: How does the salinity in ocean water cause it to form layers? **4:775**

[Optics and Optical Illusions] Optics: What is the focal length of a lens? **4:788**

[Oxidation-Reduction] Reduction: How will acid affect dirty pennies? **4:813**

[Periodic Table] Active Metals: What metals give off electrons more readily than others? **4:838**

[Potential and Kinetic Energy] Using Energy: Build a roller coaster **5:934**

[Renewable Energy] Hydropower: How does water pressure affect water energy? **5:948**

[Rivers] River Flow: How does the steepness and rate of water flow affect river erosion? **5:962**

[Seashells] Classifying Seashells **5:1025**

[Seashells] Shell Strength: Which shell is stronger: a clam shell or lobster shell? **5:1022**

[Separation and Identification] Chromatography: Can you identify a pen from the way its colors separate? **5:1034**

[Separation and Identification] Identifying a Mixture: How can determining basic properties of a substance allow you to identify the substances in a mixture? **5:1039**

[Stars] Tracking Stars: Where is Polaris? **6:1125**

[Water Properties] Adhesion: How much weight is required to break the adhesive force between an object and water? **6:1264**

3 HOURS

[Adhesives] Adhesives in the Environment: Will different environmental conditions affect the properties of different adhesives? **1:26**

[Air and Water Pollution] Pollutant Bioindicators: Can lichens provide clues to an area's air pollution? **1:51**

[Annual Growth] Lichen Growth: What can be learned from the environment by observing lichens? **1:79**

[Comets and Meteors] Comet Nucleus: Linking a Comet's Composition to its Properties. **2:218**

[Erosion] Erosion: Does soil type affect the amount of water that runs off a hillside? **2:377**

[Fish] Fish Movement: How do fins and body shape affect the movement of fish? **3:407**

[Fungi] Living Conditions: What is the ideal temperature for yeast growth? **3:544**

[Nanotechnology] Nanosize: How can the physical size affect a material's properties? **4:750**

[Volcanoes] Model of a Volcano: Will it blow its top? **6:124**

6 HOURS

[Color] Color and Flavor: How much does color affect flavor perception? **2:207**

[Dissolved Oxygen] Goldfish Breath: How does a decrease in the dissolved oxygen level affect the breathing rate of goldfish? **2:279**

[Enzymes] Stopping Enzymes: Does temperature affect enzyme action? **2:368**

1 DAY

[Adhesives] Material Adhesion: How do various glues adhere to different materials? **1:22**

[Eclipses] Phases of the Moon: What does each phase look like? **2:329**

[Enzymes] Tough and Tender: Does papain speed up the aging process? **2:365**

[Fossils] Making an Impression: In which soil environment does a fossil most easily form? **3:526**

[Osmosis and Diffusion] Changing Concentrations: Will a bag of salt water draw in fresh water? **4:803**

[Plants and Water] Transpiration: How do different environmental conditions affect plants' rates of transpiration? **5:904**

[Plants and Water] Water Flow: How do varying solutions of water affect the amount of water a plant takes in and its turgor pressure? **5:900**

[Solar Energy] Retaining the Sun's heat: What substance best stores heat for a solar system? **5:1090**

[Water Cycle] Temperature: How does temperature affect the rate of evaporation? **6:1248**

[Wood] Water Absorption: How do different woods absorb water? **6:1298**

2 DAYS

[Bacteria] Bacterial Growth: How do certain substances inhibit or promote bacterial growth? **1:90**

[Flowers] Sweet Sight: Can changing a flower's nectar and color affect the pollinators lured to the flower? **3:431**

[Genetics] Genetic Traits: Will you share certain genetic traits more with family members than non-family members? **3:556**

[Memory] Memory Mnemonics: What techniques help in memory retention? **4:701**

[Osmosis and Diffusion] Measuring Membranes: Is a plastic bag a semipermeable membrane? **4:798**

[Soil] Soil Profile: What are the different properties of the soil horizons? **5:1067**

3 DAYS

[Animal Defenses] Camouflage: Does an animal's living environment relate to the color of the animal life? **1:63**

[Chemical Properties] Chemical Patination: Producing chemical reactions on metal **1:173**

[Chemical Properties] Chemical Reactions: What happens when mineral oil, water, and iodine mix? **1:170**

[DNA (Deoxyribonucleic Acid)] Comparing DNA: Does the DNA from different species have the same appearance? **2:291**

[Dyes] Applying Dyes: How does the fiber affect the dye color? **2:301**

[Dyes] Holding the Dye: How do dye fixatives affect the colorfastness of the dye? **2:304**

[Ethnobotany] Plants and Health: Which plants have antibacterial properties? **2:392**

[Genetics] Building a Pedigree for Taste **3:559**

[Insects] Lightning Bugs: How does the environment affect a firefly's flash? **3:638**

[Oxidation-Reduction] Oxidation and Rust: How is rust produced? **4:817**

5 DAYS

[Food Spoilage] Spoiled Milk: How do different temperatures of liquid affect its rate of spoilage? **3:485**

[Nutrition] Daily Nutrition: How nutritious is my diet? **4:766**

[Osmosis and Diffusion] Changing Sizes: What effect does molecule size have on osmosis **4:806**

[Water Cycle] Surface Area: How does surface area affect the rate of evaporation? **6:1253**

6 DAYS

[Bacteria] Bacterial Resistance: Can bacteria gain resistance to a substance after exposure? **1:95**

1 WEEK

[Acid Rain] Acid Rain and Animals: How does acid rain affect brine shrimp? **1:5**

[Crystals] Crystal Structure: Will varying shape crystals form from varying substances? **2:246**

[Dissolved Oxygen] Decay and Dissolved Oxygen: How does the amount of decaying matter affect the level of dissolved oxygen in water? **2:274**

[Food Preservation] Drying Foods: Does drying fruits help prevent or delay spoilage? **3:458**

[Food Preservation] Sweet Preservatives: How does sugar affect the preservation of fruit? **3:454**

[Fungi] Decomposers: Food source for a common fungi **3:541**

[Germination] Seed Scarification: Does breaking the seed shell affect germination times? **3:573**

[Greenhouse Effect] Creating a Greenhouse: How much will the temperature rise inside a greenhouse? **3:592**

[Optics and Optical Illusions] Optical Illusions: Can the eye be fooled? **4:791**

[Oxidation-Reduction] Oxidation Reaction: Can acid change the color of copper? **4:820**

[Tropisms] Heliotropism: How does the Sun affect the movement of certain plants? **6:1201**

8 TO 12 DAYS

[Bones and Muscles] Bone Loss: How does the loss of calcium affect bone strength? **1:116**

[Caves] Cave Icicles: How does the mineral content of water affect the formation of stalactites and stalagmites? **1:135**

[Food Spoilage] Preservatives: How do different substances affect the growth of mold? **3:481**

[Pesticides] Moving through Water: How can pesticides affect nontarget plant life? **4:852**

10 DAYS

[Acid Rain] Acid Rain: Can acid rain harm structures? **1:12**

[Air and Water Pollution] Eutrophication: The effect of phosphates on water plants. **1:55**

[Microorganisms] Growing Microorganisms in a Petri Dish **4:716**

[Scientific Method] Using the Scientific Method: Do fruit flies appear out of thin air? **5:1013**

2 WEEKS

[Acid Rain] Acid Rain and Plants: How does acid rain affect plant growth? **1:9**

[Crystals] Cool Crystals: How does the effect of cooling impact crystal growth? **2:252**

[Erosion] Plants and Erosion: How do plants affect the rate of soil erosion? **2:381**

[Germination] Comparing Germination Times: How fast can seeds grow? **3:570**

[Germination] Effects of Temperature on Germination: What temperatures encourage and discourage germination? **3:566**

[Microorganisms] Microorganisms: What is the best way to grow penicillin? **4:713**

[Pesticides] Natural versus Synthetic: How do different types of pesticides compare against a pest? **4:848**

[Stars] Tracking the Motion of the Planets: Can a planet be followed? **6:1128**

[Tropisms] Geotropism: Will plant roots turn toward the pull of gravity? **6:1197**

[Weather Forecasting] Air Pressure: How can air pressure be measured? **6:1289**

[Weather Forecasting] Dewpoint: When will dew form? **6:1286**

3 TO 4 WEEKS

[Life Cycles] Insects: How does food supply affect the growth rate of grasshoppers or crickets? **4:651**

[Life Cycles] Tadpoles: Does temperature affect the rate at which tadpoles change into frogs? **4:647**

[Plant Anatomy] Water Uptake: How do different plants differ in their water needs? **5:890**

[Rivers] Weathering Erosion in Glaciers: How does a river make a trench? **5:957**

[Tropisms] Phototropism: Will plants follow a maze to reach light? **6:1193**

[Vegetative Propagation] Auxins: How do auxins affect plant growth? **6:1209**

[Vegetative Propagation] Potatoes from Pieces: How do potatoes reproduce vegetatively? **6:1216**

4 WEEKS

[Photosynthesis] Light Intensity: How does the intensity of light affect plant growth? **4:877**

[Photosynthesis] Photosynthesis: How does light affect plant growth? **4:873**

6 WEEKS

[Plant Anatomy] Plant Hormones: What is the affect of hormones on root and stem growth? **5:886**

[Soil] Soil pH: Does the pH of soil affect plant growth? **5:1074**

6 TO 14 WEEKS

[Chlorophyll] Response to Light: Do plants grow differently in different colors of light? **1:197**

[Flowers] Self versus Cross: Will there be a difference in reproduction between self-pollinated and cross-pollinated plants of the same type? **1:423**

4 MONTHS

[Composting/Landfills] Composting: Using organic material to grow plants **2:237**

[Composting/Landfills] Living Landfill: What effect do the microorganisms in soil have on the decomposition process? **2:232**

6 MONTHS

[Biomes] Building a Desert Biome **1:108**

[Biomes] Building a Temperate Forest Biome **1:107**

General Subject Index

The numeral before the colon indicates volume; numbers after the colon indicate page number. **Bold** page numbers indicate main essays. The notation (ill.) after a page number indicates a figure.

A

A groups (periodic table), *4:* 829
A layer (soil), *5:* 1066–67, 1067 (ill.)
Abscission, *1:* 192
Absolute dating, *3:* 525
Acceleration
  bottle rocket experiment, *3:* 493–501, 495 (ill.), 498 (ill.), 499 (ill.)
  build a roller coaster experiment, *5:* 934–38, 935 (ill.), 936 (ill.), 937 (ill.)
  centripetal force experiment, *3:* 501–5, 503 (ill.)
  centripetal force in, *3:* 493, 493 (ill.)
  Newtonian laws of motion on, *3:* 492, 492 (ill.)
  of planetary orbits, *3:* 579–80
Acetate, *3:* 509, 511–14, 511 (ill.), 512 (ill.), 513 (ill.)
Acetic acid, *1:* 165, *4:* 820–23, 820 (ill.), 821 (ill.), 822 (ill.)
Acetone, *3:* 511–14, 511 (ill.), 512 (ill.), 513 (ill.)
Acid/base indicators, *4:* 860
  cave formation experiment, *1:* 134, 134 (ill.)
  pH of household chemicals experiment, *4:* 861–65, 861 (ill.), 863 (ill.)
Acid rain, *1:* **1–17,** 17 (ill.)
  brine shrimp experiment, *1:* 5–8, 7 (ill.)
  damage from, *1:* 1–3, *4:* 860–61
  design an experiment for, *1:* 15–16
  formation of, *1:* 1, 164
  pH of, *1:* 1, 2 (ill.), 3 (ill.), *4:* 860–61, 861 (ill.)
  plant growth experiment, *1:* 9–12, 11 (ill.)
  structure damage experiment, *1:* 12–15, 14 (ill.), 15 (ill.), 16
Acidity
  in food preservation, *3:* 452
  in food spoilage, *3:* 478
  measurement of, *1:* 1
  neutralization of, *1:* 4
  for separation and identification, *5:* 1033, 1034 (ill.)
  of soil, *5:* 1064
  soil pH and plant growth experiment, *5:* 1074–77, 1074 (ill.), 1076 (ill.), 1079 (ill.)
  See also pH
Acids
  acid-copper reduction experiment, *4:* 813–17, 814 (ill.), 815 (ill.)
  cave formation experiment, *1:* 132–35, 134 (ill.)
  chemical properties of, *1:* 164
  chemical titration experiment, *4:* 865–68, 865 (ill.), 866 (ill.), 867 (ill.)
  copper color change experiment, *4:* 820–23, 820 (ill.), 821 (ill.), 822 (ill.)
  electricity conduction by, *2:* 334
  pH of, *4:* 859–61
  uses for, *4:* 859, 860
  See also Lemon juice; Vinegar
Acoustics, *5:* 1096
Acronyms, *4:* 700
Actions, reactions to every, *3:* 492, 494

Active solar energy systems, *5:* 1082
Adaptation, *1:* 87
Additives, food, *3:* 453
Adenine, *2:* 286–87
Adhesion
  of water, *6:* 1259–61, 1260 (ill.)
  water adhesion and weight experiment, *6:* 1264–68, 1265 (ill.), 1266 (ill.)
Adhesives, *1:* **19–32,** 20 (ill.), 21 (ill.)
  design an experiment for, *1:* 31–32
  environmental conditions experiment, *1:* 26–30, 27 (ill.), 28 (ill.), 29 (ill.)
  glue adherence experiment, *1:* 22–25, 23 (ill.), 24 (ill.)
  tape strength experiment, *4:* 688–91, 689 (ill.), 690 (ill.)
  types of, *1:* 19–22
Aeration, *3:* 609–12, 610 (ill.)
Aerobic decomposition, *2:* 231
African violets, *6:* 1207, 1207 (ill.)
Agar, *1:* 90–95, 92 (ill.), 93 (ill.), 95–100
Agriculture, *2:* 229–30, *4:* 646
Air, *1:* **33–44,** 35 (ill.), 36 (ill.), 43 (ill.), 45
  composition of, *1:* 33, 34 (ill.)
  convection current experiment, *1:* 39–42, 41 (ill.)
  density of, *1:* 34–36, 35 (ill.), 36 (ill.), *4:* 737
  design an experiment for, *1:* 42–44
  in food spoilage, *3:* 478
  in soil, *5:* 1063, 1064 (ill.)
  warm air *vs.* cool air experiment, *1:* 36–39, 36 (ill.), 38 (ill.)
  water vapor content of, *6:* 1247
Air currents
  convection, *1:* 36, 36 (ill.)
  convection current experiment, *1:* 39–42, 41 (ill.)
  in storm formation, *6:* 1147
  in weather, *6:* 1272
Air masses, *1:* 34–39, 35 (ill.), 36 (ill.), 38 (ill.)
Air pollution, *1:* **45–60,** 46 (ill.)
  acid rain from, *1:* 1
  from coal, *1:* 46, 164
  design an experiment for, *1:* 58–59
  from gases, *1:* 45–46
  greenhouse effect, *1:* 46, 47 (ill.)
  indoor, *1:* 48
  lichen bioindicator experiment, *1:* 51–55, 52 (ill.), 54 (ill.), 82
  lichen bioindicators for, *1:* 74
  from particulate matter, *1:* 45, 46–47, 59
  prevention of, *1:* 50
Air pressure
  barometric measurement of, *1:* 34, 43–44, *6:* 1284
  build a barometer experiment, *6:* 1289–92, 1290 (ill.), 1291 (ill.)
  flight and, *3:* 422
  fluids and, *3:* 439, 439 (ill.)
  in weather, *1:* 33–34, *6:* 1271, 1272 (ill.)
  on weather maps, *6:* 1285
  wind and, *1:* 33–34
Air resistance, *3:* 581–82
Airplanes, *3:* 413–15
Alcohol
  in bread making, *2:* 359
  isolation and extraction experiment, *2:* 289–91, 289 (ill.), 290 (ill.)
  safety for handling, *2:* 290, 293
  species differences in DNA experiment, *2:* 291–95, 293 (ill.)
  yeast in, *3:* 540
Algae, *1:* 131, *3:* 538, *4:* 712
  chlorophyll in, *1:* 191
  in eutrophication, *1:* 49–50, 55–58
  in lichens, *1:* 51, 73–74, 75 (ill.), *3:* 538
  photosynthesis by, *1:* 74, 75 (ill.)
Alkali earth metals, *4:* 835–38, 835 (ill.), 837 (ill.)
Alkali metals, *4:* 835–38, 835 (ill.), 837 (ill.)
Alkaline solutions. *See* Bases
Alkalinity
  pH measurement of, *1:* 1
  of soil, *5:* 1064
  soil pH and plant growth experiment, *5:* 1074–77, 1074 (ill.), 1076 (ill.), 1079 (ill.)
Alleles, *3:* 554
Allergies, food, *1:* 187
Altair, *6:* 1123
Altitude
  air density changes from, *1:* 36, 36 (ill.), *4:* 737
  dissolved oxygen level changes from, *2:* 272, 273 (ill.)

Altocumulus clouds, *6:* 1273
Altostratus clouds, *6:* 1273
Alum
  crystal formation experiment, *2:* 246–50, 246 (ill.), 249 (ill.)
  fixatives for colorfastness experiment, *2:* 304–7, 306 (ill.), 307 (ill.)
Aluminum
  acidity reaction of, *1:* 164
  build an electroscope experiment, *6:* 1135–39, 1137 (ill.), 1138 (ill.)
  decomposition of, *2:* 231
  glue adherence experiment, *1:* 22–25, 23 (ill.), 24 (ill.)
  heat conduction experiment, *3:* 618–22, 620 (ill.), 621 (ill.)
  light refraction experiment, *4:* 666–69, 666 (ill.), 667 (ill.)
  soundproofing materials experiment, *5:* 1102–5, 1104 (ill.)
Aluminum sulfate. *See* Alum
Alzheimer's disease, *4:* 699
Amazon Basin, *1:* 105
Amber, *3:* 535
Amino acids, *2:* 286
Ammonia
  comet composition experiment, *2:* 218–21, 220 (ill.)
  copper patina experiment, *1:* 173–75, 174 (ill.), 175 (ill.)
  pH of household chemicals experiment, *4:* 861–65, 861 (ill.), 863 (ill.)
  safety for, *1:* 173
Ammonium, *1:* 157–59, 157 (ill.), 158 (ill.), 159 (ill.), 164
Amnesia, *4:* 699
Ampere, André-Marie, *2:* 333, 334 (ill.)
Amperes (amps), *2:* 333
Amphibians
  acid rain damage to, *1:* 1–2
  life cycle of, *4:* 645–46, 646 (ill.)
  tadpoles and temperature experiment, *4:* 647–51, 648 (ill.), 649 (ill.), 650 (ill.)
Amplitude, *5:* 1095 (ill.)
Anaerobic decomposition, *2:* 231
Andes, *4:* 735
Andromeda Galaxy, *6:* 1124
Anemia, sickle cell, *2:* 287, *3:* 555
Anemometers, *6:* 1273–77, 1273 (ill.), 1275 (ill.), 1283 (ill.)
Angel fish, *3:* 407–9, 409 (ill.), 410
Angiosperms, *3:* 423, *6:* 1295, 1296 (ill.)
Angle of impact, *2:* 221–25, 224 (ill.)
Anglerfish, *4:* 775
Angraecum sesquipedale, 3: 426
Aniline, *2:* 300
Animal defenses, *1:* **61–69,** 62 (ill.), 63 (ill.)
  camouflage experiment, *1:* 63–65, 64 (ill.)
  design an experiment for, *1:* 68–69
  ladybug experiment, *1:* 65–68, 66 (ill.), 67 (ill.)
  overview of, *1:* 61–63
Animals
  cave, *1:* 130–31
  color perception, *2:* 214
  desert biome, *1:* 104–5
  enzymes from, *2:* 360
  living on mountains, *4:* 738
  minerals from, *6:* 1226
  ocean, *4:* 774–75
Annual growth, *1:* **71–83**
  design an experiment for, *1:* 82–83
  lichen growth experiment, *1:* 79–82, 81 (ill.)
  by lichens, *1:* 72–74, 74 (ill.)
  tree growth experiment, *1:* 74–79, 78 (ill.)
  by trees, *1:* 71–72, 72 (ill.), 73 (ill.)
  See also Plant growth
Antacids
  build a model volcano experiment, *6:* 1240–42, 1240 (ill.), 1241 (ill.)
  chemical titration experiment, *4:* 865–68, 865 (ill.), 866 (ill.), 867 (ill.)
  nanosize and reaction rate experiment, *4:* 753–55, 754 (ill.), 755 (ill.)
Antennae (insects), *3:* 632, 632 (ill.)
Anthocyanin, *1:* 192
Antibiotic resistance, *1:* 88–90, 95–100, 97 (ill.)
Antibiotics, *1:* 89–90, *3:* 539–40, *4:* 712
  anti-bacterial plant experiment, *2:* 392–95, 394 (ill.), 395 (ill.)
  growing penicillin experiment, *4:* 713–16, 713 (ill.), 715 (ill.)

Ants, *1:* 62, *3:* 634
  food for ants experiment, *3:* 635–38, 636 (ill.), 637 (ill.)
  queen, *3:* 633, 634
Appert, Nicholas, *3:* 452
Apple jelly, *3:* 467–70, 468 (ill.), 469 (ill.)
Apple juice, *6:* 1226–31, 1229 (ill.)
Apples, falling, *3:* 579, 580
Aquarium projects. *See* Fish tank projects
Aquatic plants. *See* Water plants
Aquifers, groundwater. *See* Groundwater aquifers
Arches, *6:* 1166–67, 1167–70, 1167 (ill.), 1168 (ill.), 1173 (ill.)
Archimedes, *2:* 259 (ill.)
Archimedes Principle, *2:* 259
Architecture. *See* Buildings; Structures
Arctic Ocean, *4:* 771
Aristotle, *5:* 1006, 1013
Arm muscles, *1:* 115–16, 116 (ill.)
Arrhenius, Svante, *3:* 589
Artesian wells, *3:* 601
Ascorbic acid. *See* Vitamin C
Asexual reproduction, *6:* 1208
Ashes, volcanic, *6:* 1239
Astronomers, *6:* 1109
Atlantic Ocean, *4:* 771
Atmosphere, *1:* 33–34, 35 (ill.), *3:* 589–600, 599 (ill.)
Atmospheric pressure. *See* Air pressure
Atomic clocks, *6:* 1180
Atomic mass, *4:* 828, 829
Atomic number, *4:* 828
Atomic symbol, *4:* 828
Atomic weight, *4:* 827–28
Atoms
  chemical energy of, *1:* 151
  in crystals, *2:* 244, 245 (ill.)
  density of, *2:* 257
  electrons in, *2:* 349
  in nanotechnology, *4:* 747–48
  shells of, *4:* 829, 830, 830 (ill.)
Automobiles. *See* Cars
Autotrophs, *1:* 74
Autumn, *1:* 192
Auxins
  leaf/stem cuttings and auxins experiment, *6:* 1209–16, 1213 (ill.), 1214 (ill.)
  in phototropism, *6:* 1191–92, 1193, 1193 (ill.)
  in vegetative propagation, *6:* 1208, 1209
Avery, Oswald, *2:* 286 (ill.)
Axles. *See* Wheel and axle machines

B

B groups (periodic table), *4:* 829
B layer (soil), *5:* 1067, 1067 (ill.)
Babylonia, *2:* 325–26, 375
Bacillus thuringiensis (Bt), *4:* 844–45
Bacteria, *1:* 85–102, 86 (ill.), 101 (ill.), *4:* 712
  anti-bacterial plant experiment, *2:* 392–95, 394 (ill.), 395 (ill.)
  bacterial resistance experiment, *1:* 95–100, 97 (ill.)
  blue-green, *1:* 51
  in caves, *1:* 129, 131
  for cleaning oil spills, *1:* 50
  for decomposition, *2:* 273
  design an experiment for, *1:* 100–101
  diet of, *1:* 87–88
  discovery of, *1:* 85, *4:* 711–12
  DNA, *2:* 286
  enzymes from, *2:* 362
  extremophile, *1:* 88, 88 (ill.), 101
  in food, *1:* 101
  food spoilage by, *3:* 477–80, 478 (ill.)
  growth inhibition/promotion experiment, *1:* 90–95, 92 (ill.), 93 (ill.)
  microorganisms and decomposition experiment, *2:* 233–35, 234 (ill.), 235 (ill.), 236
  safety for, *1:* 91, 96
  spoiled milk and temperature experiment, *3:* 485–88, 487 (ill.)
  structure of, *1:* 86–87, 86 (ill.)
  uses for, *1:* 101, *4:* 712
  See also Antibiotics
Bacterial diseases, *1:* 85–86, *3:* 539–40, *4:* 711–12, 712 (ill.)
Bacterial resistance, *1:* 88–90, 95–100, 97 (ill.)

Baking powder, *3:* 464
chemical titration experiment, *4:* 865–68, 865 (ill.), 866 (ill.), 867 (ill.)
leavening agents and carbon dioxide experiment, *3:* 470–73, 472 (ill.), 473 (ill.), 474
Baking soda
cave formation experiment, *1:* 133–35, 134 (ill.)
as a leavening agent, *3:* 464
leavening agents and carbon dioxide experiment, *3:* 470–73, 472 (ill.), 473 (ill.), 474
mystery powder identification experiment, *5:* 1009–13, 1011 (ill.), 1012 (ill.), 1013 (ill.)
pH of household chemicals experiment, *4:* 861–65, 861 (ill.), 863 (ill.)
soil pH and plant growth experiment, *5:* 1074–77, 1074 (ill.), 1076 (ill.), 1079 (ill.)
stalagmites and stalactite experiment, *1:* 135–39
unknown mixtures experiment, *5:* 1039–43, 1041 (ill.), 1042 (ill.)
vinegar reaction, *1:* 165
Balance/counterweight scale, *3:* 585–87, 585 (ill.), 586 (ill.), 587 (ill.), 588 (ill.)
Balloons, radiosonde, *6:* 1283
Balls, falling, *5:* 931–34, 932 (ill.), 933 (ill.)
Balsa wood, *2:* 257, 258, 258 (ill.), *6:* 1295
Baltic Sea, *5:* 996, 997
Bark (tree), *2:* 299, *6:* 1295–96
Barometers, *6:* 1284
build a barometer experiment, *6:* 1289–92, 1290 (ill.), 1291 (ill.)
experiments for, *1:* 43–44
mercury, *1:* 34
Barometric pressure. *See* Air pressure
Barringer Meteor Crater, *2:* 217, 221
Bases (basic solutions)
chemical properties of, *1:* 164
chemical titration experiment, *4:* 865–68, 865 (ill.), 866 (ill.), 867 (ill.)
for neutralization, *1:* 4
pH of, *4:* 859–61
uses for, *4:* 859, 860
Baskets, *2:* 390–91, 396–99, 398 (ill.), 399 (ill.)
Bats, *1:* 130, 131 (ill.), *3:* 425–27
Batteries, *2:* 334–35, *4:* 824 (ill.)
build a multicell battery experiment, *2:* 340–44, 341 (ill.), 342 (ill.)
electromagnet strength experiment, *4:* 678–81, 678 (ill.), 679 (ill.)
Beams, *6:* 1166–67, 1167 (ill.)
rigidity of beams experiment, *6:* 1170–72, 1171 (ill.)
strength of arches *vs.* beams experiment, *6:* 1167–70, 1168 (ill.)
Bean seeds, *3:* 566–70, 568 (ill.), 569 (ill.), 570–73, 572 (ill.)
Bedrock, *5:* 1067, 1067 (ill.)
Beef
aging meat experiment, *2:* 365–68, 366 (ill.), 367 (ill.)
ant food experiment, *3:* 635–38, 636 (ill.), 637 (ill.)
Bees, *3:* 426, 426 (ill.)
Beet dyes, *2:* 301–4, 302 (ill.), 303 (ill.), 304–7, 306 (ill.), 307 (ill.)
Beriberi, *4:* 760, *6:* 1223–24
Bernoulli, Daniel, *3:* 413, 415
Betta fish, *3:* 404–6, 405 (ill.)
Billiard balls, *5:* 911
Biodegradability, *4:* 687, 691–94, 693 (ill.), 694 (ill.), *5:* 914, 927
Bioindicators, *1:* 51–55, 52 (ill.), 54 (ill.), 82
Bioluminescence, *3:* 555, 638–42, 640 (ill.), *4:* 775, 784
Biomass, *5:* 942–43
Biomes, *1:* 103–12
desert, *1:* 103, 104–5, 104 (ill.)
desert biome experiment, *1:* 108–11, 109 (ill.), 110 (ill.), 111 (ill.)
design an experiment for, *1:* 111–12
rainforest, *1:* 105–6, 105 (ill.)
taiga, *1:* 103–4, 104 (ill.)
temperate forest experiment, *1:* 106 (ill.), 107–8, 107 (ill.), 108 (ill.)
Biopesticides, *4:* 843, 844–46, 847–52, 851 (ill.)
Birds, *1:* 50, 104, 105, *3:* 425–27, *4:* 846
Bitter taste, *1:* 177, 180, 182–86
Bivalves, *5:* 1019–20, 1020 (ill.), 1021, 1025–27, 1027 (ill.)

Black ink, *1:* 63, *5:* 1034–39, 1036 (ill.), 1037 (ill.)
Black light, *4:* 661–64, 662 (ill.), 663 (ill.)
Blanching, *3:* 466
Bleach, *4:* 812, 823
"Blending in," *1:* 61–62
Blindness, *2:* 205–6, *6:* 1224
Blood, *1:* 113, *4:* 797, 798 (ill.)
Blood spatter analysis, *3:* 508, 509 (ill.), 515–18, 516 (ill.), 517 (ill.)
Blue-green bacteria, *1:* 51
Blueshift, *6:* 1112, 1112 (ill.)
Boats, sail, *5:* 944–48, 945 (ill.), 946 (ill.)
BOD_5, *2:* 273
Boiling point, *4:* 748, 752 (ill.), *5:* 1034
Bonds, *1:* 20, 151
Bone loss, *1:* 115–20, 119 (ill.)
Bone marrow, *1:* 114
Bone tissue, *1:* 113
Bones, *1:* **113–25,** 114 (ill.)
  apatite crystals in, *2:* 243
  bone loss experiment, *1:* 116–20, 119 (ill.)
  composition and function, *1:* 113–14, 115 (ill.), 116 (ill.)
  design an experiment for, *1:* 123–25
  fossil formation experiment, *3:* 530–33, 532 (ill.)
  fossil molds of, *3:* 523
  muscle strength and fatigue experiment, *1:* 120–23, 122 (ill.)
Bony fish, *3:* 401, 402, 402 (ill.), 403 (ill.)
Book of Signs (Theophrastus), *6:* 1283–84
Borax
  polymer slime experiment, *5:* 919–23, 921 (ill.), 922 (ill.)
  white glue reaction, *1:* 167–70, 168 (ill.), 169 (ill.)
Boreal forest, *1:* 103–4, 104 (ill.)
Botany, *3:* 565
Boussingault, Jean Baptiste, *2:* 229
Bracken Cave, *1:* 130
Brahe, Tycho, *3:* 579
Braided rivers, *5:* 956
Brain
  hearing sounds, *5:* 1095
  memory and, *4:* 698–99, 699 (ill.)
  seeing optical illusions experiment, *4:* 791–94, 791 (ill.), 792 (ill.), 793 (ill.)
Bran, *4:* 760
Branches, *1:* 71, 74–79
Bread
  mold on, *3:* 478
  moldy bread experiment, *3:* 481–85, 481 (ill.), 482 (ill.), 483 (ill.)
  yeast in, *2:* 359, *3:* 464–65, 465 (ill.), 540, 544
Breathing. *See* Respiration
Bridges, *6:* 1165, 1173 (ill.)
  rigidity of beams experiment, *6:* 1170–72, 1171 (ill.)
  strength of arches *vs.* beams experiment, *6:* 1167–70, 1168 (ill.)
Brightness, *2:* 206–7, *6:* 1124, 1124 (ill.)
Brine shrimp, *1:* 5–8, 7 (ill.)
Bromelain, *2:* 368–72, 370 (ill.), 371 (ill.)
Bronze Age, *2:* 231, *5:* 969
Browning reaction. *See* Maillard reaction
Bt *(Bacillus thuringiensis), 4:* 844–45
Budding, *1:* 143–44, *3:* 539, 540 (ill.)
Buds, *1:* 72, 72 (ill.), 73 (ill.)
Building materials, *2:* 321
Buildings, *6:* 1165
  acid rain damage to, *1:* 3, 12–15, 14 (ill.), 15 (ill.), 16
  building properties of wood experiment, *6:* 1302–6, 1304 (ill.), 1305 (ill.)
  earthquake destruction experiment, *2:* 317–21, 319 (ill.), 320 (ill.), 321 (ill.)
  See also Structures
Buoyancy, *2:* **257–69,** 257 (ill.), 259, 259 (ill.)
  design an experiment for, *2:* 267–69
  make a hydrometer experiment, *5:* 997–1000, 998 (ill.), 999 (ill.)
  relative density and floating experiment, *2:* 260–64, 262 (ill.), 263 (ill.)
  water pressure experiment, *2:* 264–67, 265 (ill.), 266 (ill.)
Burn test, *3:* 513, 513 (ill.)
Burrs, *4:* 685, 686 (ill.)
Butter, rancid, *3:* 480
Butterflies
  life cycle of, *3:* 633–34, *4:* 645, 656 (ill.)
  mimicry by, *1:* 62
  pollination by, *3:* 425–27

C

C layer (soil), *5:* 1067, 1067 (ill.)
Cabbage, purple, *2:* 304–7, 306 (ill.), 307 (ill.)
Cactus, *5:* 899–900, 908, 908 (ill.)
desert biome experiment, *1:* 108–11, 109 (ill.), 110 (ill.), 111 (ill.)
saguaro, *1:* 105, *5:* 900
water storage by, *5:* 884, 884 (ill.), 885
Calcite, *1:* 129–30, *4:* 862
Calcium
bone loss experiment, *1:* 115–20, 119 (ill.)
in bones, *1:* 114
hard water sources experiment, *6:* 1231–34, 1232 (ill.)
for nutrition, *4:* 761, *6:* 1226
periodic table location for, *4:* 829
in soil, *5:* 1064
in water, *6:* 1225–26
Calcium carbonate
bone loss experiment, *1:* 116–20, 119 (ill.)
seashells of, *5:* 1020, 1022
soil pH and plant growth experiment, *5:* 1074–77, 1074 (ill.), 1076 (ill.), 1079 (ill.)
solubility of elements experiment, *4:* 835–38, 835 (ill.), 837 (ill.)
stalagmites and stalactite experiment, *1:* 135–39, 137 (ill.)
Calcium chloride, *1:* 157–59, 157 (ill.), 158 (ill.), 159 (ill.)
Calories, *4:* 766–69, 768 (ill.), 769 (ill.)
Cambium, *6:* 1296, 1297 (ill.)
Camera lenses, *4:* 795 (ill.)
Cameras, *6:* 1125–28, 1126 (ill.), 1127 (ill.)
Camouflage, *1:* 61–62, 63–65, 64 (ill.), *5:* 1021
Canals, *2:* 375
Cancellous bone, *1:* 114
Canned food, *3:* 452–53, 479, 479 (ill.)
Capillary action, *6:* 1260
Carbohydrates
dietary carbohydrate sources experiment, *4:* 761–64, 763 (ill.), 764 (ill.)
muscle strength and fatigue experiment, *1:* 123
for nutrition, *4:* 760, 761 (ill.)
Carbon, *2:* 230, 246 (ill.), *4:* 749, 829, *5:* 912
Carbon-carbon bonds, *5:* 912
Carbon dating, *3:* 525
Carbon dioxide
in air, *1:* 33
in bread making, *2:* 359
burning fossil fuels experiment, *3:* 596–98, 596 (ill.), 597 (ill.)
in cave formation, *1:* 127–29, 128 (ill.)
comet composition experiment, *2:* 218–21, 220 (ill.)
in dry ice, *2:* 220
from fish, *3:* 402
greenhouse effect, *1:* 46, 47 (ill.), *3:* 589–90, *5:* 941
from leavening agents, *3:* 464
leavening agents and carbon dioxide experiment, *3:* 470–73, 472 (ill.), 473 (ill.), 474
nanosize and reaction rate experiment, *4:* 753–55, 754 (ill.), 755 (ill.)
in plant respiration, *4:* 871, 872
from power plants, *1:* 46
temperature for yeast growth experiment, *3:* 544–49, 547 (ill.), 548 (ill.)
from yeast, *2:* 359, *3:* 540–41
Carbon monoxide, *1:* 45, *2:* 231
Carbon nanotubes, *4:* 749
Carbonic acid, *1:* 127–29, 128 (ill.), 132–35, 134 (ill.), *3:* 544
Cardboard soundproofing, *5:* 1102–5, 1104 (ill.)
Cardiac muscles, *1:* 115, 115 (ill.)
Carlsbad Caverns, *1:* 129
Carotene, *1:* 192, 201 (ill.), *4:* 872
Cars, *1:* 3–4, 46, *3:* 590
Carson, Rachel, *4:* 846
Carson River, *5:* 955
Cartier, Jacques, *4:* 759
Cartilage, *1:* 114
Cartilaginous fish, *3:* 401
Casts, fossil, *3:* 523, 526–29, 528 (ill.)
Catalase, *2:* 361 (ill.), 362–65, 363 (ill.), 364 (ill.)
Catalysts, *2:* 359–60, 360 (ill.)
Catalytic converters, *1:* 3–4
Caterpillars, *3:* 633–34, *4:* 645
Caventou, Joseph Biernaime, *1:* 191
Caverns. *See* Caves

Caves, *1:* **127–40,** 140 (ill.)
- cave formation experiment, *1:* 132–35, 134 (ill.)
- design an experiment for, *1:* 139–40
- formation of, *1:* 127–29, 128 (ill.)
- life forms in, *1:* 130–31, 131 (ill.)
- sea, *1:* 129, 129 (ill.)
- stalagmites and stalactite experiment, *1:* 135–39, 137 (ill.)
- stalagmites and stalactite formation, *1:* 129–30, 130 (ill.)

Cell division, *1:* 143–44

Cell membrane, *1:* 142
- bacteria, *1:* 86, 87 (ill.)
- diffusion through, *4:* 797, 798 (ill.)
- osmosis through, *4:* 798, *5:* 898

Cell nucleus, *1:* 86, 142–43, *2:* 285, 289–91, 289 (ill.), 290 (ill.)

Cell theory, *1:* 141–42

Cells, *1:* **141–50,** 142 (ill.)
- design an experiment for, *1:* 148–50
- microscopes for, *1:* 141, 141 (ill.)
- monocot *vs.* dicot plant experiment, *1:* 145–47, 145 (ill.), 146 (ill.), 147 (ill.), 148
- multicellular/unicellular experiment, *1:* 144–45, 144 (ill.)
- osmosis, *5:* 898–99, 898 (ill.), 899 (ill.)
- reproduction of, *1:* 143–44
- structure of, *1:* 142, 142 (ill.)
- yeast reproduction experiment, *1:* 147–48, 147 (ill.), 148 (ill.), 149 (ill.), 150

Cellulose, *4:* 872

Cement, contact/rubber, *1:* 20, 22–25

Centrifugal force, *5:* 983–83, 983 (ill.), 989–92, 990 (ill.)

Centrifuge, *4:* 724–25

Centripetal force, *3:* 492–93, 493 (ill.)
- distance/force relationship experiment, *3:* 501–5, 503 (ill.)
- helicopter and propeller experiment, *3:* 418–21, 418 (ill.), 419 (ill.), 420 (ill.)
- orbits and, *3:* 493, 504 (ill.), 505

Ceramics, *4:* 686

Cerebral cortex, *4:* 698–99, 699 (ill.)

CFCs (Chlorofluorocarbons), *1:* 46

Chain, Ernst, *3:* 539–40

Chalk
- acid rain damage to, *1:* 12–15, 14 (ill.), 15 (ill.), 16
- cave formation experiment, *1:* 132–35, 134 (ill.)
- hard water sources experiment, *6:* 1231–34, 1232 (ill.)
- solubility of elements experiment, *4:* 835–38, 835 (ill.), 837 (ill.)

Chanute, Octave, *3:* 414

Chase, Martha, *2:* 286

Chemical energy, *1:* **151–61,** 152 (ill.)
- definition of, *1:* 151, *5:* 929
- design an experiment for, *1:* 160–61
- endothermic *vs.* exothermic experiment, *1:* 156–60, 157 (ill.), 158 (ill.), 159 (ill.)
- production of, *1:* 151–52
- rusting experiment, *1:* 152–56, 155 (ill.)

Chemical pesticides, *4:* 843–44, 844 (ill.), 848–52, 851 (ill.)

Chemical properties, *1:* **163–76,** 164 (ill.), 165 (ill.), *4:* 687
- in chemical reactions, *1:* 163–66, 164 (ill.)
- copper patina experiment, *1:* 173–75, 174 (ill.), 175 (ill.)
- design an experiment for, *1:* 175–76
- mineral oil, water and iodine experiment, *1:* 170–73, 170 (ill.), 171 (ill.), 172 (ill.)
- white glue and borax experiment, *1:* 167–70, 168 (ill.), 169 (ill.)

Chemical reactions
- chemical properties in, *1:* 163–66, 164 (ill.)
- copper patina experiment, *1:* 173–75, 174 (ill.), 175 (ill.)
- definition of, *1:* 163
- design an experiment for, *1:* 160–61, 175–76
- endothermic, *1:* 151, 152, 165
- endothermic *vs.* exothermic experiment, *1:* 156–60, 157 (ill.), 158 (ill.), 159 (ill.)
- energy from, *1:* 151
- enzymes in, *2:* 359–60, 360 (ill.), 361 (ill.), 362–65, 363 (ill.), 364 (ill.)
- examples of, *1:* 164
- exothermic, *1:* 151–52, 152 (ill.), 165, 165 (ill.)
- in food spoilage, *3:* 451
- of leavening agents, *3:* 464–65

mineral oil, water and iodine experiment, *1:* 170–73, 170 (ill.), 171 (ill.), 172 (ill.)
mystery powder identification experiment, *5:* 1009–13, 1011 (ill.), 1012 (ill.), 1013 (ill.)
nanosize and reaction rate experiment, *4:* 753–55, 754 (ill.), 755 (ill.)
process of, *1:* 164–65
rusting experiment, *1:* 152–56, 155 (ill.)
safety for, *1:* 158
synthesis, *1:* 163
taste as, *1:* 179
white glue and borax experiment, *1:* 167–70, 168 (ill.), 169 (ill.)

Chemosenses, *1:* 177–90
design an experiment for, *1:* 189–90
smell, *1:* 177, 179–80, 179 (ill.), 180 (ill.)
smell-taste relationship experiment, *1:* 186–89, 187 (ill.)
supertaster experiment, *1:* 180–86, 184 (ill.)
taste, *1:* 177–79, 178 (ill.)

Chili peppers, *4:* 848–52, 851 (ill.)
China, *2:* 389, *6:* 1123
Chitin exoskeleton, *5:* 1020–21, 1022–25, 1023 (ill.), 1024 (ill.), 1025 (ill.)
Chloride, *5:* 995, *6:* 1226
Chlorine, *4:* 812
Chlorofluorocarbons (CFCs), *1:* 46

Chlorophyll, *1:* 191–201, 191 (ill.)
color change from cooking, *3:* 465–66
color change in leaves, *1:* 192, 192 (ill.), 201 (ill.)
in cyanobacteria, *1:* 74
design an experiment for, *1:* 200–201
light colors and plant growth experiment, *1:* 197–200, 197 (ill.), 199 (ill.), 200 (ill.)
in photosynthesis, *1:* 191–201, 191 (ill.), *4:* 871–72, *5:* 884–85
pigment separation experiment, *1:* 193–97, 195 (ill.), 196 (ill.)

Chloroplasts, *1:* 191, *4:* 871–72
Chromatography, *5:* 1032–33, 1034 (ill.)
paper chromatography and ink experiment, *5:* 1034–39, 1036 (ill.), 1037 (ill.)
plant pigment separation experiment, *1:* 193–97, 195 (ill.), 196 (ill.)

Chromium, *6:* 1226
Chromosomes, *3:* 553–54, 554 (ill.)
Chrysalis, *3:* 634
Cilia, *1:* 179
Circles, pi of, *4:* 701–4, 701 (ill.), 702 (ill.), 703 (ill.)
Circular motion, *3:* 492–93, 493 (ill.), 501–5, 503 (ill.)
Cirrocumulus clouds, *6:* 1273
Cirrostratus clouds, *6:* 1273
Cirrus clouds, *6:* 1272, 1273
Citric acid, *2:* 334, 340–44, 341 (ill.), 342 (ill.)
Clam shells, *5:* 1022–25, 1023 (ill.), 1024 (ill.), 1025 (ill.)

Clay
density of, *2:* 257, 258, 258 (ill.)
in soil, *5:* 1065, 1066, 1066 (ill.)
soil horizon properties experiment, *5:* 1067–73, 1071 (ill.), 1072 (ill.)
soil type and runoff experiment, *2:* 377–80, 378 (ill.), 379 (ill.)

Clean Air Act, *1:* 50
Clean Water Act, *1:* 50
Cleaning products, *1:* 164
Climate, *4:* 741–44, 742 (ill.), 743 (ill.), *6:* 1271
Climate change, *1:* 46, 72, *3:* 589
Climbing plants, *6:* 1192, 1205 (ill.)

Clocks, *6:* 1177–78
atomic, *6:* 1180
pendulum, *6:* 1178
water, *6:* 1177, 1177 (ill.), 1185–88, 1187 (ill.)

Clostridium, 3: 478

Clouds, *6:* 1271, 1272–73
formation of, *6:* 1147–48, 1148 (ill.), 1272
funnel, *6:* 1150–51, 1150 (ill.)
lightning formation in, *6:* 1135
temperature and cloud formation experiment, *6:* 1277–80
types of, *6:* 1272–73, 1272 (ill.)

Coagulation, *3:* 609–12, 610 (ill.), *4:* 724
Coal, *1:* 1, 3, 46, 164
Coatings, *4:* 749
Cohesion, *6:* 1259–61, 1261–64, 1261 (ill.), 1263 (ill.), 1268 (ill.)
Coiling reeds, *2:* 396–99, 398 (ill.), 399 (ill.)
Cold fronts, *1:* 35, *6:* 1285
Cold packs, *1:* 152, 152 (ill.), 160, 161 (ill.)

Cold temperature
- adhesives experiment, *1:* 26–30, 27 (ill.), 28 (ill.), 29 (ill.)
- cool temperature and crystal growth experiment, *2:* 250–53, 252 (ill.)
- for food preservation, *3:* 453, 453 (ill.), 479–80
- magnetic strength effect experiment, *4:* 674–78, 674 (ill.), 676 (ill.)
- mountain altitude and, *4:* 737

Coliform bacteria, *3:* 485

Collagen, *1:* 114, *2:* 368–72, 370 (ill.), 371 (ill.)

Colloids, *4:* 723–24, 724 (ill.), 725, 725 (ill.)
- separation of, *4:* 724–25
- Tyndall effect experiment, *4:* 730–32, 731 (ill.), 732 (ill.)

Colonies, bacteria, *1:* 87

Color-blindness, *2:* 205–6

Colorfastness of dyes, *2:* 300, 304–7, 306 (ill.), 307 (ill.)

Colors, *2:* **203–14,** 203 (ill.), 204 (ill.), 205 (ill.)
- as animal defenses, *1:* 65–68, 66 (ill.), 67 (ill.)
- animals perception of, *2:* 214
- camouflage, *1:* 61–62, 63–65, 64 (ill.)
- cooking changes in, *3:* 465–66
- copper color change experiment, *4:* 820–23, 820 (ill.), 821 (ill.), 822 (ill.)
- design an experiment for, *2:* 213–14
- in dyes, *5:* 1033
- fiber type and dye color experiment, *2:* 301–4, 302 (ill.), 303 (ill.)
- heat absorption and reflection by, *3:* 617
- how we perceive them, *2:* 205–6, 205 (ill.)
- hue, saturation and brightness of, *2:* 206–7, 214
- interference fringes, *4:* 660
- leaves changing, *1:* 192, 192 (ill.), 200 (ill.)
- light colors and plant growth experiment, *1:* 197–200, 197 (ill.), 198 (ill.), 199 (ill.), *4:* 873–77, 875 (ill.), 876 (ill.)
- make a rainbow experiment, *4:* 664–65, 664 (ill.), 665 (ill.)
- in nanotechnology, *4:* 748
- overview, *2:* 203–7
- paper chromatography and ink experiment, *5:* 1034–39, 1036 (ill.), 1037 (ill.)
- pollinators attracted by, *3:* 426, 431–35, 433 (ill.)
- primary, *2:* 205
- in separation and identification, *5:* 1033
- taste perception experiment, *2:* 207–10, 208 (ill.), 209 (ill.)
- temperature of different colors experiment, *2:* 210–12, 211 (ill.), 212 (ill.), 213
- testing mineral characteristics experiment, *5:* 971–75, 973 (ill.), 974 (ill.)
- of visible light, *6:* 1112
- *See also* Pigments

Columbus, Christopher, *3:* 462

Coma (comet), *2:* 216

Combustion, *1:* 152, *3:* 596–98, 596 (ill.), 597 (ill.)

Comets and meteors, *2:* **215–27,** 216 (ill.), 217 (ill.), 218 (ill.)
- composition and properties experiment, *2:* 218–21, 220 (ill.)
- composition of, *2:* 215, 216, 216 (ill.)
- crater shape experiment, *2:* 221–25, 224 (ill.)
- craters from, *2:* 217, 218 (ill.)
- design an experiment for, *2:* 225–27
- models of, *2:* 227
- orbital path of, *2:* 215–16, 216 (ill.)

Complex craters, *2:* 217, 218 (ill.)

Composting, *2:* **229–41,** 230 (ill.)
- design an experiment for, *2:* 239–40
- microorganisms and decomposition experiment, *2:* 232–35, 234 (ill.), 235 (ill.)
- organic waste for plant growth experiment, *2:* 235–39, 236 (ill.), 238 (ill.), 239 (ill.)
- process of, *2:* 230, 230 (ill.), 231 (ill.)

Compound eyes, *3:* 632

Compound microscopes, *1:* 141, 141 (ill.)

Compressional strength, *4:* 687, 687 (ill.)

Computers, *4:* 750, *6:* 1283, 1285

Concave lens, *4:* 788–91, 788 (ill.), *6:* 1110, 1113–17, 1114 (ill.), 1116 (ill.)

Condensation, *6:* 1272

Conduction
- conductivity of elements experiment, *4:* 830–35, 833 (ill.)
- of electricity, *4:* 687, *6:* 1133
- of heat, *3:* 615–16
- heat conduction experiment, *3:* 618–22, 620 (ill.), 621 (ill.)

Cones (eye), *2:* 205, 205 (ill.)

Confined aquifers, *3:* 601, 603 (ill.)

Conifers, *1:* 103, 104 (ill.), *6:* 1295
Conservation of energy, *5:* 1047
Constellations, *6:* 1124
Contact cement, *1:* 20
Continental drift, *6:* 1237–38
Contractions, muscle, *1:* 115–16, 116 (ill.), 120–23, 122 (ill.)
Control experiment, *5:* 1007
Convection box, *1:* 44
Convection currents
- in air, *1:* 36, 36 (ill.)
- air currents experiment, *1:* 39–42, 41 (ill.)
- for heat transfer, *3:* 615, 616
- ocean currents experiment, *4:* 780–83, 782 (ill.)
- in oceans, *4:* 773, 774 (ill.)
- in water, *1:* 44

Convex lens, *4:* 788–91, 788 (ill.), *6:* 1110, 1113–17, 1114 (ill.), 1116 (ill.)
Cooking, *1:* 194, *3:* 463–64, 465–66
Cool air, *6:* 1147–48, 1271
- convection current experiment, *1:* 39–42, 41 (ill.)
- transpiration rate and environment experiment, *5:* 904–7, 906 (ill.)
- warm air *vs.* cool air experiment, *1:* 36–39, 36 (ill.), 38 (ill.)
- *See also* Cold temperature

Copernicus, Nicolaus, *5:* 981, *6:* 1178
Copper
- acid-copper reduction experiment, *4:* 813–17, 814 (ill.), 815 (ill.)
- conductivity of, *6:* 1133
- construct a multicell battery experiment, *2:* 340–44, 341 (ill.), 342 (ill.)
- copper color change experiment, *4:* 820–23, 820 (ill.), 821 (ill.), 822 (ill.)
- electrons released by metals experiment, *4:* 838–40, 840 (ill.), 841 (ill.), 842
- electroplating experiment, *2:* 344–45, 344 (ill.), 345 (ill.)
- heat conduction experiment, *3:* 618–22, 620 (ill.), 621 (ill.)
- hydrochloric acid reaction, *1:* 165
- for nutrition, *6:* 1226
- patina reaction experiment, *1:* 173–75, 174 (ill.), 175 (ill.)

Copper Age, *5:* 969
Coprolites, *3:* 524
Coral snakes, *1:* 62
Coriolis, Gustave-Gaspard, *5:* 984
Coriolis force, *5:* 984–85
Corn, genetically engineered, *4:* 845, 846 (ill.)
Corn oil, *5:* 942
Cornstarch, *5:* 1009–13, 1011 (ill.), 1012 (ill.), 1013 (ill.)
Corona, *2:* 326
Corrosion. *See* Rusting
Cotton, *3:* 508
Cotyledons, *3:* 566, 566 (ill.)
Counterweights, *3:* 585–87, 585 (ill.), 586 (ill.), 587 (ill.), 588 (ill.)
Cowry shell, *5:* 1021
Cows, *1:* 48
Craters, meteor impact, *2:* 217, 218 (ill.), 221–25, 224 (ill.), 227
Cream heat capacity, *3:* 625–28, 626 (ill.), 627 (ill.), 628 (ill.)
Cream of tarter. *See* Tartaric acid
Crest, *4:* 773, 774 (ill.)
Crick, Francis, *2:* 286–87, 287 (ill.)
Crickets, *4:* 651–55, 653 (ill.), 654 (ill.)
Crime scene
- blood spatter analysis experiment, *3:* 515–18, 516 (ill.), 517 (ill.)
- DNA fingerprinting, *2:* 296, *3:* 509–10, 510 (ill.)
- forensic techniques for, *3:* 507–11

Cross-pollination, *3:* 424–25, 425 (ill.), 427–31, 430 (ill.)
Crust. *See* Earth's crust
Crustaceans, *5:* 1020–21, 1022 (ill.)
- classifying seashells experiment, *5:* 1025–27, 1027 (ill.)
- strength of shells experiment, *5:* 1022–25, 1023 (ill.), 1024 (ill.), 1025 (ill.)

Crustose lichens, *1:* 52, 52 (ill.)
Crystal lattice, *2:* 243
Crystals, *2:* **243–55,** 246 (ill.)
- artificial, *2:* 245–46
- cool temperature and crystal growth experiment, *2:* 250–53, 252 (ill.)
- design an experiment for, *2:* 254–55

formation of, *2:* 245–46
forming different crystal shapes experiment, *2:* 246–50, 246 (ill.), 249 (ill.), 254 (ill.)
shape and structure of, *2:* 243, 244–45, 244 (ill.), 245 (ill.), 254 (ill.)
uses for, *2:* 243–44, 244 (ill.)
Cultures (social), *2:* 389, 391
Cumulonimbus clouds, *6:* 1148, 1273
See also Thunderstorms
Cumulus clouds, *6:* 1272, 1273
Curing food, *3:* 452
Currents. *See* Air currents; Convection currents; Ocean currents
Curves, *5:* 984–85
Cuttle fish, *1:* 63
Cyanoacrylate glue, *1:* 20, 21, 22–25, 24, 24 (ill.)
Cyanobacteria, *1:* 74, 75 (ill.)
Cytology, *1:* 142
Cytoplasms, *1:* 86, 142
Cytosine, *2:* 286–87

D

D-cell batteries, *2:* 334–35, 340–44, 341 (ill.), 342 (ill.)
da Vinci, Leonardo *3:* 413, 422 (ill.), *6:* 1247
Daily Value, *4:* 767
Darwin, Charles, *6:* 1191, 1191 (ill.), 1209
Data recording, *1:* 16, 31, 43
Dating techniques, *3:* 524–25
Days, *6:* 1175, 1176
DDT (Dichlorodiphenyltrichloroethane), *4:* 846, 847
Dead zones, *2:* 271, 273
Decanting, *4:* 724
Decay. *See* Decomposition
Decibels, *5:* 1096
Deciduous trees, *1:* 107–8, 107 (ill.), 192
Decomposition
aerobic, *2:* 231
anaerobic, *2:* 231
bacteria for, *1:* 85, 101 (ill.), *2:* 273
BOD_5 needed for, *2:* 273
chemical reaction, *1:* 163
in composting, *2:* 229–30
decay and dissolved oxygen changes experiment, *2:* 274–79, 276 (ill.), 277 (ill.)
dissolved oxygen level changes from, *2:* 272–73, 273–74
in fossil formation, *3:* 522–23, 522 (ill.)
fungi for, *3:* 537, 538, 538 (ill.)
in landfills, *2:* 231, 232–35, 234 (ill.), 235 (ill.)
in radioactive decay, *3:* 525, *6:* 1238
yeast decomposition experiment, *3:* 541–43, 543 (ill.)
Deep ocean currents, *4:* 773
Deep sea life, *4:* 775
Defense mechanisms. *See* Animal defenses
Deficiency diseases, *6:* 1223, 1224
Defraction grating, *4:* 664–65, 664 (ill.), 665 (ill.)
Democritus, *6:* 1123
Denatured proteins, *3:* 463
Density, *2:* **257–69,** 257 (ill.), 259 (ill.)
of air, *1:* 34–36, 35 (ill.), 36 (ill.), *4:* 737
of balsa wood, *2:* 257, 258, 258 (ill.), *6:* 1295
of clay, *2:* 257, 258, 258 (ill.)
convection current experiment, *1:* 39–42, 41 (ill.)
definition of, *1:* 36, *2:* 257
density ball measurement experiment, *5:* 1000–1003, 1001 (ill.), 1002 (ill.)
design an experiment for, *2:* 267–69
of fluids, *3:* 439
mountain altitude and, *4:* 737
ocean convection currents experiment, *4:* 780–83, 782 (ill.)
relative, *2:* 258–59, 258 (ill.), 260–64, 262 (ill.), 263 (ill.)
relative density and floating experiment, *2:* 260–64, 262 (ill.), 263 (ill.)
salinity and, *4:* 772
salinity and stratification experiment, *4:* 775–80, 778 (ill.)
of seawater, *4:* 772
temperature and, *4:* 772
warm air *vs.* cool air experiment, *1:* 34–39, 35 (ill.), 36 (ill.)
water pressure and buoyancy experiment, *2:* 264–67, 265 (ill.), 266 (ill.)
of wood, *6:* 1295
Density ball, *5:* 1000–1003, 1001 (ill.), 1002 (ill.)
Density-driven currents. *See* Convection currents

Deoxyribonucleic acid. *See* DNA
Dependent variable, *5:* 1008
Desert
  biome, *1:* 103, 104–5, 104 (ill.)
  desert biome experiment, *1:* 108–11, 109 (ill.), 110 (ill.), 111 (ill.)
  mountains and desert formation experiment, *4:* 741–44, 742 (ill.), 743 (ill.)
Desert plants, *1:* 105, *5:* 898, 899–900, 908, 908 (ill.)
Detergents
  action of, *6:* 1260
  borax in, *1:* 167
  DNA isolation and extraction experiment, *2:* 289–91, 289 (ill.), 290 (ill.)
  enzymes in, *2:* 362
  eutrophication from, *1:* 55
  species differences in DNA experiment, *2:* 291–95, 293 (ill.)
Deveron River, *5:* 956
Dewpoint temperature, *6:* 1285 (ill.), 1286–89, 1287 (ill.), 1288 (ill.)
Diamonds, *2:* 243, 244, 246 (ill.), *4:* 747, 749, 750 (ill.)
Dichlorodiphenyltrichloroethane (DDT), *4:* 846, 847
Dicot plants, *1:* 145–47, 145 (ill.), 146 (ill.), 147 (ill.), 148
Diesel vehicles, *1:* 46
Diet
  of bacteria, *1:* 87–88
  dietary carbohydrate and fat sources experiment, *4:* 761–64, 763 (ill.), 764 (ill.)
  dietary proteins and salt sources experiment, *4:* 764–66, 765 (ill.), 766 (ill.)
  how good is my diet experiment, *4:* 766–69, 768 (ill.), 769 (ill.)
  vitamins and minerals in, *6:* 1226, 1235 (ill.)
  See also Food; Nutrition
Diffraction of light, *4:* 660
Diffusion. *See* Osmosis and diffusion
Digestion, *1:* 85, 164, *2:* 359, 360
Digital pH meter, *4:* 860, 860 (ill.)
Dimples, *3:* 554–55, 556–59, 558 (ill.), 559 (ill.)
Dinosaurs, *1:* 85
Dioscorides, *2:* 389
Dirt. *See* Soil
Diseases, *1:* 85–86, 86, 88–90, *3:* 539
Dishwasher detergents. *See* Detergents
Disinfection, *3:* 609–12, 610 (ill.)
Dissolved oxygen, *2:* **271–84,** 272 (ill.), 273 (ill.), 274 (ill.)
  decay and dissolved oxygen changes experiment, *2:* 274–79, 276 (ill.), 277 (ill.)
  design an experiment for, *2:* 282–84
  factors effecting levels of, *2:* 271–73
  goldfish breathing rate experiment, *2:* 279–84, 281 (ill.), 282 (ill.), 283
Distance, *3:* 501–5, 503 (ill.), *5:* 1047
Distillation, *4:* 724, 725 (ill.)
DNA (Deoxyribonucleic acid), *2:* **285–97,** 286 (ill.), 295 (ill.), *3:* 553–54
  bacteria, *1:* 86, 87
  cell nucleus, *1:* 142–43
  design an experiment for, *2:* 295–96
  of different species, *2:* 287–88
  isolation and extraction experiment, *2:* 289–91, 289 (ill.), 290 (ill.)
  mutations, *3:* 555
  replication of, *2:* 287, 288 (ill.)
  sequencing, *2:* 287–88, 295 (ill.), *3:* 553
  species differences in DNA experiment, *2:* 291–95, 293 (ill.)
  structure of, *2:* 286–87, 287 (ill.), *3:* 554 (ill.)
DNA fingerprinting, *2:* 296, *3:* 509–10, 510 (ill.), 562
DNA transformation, *2:* 296
Dolphins, *3:* 402
Dominant inheritance, *3:* 554–55
Doppler effect, *6:* 1111, 1112, 1112 (ill.), 1118–20, 1119 (ill.)
Double-acting baking powder, *3:* 464, 470–73, 472 (ill.), 473 (ill.), 474
Double-helix structure, *2:* 286–87, 287 (ill.), *3:* 554 (ill.)
Dried food, *3:* 451, 479, 479 (ill.)
  food drying experiment, *3:* 458–61, 458 (ill.), 459 (ill.), 460 (ill.)
  process of, *3:* 453
Drinking water, *3:* 604, 605–9, 608 (ill.), 609–12, 610 (ill.)
Drugs, plant-based, *2:* 389–90, 390 (ill.)
  See also Antibiotics

Dry cell batteries, *2:* 334
Dry environments, *5:* 899–900
See also Desert
Dry ice, *2:* 220, *6:* 1158–61, 1159 (ill.), 1160 (ill.), 1161 (ill.), 1162
Dung, *3:* 524
Dust
in cloud formation, *6:* 1148
in comets, *2:* 218–21, 220 (ill.)
in star formation, *6:* 1123–24
Dust Bowl, *2:* 375, 375 (ill.)
Dust tail (comet), *2:* 216
Dutchman's pipe, *3:* 427
Dyes, *2:* **299–309,** 299 (ill.), 300 (ill.)
colorfastness experiment, *2:* 304–7, 306 (ill.)
design an experiment for, *2:* 308–9
fiber type and dye color experiment, *2:* 301–4, 302 (ill.), 303 (ill.)
fixatives for, *2:* 300–301, 300 (ill.), 304–7, 306 (ill.), 307 (ill.)
natural, *2:* 299, 301–4, 302 (ill.), 303 (ill.), 304–7, 306 (ill.), 307 (ill.), 391
separation of colors in, *5:* 1033
synthetic, *2:* 299–300, 304–7, 306 (ill.), 307 (ill.)
Dynamic equilibrium, *4:* 798

E

Eardrum, *5:* 1095, 1106 (ill.)
Earlobes, *3:* 556–59, 558 (ill.), 559 (ill.)
Ears, *3:* 403, *5:* 1095, 1106 (ill.)
Earth
centrifugal force and gravity experiment, *5:* 989–92, 990 (ill.)
circumference of, *5:* 985
formation of, *5:* 982–83
geologic history of, *5:* 969–70, 970 (ill.)
gravity, *3:* 579, 580
pendulum rotation experiment, *5:* 985–89, 988 (ill.)
rotation and orbit of, *5:* 981–85, 982 (ill.), 983 (ill.), 984 (ill.), 985 (ill.), 986 (ill.)
Earthquakes, *2:* **311–23,** 322 (ill.)
build a seismograph experiment, *2:* 314–16, 315 (ill.), 316 (ill.)
design an experiment for, *2:* 322–23
epicenter destruction experiment, *2:* 317–21, 319 (ill.), 320 (ill.), 321 (ill.)
epicenter of, *2:* 312
measurement of, *2:* 312–13
Earth's axis, *5:* 982, 983
Earth's core, *5:* 969–70, *6:* 1238
Earth's crust, *5:* 970
earthquake movement experiment, *2:* 314–16, 315 (ill.), 316 (ill.)
in mountain formation, *4:* 735–37, 737 (ill.)
mountain formation experiment, *4:* 738–41, 739 (ill.), 740 (ill.)
Earth's mantle, *5:* 970, *6:* 1238
Earthworms, *2:* 230, 231 (ill.)
Echinoderms, *5:* 1025–27, 1027 (ill.)
Eclipses, *2:* **325–32,** 325 (ill.)
design an experiment for, *2:* 330–32
eclipse model experiment, *2:* 327–29, 328 (ill.), 329 (ill.)
history of, *2:* 325–26
lunar, *2:* 326, 326 (ill.), 327–29, 328 (ill.), 329 (ill.)
phases of the moon experiment, *2:* 329–30, 330 (ill.), 331 (ill.)
solar, *2:* 325–29, 325 (ill.), 328 (ill.), 329 (ill.)
Ecosystem, *2:* 381, *4:* 737–38
See also Biomes
Eels, electric, *1:* 63, 63 (ill.)
Effort, *5:* 1047
Egg whites, *3:* 465, 465 (ill.)
Eggs, *4:* 806–9, 808 (ill.), 809 (ill.)
Eggshells, *4:* 806–9, 808 (ill.), 809 (ill.), 846, *5:* 1019
Egyptians, *2:* 389, *5:* 1048, *6:* 1175, 1177
Einstein, Albert, *6:* 1179
Elasticity, *2:* 321, *5:* 912
Electric eels, *1:* 63, 63 (ill.)
Electric motors, *2:* 358 (ill.), *5:* 1087–89, 1088 (ill.), 1089 (ill.)
Electric power plants, *1:* 1, 46, *3:* 590
Electricity, *2:* **333–47,** 334 (ill.)
conduction of, *4:* 687, *6:* 1133
conductivity of elements experiment, *4:* 830–35, 833 (ill.)

construct a multicell battery experiment, *2:* 340–44, 341 (ill.), 342 (ill.)
definition of, *5:* 929
design an experiment for, *2:* 346–47
electrolyte solution experiment, *2:* 335–40, 337 (ill.), 338 (ill.), 339 (ill.)
electromagnet creation experiment, *2:* 354–57, 354 (ill.), 356 (ill.)
electromagnet strength experiment, *4:* 678–81, 678 (ill.), 679 (ill.)
electroplating experiment, *2:* 344–45, 344 (ill.), 345 (ill.)
magnetic field creation experiment, *2:* 351–54, 353 (ill.)
in magnetism, *2:* 349–50, *4:* 672–73
production of, *2:* 333–34, 349
from renewable sources, *5:* 941–43
safety for, *2:* 352, 358
from solar energy, *5:* 1083
Volta Pile, *2:* 335 (ill.), 344
See also Static electricity

Electrodes, *2:* 333, 334

Electrolytes
construct a multicell battery experiment, *2:* 340–44, 341 (ill.), 342 (ill.)
for electricity conduction, *2:* 333–34
electrolyte solution experiment, *2:* 335–40, 337 (ill.), 338 (ill.), 339 (ill.)
Volta Pile, *2:* 344

Electromagnetic spectrum, *2:* 203, 350, 350 (ill.), *4:* 659, 660 (ill.), 787

Electromagnetic waves, *2:* 203, 204–5, 204 (ill.), 350, 350 (ill.), *3:* 616–17

Electromagnetism, *2:* **349–58,** 349 (ill.), 350 (ill.), 357 (ill.), 358 (ill.), *4:* 672–73, 681 (ill.)
design an experiment for, *2:* 356–57
electricity in, *2:* 349–50, *4:* 672–73
electromagnet creation experiment, *2:* 354–57, 354 (ill.), 356 (ill.)
electromagnet strength experiment, *4:* 678–81, 678 (ill.), 679 (ill.)
magnetic field creation experiment, *2:* 351–54, 353 (ill.)
production of, *2:* 349–50

Electronics, *4:* 750

Electrons
in electricity, *2:* 333, 349
electrons released by metals experiment, *4:* 838–40, 840 (ill.), 841 (ill.), 842
in oxidation-reduction reactions, *4:* 811
in static electricity, *6:* 1133–35, 1134 (ill.)

Electrophoresis, gel, *3:* 562

Electroplating, *2:* 335, 344–45, 344 (ill.), 345 (ill.)

Electroscope, *6:* 1135–39, 1137 (ill.), 1138 (ill.), 1140

Electrostatic cleaners, *4:* 724

Elements
conductivity of elements experiment, *4:* 830–35, 833 (ill.)
periodic table of, *4:* 827–42
properties of, *4:* 828
solubility of elements experiment, *4:* 835–38, 835 (ill.), 837 (ill.)

Elevation. *See* Altitude

Elliptical orbits, *3:* 579, *5:* 981

Elongation, *5:* 912–13, 915, 919

Embryos, plant, *3:* 565

Emeralds, *2:* 243

Endoskeleton, *3:* 530

Endothermic reactions, *1:* 151, 152, 165
from cold packs, *1:* 152, 152 (ill.), 160, 161 (ill.)
design an experiment for, *1:* 160–61
vs. exothermic, *1:* 156–60, 157 (ill.), 158 (ill.), 159 (ill.)
rusting experiment, *1:* 152–56, 155 (ill.)

Energy
conservation of, *5:* 1047
food, *1:* 160
laws of, *5:* 929–32
See also Chemical energy; Heat; Kinetic energy; Potential energy; Renewable energy; Solar energy

Energy Information Administration, *2:* 231

Entomology, *3:* 631

Environmental conditions
adhesives experiment, *1:* 26–30, 27 (ill.), 28 (ill.), 29 (ill.)
camouflage experiment, *1:* 63–65, 64 (ill.)
extreme, *1:* 88, 101
pollution effects, *1:* 45

Environmental Protection Agency (EPA), *2:* 271

Enzymes, *2:* **359–73**

aging meat experiment, *2:* 365–68, 366 (ill.), 367 (ill.)

in chemical reactions, *2:* 359–60, 360 (ill.), 361 (ill.), 362–65, 363 (ill.), 364 (ill.)

design an experiment for, *2:* 372–73

in digestion, *2:* 359, 360

discovery of, *2:* 359–60

DNA isolation and extraction experiment, *2:* 289–91, 289 (ill.), 290 (ill.)

hydrogen peroxide break down experiment, *2:* 361 (ill.), 362–65, 363 (ill.), 364 (ill.)

production of, *2:* 360–62

species differences in DNA experiment, *2:* 291–95, 293 (ill.)

temperature and enzyme action experiment, *2:* 368–72, 370 (ill.), 371 (ill.)

EPA (Environmental Protection Agency), *2:* 271

Epicenter, *2:* 312, 317–21, 319 (ill.), 320 (ill.), 321 (ill.)

Epiphytes, *5:* 883–84

Epoxies, *1:* 20

Epsom salts, *1:* 135–39, *2:* 246–50, 246 (ill.), 249 (ill.)

Equator, *5:* 985

Equilibrium, *4:* 798, *6:* 1165–66

Erosion, *2:* **375–88,** 375 (ill.), 376 (ill.), 386 (ill.), *5:* 1065

design an experiment for, *2:* 386–87

glacier erosion trench experiment, *5:* 957–60, 958 (ill.), 959 (ill.)

of mountains, *4:* 737

plants and the rate of erosion experiment, *2:* 381–86, 382 (ill.), 383 (ill.), 384 (ill.)

river erosion experiment, *5:* 962–65, 963 (ill.), 964 (ill.), 965 (ill.), 966

soil type and runoff experiment, *2:* 377–80, 378 (ill.), 379 (ill.)

Eruptions. *See* Volcanoes

Ethics, *2:* 296, *3:* 562, *4:* 750

Ethnobotany, *2:* **389–400,** 390 (ill.)

anti-bacterial plant experiment, *2:* 392–95, 394 (ill.), 395 (ill.)

coiling reeds experiment, *2:* 396–99, 398 (ill.), 399 (ill.)

design an experiment for, *2:* 399–400

plants as medicine, *2:* 389–90, 390 (ill.), 400

tools from plants, *2:* 390–92, 392 (ill.), 400

Eukaryotes, *3:* 537–38

Euphotic zone, *4:* 873

Eutrophication

dissolved oxygen level changes from, *2:* 273, 274 (ill.), 278–79

nutrients in, *1:* 49–50, 50 (ill.)

process of, *1:* 55–58

Evaporation

evaporation and surface area experiment, *6:* 1253–56, 1253 (ill.), 1254 (ill.), 1255 (ill.)

evaporation and temperature experiment, *6:* 1248–53, 1250 (ill.), 1251 (ill.)

of mixtures, *5:* 1032

in PVA glue, *1:* 20–21

of seawater, *4:* 724

stalagmites and stalactite experiment, *1:* 135–39, 137 (ill.)

suspensions *vs.* solutions experiment, *4:* 725–30, 729 (ill.)

in the water cycle, *6:* 1247

wind and, *6:* 1252–53

Evidence, *3:* 507–11, 508–9, 511–14, 511 (ill.), 512 (ill.), 513 (ill.)

Excavations, *2:* 230–31

Exhaust, car. *See* Cars

Exoskeleton

chitin, *5:* 1020–21, 1022–25, 1023 (ill.), 1024 (ill.), 1025 (ill.)

fossils of, *3:* 530

of insects, *3:* 631, *5:* 1019

seashells as, *5:* 1019–21, 1020 (ill.)

Exothermic reactions, *1:* 151–52, 152 (ill.), 165, 165 (ill.)

design an experiment for, *1:* 160–61

vs. endothermic, *1:* 156–60, 157 (ill.), 158 (ill.), 159 (ill.)

rusting experiment, *1:* 152–56, 155 (ill.)

Experiments, *5:* 1006–8

Extinction, *3:* 410–11

Extreme environments, *1:* 88, 88 (ill.)

Extremophiles, *1:* 88, 88 (ill.), 101

Eyes
color vision by, *2:* 205–6, 205 (ill.)
compound, *3:* 632
of fish, *3:* 403
perception of light, *4:* 787
seeing optical illusions experiment, *4:* 791–94, 791 (ill.), 792 (ill.), 793 (ill.)

F

Fabrics
fiber evidence from, *3:* 508–9, 511–14, 511 (ill.), 512 (ill.), 513 (ill.)
nanotechnology for, *4:* 749
natural *vs.* synthetic, *2:* 301–4, 302 (ill.), 303 (ill.)
properties of, *4:* 696
soundproofing materials experiment, *5:* 1102–5, 1104 (ill.)
Falling objects, *3:* 579, 580, 581–84, 582 (ill.), 583 (ill.), 584 (ill.)
See also Gravity
False memory, *4:* 699–700, 705–7, 707 (ill.)
Family genetics, *3:* 556–59, 558 (ill.), 559 (ill.)
Farming, *2:* 229–30, *4:* 646
Fat-soluble vitamins, *6:* 1224–25, 1224 (ill.)
Fatigue, *1:* 120–23, 122 (ill.)
Fats, *4:* 760–64, 763 (ill.), 764 (ill.)
Faulds, Henry, *3:* 507
Fault-block mountains, *4:* 736
Faults (earthquake), *2:* 311, 322 (ill.)
Feathers, *3:* 530–33, 532 (ill.)
Fermentation, *3:* 540–41, 544–49, 547 (ill.), 548 (ill.)
Ferns, *1:* 131
Fertilizer, *1:* 49, 55, *2:* 279, 386
Fiber evidence, *3:* 508–9, 511–14, 511 (ill.), 512 (ill.), 513 (ill.)
Fibers, natural *vs.* synthetic, *2:* 301–4, 302 (ill.), 303 (ill.)
Filtration
for separating mixtures, *4:* 724, *5:* 1032
suspensions *vs.* solutions experiment, *4:* 725–30, 729 (ill.)
water cleaning experiment, *3:* 609–12, 610 (ill.)
Fingerprinting, DNA, *2:* 296, *3:* 509–10, 510 (ill.), 562
Fingerprints, *3:* 507–8, 508 (ill.), 509 (ill.), 519
Fins, *3:* 402–3, 407–9, 409 (ill.), 410
Fir trees, *1:* 103, 104 (ill.)
Fireballs, *2:* 217
Fireflies, *3:* 638–42, 640 (ill.)
Fireworks, *1:* 165, 165 (ill.)
First-class lever, *5:* 1049–50
First law of motion, *3:* 491–92, 494, 579
Fish, *3:* **401–11,** 402 (ill.)
acid rain damage to, *1:* 1–2
bioluminescent, *4:* 775, 784
characteristics of, *3:* 401–2, 402 (ill.)
defense mechanisms of, *1:* 61, 63
design an experiment for, *3:* 409–11
dissolved oxygen changes experiment, *2:* 279–84, 281 (ill.), 282 (ill.), 283
dissolved oxygen levels for, *2:* 271, 272, 273
fish breathing experiment, *3:* 404–6, 405 (ill.)
how they breathe, *3:* 402, 403 (ill.)
how they move, *3:* 402–3, 403 (ill.)
movement of fish experiment, *3:* 407–9, 410
ocean, *4:* 774–75
senses of, *3:* 403–4
water pollution and, *1:* 50, *3:* 411
Fish tank projects
desert biome experiment, *1:* 108–11, 109 (ill.), 110 (ill.), 111 (ill.)
dissolved oxygen changes experiment, *2:* 279–84, 281 (ill.), 282 (ill.), 283
fish breathing experiment, *3:* 404–6, 405 (ill.)
movement of fish experiment, *3:* 407–9, 409 (ill.), 410
temperate forest biome, *1:* 106–8, 106 (ill.), 107 (ill.), 108 (ill.)
Fish tanks, care of, *3:* 406
Fixatives for dyes, *2:* 300–301, 300 (ill.), 304–7, 306 (ill.)
Flagella, *1:* 87
Flammability, *1:* 164
Flashlight fish, *4:* 775
Flavor, *2:* 207–10, 208 (ill.), 209 (ill.), *3:* 463–64
See also Taste

Fleas, *3:* 633
Fleming, Alexander, *3:* 539
Flight, *3:* **413–22,** 414 (ill.)
  centripetal force experiment, *3:* 418–21, 418 (ill.), 419 (ill.), 420 (ill.)
  design an experiment for, *3:* 421–22
  history of, *3:* 413–15, 415 (ill.), 422 (ill.)
  by insects, *3:* 632–33
  making gliders fly experiment, *3:* 415–18, 416 (ill.), 417 (ill.)
Floating
  density and buoyancy in, *2:* 257 (ill.), 259, 259 (ill.)
  relative density and floating experiment, *2:* 260–64, 262 (ill.), 263 (ill.)
  water pressure and buoyancy experiment, *2:* 264–67, 265 (ill.), 266 (ill.)
  water surface tension cohesion experiment, *6:* 1261–64, 1261 (ill.), 1263 (ill.)
Florey, Howard, *3:* 539–40
Flour
  mystery powder identification experiment, *5:* 1009–13, 1011 (ill.), 1012 (ill.), 1013 (ill.)
  unknown mixtures experiment, *5:* 1039–43, 1041 (ill.), 1042 (ill.)
Flowers, *3:* **423–37,** 424 (ill.)
  attracting pollinators experiment, *3:* 431–35, 433 (ill.)
  design an experiment for, *3:* 435–37
  parts of, *3:* 423–24, 424 (ill.), 426 (ill.), 436–37
  pollination of, *3:* 423–27, 425 (ill.), 426 (ill.)
  self-pollination *vs.* cross-pollination experiment, *3:* 427–31, 430 (ill.)
Fluids, *3:* **439–49**
  categories of, *3:* 440–41
  design an experiment for, *3:* 447–48
  properties of, *3:* 439–40, 439 (ill.), 440 (ill.)
  spinning rod experiment, *3:* 444–47, 446 (ill.), 447 (ill.)
  viscosity and temperature experiment, *3:* 441–44, 442 (ill.), 443 (ill.)
Fluorescence, *4:* 660, 661–64, 662 (ill.), 663 (ill.)
Fluoride, *6:* 1226
Fold mountains, *4:* 736
Foliose lichens, *1:* 52, 52 (ill.)
Food
  acidic, *1:* 164
  allergies, *1:* 187
  bacteria and, *1:* 87–88, 101
  canned, *3:* 452–53, 452 (ill.), 479, 479 (ill.)
  chlorophyll production of, *1:* 192
  curing, *3:* 452
  decay and dissolved oxygen changes experiment, *2:* 274–79, 276 (ill.), 277 (ill.)
  dietary carbohydrate and fat sources experiment, *4:* 761–64, 763 (ill.), 764 (ill.)
  dietary proteins and salt sources experiment, *4:* 764–66, 765 (ill.), 766 (ill.)
  dried, *3:* 451, 453, 458–61, 458 (ill.), 459 (ill.), 460 (ill.), 479, 479 (ill.)
  food supply and growth rate experiment, *4:* 651–55, 653 (ill.), 654 (ill.)
  frozen, *3:* 451, 453
  fungi as, *3:* 537
  heating, *3:* 465–66
  how good is my diet experiment, *4:* 766–69, 768 (ill.), 769 (ill.)
  organic, *4:* 855–56
  pesticides on, *4:* 848
  processed, *4:* 760
  salting, *3:* 452, 452 (ill.)
  smell-taste relationship experiment, *1:* 186–89, 187 (ill.)
  supertaster experiment, *1:* 180–86, 184 (ill.)
  taste of, *1:* 177–79, 178 (ill.)
  See also Diet; Nutrition; Taste
Food additives, *3:* 453
Food coloring, *2:* 207–10, 208 (ill.), 209 (ill.)
Food energy, *1:* 160
Food poisoning, *3:* 477
Food preservation, *3:* **451–62**
  design an experiment for, *3:* 461–62
  food drying experiment, *3:* 458–61, 458 (ill.), 459 (ill.), 460 (ill.)
  history of, *3:* 478–80
  methods of, *3:* 451–53, 452 (ill.), 453 (ill.)
  moldy bread experiment, *3:* 481–85, 481 (ill.), 482 (ill.), 483 (ill.)
  sugar fruit preservation experiment, *3:* 454–57, 455 (ill.), 456 (ill.)
  vinegar for, *3:* 452, 452 (ill.), 479

Food preservatives, *3:* 452, 453, 462, 478–79, 481–85, 481 (ill.), 482 (ill.), 483 (ill.)
Food science, *3:* 463–75
design an experiment for, *3:* 473–75
heating food, *3:* 465–66
jelly and pectin experiment, *3:* 467–70, 468 (ill.), 469 (ill.)
leavening agents, *3:* 464–65, 465 (ill.)
leavening agents and carbon dioxide experiment, *3:* 470–73, 472 (ill.), 473 (ill.), 474
Maillard reaction in, *3:* 463–64
Food spoilage, *3:* 477–90
design an experiment for, *3:* 461–62, 488–90
food drying experiment, *3:* 458–61, 458 (ill.), 459 (ill.), 460 (ill.)
microorganisms in, *3:* 451–53, 477–80, 478 (ill.)
moldy bread experiment, *3:* 481–85, 481 (ill.), 482 (ill.), 483 (ill.)
prevention of, *3:* 478–80, 479 (ill.), 480 (ill.)
process of, *3:* 451, 477–78
spoiled milk and temperature experiment, *3:* 485–88, 487 (ill.)
sugar fruit preservation experiment, *3:* 454–57, 455 (ill.), 456 (ill.)
Food webs, *6:* 1193
Footprints, *3:* 524
Forces, *3:* 491–505, 492–93, 504 (ill.)
arch distribution of, *6:* 1166–67
bottle rocket experiment, *3:* 493–501, 495 (ill.), 498 (ill.), 499 (ill.), 500 (ill.)
centripetal force experiment, *3:* 501–5, 503 (ill.)
design an experiment for, *3:* 504–5
effect on structures, *6:* 1165–66, 1166 (ill.)
machines can change, *5:* 1047
Newtonian laws of motion, *3:* 491–93, 492 (ill.), 493 (ill.), 579–80
planetary orbits and, *3:* 579–80
wheel size and effort experiment, *5:* 1051–55, 1054 (ill.)
Forensic science, *3:* 507–19
blood spatter analysis experiment, *3:* 515–18, 516 (ill.), 517 (ill.)
design an experiment for, *3:* 518–19
DNA fingerprinting, *2:* 298, *3:* 509–10, 510 (ill.), 562
fiber evidence experiment, *3:* 511–14, 511 (ill.), 512 (ill.), 513 (ill.)
techniques for, *3:* 507–11, 508 (ill.), 509 (ill.), 510 (ill.)
Forests
acid rain damage to, *1:* 2, 3 (ill.)
biomes, *1:* 103–4
boreal, *1:* 103–4, 104 (ill.)
carbon dioxide absorbed by, *3:* 590
temperate forest experiment, *1:* 106 (ill.), 107–8, 107 (ill.), 108 (ill.)
See also Rainforests; Trees
Fossil casts, *3:* 523, 526–29, 528 (ill.)
Fossil fuels
acid rain from, *1:* 1, 2 (ill.), 4
burning fossil fuels experiment, *3:* 596–98, 596 (ill.), 597 (ill.)
efficiency of, *5:* 1083
greenhouse gases from, *3:* 590, *5:* 941
Fossil molds, *3:* 523, 535
Fossils, *3:* 521–36, 524 (ill.), 525 (ill.), 534 (ill.)
collection of, *3:* 535
dating techniques for, *3:* 524–25
design an experiment for, *3:* 533–35
formation of, *3:* 521–24, 522 (ill.), 523 (ill.)
fossil formation experiment, *3:* 530–33, 532 (ill.)
soils for fossil casts experiment, *3:* 526–29, 528 (ill.)
Foucault, Jean-Bernard-Leon, *5:* 985
Fourier, Jean-Baptiste-Joseph, *3:* 589
Franklin, Benjamin, *6:* 1134 (ill.), 1135
Franklin, Rosalind, *2:* 287
Freeze drying, *3:* 453
Frequency, *2:* 350, *5:* 1095 (ill.), *6:* 1112, 1112 (ill.)
Fresh Kills landfill, *2:* 231
Freshwater. *See* Water
Friction, *6:* 1133
lightning sparks experiment, *6:* 1152–55, 1154 (ill.)
static electricity from, *6:* 1133–34, 1134 (ill.)
Frogs
leaf, *1:* 61–62
life cycle of, *4:* 645–46, 646 (ill.)
tadpoles and temperature experiment, *4:* 647–51, 648 (ill.), 649 (ill.), 650 (ill.)

Fronts (weather), *1:* 34–35
Frozen food, *3:* 451, 453
Fruit
  food drying experiment, *3:* 458–61, 458 (ill.), 459 (ill.), 460 (ill.)
  how fruit flies appear experiment, *5:* 1013–16, 1015 (ill.), 1016 (ill.)
  jelly and pectin experiment, *3:* 467–70, 468 (ill.), 469 (ill.)
  for scurvy, *4:* 759, 760 (ill.)
  sources of vitamin C experiment, *6:* 1226–31, 1229 (ill.)
  sugar fruit preservation experiment, *3:* 454–57, 455 (ill.), 456 (ill.)
  yeast decomposition experiment, *3:* 541–43, 543 (ill.)
Fruit flies, *5:* 1013–16, 1015 (ill.), 1016 (ill.)
Fruticose lichens, *1:* 52, 52 (ill.)
Fulcrum, *5:* 1049–51, 1050 (ill.), 1055–57, 1057 (ill.)
Full moon, *6:* 1175
Fungal diseases, *3:* 539
Fungi, *3:* **537–51,** 538 (ill.), 539 (ill.), 550 (ill.), *4:* 712
  as biopesticides, *4:* 844–45
  in caves, *1:* 131
  design an experiment for, *3:* 549–50
  in lichens, *1:* 51, 73–74, 75 (ill.)
  microorganisms and decomposition experiment, *2:* 233–35, 234 (ill.), 235 (ill.), 236
  reproduction by, *3:* 539, 540 (ill.)
  safety for, *1:* 81
  sugar fruit preservation experiment, *3:* 454–57, 455 (ill.), 456 (ill.)
  temperature for yeast growth experiment, *3:* 544–49, 547 (ill.), 548 (ill.)
  types of, *3:* 537, 538
  uses for, *3:* 537, 538, 539–41, *4:* 712
  yeast decomposition experiment, *3:* 541–43, 543 (ill.)
Fungicides, *4:* 843
Funk, Casimir, *4:* 760
Funnel clouds, *6:* 1150–51, 1150 (ill.)

G

Galaxies, *6:* 1123, 1124–25
Galileo Galilei, *6:* 1109, 1123, 1123 (ill.), 1178, 1178 (ill.)
Garbage, *2:* 230–31, 232–35, 234 (ill.), 235 (ill.)
  See also Landfills
Garlic, *2:* 392–95, 394 (ill.), 395 (ill.), *4:* 848–52, 851 (ill.)
Gas chromatography, *5:* 1033
Gases
  in air, *1:* 33
  air pollution, *1:* 45–46
  in comets, *2:* 216
  as fluids, *3:* 439–41
  greenhouse, *1:* 46, 47 (ill.), 48, *3:* 589–91
  noble, *4:* 830
Gastropods, *5:* 1019–20, 1025–27, 1027 (ill.)
Gecko, *1:* 19, 20 (ill.)
Gel, *3:* 467–70, 468 (ill.), 469 (ill.)
Gel electrophoresis, *3:* 562
Gelatin, *1:* 92, 97
  how color affects taste experiment, *2:* 207–10, 208 (ill.), 209 (ill.)
  medium preparation experiment, *4:* 716–20, 718 (ill.), 719 (ill.)
  temperature and enzyme action experiment, *2:* 368–72, 370 (ill.), 371 (ill.)
Gemstones, *2:* 243
Genes, *3:* 553
Genetic engineering, *3:* 555, 556 (ill.), 562, *4:* 845, 846 (ill.), 848
Genetic traits, *3:* 554–55, 556–59, 558 (ill.), 559 (ill.), 562
Genetics, *3:* **553–63,** 554 (ill.), 555 (ill.)
  color-blindness, *2:* 206
  cross-pollination, *3:* 425, 425 (ill.)
  design an experiment for, *3:* 561–62
  genetic traits experiment, *3:* 556–59, 558 (ill.), 559 (ill.)
  pedigree for taste experiment, *3:* 559–61, 561 (ill.)
  pollination, *3:* 425, 425 (ill.), *6:* 1207, 1207 (ill.), 1208 (ill.)

smell, *1:* 179–80, 189
taste, *1:* 180
vegetative propagation, *6:* 1208, 1208 (ill.)
Geology, *5:* 969–70, 970 (ill.)
Geometric patterns (crystals), *2:* 243, 244–45, 244 (ill.)
Geothermal energy, *5:* 943
Geotropism, *6:* 1191, 1192, 1197–1201, 1198 (ill.), 1199 (ill.), 1200 (ill.)
Germ theory of disease, *1:* 86, *4:* 712
Germination, *3:* **565–78,** 566 (ill.)
design an experiment for, *3:* 576–77
germination time experiment, *3:* 570–73, 572 (ill.)
process of, *3:* 565–66
seed scarification experiment, *3:* 573–76, 574 (ill.), 575 (ill.), 576 (ill.)
temperature for germination experiment, *3:* 566–70, 568 (ill.), 569 (ill.)
Gibberellic acid, *5:* 886–90, 888 (ill.), 889 (ill.)
Gills, *3:* 401, 402, 404–6, 405 (ill.)
Glaciers, *5:* 957–60, 958 (ill.), 959 (ill.)
Glass, *2:* 231, *3:* 618–22, 620 (ill.), 621 (ill.), *4:* 823
Glauber's salt, *5:* 1090–92, 1092 (ill.), 1093
Gliders, *3:* 414, 415–18, 416 (ill.), 417 (ill.)
Global warming, *1:* 46, *3:* 589, 590 (ill.)
Glucose, *4:* 872
Glues, *1:* 19–21
glue adherence experiment, *1:* 22–25, 23 (ill.), 24 (ill.)
light refraction experiment, *4:* 666–69, 666 (ill.), 667 (ill.)
Glutamate, *1:* 177
GMT (Greenwich Mean Time), *6:* 1179
Gnomon, *6:* 1177
Gold, *4:* 828
Goldfish, *2:* 279–84, 281 (ill.), 282 (ill.), 283
Golgi bodies, *1:* 142
Grain, wood, *6:* 1297, 1298 (ill.)
Grapefruit, *6:* 1226–31, 1229 (ill.)
Graphite, *2:* 244, 246 (ill.), *4:* 749, 750 (ill.)
Grasses, *2:* 381–86, 382 (ill.), 383 (ill.), 390–91
Grasshoppers, *3:* 633, *4:* 651–55, 653 (ill.), 654 (ill.)
Gravity, *3:* **579–88,** 580 (ill.)
build a roller coaster experiment, *5:* 934–38, 935 (ill.), 936 (ill.), 937 (ill.)
center of, *5:* 983
centrifugal force and gravity experiment, *5:* 989–92, 990 (ill.)
definition of, *3:* 491
in density determination, *2:* 259
design an experiment for, *3:* 587–88
geotropism effect, *6:* 1191, 1192
height of objects experiment, *5:* 931–34, 932 (ill.), 933 (ill.)
measuring mass experiment, *3:* 585–87, 585 (ill.), 586 (ill.), 587 (ill.), 588 (ill.)
Newtonian laws of motion on, *3:* 492, 579–80
orbits, *5:* 982
root growth and gravity experiment, *6:* 1197–1201, 1198 (ill.), 1199 (ill.), 1200 (ill.)
specific, *2:* 258, *5:* 997–1000, 998 (ill.), 999 (ill.)
speed of falling objects experiment, *3:* 581–84, 582 (ill.), 583 (ill.), 584 (ill.)
star formation, *6:* 1124
tides, *4:* 774, 775 (ill.)
Grease, *6:* 1260
Greeks, ancient, *2:* 389, *3:* 565, *4:* 827, *5:* 1006, *6:* 1123
Green algae, *3:* 538
Greenhouse effect, *3:* **589–600,** 590 (ill.), 591 (ill.), 599 (ill.)
burning fossil fuels experiment, *3:* 596–98, 596 (ill.)
design an experiment for, *3:* 598–600
from fossil fuel combustion, *3:* 590, *5:* 941
gases in, *1:* 46, 47 (ill.), 48, *3:* 589–91
greenhouse temperature increase experiment, *3:* 592–96, 593 (ill.), 594 (ill.)
history of, *3:* 589–90
how it works, *1:* 46, 47 ll, *3:* 589, 617 (ill.)
particulate matter in, *1:* 46–47
Greenhouses, *5:* 1082, 1084–87, 1084 (ill.), 1086 (ill.)
Greenwich Mean Time (GMT), *6:* 1179
Groundwater aquifers, *3:* **601–13,** 603 (ill.)
aquifer contamination experiment, *3:* 605–9, 608 (ill.)
design an experiment for, *3:* 612–13
formation of, *3:* 601, 602 (ill.), 603 (ill.)
pollution of, *3:* 604–5, 605 (ill.), 606 (ill.)
water cleaning experiment, *3:* 609–12, 610 (ill.)

Growth
of bacteria, *1:* 90–95, 92 (ill.), 93 (ill.)
of crystals, *2:* 245–46, 250–53, 252 (ill.)
insect food supply and growth rate experiment, *4:* 651–55, 653 (ill.), 654 (ill.)
See also Annual growth; Plant growth
Guanine, *2:* 286–87
Guar gum, *5:* 919–23, 921 (ill.), 922 (ill.)
Gulf Stream, *4:* 773
Guppies, *3:* 404–6, 405 (ill.)
Gymnosperms, *6:* 1295

H

Hailstones, *6:* 1151–52, 1151 (ill.), 1158–61, 1159 (ill.), 1160 (ill.), 1161 (ill.), 1162
Hair, mid-finger, *3:* 556–59, 559 (ill.)
Hair dyes, *2:* 300
Hairline, straight, *3:* 556–59, 556 (ill.), 559 (ill.)
Halley, Edmond, *2:* 215–16, 216 (ill.), 326, *6:* 1248
Halley's Comet, *2:* 215–16, 216 (ill.)
Han Hsin, *3:* 413
Hard water, *6:* 1226, 1231–34, 1232 (ill.)
Hardness, *4:* 748, *5:* 971–75, 973 (ill.), 974 (ill.)
Hardwood, *6:* 1295, 1302–6, 1304 (ill.), 1305 (ill.)
Hawkmoths, *3:* 426
Health effects
of pesticides, *4:* 844
of pollution, *1:* 59
of vitamins and minerals, *4:* 761, *6:* 1223–36, 1224 (ill.), 1225 (ill.), 1226, 1227 (ill.), 1234 (ill.), 1235 (ill.)
Hearing, *5:* 1095, 1106 (ill.)
Heartwood, *6:* 1296
Heat, *1:* 151–52, *3:* **615–29,** 615 (ill.), 616 (ill.)
conduction in solids experiment, *3:* 618–22, 620 (ill.), 621 (ill.)
convection in liquids experiment, *3:* 622–25, 623 (ill.), 624 (ill.)
for cooking food, *3:* 465–66, 479–80
definition of, *3:* 615, *5:* 929
design an experiment for, *3:* 628–29
endothermic reactions, *1:* 165
endothermic *vs.* exothermic experiment, *1:* 156–60, 157 (ill.), 158 (ill.), 159 (ill.)
exothermic reactions, *1:* 165
heat capacity experiment, *3:* 625–28, 626 (ill.), 627 (ill.), 628 (ill.)
magnetic strength effect experiment, *4:* 674–78, 676 (ill.)
movement of, *3:* 615–17, 616 (ill.), 617 (ill.)
for separation and identification, *5:* 1034
solar heat storage experiment, *5:* 1090–92, 1092 (ill.), 1093
from sunlight, *3:* 589
temperature of different colors experiment, *2:* 210–12, 211 (ill.), 212 (ill.), 213
thermal properties of materials, *4:* 687
transfer of, *3:* 615–16, *5:* 930
wood for, *5:* 942
Heat capacity, *3:* 617, 625–28, 626 (ill.), 627 (ill.), 628 (ill.)
Heat energy. *See* Heat
Heat lamp safety, *1:* 28
Heavy metals, *1:* 49
Helicopters, *3:* 413, 418–21, 418 (ill.), 419 (ill.), 420 (ill.)
Heliotropism, *6:* 1201–4, 1202 (ill.), 1203 (ill.)
Helium, *4:* 829, *6:* 1123–24
Helmholtz, Hermann von, *5:* 1096
Heng, Chang, *2:* 312–13
Herbal medicine, *2:* 389–90, 390 (ill.), 400
Herbicides, *1:* 49, *4:* 843
Heredity. *See* Genetics
Hershey, Alfred, *2:* 286
Heterogeneous mixtures, *5:* 1031–32, 1032 (ill.), 1033 (ill.)
High tide, *4:* 774, *5:* 984, 992 (ill.)
Hippocampus, *4:* 698–99, 699 (ill.)
H.M.S. *Challenger, 5:* 995, 995 (ill.), 996
Homogenous mixtures, *5:* 1032, 1033 (ill.)
Honey
ant food experiment, *3:* 635–38, 636 (ill.), 637 (ill.)
viscosity and temperature experiment, *3:* 441–44, 442 (ill.), 443 (ill.)
Hooke, Robert, *1:* 141
Hormones, plant. *See* Plant hormones

Horned lizards, *1:* 63
Hot environments
  adhesives experiment, *1:* 26–30, 27 (ill.), 28 (ill.), 29 (ill.)
  transpiration rate and environment experiment, *5:* 904–7, 906 (ill.)
Hot springs, *1:* 88
Hours, *6:* 1177
Household chemicals, *4:* 861–65, 861 (ill.), 863 (ill.)
Howard, Albert, *2:* 229
Howard, Luke, *6:* 1272
Hubble Space Telescope, *6:* 1110, 1110 (ill.)
Hue (color), *2:* 206–7
Human Genome Project, *3:* 555–56
Humans, *1:* 85, *2:* 287, 288, *3:* 553–55, 555–56
Humidity
  adhesives experiment, *1:* 26–30, 27 (ill.), 28 (ill.), 29 (ill.)
  in weather, *6:* 1271, 1284
Humonogous fungus, *3:* 537
Humus, *2:* 229, 230, *5:* 1063, 1066, 1067 (ill.)
Hunting weapons, *2:* 391
Hurricanes, *6:* 1284 (ill.), 1286
Hutton, James, *5:* 969, 970 (ill.)
Huygens, Christian, *4:* 660
Hydrangea, *4:* 860
Hydrocarbons, *3:* 596
Hydrochloric acid, *1:* 164, 165, *4:* 865–68, 865 (ill.), 866 (ill.), 867 (ill.)
Hydrogen
  density of, *2:* 257
  nanotechnology, *4:* 747
  periodic table location for, *4:* 829
  in polymers, *5:* 912
  in star formation, *6:* 1123–24
  in water molecules, *1:* 20, 21 (ill.), *4:* 747, 748 (ill.), *6:* 1259
Hydrogen ions, *1:* 1, *2:* 334, *4:* 859, 865
Hydrogen peroxide, *1:* 163, *2:* 361 (ill.), 362–65, 363 (ill.), 364 (ill.)
Hydrogen sulfide, *1:* 129
Hydrologic cycle. *See* Water cycle
Hydrologists, *6:* 1248
Hydrometers, *5:* 997–1000, 998 (ill.), 999 (ill.)
Hydrophilic substances, *3:* 465, 465 (ill.), *6:* 1260
Hydrophobic substances
  attraction to water, *6:* 1260
  proteins, *3:* 465, 465 (ill.), *6:* 1260
  water adhesion and weight experiment, *6:* 1264–68, 1265 (ill.), 1266 (ill.)
Hydroponics, *5:* 895
Hydropower, *5:* 943, 943 (ill.), 948–51, 948 (ill.), 949 (ill.), 950 (ill.)
Hydroxide ions, *4:* 865
Hypertonic solutions, *4:* 798
Hyphae, *3:* 538, 539, 539 (ill.), 540
Hypothesis formation, *5:* 1006, 1007 (ill.)
Hypotonic solutions, *4:* 798

I

Ice
  in comets, *2:* 215, 216, 218–21, 220 (ill.)
  dry, *2:* 220
Ichthyosaur, *3:* 521
Igneous rocks, *5:* 970, 975–78, 975 (ill.), 976 (ill.), 977 (ill.)
Iguanodon, *3:* 521
Imperfect flowers, *3:* 424
Incandescent lights, *1:* 198, 198 (ill.)
Inclined plane, *5:* 1047–48, 1048 (ill.), 1049 (ill.)
Independent assortment, law of, *3:* 554
Independent variables, *5:* 1008
Indian Ocean, *4:* 771
Indicators, pH. *See* Acid/base indicators
Indigo, *2:* 299
Indoor air pollution, *1:* 48
Indore method, *2:* 229
Industrial chemicals, *1:* 49
Inertia, *3:* 491–92, 493, 494, 579, 581
Information gathering, *5:* 1006
Infrared radiation, *3:* 589, 616–17
Ingenhousz, Jan, *4:* 871, 871 (ill.)
Inheritance, dominant *vs.* recessive, *3:* 554–55
  See also Genetics
Inhibition, zone of, *1:* 90–91
Ink, *1:* 63, *5:* 1034–39, 1036 (ill.), 1037 (ill.)
Insecticides, *4:* 843

Insects, *3:* **631–44**
ant food experiment, *3:* 635–38, 636 (ill.), 637 (ill.)
characteristics of, *3:* 631–32, 632 (ill.)
design an experiment for, *3:* 642–43
dyes from, *2:* 299
exoskeleton of, *3:* 631, *5:* 1019
food supply and growth rate experiment, *4:* 651–55, 653 (ill.), 654 (ill.)
fossils of, *3:* 523–24
life cycle of, *3:* 633–34, 643 (ill.), *4:* 645, 645 (ill.), 646
lightning bug experiment, *3:* 638–42, 640 (ill.)
movement by, *3:* 632–33, 633 (ill.)
natural adhesives from, *1:* 19
pheromones, *4:* 844
pollination by, *3:* 425–27
social, *3:* 634
taiga biome, *1:* 104
temperate forest biome, *1:* 108
Insulin, *3:* 555
Interference fringes, *4:* 660
International Hydrographic Organization, *4:* 771
Invertebrates, *5:* 1019
Involuntary muscles, *1:* 115
Iodine
mineral oil, water and iodine experiment, *1:* 170–73, 170 (ill.), 171 (ill.), 172 (ill.)
mystery powder identification experiment, *5:* 1009–13, 1011 (ill.), 1012 (ill.), 1013 (ill.)
for nutrition, *6:* 1226
plastic bag membrane experiment, *4:* 798–803, 799 (ill.), 800 (ill.), 801 (ill.), 802 (ill.)
sources of vitamin C experiment, *6:* 1226–31, 1229 (ill.)
Ion tail, *2:* 216
Ionic cleaners, *4:* 724
Ionic conduction, *2:* 333–34
Ions, *2:* 244, 245 (ill.)
Iron
for bacteria, *1:* 88
magnetized, *4:* 671–72, 671 (ill.), 672 (ill.)
for nutrition, *6:* 1226
oxidation-reduction reactions, *4:* 812
rusting, *1:* 151, 152 (ill.), 163, 165, *4:* 812
rusting experiment, *1:* 152–56, 155 (ill.)
in soil, *5:* 1064
steel wool rust experiment, *4:* 817–20, 818 (ill.)
synthesis reactions, *1:* 163
in water, *6:* 1225–26
Iron Age, *5:* 969
Iron oxide, *1:* 151, 152–56, 155 (ill.), *4:* 812
Irrigation, *2:* 375
Isobars, *6:* 1285
Isotonic solutions, *4:* 798
Ivory, *5:* 911

J

Janssen, Hans, *1:* 141
Janssen, Zacharius, *1:* 141
Jawless fish, *3:* 401, 402 (ill.)
Jelly, *3:* 467–70, 468 (ill.), 469 (ill.)
Jellyfish, *1:* 149
Joints, *1:* 113–14
Juices, fruit, *6:* 1226–31, 1229 (ill.)
Jumping spiders, *1:* 62
Jumps, *3:* 633
Jupiter (planet), *6:* 1109

K

Kangaroo rats, *1:* 105
Kepler, Johannes, *3:* 579, *5:* 981
Kinetic energy, *5:* **929–40,** 930 (ill.)
build a roller coaster experiment, *5:* 934–38, 935 (ill.), 936 (ill.), 937 (ill.)
design an experiment for, *5:* 939–40
height of objects experiment, *5:* 931–34, 932 (ill.), 933 (ill.)
laws of, *5:* 929–31
Kingdoms, *3:* 537
Kites, *3:* 413
Koch, Robert, *1:* 86
Kuhne, Willy, *2:* 359–60

L

Labyrinth, *3:* 404–6, 405 (ill.)
Lactic acid, *3:* 485

Ladybugs, *1:* 65–68, 66 (ill.), 67 (ill.)
Lady's Slipper, *3:* 426, 427 (ill.)
Lakes
acid rain damage to, *1:* 1–2
dissolved oxygen in, *2:* 271–84
eutrophication of, *1:* 49–50, 50 (ill.), 55–58, 57 (ill.)
neutralization of, *1:* 4
water pollution, *1:* 48
Landfills, *2:* **229–41,** 231 (ill.)
biomass energy from, *5:* 942–43
decomposition in, *2:* 231
design an experiment for, *2:* 239–40
history of, *2:* 230–31
microorganisms and decomposition experiment, *2:* 232–35, 234 (ill.), 235 (ill.)
sanitary, *2:* 231
Langley, Samuel Pierpont, *3:* 414
Larva, *3:* 633–34, *4:* 645
Lattice, crystal, *2:* 243
Laundry detergents. *See* Detergents
Lava, *5:* 970
Lava caves, *1:* 129
Lavoisier, Antoine, *4:* 827
Law of independent assortment, *3:* 554
Laws of motion. *See* Newtonian laws of motion
Leaching, *4:* 847, 847 (ill.), 851–55, 854 (ill.)
Lead
air pollution, *1:* 45, 46
atomic symbol for, *4:* 828
density of, *2:* 257, 258, 258 (ill.)
safety for handling, *6:* 1167
Leaf cuttings, *6:* 1208, 1209–16, 1213 (ill.), 1214 (ill.)
Leaf frog, *1:* 61–62
Leaf litter, *2:* 381–86, 382 (ill.), 383 (ill.)
Leather dyes, *2:* 300
Leavening agents, *3:* 464–65, 465 (ill.), 470–73, 472 (ill.), 473 (ill.), 474
See also Baking powder; Baking soda; Yeast
Leaves, *5:* 885, 885 (ill.)
chlorophyll in, *1:* 191–201, 191 (ill.)
color change by, *1:* 192, 192 (ill.), 201 (ill.)
falling in autumn, *1:* 192
fossil formation experiment, *3:* 530–33, 532 (ill.)
in photosynthesis, *4:* 871–72, *5:* 884–85
pigment separation experiment, *1:* 193–97, 195 (ill.), 196 (ill.)
transpiration rate and environment experiment, *5:* 904–7, 906 (ill.)
water in, *5:* 898
LED (Light emitting diode), *4:* 666–69, 666 (ill.), 667 (ill.)
Leeuwenhoek, Anton van, *1:* 85, 141, *4:* 711
Legs (insect), *3:* 631, 633
Lemon juice
acid-copper reduction experiment, *4:* 813–17, 814 (ill.), 815 (ill.)
construct a multicell battery experiment, *2:* 340–44, 341 (ill.), 342 (ill.)
copper patina experiment, *1:* 173–75, 174 (ill.), 175 (ill.)
electrolyte function, *2:* 334
electrolyte solution experiment, *2:* 335–40, 337 (ill.), 338 (ill.), 339 (ill.)
jelly and pectin experiment, *3:* 467–70, 468 (ill.), 469 (ill.)
moldy bread experiment, *3:* 481–85, 481 (ill.), 482 (ill.), 483 (ill.)
pH of, *4:* 859 (ill.)
pH of household chemicals experiment, *4:* 861–65, 861 (ill.), 863 (ill.)
Lenses
camera, *4:* 795 (ill.)
focal length of lens experiment, *4:* 788–91, 788 (ill.)
telescope, *6:* 1110
telescope lenses experiment, *6:* 1113–17, 1114 (ill.), 1116 (ill.)
Levers, *5:* 1049–51, 1050 (ill.), 1055–57, 1057 (ill.)
Lichens
air pollution experiment, *1:* 51–55, 54 (ill.)
annual growth of, *1:* 72–74, 74 (ill.)
fungi in, *1:* 51, 73–74, 75 (ill.), *3:* 538
growth experiment, *1:* 79–82, 81 (ill.)
structure of, *3:* 538
types of, *1:* 52, 52 (ill.)
Life cycle, *4:* **645–57,** 656 (ill.)
of amphibians, *4:* 645–46, 646 (ill.)
design an experiment for, *4:* 655–56

food supply and growth rate experiment, *4:* 651–55, 653 (ill.), 654 (ill.)
of insects, *3:* 633–34, 643 (ill.), *4:* 645, 645 (ill.), 646
pesticide disruption of, *4:* 843
tadpoles and temperature experiment, *4:* 647–51, 648 (ill.), 649 (ill.), 650 (ill.)
Lift (airplane wing), *3:* 413, 415–18, 416 (ill.), 417 (ill.)
Lifting loads
inclined plane for, *5:* 1047–48, 1048 (ill.), 1049 (ill.)
lever lifting experiment, *5:* 1055–57, 1057 (ill.)
levers for, *5:* 1049–51, 1050 (ill.), 1051 (ill.)
wheel size and effort experiment, *5:* 1051–55, 1054 (ill.)
Ligaments, *1:* 113–14
Light, *4:* **659–70,** 659 (ill.)
bending, *2:* 203–5, 205 (ill.)
black, *4:* 661–64, 662 (ill.), 663 (ill.)
black light experiment, *4:* 661–64, 662 (ill.), 663 (ill.)
colors as, *2:* 203–5
design an experiment for, *4:* 669–70
electromagnetic spectrum, *2:* 203, *4:* 659, 660 (ill.), 787
focal length of lens experiment, *4:* 788–91, 788 (ill.)
how we view it, *4:* 787
light colors and plant growth experiment, *1:* 197–200, 197 (ill.), 199 (ill.), 200 (ill.), *4:* 873–77, 875 (ill.), 876 (ill.)
lightning bug experiment, *3:* 639–42, 640 (ill.)
make a rainbow experiment, *4:* 664–65, 664 (ill.), 665 (ill.)
passing through colloids, *4:* 725, 725 (ill.)
in photosynthesis, *4:* 871–73
phototropism effect, *6:* 1191–93
properties of, *4:* 659–60
red, *2:* 203, 204–5, 210–12, 211 (ill.), 212 (ill.), 213, *4:* 873–77, 875 (ill.), 876 (ill.)
refraction experiment, *4:* 666–69, 666 (ill.), 667 (ill.)
in space, *6:* 1109, 1111–12, 1112 (ill.)
speed of, *6:* 1149, 1179
splitting, *2:* 244–45
telescope magnification of, *6:* 1110
temperature of different colors experiment, *2:* 210–12, 211 (ill.), 212 (ill.), 213
Tyndall effect experiment, *4:* 730–32, 731 (ill.), 732 (ill.)
violet, *2:* 203, 204–5, 210–12, 211 (ill.), 212 (ill.), 213, *4:* 873–77, 875 (ill.), 876 (ill.)
visible, *4:* 659, 660, 787, *6:* 1112
white, *2:* 203–5, 205 (ill.), *4:* 873–77, 875 (ill.), 876 (ill.)
yellow, *4:* 873–77, 875 (ill.), 876 (ill.)
Light bulbs
incandescent, *1:* 198, 198 (ill.)
light intensity and plant growth experiment, *4:* 877–80, 878 (ill.), 879 (ill.), 880 (ill.)
Light emitting diode (LED), *4:* 666–69, 666 (ill.), 667 (ill.)
Light sensitivity, *1:* 164
Light-years, *6:* 1124
Lightning
formation of, *6:* 1135, 1135 (ill.), 1148–49, 1149 (ill.)
lightning sparks experiment, *6:* 1152–55, 1154 (ill.)
Lightning bugs, *3:* 638–42, 640 (ill.)
Lilienthal, Otto, *3:* 414, 414 (ill.)
Lime, *1:* 4, *4:* 860, *5:* 1074–77, 1074 (ill.), 1076 (ill.), 1079 (ill.)
Limestone
acid rain damage to, *1:* 3, 12–15, 14 (ill.), 15 (ill.), 16, 17 (ill.)
caves, *1:* 127–29, 128 (ill.), 132–35, 134 (ill.)
stalagmites and stalactite experiment, *1:* 135–39, 137 (ill.)
stalagmites and stalactite formation, *1:* 129–30, 130 (ill.)
See also Chalk
Lind, James, *4:* 759, 760 (ill.)
Linen, *3:* 509
Lippershey, Hans, *1:* 141
Liquid chromatography, *5:* 1033
Liquids
density of, *2:* 259
electricity conduction through, *2:* 333–34

as fluids, *3:* 439–41
heat capacity experiment, *3:* 625–28, 626 (ill.), 627 (ill.), 628 (ill.)
heat convection experiment, *3:* 622–25, 623 (ill.), 624 (ill.)
relative density and floating experiment, *2:* 260–64, 262 (ill.), 263 (ill.)
viscosity and temperature experiment, *3:* 441–44, 442 (ill.), 443 (ill.)
Lisbon, Portugal earthquake of 1755, *2:* 311–12, 312 (ill.)
Litmus paper, *4:* 860
Litter, *1:* 50
Liver, *2:* 361 (ill.), 362–65, 363 (ill.), 364 (ill.)
Lizards, *1:* 19, 20 (ill.), 63, 104–5
Lobsters, *5:* 1022–25, 1022 (ill.), 1023 (ill.), 1024 (ill.), 1025 (ill.)
Lockyer, Joseph Norman, *2:* 326 (ill.)
Long-term memory, *4:* 697–98, 698 (ill.)
Low tide, *4:* 774, *5:* 984, 992 (ill.)
Luciferin, *3:* 639, 640 (ill.)
Luminol, *3:* 508
Lunar eclipse, *2:* 326, 326 (ill.), 327–29, 328 (ill.), 329 (ill.)
Lungfish, *3:* 402
Luster of minerals, *5:* 971–75, 973 (ill.), 974 (ill.)

M

Machines. *See* Simple machines
Macrominerals, *6:* 1226
Macroorganisms, *2:* 230, 231 (ill.)
Magma, *5:* 970, *6:* 1238, 1239
Magnesium
chemical properties of, *1:* 165
hard water sources experiment, *6:* 1231–34, 1232 (ill.)
for nutrition, *4:* 761
periodic table location for, *4:* 829
in water, *6:* 1225–26
Magnetism, *4:* **671–83,** 671 (ill.), 681 (ill.)
design an experiment for, *4:* 681–82
domain alignment for, *4:* 671–72, 672 (ill.)
electricity in, *2:* 349–50, *4:* 672–73
electromagnet creation experiment, *2:* 354–57, 354 (ill.), 356 (ill.)
electromagnet strength experiment, *4:* 678–81, 678 (ill.), 679 (ill.)
magnetic strength experiment, *4:* 674–78, 674 (ill.), 676 (ill.)
production of, *2:* 349–50, *4:* 672–73
See also Electromagnetism
Magnifying lens, *5:* 1081
Maillard, Louis Camille, *3:* 463–64
Maillard reaction, *3:* 463–64
Malnutrition, *4:* 759–60
Mammals, *1:* 50, 104, *3:* 524
See also Animals
Manganese, *6:* 1226
Manure, *2:* 229, *5:* 943
Marble, *1:* 12–15, 14 (ill.), 15 (ill.), 16
Marine mammals, *1:* 50, *3:* 524
Mariotte, Edme, *6:* 1248
Mass
acceleration and, *3:* 492
atomic, *4:* 828, 829
center of, *5:* 983
density determination, *2:* 257, 259
of fluids, *3:* 439
gravity's effect on, *3:* 580, 581
inertia and, *3:* 491–92
measuring mass experiment, *3:* 585–87, 585 (ill.), 586 (ill.), 587 (ill.), 588 (ill.)
second law of motion on, *3:* 579–80
Materials science, *4:* **685–96,** 686 (ill.)
design an experiment for, *4:* 695–96
nanosize and properties experiment, *4:* 750–53, 752 (ill.)
nanotechnology in, *4:* 749
properties of materials, *4:* 686–87, 687 (ill.)
renewable packing material experiment, *4:* 691–94, 693 (ill.), 694 (ill.)
soundproofing materials experiment, *5:* 1102–5, 1104 (ill.)
tape strength experiment, *4:* 688–91, 689 (ill.), 690 (ill.)
types of materials, *4:* 685–86
Mauve, *2:* 300

Meandering rivers
course of, *5:* 956, 967 (ill.)
stream pattern experiment, *5:* 960–62, 961 (ill.), 964 (ill.), 965 (ill.), 966
Meap tides, *3:* 580
Meat
aging meat experiment, *2:* 365–68, 366 (ill.), 367 (ill.)
ant food experiment, *3:* 635–38, 636 (ill.), 637 (ill.)
cooking, *3:* 463–64
curing, *3:* 452
safety for, *2:* 366
Meat tenderizer
aging meat experiment, *2:* 365–68, 366 (ill.), 367 (ill.)
DNA isolation and extraction experiment, *2:* 289–91, 289 (ill.), 290 (ill.)
species differences in DNA experiment, *2:* 291–95, 293 (ill.)
Mechanical bonding, *1:* 20
Medicinal plants, *2:* 389–90, 390 (ill.), 400
Medicine, *2:* 389–90, 390 (ill.), 400, *4:* 749
See also Health effects
Medium, for microorganisms, *4:* 716–20, 718 (ill.), 719 (ill.)
Megalosaurus, *3:* 521
Melanin, *1:* 200
Melting point, *4:* 748, 752 (ill.), *5:* 1034
Membranes
cell, *1:* 86, 87 (ill.), 142, *4:* 797, 798, 798 (ill.), *5:* 898
semipermeable, *3:* 452, *4:* 797, 798–803, 799 (ill.), 800 (ill.), 801 (ill.), 802 (ill.), 806–9, 808 (ill.), 809 (ill.)
Memory, *4:* **697–709**
design an experiment for, *4:* 707–8
false, *4:* 699–700, 705–7, 707 (ill.)
how it works, *4:* 698–99, 699 (ill.)
make a false memory experiment, *4:* 705–7, 707 (ill.)
memory mnemonics experiment, *4:* 701–4, 701 (ill.), 702 (ill.), 703 (ill.)
problems with, *4:* 699–700, 699 (ill.)
techniques to help, *4:* 700
types of, *4:* 697–98, 698 (ill.)
Mendel, Gregor, *3:* 554, 555 (ill.)
Mendeleev, Dmitri, *4:* 827–28, 828 (ill.)
Meniscus, *6:* 1260
Mercury, *4:* 828
Mercury barometers, *1:* 34
Mestral, George de, *4:* 685, 686 (ill.)
Metals, *4:* 686
conductivity of elements experiment, *4:* 830–35, 833 (ill.)
electricity conduction through, *2:* 333
electrons released by metals experiment, *4:* 838–40, 840 (ill.), 841 (ill.), 842
glue adherence experiment, *1:* 22–25, 23 (ill.), 24 (ill.)
heavy, *1:* 49
oxidation-reduction reactions in, *4:* 811 (ill.)
periodic table location for, *4:* 829
See also Copper; Iron
Metamorphic rocks, *5:* 971, 975–78, 975 (ill.), 976 (ill.), 977 (ill.)
Metamorphosis
amphibians, *4:* 645–46, 645 (ill.)
insects, *3:* 633–34
tadpoles and temperature experiment, *4:* 647–51, 648 (ill.), 649 (ill.), 650 (ill.)
Meteor showers, *2:* 218, 218 (ill.), 227
Meteorites, *2:* 217, 217 ll, 218 (ill.)
Meteoroids, *2:* 216–17, 217 (ill.)
Meteorologists, *1:* 34, *6:* 1284
Meteors. *See* Comets and meteors
Methane, *1:* 46, 48, *2:* 231, *5:* 943
Mexican free-tail bats, *1:* 130
Michell, John, *2:* 312
Microclimates, *3:* 592–96, 593 (ill.), 594 (ill.)
Microorganisms, *4:* **711–21,** 711 (ill.)
as biopesticides, *4:* 844–45
for composting, *2:* 229
design an experiment for, *4:* 720–21
discovery of, *4:* 711–12, 712 (ill.)
in food spoilage, *3:* 451–53, 477–80, 478 (ill.)
growing penicillin experiment, *4:* 713–16, 713 (ill.), 715 (ill.)
in landfills, *2:* 231, 232–35, 234 (ill.), 235 (ill.)
medium preparation experiment, *4:* 716–20, 718 (ill.), 719 (ill.)

in soil, *2:* 229, *5:* 1063, 1067
types of, *4:* 712
See also Bacteria; Fungi
Microscopes
compound, *1:* 141, 141 (ill.)
development of, *1:* 85, 141
for forensic science, *3:* 507, 511
for microorganisms, *4:* 711
for nanotechnology, *4:* 748
scanning tunneling, *4:* 748
Mid-finger hair, *3:* 556–59, 558 (ill.), 559 (ill.)
Milk
ant food experiment, *3:* 635–38, 636 (ill.), 637 (ill.)
pasteurization of, *3:* 480, 485
spoiled milk and temperature experiment, *3:* 485–88, 487 (ill.)
Milky Way, *6:* 1123, 1124
Mimicry, *1:* 62
Mineral oil, *1:* 170–73, 170 (ill.), 171 (ill.), 172 (ill.)
Minerals, *5:* **969–79,** 970 (ill.), *6:* **1223–36,** 1234 (ill.)
in bones, *1:* 113, 114
crystalline, *2:* 243, 244
definition of, *5:* 969
design an experiment for, *5:* 978, *6:* 1234–36
dyes from, *2:* 299
formation of, *5:* 970
in fossil formation, *3:* 523
hard water sources experiment, *6:* 1231–34, 1232 (ill.)
health effects of, *4:* 761, *6:* 1223–36, 1224 (ill.), 1225 (ill.), 1226 (ill.), 1227 (ill.), 1234 (ill.), 1235 (ill.)
in soil, *5:* 1063, 1064, 1064 (ill.)
stalagmites and stalactite experiment, *1:* 135–39, 137 (ill.)
testing mineral characteristics experiment, *5:* 971–75, 973 (ill.), 974 (ill.)
trace, *6:* 1226
in water, *6:* 1225–26
Mini-biomes, *1:* 106–8, 106 (ill.), 107 (ill.)
Miniaturization, *4:* 750
Mirrors, *6:* 1110–11
Mississippi River, *5:* 955
Mixtures and solutions, *4:* **723–34,** 723 (ill.)
design an experiment for, *4:* 732–33
hypertonic *vs.* hypotonic, *4:* 798
osmosis of, *4:* 798
separation of, *4:* 724–25, 725 (ill.), *5:* 1031–34, 1032 (ill.)
suspensions *vs.* solutions experiment, *4:* 725–30, 729 (ill.)
Tyndall effect experiment, *4:* 730–32, 731 (ill.), 732 (ill.)
types of, *4:* 723–24, 724 (ill.), *5:* 1031–32, 1033 (ill.)
unknown mixtures experiment, *5:* 1039–43, 1041 (ill.), 1042 (ill.)
Mnemonics, *4:* 700, 701–4, 701 (ill.), 702 (ill.), 703 (ill.)
Moh's Hardness Scale, *5:* 974
Molds
antibiotics from, *3:* 539–40, *4:* 712
diffusion of, *4:* 797
food spoilage by, *3:* 477–80, 478 (ill.)
growing penicillin experiment, *4:* 713–16, 713 (ill.), 715 (ill.)
moldy bread experiment, *3:* 481–85, 481 (ill.), 482 (ill.), 483 (ill.)
Molecules
carbon, *4:* 749
crystals, *2:* 244
molecule size and osmosis experiment, *4:* 806–9, 808 (ill.), 809 (ill.)
in nanotechnology, *4:* 747–48
salt, *4:* 747
water, *1:* 20, 21 (ill.), *4:* 747, 748 (ill.), *6:* 1259, 1259 (ill.)
Mollusks, *5:* 1019–20, 1020 (ill.), 1021
Molting, *3:* 631, *5:* 1020–21
Monocot plants, *1:* 145–47, 145 (ill.), 146 (ill.), 147 (ill.), 148
Monosodium glutamate (MSG), *1:* 177
Months, *6:* 1175
Moon
gravity and, *3:* 579, 580
of Jupiter, *6:* 1109
lunar eclipse, *2:* 326, 326 (ill.), 327–29, 328 (ill.), 329 (ill.)
mountains on, *6:* 1109

orbit of, *5:* 982, 986 (ill.)
phases of, *2:* 329–30, 330 (ill.), 331 (ill.)
tides and, *4:* 774, 775 (ill.), *5:* 983–84
in timekeeping, *6:* 1175
Mordants, *2:* 300–301, 300 (ill.), 304–7, 306 (ill.), 307 (ill.)
Mosses, *1:* 131
Motion
circular, *3:* 492–93, 493 (ill.), 501–5, 503 (ill.)
three laws of, *3:* 491–93, 492 (ill.), 493 (ill.)
Motors, electric, *2:* 358 (ill.), *5:* 1087–89, 1088 (ill.), 1089 (ill.)
Mount Everest, *4:* 735, 736 (ill.)
Mount Vesuvius, *6:* 1237, 1237 (ill.), 1239
Mountain range, *4:* 735
Mountains, *4:* **735–45,** 736 (ill.)
air density and, *1:* 36, 36 (ill.)
desert formation experiment, *4:* 741–44, 742 (ill.), 743 (ill.)
design an experiment for, *4:* 744–45
ecosystem of, *4:* 737–38
formation of, *4:* 735–37, 736 (ill.), 737 (ill.)
on the moon, *6:* 1109
mountain formation experiment, *4:* 738–41, 739 (ill.), 740 (ill.)
Mouths (insect), *3:* 632
Movement
by fish, *3:* 402–3, 403 (ill.), 407–9, 409 (ill.), 410
of heat, *3:* 615–17, 616 (ill.), 617 (ill.)
water bottle rocket experiment, *3:* 493–501, 495 (ill.), 498 (ill.), 499 (ill.), 500 (ill.)
See also Motion
MSG (Monosodium glutamate), *1:* 177
Mucus, *1:* 179
Multicellular organisms, *1:* 141, 144 (ill.)
Municipal water supply, *3:* 609–12, 610 (ill.)
Murray, John, *5:* 995
Muscle contractions, *1:* 115–16, 116 (ill.), 120–23, 122 (ill.)
Muscle fibers, *1:* 115, 115 (ill.), 124
Muscle strength, *1:* 115–16, 115 (ill.), 120–23, 122 (ill.)
Muscles, *1:* **113–25**
design an experiment for, *1:* 123–25
muscle strength and fatigue experiment, *1:* 120–23, 122 (ill.)
strength of, *1:* 115–16, 115 (ill.)
Mushrooms, *1:* 81, 108, *3:* 540, 550 (ill.)
Music, *4:* 700, 701–4, 701 (ill.), 702 (ill.), 703 (ill.)
Mutations, DNA, *3:* 555
Mycelium, *3:* 538, 539 (ill.)
Mystery powders experiment, *5:* 1009–13, 1011 (ill.), 1012 (ill.), 1013 (ill.)

N

Nails, magnetized, *4:* 674–78, 674 (ill.), 676 (ill.)
Nanometers, *4:* 787
Nanorobots (nanobots), *4:* 749, 750
Nanotechnology, *4:* **747–57,** 748 (ill.), 749 (ill.)
building blocks of, *4:* 747–48, 748 (ill.), 750 (ill.)
design an experiment for, *4:* 756–57
nanosize and properties of materials experiment, *4:* 750–53, 752 (ill.)
nanosize and reaction rate experiment, *4:* 753–55, 754 (ill.), 755 (ill.)
uses for, *4:* 749–50
Nansen bottles, *5:* 997
Napoleon Bonaparte, *3:* 452, 479
Nares, *3:* 403–4
National Weather Service, *6:* 1273, 1275 (ill.)
Native American baskets, *2:* 390–91, 396
Natural dyes, *2:* 299, 301–4, 302 (ill.), 303 (ill.), 304–7, 306 (ill.), 307 (ill.), 391
Natural fibers, *2:* 301–4, 302 (ill.), 303 (ill.)
Natural pesticides, *4:* 843, 844–46, 847–52, 851 (ill.)
Natural pollutants, *1:* 48
Nebula, *6:* 1124, 1124 (ill.)
Nectar, *3:* 425–26, 431–35, 433 (ill.)
Needles (tree), *1:* 103
Nervous system, *4:* 843–44, 844 (ill.)
Neutralization, *1:* 4, *4:* 860
Neutrons, *4:* 828
Newton, Isaac
energy, *5:* 930–31
gravity, *5:* 982
laws of motion, *3:* 491, 579, 580 (ill.), *6:* 1165
light, *2:* 203–5, 203 (ill.), 205 (ill.), *4:* 659–60, 659 (ill.)
tides, *4:* 774

Newtonian fluids, *3:* 440–41, 444–47, 446 (ill.), 447 (ill.)
Newtonian laws of motion, *3:* 491–93, 492 (ill.), 493 (ill.)
bottle rocket experiment, *3:* 493–501, 495 (ill.), 498 (ill.), 499 (ill.), 500 (ill.)
planetary orbits and, *3:* 579–80
on structures, *6:* 1165
Niagara River, *5:* 955 (ill.), 956
Nickel electroplating, *2:* 344–45, 344 (ill.), 345 (ill.)
Nile River, *5:* 955, 956 (ill.)
Nimbostratus clouds, *6:* 1273
Nimbus clouds, *6:* 1272
Nitrates, *1:* 49
Nitric acid, *1:* 164
Nitrogen, *1:* 33, 85, *2:* 230, 386
Nitrogen dioxide, *1:* 45
Nitrogen oxides, *1:* 1, 46
Noble gases, *4:* 830
Non-Newtonian fluids, *3:* 440–41, 444–47, 446 (ill.), 447 (ill.)
Nonpoint source pollution, *3:* 604, 605 (ill.)
Nontarget organisms, *4:* 846
Nontasters, *1:* 180–86
North Star, *6:* 1125–28, 1126 (ill.), 1127 (ill.)
Notes, sticky, *1:* 22, 22 (ill.), 26–30, 27 (ill.), 28 (ill.), 29 (ill.)
Nuclear fusion, *6:* 1124
Nucleation, *2:* 246
Nucleotides, *2:* 286–87, 291
Nucleus
cell, *1:* 86, 142–43, *2:* 285, 289–91, 289 (ill.), 290 (ill.)
comet, *2:* 216
Number, atomic, *4:* 828
Nutrients
dissolved oxygen level changes from, *2:* 272–73, 279
in eutrophication, *1:* 49–50, 50 (ill.)
how good is my diet experiment, *4:* 766–69, 768 (ill.), 769 (ill.)
needed for health, *4:* 760–61, 761 (ill.)
for plants, *5:* 883, 895
role of, *4:* 759
Nutrition, *4:* **759–70,** 760 (ill.)
design an experiment for, *4:* 769–70
dietary carbohydrate and fat sources experiment, *4:* 761–64, 763 (ill.), 764 (ill.)
dietary proteins and salt sources experiment, *4:* 764–66, 765 (ill.), 766 (ill.)
essential nutrients in, *4:* 760–61, 761 (ill.)
how good is my diet experiment, *4:* 766–69, 768 (ill.), 769 (ill.)
muscle strength and fatigue experiment, *1:* 123, 124 (ill.)
vitamins and minerals in, *6:* 1223–26, 1224 (ill.), 1225 (ill.), 1226 (ill.), 1227 (ill.), 1234 (ill.), 1235 (ill.)
Nutrition Fact Labels, *4:* 767–69, 768 (ill.), 769 (ill.)
Nylon, *3:* 509, *6:* 1139–44, 1141 (ill.), 1143 (ill.)
Nymphs, *4:* 645

O

O layer (soil), *5:* 1066, 1067 (ill.)
Observation, controlled, *5:* 1007
Occluded fronts, *1:* 35
Ocean currents, *4:* 772–74, 774 (ill.), 780–83, 782 (ill.)
Ocean water. *See* Seawater
Ocean waves, *4:* 773, 774 (ill.), 784
Oceanographers, *4:* 771
Oceans, *4:* **771–85**
biome, *1:* 103
convection current experiment, *4:* 780–83, 782 (ill.)
design an experiment for, *4:* 783–84
eutrophication experiment, *1:* 55–58, 57 (ill.)
life in, *4:* 774–75, 775 (ill.)
photosynthesis in, *4:* 872–73, 873 (ill.)
salinity and stratification experiment, *4:* 775–80, 778 (ill.)
seawater properties, *4:* 771–72, 772 (ill.), 773 (ill.)
size of, *1:* 48, *4:* 772
See also Tides

Octopi, *1:* 63
Odors
as animal defenses, *1:* 62–63, 62 (ill.), 65–68, 66 (ill.), 67 (ill.)
pollinators attracted by, *3:* 426–27
smell-taste relationship experiment, *1:* 186–89, 187 (ill.)
See also Smell, sense of
Oersted, Hans Christian, *4:* 672, 672 (ill.)
Ogallala aquifer, *3:* 602
Oil pollution, *1:* 48–49, 49 (ill.), 58
Oil power plants, *1:* 1, 46
Oil spills, *1:* 48–49, 49 (ill.), 50
Oils
heat capacity experiment, *3:* 625–28, 626 (ill.), 627 (ill.), 628 (ill.)
viscosity and temperature experiment, *3:* 441–44, 442 (ill.), 443 (ill.)
Old Farmers Almanac, 6: 1284
Olfactory cells, *1:* 179, 179 (ill.), 189
Olive oil, *3:* 625–28, 626 (ill.), 627 (ill.), 628 (ill.)
Onions, *2:* 392–95, 394 (ill.), 395 (ill.)
Oobleck, *3:* 448
Oort cloud, *2:* 215
Opossums, *1:* 61
Optics and optical illusions, *4:* **787–96,** 787 (ill.), 795 (ill.)
design an experiment for, *4:* 794–95
focal length of lens experiment, *4:* 788–91, 788 (ill.)
light and how we view it, *4:* 787–88
seeing optical illusions experiment, *4:* 791–94, 791 (ill.), 792 (ill.), 793 (ill.)
See also Light
Orange juice
ant food experiment, *3:* 635–38, 636 (ill.), 637 (ill.)
sources of vitamin C experiment, *6:* 1226–31, 1229 (ill.)
Orbits, *5:* **981–94,** 982 (ill.), 983 (ill.), 984 (ill.), 985 (ill.), 992 (ill.)
centrifugal force and gravity experiment, *5:* 989–92, 990 (ill.)
centripetal force in, *3:* 493, 504 (ill.), 505
of comets, *2:* 215–16, 216 (ill.)
design an experiment for, *3:* 505, *5:* 992–94
discovery of, *5:* 981–82, *6:* 1109–10
elliptical, *3:* 579, *5:* 981
of the moon, *5:* 982, 986 (ill.)
Newtonian laws of motion and, *3:* 579–80
pendulum rotation experiment, *5:* 985–89, 988 (ill.)
star movement and, *6:* 1124
Organelles, *1:* 86, 142
Organic farming, *2:* 229–30
Organic food, *4:* 855–56
Organic matter, *5:* 1063, 1066
Organic waste, *2:* 229, 230, 235–39, 236 (ill.), 238 (ill.), 239 (ill.)
Organisms, nontarget, *4:* 846
Organophosphates, *4:* 843–44, 844 (ill.)
Orion nebula, *6:* 1124 (ill.)
Oscillation, *6:* 1180–85, 1182 (ill.), 1183 (ill.)
Osmosis and diffusion, *4:* **797–810,** 797 (ill.)
design an experiment for, *4:* 809–10
molecule size experiment, *4:* 806–9, 808 (ill.), 809 (ill.)
of nutrients, *5:* 883
plastic bag membrane experiment, *4:* 798–803, 799 (ill.), 800 (ill.), 801 (ill.), 802 (ill.)
process of, *4:* 797, 798
salt water osmosis experiment, *4:* 803–6, 803 (ill.), 804 (ill.), 805 (ill.)
through semipermeable membranes, *3:* 452, *4:* 797
of water for plants, *4:* 798, *5:* 897–98, 898 (ill.), 899 (ill.)
Osteoporosis, *1:* 114, 116 (ill.)
Overfishing, *3:* 411
Oxidation-reduction reactions, *4:* **811–25,** 811 (ill.), 823 (ill.), 824 (ill.)
acid-copper reduction experiment, *4:* 813–17, 814 (ill.), 815 (ill.)
copper color change experiment, *4:* 820–23, 820 (ill.), 821 (ill.), 822 (ill.)
design an experiment for, *4:* 823–25
examples of, *4:* 812–13
process of, *1:* 164, *4:* 811
rusting experiment, *1:* 152–56, 155 (ill.)
rusting process as, *1:* 151, 152 (ill.), *4:* 812, 823 (ill.)
steel wool rust experiment, *4:* 817–20, 818 (ill.)

Oxygen
- in air, *1:* 33
- altitude and, *1:* 36
- for composting, *2:* 230
- diffusion in blood, *4:* 797, 798 (ill.)
- for fish, *3:* 402, 404–6, 405 (ill.)
- in landfills, *2:* 231
- from photosynthesis, *5:* 884–85
- in plant respiration, *4:* 871, 872, *5:* 883
- rust reaction, *1:* 163, 165
- in water molecules, *1:* 20, 21 (ill.), *4:* 747, 748 (ill.), *6:* 1259, 1259 (ill.)
- *See also* Dissolved oxygen

Ozone, *1:* 46

P

Pacific Ocean, *4:* 771
Packing peanuts, *4:* 691–94, 693 (ill.), 694 (ill.)
Packing tape, *1:* 21
Paleontologists, *3:* 521, 534 (ill.), 535
Palmieri, Luigi, *2:* 313
Papain, *2:* 360, 365–68, 366 (ill.), 367 (ill.)
Papaya, *2:* 360, 365–68, 366 (ill.), 367 (ill.)
Paper chromatography, *5:* 1033, 1034–39, 1036 (ill.), 1037 (ill.)
Papillae, *1:* 178, 179, 181
Papyrus, *1:* 19
Parasites, *3:* 538
Parents, genetics from, *3:* 553–55
Parrot fish, *1:* 61
Particulate matter, *1:* 45, 46–47, 59
Pascal, Blaise, *1:* 34
Pascal (unit of measure), *1:* 34
Passive solar energy systems, *5:* 1082, 1084–87, 1084 (ill.), 1086 (ill.)
Pasteur, Louis, *1:* 86, *3:* 452, *4:* 711–12, 712 (ill.)
Pasteurization, *3:* 480, 480 (ill.), 485, *4:* 712
Patinas, *1:* 173–75, 174 (ill.), 175 (ill.)
Patterns, camouflage, *1:* 61–62
Pea plants, *3:* 554
Pectin, *3:* 467–70, 468 (ill.), 469 (ill.)
Pelletier, Pierre Joseph, *1:* 191
Pencil lead. *See* Graphite

Pendulums
- pendulum oscillation time experiment, *6:* 1180–85, 1182 (ill.), 1183 (ill.)
- pendulum rotation experiment, *5:* 985–89, 988 (ill.)
- in timekeeping, *6:* 1178

Penicillin
- discovery of, *3:* 539–40, *4:* 712, 712 (ill.)
- growing penicillin experiment, *4:* 713–16, 713 (ill.), 715 (ill.)

Pennies, *4:* 813–17, 814 (ill.), 815 (ill.)
Pepsin, *2:* 360
Perception, *4:* 791–94, 791 (ill.), 792 (ill.), 793 (ill.)
Perfect flowers, *3:* 424
Periodic table, *4:* **827–42,** 831 (ill.)
- conductivity of elements experiment, *4:* 830–35, 833 (ill.)
- design an experiment for, *4:* 840–42
- development of, *4:* 827–28, 828 (ill.)
- electrons released by metals experiment, *4:* 838–40, 840 (ill.), 841 (ill.), 842
- how to read, *4:* 828–30, 829 (ill.), 830 (ill.)
- solubility of elements experiment, *4:* 835–38, 835 (ill.), 837 (ill.)

Perkin, William Henry, *2:* 299–300, 299 (ill.)
Permineralization, *3:* 522, 522 (ill.), 523, 523 (ill.)
Perrault, Claude, *5:* 955
Perroult, Pierre, *6:* 1247–48
Pesticides, *4:* **843–57,** 846 (ill.), 848 (ill.)
- benefits and dangers of, *4:* 845–48
- chemical, *4:* 843–44, 844 (ill.)
- degradation of, *4:* 847
- design an experiment for, *4:* 855–57
- natural, *4:* 843, 844–46, 847–48
- natural *vs.* chemical pesticides experiment, *4:* 848–52, 851 (ill.)
- safe handling of, *4:* 851
- water movement of pesticides experiment, *4:* 851–55, 854 (ill.)
- water pollution by, *1:* 49, *4:* 846–47, 847 (ill.)

Pests, definition of, *4:* 843
Petals, *3:* 424, 424 (ill.)
Petri dishes, *4:* 716–20, 718 (ill.), 719 (ill.)
Petrifaction, *3:* 523, 535
Petrified Forest, *3:* 523

pH, *4:* **859–69**
of acid rain, *1:* 1, 2 (ill.), 3 (ill.), *4:* 860–61, 861 (ill.)
brine shrimp experiment, *1:* 5–8, 7 (ill.)
chemical titration experiment, *4:* 865–68, 865 (ill.), 866 (ill.), 867 (ill.)
definition of, *1:* 1, *4:* 859
design an experiment for, *4:* 868–69
dye colorfastness and, *2:* 307
household chemicals pH experiment, *4:* 861–65, 861 (ill.), 863 (ill.)
jelly and pectin experiment, *3:* 467–70, 468 (ill.), 469 (ill.)
measurement of, *4:* 859–60, 859 (ill.), 860 (ill.)
microorganisms and decomposition experiment, *2:* 233–35, 234 (ill.), 235 (ill.), 236
neutral, *1:* 9
plant growth experiment, *1:* 9–12, 11 (ill.)
rate of erosion experiment, *2:* 386
for separation and identification, *5:* 1033, 1034 (ill.)
soil, *4:* 860, *5:* 1064
soil pH and plant growth experiment, *5:* 1074–77, 1074 (ill.), 1076 (ill.), 1079 (ill.)
unknown mixtures experiment, *5:* 1039–43, 1041 (ill.), 1042 (ill.)
pH indicators. *See* Acid/base indicators
pH meter, digital, *4:* 860, 860 (ill.)
Phenylthiocarbamide (PTC), *3:* 559–61, 561 (ill.)
Pheromones, *4:* 844
Phloem, *4:* 872, *5:* 884, *6:* 1296
Phosphates, *1:* 49, 55–58, 57 (ill.)
Phosphorescence, *4:* 660
Phosphorus, *1:* 55, *2:* 386, *4:* 761, *5:* 1064
Photo-chromic glass, *4:* 823
Photosynthesis, *4:* **871–82,** 871 (ill.), 872 (ill.), 873 (ill.)
by algae, *1:* 74, 75 (ill.)
chlorophyll in, *1:* 191–201, 191 (ill.), *4:* 871–72, *5:* 884–85
design an experiment for, *4:* 880–81
discovery of, *4:* 871
dissolved oxygen from, *2:* 271–72
light colors and plant growth experiment, *1:* 197–200, 197 (ill.), 199 (ill.), 200 (ill.), *4:* 873–77, 875 (ill.), 876 (ill.)
light intensity and plant growth experiment, *4:* 877–80, 878 (ill.), 879 (ill.), 880 (ill.)
process of, *1:* 191–201, 191 (ill.), *4:* 871–72, *5:* 884–85, 885 (ill.), 897
Phototropism, *6:* 1191–93, 1192 (ill.), 1193 (ill.)
auxins in, *6:* 1191–92, 1193, 1193 (ill.), 1209
phototropism maze experiment, *6:* 1193–97, 1195 (ill.), 1196 (ill.)
Photovoltaic cells, *5:* 1083, 1087–89, 1088 (ill.), 1089 (ill.)
Physical changes, *1:* 163, 164 (ill.)
Physical properties, *1:* 163
Phytoplankton, *4:* 873, 873 (ill.)
Pi, *4:* 701–4, 701 (ill.), 702 (ill.), 703 (ill.)
Pickling, *3:* 452, 452 (ill.)
Pigments
colors, *2:* 205
in leaves, *1:* 192
light colors and plant growth experiment, *1:* 197–200, 197 (ill.), 199 (ill.), 200 (ill.)
plant pigment separation experiment, *1:* 193–97, 195 (ill.), 196 (ill.)
Pill bugs, *1:* 68
Pineapple, *2:* 368–72, 370 (ill.), 371 (ill.)
Pistil, *3:* 423–24, 424 (ill.)
Pitch (sound), *5:* 1095 (ill.), 1099–1102, 1100 (ill.), 1101 (ill.)
Planetary orbits. *See* Orbits
Plankton, *2:* 279, *4:* 774
Plant anatomy, *5:* **883–95,** 883 (ill.), 884 (ill.), 885 (ill.)
design an experiment for, *5:* 893–95
in photosynthesis, *5:* 884–85, 885 (ill.)
plant hormones and growth experiment, *5:* 886–90, 888 (ill.), 889 (ill.)
for pollination, *3:* 423–27, 425 (ill.), 426 (ill.), 427 (ill.)
water uptake experiment, *5:* 890–93, 892 (ill.), 893 (ill.)
Plant cells. *See* Cells
Plant growth, *5:* 1084–87, 1084 (ill.), 1086 (ill.)
acid rain experiment, *1:* 9–12, 11 (ill.)
annual, *1:* 71–74, 72 (ill.), 73 (ill.), 74 (ill.)
auxins in, *6:* 1191–92, 1209
design an experiment for, *1:* 82–83

heliotropism and plant movement experiment, *6:* 1201–4, 1202 (ill.), 1203 (ill.)
lichen growth experiment, *1:* 79–82, 81 (ill.)
by lichens, *1:* 72–74, 74 (ill.)
light colors and plant growth experiment, *1:* 197–200, 197 (ill.), 199 (ill.), 200 (ill.), *4:* 873–77, 875 (ill.), 876 (ill.)
light intensity and plant growth experiment, *4:* 877–80, 878 (ill.), 879 (ill.), 880 (ill.)
organic waste for plant growth experiment, *2:* 236–39, 236 (ill.), 238 (ill.), 239 (ill.)
phototropism effect on, *6:* 1191–93, 1192 (ill.), 1193 (ill.)
phototropism maze experiment, *6:* 1193–97, 1195 (ill.), 1196 (ill.)
plant hormones and growth experiment, *5:* 886–90, 888 (ill.), 889 (ill.)
soil pH and plant growth experiment, *5:* 1074–77, 1074 (ill.), 1076 (ill.), 1079 (ill.)
tree growth experiment, *1:* 74–79, 78 (ill.)
by trees, *1:* 71–72, 72 (ill.), 73 (ill.)
water movement of pesticides experiment, *4:* 851–55, 854 (ill.)

Plant hormones
leaf/stem cuttings and auxins experiment, *6:* 1209–16, 1213 (ill.), 1214 (ill.)
in phototropism, *6:* 1191–92, 1193, 1193 (ill.)
plant hormones and growth experiment, *5:* 886–90, 888 (ill.), 889 (ill.)
in vegetative propagation, *6:* 1208, 1209

Plants
acid rain damage to, *1:* 2
anti-bacterial plant experiment, *2:* 392–95, 394 (ill.), 395 (ill.)
cave, *1:* 131
climbing, *6:* 1192, 1205 (ill.)
color perception, *2:* 214
cultural uses of, *2:* 389, 390–92, 392 (ill.), 400, *5:* 897
desert, *1:* 105, *5:* 898, 899–900, 908, 908 (ill.)
dicot, *1:* 145–47, 145 (ill.), 146 (ill.), 147 (ill.), 148
enzymes from, *2:* 360
fossils of, *3:* 524 (ill.)
genetic engineering of, *4:* 845, 846 (ill.), 848
heliotropic, *6:* 1201–4, 1202 (ill.), 1203 (ill.)
how they stand up, *5:* 898–99, 899 (ill.)
medicinal, *2:* 389–90, 390 (ill.), 400
minerals absorbed by, *6:* 1226
monocot *vs.* dicot, *1:* 145–47, 145 (ill.), 146 (ill.), 147 (ill.), 148
nutrients for, *5:* 883, 895
organic waste for plant growth experiment, *2:* 235–39, 236 (ill.), 238 (ill.)
pigment separation experiment, *1:* 193–97, 195 (ill.), 196 (ill.)
rainforest, *1:* 106
respiration by, *4:* 871, 872, *5:* 883, 898
shade, *5:* 885, *6:* 1191
wilting, *5:* 899, 900 (ill.)
See also Flowers; Photosynthesis; Pollination; Water plants

Plants and water, *5:* **897–909,** 897 (ill.), 900 (ill.), 908 (ill.)
design an experiment for, *5:* 907–9
in dry environments, *5:* 899–900
osmosis for, *4:* 798, *5:* 897–98, 897 (ill.), 898 (ill.), 899 (ill.)
rate of erosion experiment, *2:* 381–86, 382 (ill.), 383 (ill.), 384 (ill.)
transpiration rate and environment experiment, *5:* 904–7, 906 (ill.)
turgor pressure experiment, *5:* 900–904, 900 (ill.), 902 (ill.), 903 (ill.)

Plasmolysis, *5:* 899

Plastics
adhesives from, *1:* 19
decomposition of, *2:* 231
glue adherence experiment, *1:* 22–25, 23 (ill.), 24 (ill.)
light refraction experiment, *4:* 666–69, 666 (ill.), 667 (ill.)
litter, *1:* 50
plastic bag membrane experiment, *4:* 798–803, 799 (ill.), 800 (ill.), 801 (ill.), 802 (ill.)
polymer strength experiment, *5:* 914–15, 917 (ill.), 918 (ill.)
properties of different plastics experiment, *5:* 923–25, 924 (ill.), 925 (ill.), 926
recycling, *5:* 923
See also Polymers

Plate tectonics
  earthquakes, *2:* 311
  formation of, *5:* 970
  mountain formation, *4:* 735–37, 736 (ill.), 737 (ill.)
  mountain formation experiment, *4:* 738–41, 739 (ill.), 740 (ill.)
  volcanic eruptions, *6:* 1238–39
Playing dead, *1:* 61, 65–68, 66 (ill.), 67 (ill.)
Plywood, *6:* 1298
Pnematocyst, *1:* 149
Point source pollution, *3:* 604, 605 (ill.)
Poisoning, food, *3:* 477
Polaris (North Star), *6:* 1125–28, 1126 (ill.), 1127 (ill.)
Poles, magnetic, *4:* 671–72
Pollen, *3:* 424, 425, 426, 437
Pollination
  of flowers, *3:* 423–27, 425 (ill.), 426 (ill.), 427 (ill.)
  genetics of, *3:* 425, 425 (ill.), *6:* 1207, 1207 (ill.), 1208 (ill.)
  self-pollination *vs.* cross-pollination experiment, *3:* 427–31, 430 (ill.)
Pollinators, *3:* 425–27, 431–35, 433 (ill.)
Pollution. *See* Air pollution; Water pollution
Polyester, *3:* 509
Polyethylene, *5:* 912, 914–15, 917 (ill.), 918 (ill.)
Polymerization, *5:* 912
Polymers, *4:* 686, *5:* **911–27,** 912 (ill.), 913 (ill.)
  adhesives from, *1:* 19, 21
  chains of, *5:* 911–12, 912 (ill.), 913, 913 (ill.), 914–15, 914 (ill.), 917 (ill.), 918 (ill.), 919
  design an experiment for, *5:* 925–27
  polymer slime experiment, *5:* 919–23, 921 (ill.), 922 (ill.)
  properties of, *5:* 912–13
  properties of different plastics experiment, *5:* 923–25, 924 (ill.), 925 (ill.), 926
  synthetic, *5:* 911–12
  tensile strength experiment, *5:* 914–19, 917 (ill.), 918 (ill.)
Polysaccharides, *5:* 919–23, 921 (ill.), 922 (ill.)
Polyvinyl acetate (PVA), *1:* 20, 22–25, 23 (ill.), 167–70, 168 (ill.), 169 (ill.)
Pombal, Marquis de, *2:* 312
Pomo Indians, *2:* 390–91, 396
Pompeii, *6:* 1237, 1237 (ill.), 1239
Pores, *3:* 601
Potassium, *4:* 761, *5:* 1034, 1064, *6:* 1226
Potassium carbonate, *4:* 835–38, 835 (ill.), 837 (ill.)
Potatoes, *6:* 1208, 1216–19, 1218 (ill.)
Potential energy, *5:* **929–40,** 929 (ill.)
  build a roller coaster experiment, *5:* 934–38, 935 (ill.), 936 (ill.), 937 (ill.)
  definition of, *5:* 929
  design an experiment for, *5:* 939–40
  height of objects experiment, *5:* 931–34, 932 (ill.), 933 (ill.)
Potometers, *5:* 890–93, 892 (ill.), 893 (ill.)
Potter, Beatrix, *1:* 73
Power plants, *1:* 1, 46, *3:* 590
Precipitation
  mountain ecosystems, *4:* 737
  mountains and desert formation experiment, *4:* 741–44, 742 (ill.), 743 (ill.)
  in the water cycle, *5:* 955, *6:* 1247
  in weather, *6:* 1271
  See also Rain
Predators, *1:* 61–63
Preservation of food. *See* Food preservation
Pressure. *See* Air pressure; Turgor pressure; Water pressure
Priestley, Joseph, *4:* 871
Primary colors, *2:* 205
Prisms, *2:* 204, 205 (ill.), 210–12, 211 (ill.), 212 (ill.), 213
Processed food, *4:* 760
Products, of chemical reactions, *1:* 151, 164–65
Prokaryotes, *1:* 86
Prominences, solar, *2:* 326
Propagation. *See* Vegetative propagation
Propellers, *3:* 418–21, 418 (ill.), 419 (ill.), 420 (ill.)
Proteins
  denatured, *3:* 463
  dietary protein sources experiment, *4:* 764–66, 765 (ill.), 766 (ill.)
  DNA isolation experiment, *2:* 289–91, 289 (ill.), 290 (ill.)
  in food spoilage, *3:* 478

hydrophilic *vs.* hydrophobic, *3:* 465, 465 (ill.)
for nutrition, *4:* 761
temperature and enzyme action experiment, *2:* 368–72, 370 (ill.), 371 (ill.)
Protists, *4:* 712
Protons, *2:* 349, *4:* 828
Protozoa, *4:* 711, 712
PTC (Phenylthiocarbamide), *3:* 559–61, 561 (ill.)
Puffer fish, *1:* 63
Pulleys, *5:* 1049, 1051–55, 1054 (ill.)
Pupa, *3:* 633–34, *4:* 645
Purple cabbage, *2:* 304–7, 306 (ill.), 307 (ill.)
Purple dyes, *2:* 299
PVA (Polyvinyl acetate), *1:* 20, 22–25, 23 (ill.)
Pyramids, *5:* 1048
Pythagoras, *5:* 1096

Q

Quadricep muscles, *1:* 120–23, 122 (ill.)
Quarters (coin), *2:* 344–45, 344 (ill.), 345 (ill.)
Queen ants, *3:* 633, 634

R

Radiation
of heat, *3:* 615, 616–17
infrared, *3:* 616–17
Radioactive decay, *3:* 525, *6:* 1238
Radioactivity (chemical reaction), *1:* 164
Radioisotope dating, *3:* 525
Radiometers, *1:* 43
Radiosonde balloons, *6:* 1283
Radish seeds, *3:* 570–73, 572 (ill.)
Radon, *1:* 48
Rain
dissolved oxygen level changes from, *2:* 272
mountain effect on, *4:* 737
normal pH level, *1:* 1, 2 (ill.)
in the water cycle, *5:* 955, *6:* 1247
See also Acid rain
Rain shadow, *4:* 741–44, 742 (ill.), 743 (ill.)
Rainbows, *2:* 204 (ill.), 205, *4:* 664–65, 664 (ill.), 665 (ill.)
Raindrops, *4:* 659–60, *6:* 1272
Rainforests, *1:* 105–6, 105 (ill.), *2:* 390
Ramps, *5:* 1047–48, 1048 (ill.), 1049 (ill.)
Rats, kangaroo, *1:* 105
Rayon, *3:* 509, *5:* 911
RDA (Recommended Daily Allowance), *6:* 1223, 1226
Reactants, *1:* 151, 164–65
Reactions, chemical. *See* Chemical reactions
Reactions, for every action, *3:* 492, 494
Reaumur, Rene Antoine de, *2:* 359
Recessive inheritance, *3:* 554–55
Recombinant DNA technology, *3:* 555
Recommended Daily Allowance (RDA), *6:* 1223, 1226
Recycling, *2:* 231, 240, *5:* 914, 915 (ill.), 923
Red cabbage juice
chemical titration experiment, *4:* 865–68, 865 (ill.), 866 (ill.), 867 (ill.)
pH of household chemicals experiment, *4:* 861–65, 861 (ill.), 863 (ill.)
unknown mixtures experiment, *5:* 1039–43, 1041 (ill.), 1042 (ill.)
Red hair, *3:* 555
Red light
bending, *2:* 204–5
light colors and plant growth experiment, *4:* 873–77, 875 (ill.), 876 (ill.)
temperature of different colors experiment, *2:* 210–12, 211 (ill.), 212 (ill.), 213
wavelength of, *2:* 203
Red Sea, *5:* 996–97, 996 (ill.)
Redshift, *6:* 1112, 1112 (ill.)
Reduction reactions. *See* Oxidation-reduction reactions
Reeds, *2:* 390–91, 396–99, 398 (ill.), 399 (ill.)
Reflection, in raindrops, *4:* 659–60
Reflector telescopes, *6:* 1110–11, 1111 (ill.)
Reflectors, solar, *5:* 1082–83
Refraction
light refraction experiment, *4:* 666–69, 666 (ill.), 667 (ill.)
make a rainbow experiment, *4:* 664–65, 664 (ill.), 665 (ill.)
in raindrops, *4:* 659–60
Refractor telescopes, *6:* 1110, 1111 (ill.)

Refrigeration, *3:* 453, 479–80
Relative age dating, *3:* 524
Relative density, *2:* 260–64, 262 (ill.), 263 (ill.)
Relativity, special, *6:* 1179, 1180 (ill.)
Renaissance age, *5:* 981
Renewable energy, *5:* **941–53**
design an experiment for, *5:* 951–52
hydropower and water pressure experiment, *5:* 948–51, 948 (ill.), 949 (ill.), 950 (ill.)
sources of, *5:* 942–43, 942 (ill.), 943 (ill.)
wind energy experiment, *5:* 944–48, 945 (ill.), 946 (ill.)
See also Solar energy
Renewable materials, *4:* 691–94, 693 (ill.), 694 (ill.), *6:* 1297–98
Rennin, *2:* 360
Reproduction
asexual, *6:* 1208
by bacteria, *1:* 87
cellular, *1:* 143–44
sexual, *6:* 1207
by yeast, *1:* 143–44, 147–48, 147 (ill.), 148 (ill.), 149 (ill.), 150
Resins, tree, *3:* 523–24
Resistance, bacterial, *1:* 88–90, 95–100, 97 (ill.)
Respiration
dissolved oxygen changes experiment, *2:* 279–84, 281 (ill.), 282 (ill.), 283
by fish, *3:* 402, 403 (ill.), 404–6, 405 (ill.)
in germination, *3:* 565–66
by plants, *4:* 871, 872, *5:* 883, 898
Resultants, *6:* 1165
Results of experiments, *5:* 1008
Retina, *2:* 205, 205 (ill.), *4:* 787
Retinal, *6:* 1224
Revolving levers, *5:* 1051, 1051 (ill.)
Ribosomes, *1:* 86
Rice, *4:* 760, *6:* 1223–24, 1226 (ill.)
Richter, Charles F., *2:* 312 (ill.), 313
Richter Scale, *2:* 312 (ill.), 313
Rings, tree, *1:* 71–72
Ringworm, *3:* 538
Rivers, *5:* **955–67,** 955 (ill.), 967 (ill.)
course of, *5:* 956, 967 (ill.)
design an experiment for, *5:* 965–66
dissolved oxygen in, *2:* 271–84
glacier erosion trench experiment, *5:* 957–60, 958 (ill.), 959 (ill.)
river erosion experiment, *5:* 962–65, 963 (ill.), 964 (ill.), 965 (ill.), 966
stream pattern experiment, *5:* 960–62, 961 (ill.)
water pollution of, *1:* 48
Rocket launcher, *3:* 495–98, 498 (ill.), 499 (ill.), 500 (ill.)
Rockets, water bottle, *3:* 493–501, 495 (ill.), 498 (ill.), 499 (ill.), 500 (ill.)
Rocks, *5:* **969–79,** 970 (ill.), 971 (ill.)
classification of, *5:* 970–71
classifying rocks experiment, *5:* 975–78, 975 (ill.), 976 (ill.), 977 (ill.)
crystalline, *2:* 243, 244, 255
definition of, *5:* 969
design an experiment for, *5:* 978
igneous, *5:* 970, 975–78, 975 (ill.), 976 (ill.), 977 (ill.)
lichen on, *1:* 74, 79
metamorphic, *5:* 971, 975–78, 975 (ill.), 976 (ill.), 977 (ill.)
molten, *6:* 1238
sedimentary, *3:* 522, *5:* 971, 975–78, 975 (ill.), 976 (ill.), 977 (ill.)
in soil formation, *5:* 1063–65, 1064 (ill.), 1065 (ill.)
weathering of, *5:* 1063–65
Rocky Mountains, *4:* 735
Rodale, J. I., *2:* 229
Rodenticides, *4:* 843
Rodents, desert, *1:* 104–5
Rods (eye), *2:* 205, 205 (ill.)
Rohrer, Heinrich, *4:* 749 (ill.)
Roller coasters, *5:* 934–38, 935 (ill.), 936 (ill.), 937 (ill.)
Romans, *2:* 389
Rooting hormones, *6:* 1209–16, 1213 (ill.), 1214 (ill.)
Roots
acid rain experiment, *1:* 9–12, 11 (ill.)
annual growth of, *1:* 71
plant hormones and growth experiment, *5:* 886–90, 888 (ill.), 889 (ill.)

plant water uptake experiment, *5:* 890–93, 892 (ill.), 893 (ill.)
plants and the rate of erosion experiment, *2:* 381–86, 382 (ill.), 383 (ill.), 384 (ill.)
role of, *5:* 883–84, 883 (ill.)
root growth and gravity experiment, *6:* 1197–1201, 1198 (ill.), 1199 (ill.), 1200 (ill.)
tropism effect on, *6:* 1192
water absorbed by, *5:* 897–98, 897 (ill.), 898 (ill.)

Rotation, *5:* **981–94,** 982 (ill.), 983 (ill.), 984 (ill.), 992 (ill.)
centrifugal force and gravity experiment, *5:* 989–92, 990 (ill.)
Coriolis force, *5:* 984–85, 985 (ill.)
design an experiment for, *5:* 992–94
effect on tides, *5:* 983–84
pendulum rotation experiment, *5:* 985–89, 988 (ill.)
in timekeeping, *6:* 1176, 1178
velocity of, *5:* 985, 985 (ill.)

Rubber adhesives, *1:* 20, 22–25, 24 (ill.)
Rubbing. *See* Friction
Runoff of pesticides, *4:* 847, 847 (ill.), 851–55, 854 (ill.)
Rusting
process of, *1:* 151, 152 (ill.), *4:* 812, 823 (ill.)
steel wool rust experiment, *4:* 817–20, 818 (ill.)
synthesis reaction, *1:* 153–54, 155 (ill.), 163

S

Saccharomyces cerevisiae, 3: 544–49, 547 (ill.), 548 (ill.)
Sachs, Julius von, *1:* 191
Safe Water Drinking Act, *1:* 50
Saguaro cactus, *1:* 105, *5:* 900
Sail boats, *5:* 944–48, 945 (ill.), 946 (ill.)
Sailors, *4:* 759, *6:* 1223

Salinity, *5:* **995–1004,** 995 (ill.), 996 (ill.)
acid-copper reduction experiment, *4:* 813–17, 814 (ill.), 815 (ill.)
copper patina experiment, *1:* 173–75, 174 (ill.), 175 (ill.)
density ball experiment, *5:* 1000–1003, 1001 (ill.), 1002 (ill.)
design an experiment for, *5:* 1003–4
dissolved oxygen level changes from, *2:* 272
electrons released by metals experiment, *4:* 838–40, 840 (ill.), 841 (ill.), 842
make a hydrometer experiment, *5:* 997–1000, 998 (ill.), 999 (ill.)
ocean convection currents experiment, *4:* 780–83, 782 (ill.)
salinity and turgor pressure experiment, *5:* 900–904, 900 (ill.), 902 (ill.), 903 (ill.)
salt water osmosis experiment, *4:* 803–6, 803 (ill.), 804 (ill.), 805 (ill.)
of seawater, *4:* 771–72, 772 (ill.), *5:* 995–97, 995 (ill.), 996 (ill.)
solar heat storage experiment, *5:* 1090–92, 1092 (ill.), 1093

Saliva, *1:* 178
Salt
attraction to water, *6:* 1260
crystal formation experiment, *2:* 246–50, 246 (ill.), 249 (ill.), 254 (ill.)
dietary salt sources experiment, *4:* 764–66, 765 (ill.), 766 (ill.)
for food preservation, *3:* 452, 452 (ill.), 479, 480
formation of, *4:* 812, *5:* 996
moldy bread experiment, *3:* 481–85, 481 (ill.), 482 (ill.), 483 (ill.)
molecules of, *4:* 747
for nutrition, *4:* 761
See also Salinity

Salt water. *See* Seawater
Salty taste, *1:* 177, 179, 182–86
San Andreas Fault, *2:* 322 (ill.)
Sand
in soil, *5:* 1065, 1066 (ill.)
soil horizon properties experiment, *5:* 1067–73, 1071 (ill.), 1072 (ill.)
soil type and runoff experiment, *2:* 377–80, 378 (ill.), 379 (ill.)
soils for fossil casts experiment, *3:* 526–29, 528 (ill.)

Sandy water, *4:* 723, 723 (ill.)
Sanitary landfills, *2:* 231
Sapwood, *6:* 1296
Satellite images, *2:* 376
Saturation of colors, *2:* 206–7, 214

Sauveur, Joseph, *5:* 1096
Scallop shells, *5:* 1028
Scanning tunneling microscope (STM), *4:* 748
Scarification of seeds, *3:* 573–76, 574 (ill.), 575 (ill.), 576 (ill.)
Scents. *See* Odors; Smell, sense of
Schleiden, Matthias, *1:* 142
Schwann, Theodor, *1:* 142
Scientific method, *5:* **1005–18,** 1006 (ill.), 1007 (ill.), 1008 (ill.)
  design an experiment for, *5:* 1017–18
  how fruit flies appear experiment, *5:* 1013–16, 1015 (ill.), 1016 (ill.)
  mystery powder identification experiment, *5:* 1009–13, 1011 (ill.), 1012 (ill.), 1013 (ill.)
  steps in, *5:* 1005–8
Screws, *5:* 1048–49, 1050 (ill.), 1057–60, 1058 (ill.), 1059 (ill.), 1060 (ill.)
Scurvy, *4:* 759–60, 760 (ill.), *6:* 1223
Sea anemones, *1:* 149
Seabirds, *1:* 50
Seashells, *5:* **1019–29,** 1020 (ill.), 1022 (ill.)
  cave formation experiment, *1:* 133–35, 134 (ill.)
  classifying seashells experiment, *5:* 1025–27, 1027 (ill.)
  design an experiment for, *5:* 1027–28
  formation of, *5:* 1020–21
  fossil casts experiment, *3:* 526–29, 528 (ill.)
  fossil formation experiment, *3:* 530–33, 532 (ill.)
  strength of shells experiment, *5:* 1022–25, 1023 (ill.), 1024 (ill.), 1025 (ill.)
Seasons, *5:* 981, 983, 983 (ill.), 984 (ill.)
Seawater
  amount on the Earth, *3:* 602
  density of, *4:* 772
  freshwater from, *4:* 724–25
  properties of, *4:* 771–72, 772 (ill.), 773 (ill.)
  salinity and stratification experiment, *4:* 775–80, 778 (ill.)
  salinity of, *4:* 771–72, 772 (ill.), *5:* 995–97, 995 (ill.), 996 (ill.)
  stratification of, *4:* 772
Second-class lever, *5:* 1051, 1051 (ill.)
Second law of motion, *3:* 492, 492 (ill.), 494, 579–80
Sediment, *3:* 522, 524, 526–29, 528 (ill.)
Sedimentary rocks, *3:* 522, *5:* 971, 975–78, 975 (ill.), 976 (ill.), 977 (ill.)
Sedimentation, *3:* 609–12, 610 (ill.)
Seed crystals, *2:* 246
Seedlings, *3:* 566, 566 (ill.), *5:* 1084–87, 1084 (ill.), 1086 (ill.)
Seeds
  development of, *3:* 423
  germination of, *3:* 565–78, 566 (ill.)
  germination time experiment, *3:* 570–73, 572 (ill.)
  seed scarification experiment, *3:* 573–76, 574 (ill.), 575 (ill.), 576 (ill.)
  shells of, *5:* 1019
  temperature for germination experiment, *3:* 566–70, 568 (ill.), 569 (ill.)
Seesaws, *5:* 1050 (ill.)
Seismic belts, *5:* 970
Seismic waves, *2:* 311
Seismographs
  build a seismograph experiment, *2:* 314–16, 315 (ill.), 316 (ill.)
  detecting volcanic eruptions experiment, *6:* 1242–44, 1242 (ill.), 1243 (ill.), 1244 (ill.)
  for earthquakes, *2:* 313
  for volcanic eruptions, *6:* 1239
Seismology, *2:* 312
Selenium, *6:* 1226
Self-pollination, *3:* 424, 425 (ill.), 427–31, 430 (ill.)
Semiconductors, *4:* 686
Semipermeable membranes
  molecule size and osmosis experiment, *4:* 806–9, 808 (ill.), 809 (ill.)
  osmosis through, *3:* 452, *4:* 797
  plastic bag membrane experiment, *4:* 798–803, 799 (ill.), 800 (ill.), 801 (ill.), 802 (ill.)
Sensory memory, *4:* 697, 698 (ill.)
Sepals, *3:* 424, 424 (ill.)
Separation and identification, *4:* 724–25, 725 (ill.), *5:* **1031–45,** 1032 (ill.), 1033 (ill.)
  design an experiment for, *5:* 1043–44
  paper chromatography and ink experiment, *5:* 1034–39, 1036 (ill.), 1037 (ill.)
  techniques for, *5:* 1032–34, 1034 (ill.)
  unknown mixtures experiment, *5:* 1039–43, 1041 (ill.), 1042 (ill.)

Settling (separation technique), *5:* 1032
Sewage, *1:* 49
Sexual reproduction, *6:* 1207
Shade plants, *5:* 885, *6:* 1191
Sharks, *3:* 402
Shear stress, *3:* 441
Shells
 of atoms, *4:* 829, 830, 830 (ill.)
 of eggs, *4:* 806–9, 808 (ill.), 809 (ill.), 846, *5:* 1019
 of seeds, *5:* 1019
 See also Seashells
Shelter, *2:* 391
Ships, *2:* 257 (ill.), 259
 See also Sail boats
Shooting stars. *See* Comets and meteors
Shoreline extension, *2:* 231
Short-term memory, *4:* 697, 698 (ill.)
Shrimp, *1:* 5–8, 7 (ill.), *4:* 775
Shutters, *4:* 659
Sickle cell anemia, *2:* 287, *3:* 555
Sidereal day, *5:* 981, *6:* 1176
Sieve, *5:* 1032
Silent Spring (Carson), *4:* 846
Silk, *3:* 509, *4:* 685, 686 (ill.)
Silkworms, *4:* 712
Silt, *5:* 1065, 1066 (ill.), 1067–73, 1071 (ill.), 1072 (ill.)
Silver, *6:* 1133
Simple craters, *2:* 217, 218 (ill.)
Simple machines, *5:* **1047–62,** 1061 (ill.)
 design an experiment for, *5:* 1060–62
 examples of, *5:* 1047–51, 1048 (ill.), 1049 (ill.), 1050 (ill.), 1051 (ill.)
 lever lifting experiment, *5:* 1055–57, 1057 (ill.)
 screw thread size experiment, *5:* 1057–60, 1058 (ill.), 1059 (ill.), 1060 (ill.)
 wheel size and effort experiment, *5:* 1051–55, 1054 (ill.)
Single-acting baking powder, *3:* 464
Sirius (star), *6:* 1124, 1124 (ill.)
Skeletal muscles, *1:* 115, 115 (ill.), 120–23, 122 (ill.)
Skeletons, *1:* 113, 114 (ill.), *5:* 1019
Skunks, *1:* 62–63, 62 (ill.)
Slugs, *5:* 1019
Smell
 design an experiment for, *1:* 189
 in fish, *3:* 403–4
 how it works, *1:* 177, 179–80, 179 (ill.), 180 (ill.)
 smell-taste relationship experiment, *1:* 186–89, 187 (ill.)
 vanilla, *4:* 797
 See also Odors
Smith, Robert Angus, *1:* 3
Smog, *1:* 47, 48 (ill.)
Smoke, *1:* 165
Smooth muscles, *1:* 115, 115 (ill.)
Snails, *2:* 299, *5:* 1019
Snakes, *1:* 62, 104–5
Snow, *4:* 737
Snowflakes, *2:* 245
Soaps, *1:* 95–100, 97 (ill.), *6:* 1231–34, 1232 (ill.)
 See also Detergents
Social insects, *3:* 634
Sodium, *4:* 812, *5:* 995, 1034, *6:* 1226
Sodium borate. *See* Borax
Sodium carbonate, *4:* 835–38, 835 (ill.), 837 (ill.)
Sodium chloride. *See* Salinity; Salt
Sodium hydrocarbonate, *1:* 157–59, 157 (ill.), 158 (ill.), 159 (ill.)
Sodium hydroxide, *4:* 865–68, 865 (ill.), 866 (ill.), 867 (ill.)
Sodium sulfate decahydrate (Glauber's salt), *5:* 1090–92, 1092 (ill.), 1093
Softwood, *6:* 1295, 1302–6, 1304 (ill.), 1305 (ill.)
Soil, *2:* 232–35, *5:* **1063–79**
 bacteria in, *1:* 85
 composition of, *5:* 1064, 1064 (ill.), 1065–66, 1066 (ill.)
 design an experiment for, *5:* 1078–79
 formation of, *5:* 1064 (ill.), 1065 (ill.)
 humus in, *2:* 229, 230, *5:* 1063, 1066
 layers of, *5:* 1066–67, 1067 (ill.)
 life in, *5:* 1067, 1068 (ill.)
 microorganisms and decomposition experiment, *2:* 232–35, 234 (ill.), 235 (ill.)
 microorganisms in, *2:* 229, *5:* 1063, 1067
 oxygen pockets in, *5:* 883

pH and plant growth experiment, *5:* 1074–77, 1074 (ill.), 1076 (ill.)
pH of, *4:* 860, *5:* 1064
properties of soil horizons experiment, *5:* 1067–73
soil horizon properties experiment, *5:* 1071 (ill.), 1072 (ill.)
soil type and runoff experiment, *2:* 377–80, 378 (ill.), 379 (ill.)
soils for fossil casts experiment, *3:* 526–29, 528 (ill.)
terraces, *2:* 386
uses of, *5:* 1063
Soil erosion. *See* Erosion
Soil horizons, *5:* 1066–67, 1067–73, 1067 (ill.), 1071 (ill.), 1072 (ill.)
Soil profile, *5:* 1066, 1067–73, 1067 (ill.), 1071 (ill.), 1072 (ill.)
Soil test kit, *2:* 386
Solar (photovoltaic) cells, *5:* 1083, 1087–89, 1088 (ill.), 1089 (ill.)
Solar collectors, *5:* 1082, 1082 (ill.)
Solar days, *6:* 1176
Solar eclipse, *2:* 325–29, 325 (ill.), 328 (ill.), 329 (ill.)
Solar energy, *5:* 942, **1081–94,** 1081 (ill.)
design an experiment for, *5:* 1093–94
heat storage substances experiment, *5:* 1090–92, 1092 (ill.), 1093
seedling growth in greenhouses experiment, *5:* 1084–87, 1084 (ill.), 1086 (ill.)
solar cells to run a motor experiment, *5:* 1087–89, 1088 (ill.), 1089 (ill.)
ways to collect it, *5:* 1082–83, 1082 (ill.)
where it comes from, *5:* 1081–82, 1081 (ill.)
Solar reflectors, *5:* 1082–83
Solar system, *2:* 215, *5:* 982–83
Solids
density of, *2:* 259
heat conduction experiment, *3:* 618–22, 620 (ill.), 621 (ill.)
relative density and floating experiment, *2:* 260–64, 262 (ill.), 263 (ill.)
Solubility
separation techniques for, *5:* 1033
solubility of elements experiment, *4:* 835–38, 835 (ill.), 837 (ill.)
unknown mixtures experiment, *5:* 1039–43, 1041 (ill.), 1042 (ill.)
Solutions. *See* Mixtures and solutions
Solvents, *5:* 1032
Songs, *4:* 700, 701–4, 701 (ill.), 702 (ill.), 703 (ill.)
Sorensen, Margarethe Hoyrup, *4:* 859
Sorensen, Soren Peter Lauritz, *4:* 859
Sound, *5:* **1095–1107,** 1095 (ill.), 1096 (ill.), 1106 (ill.)
design an experiment for, *5:* 1105–7
Doppler effect experiment, *6:* 1118–20, 1119 (ill.)
measurement of, *5:* 1095–96, 1095 (ill.)
soundproofing materials experiment, *5:* 1102–5, 1104 (ill.)
speed of, *6:* 1149
string length and sound experiment, *5:* 1096–99, 1097 (ill.), 1098 (ill.)
string thickness and sound experiment, *5:* 1099–1102, 1100 (ill.), 1101 (ill.)
Soundproofing, *5:* 1102–5, 1104 (ill.)
Sour taste, *1:* 177
Southern Ocean, *4:* 771
Space observation, *6:* **1109–22**
bacteria in, *1:* 88
design an experiment for, *6:* 1120–22
Doppler effect experiment, *6:* 1118–20, 1119 (ill.)
light in, *6:* 1109, 1111–12, 1112 (ill.)
telescope lenses experiment, *6:* 1113–17, 1114 (ill.), 1116 (ill.)
telescopes for, *6:* 1109–10, 1110 (ill.), 1111 (ill.)
Space-time, *6:* 1179–80, 1180 (ill.)
Special relativity, theory of, *6:* 1179, 1180 (ill.)
Species DNA differences, *2:* 287–88, 291–95, 293 (ill.)
Specific gravity, *2:* 258, *5:* 997–1000, 998 (ill.), 999 (ill.)
Spectrum, electromagnetic, *2:* 203, 350, 350 (ill.), *4:* 659, 660 (ill.), 787
Speed
centrifugal force and gravity experiment, *5:* 989–92, 990 (ill.)
in chromatography, *5:* 1032–33
crater shape experiment, *2:* 221–25, 224 (ill.)
of fluids, *3:* 441
of light, *6:* 1149, 1179

measuring wind speed experiment, *6:* 1273, 1275 (ill.)
Newtonian laws of motion on, *3:* 491–92
of sound, *6:* 1149
speed of falling objects experiment, *3:* 581–84, 582 (ill.), 583 (ill.), 584 (ill.)
of wind, *6:* 1273 (ill.), 1283 (ill.)
Speleology, *1:* 127, 132
Spelunking, *1:* 132
Sperm cells, *3:* 423, 424
Spices, *3:* 462
Spiders, *1:* 62, 108, *4:* 685, 686 (ill.)
Spinning rod experiment, *3:* 444–47, 446 (ill.), 447 (ill.)
Spoiled food. *See* Food spoilage
Spores, *3:* 481, 539
Sports equipment, *4:* 749
Spring tides, *3:* 580
Springs, hot, *1:* 88
Spruce trees, *1:* 103, 104 (ill.)
Squats (exercise), *1:* 120–23, 122 (ill.)
Squid, giant, *4:* 775 (ill.)
Stalactities, *1:* 129–30, 130 (ill.), 135–39, 137 (ill.)
Stalagmites, *1:* 129–30, 130 (ill.), 135–39, 137 (ill.)
Stamen, *3:* 423, 424, 424 (ill.)
Staphylococcus bacteria, *3:* 539
Starches
dietary carbohydrate sources experiment, *4:* 761–64, 763 (ill.), 764 (ill.)
for nutrition, *4:* 760
in photosynthesis, *4:* 872
plastic bag membrane experiment, *4:* 798–803, 799 (ill.), 800 (ill.), 801 (ill.), 802 (ill.)
Stars, *6:* **1123–31,** 1124 (ill.)
design an experiment for, *6:* 1130–31
discovery of, *6:* 1123, 1123 (ill.)
formation of, *6:* 1123–24
for timekeeping, *6:* 1177
tracking the North Star experiment, *6:* 1125–28, 1126 (ill.), 1127 (ill.)
tracking the planets experiment, *6:* 1128–30, 1128 (ill.), 1129 (ill.), 1130 (ill.)
Stars, shooting. *See* Comets and meteors
Static electricity, *6:* **1133–46,** 1135 (ill.)
build an electroscope experiment, *6:* 1135–39, 1137 (ill.), 1138 (ill.)
design an experiment for, *6:* 1144–45
how to make it, *6:* 1133–34, 1134 (ill.)
in lightning, *6:* 1135, 1135 (ill.), 1148–49
lightning sparks experiment, *6:* 1152–55, 1154 (ill.)
measuring the charge experiment, *6:* 1139–44, 1141 (ill.), 1143 (ill.)
Statues, *1:* 12–15, 14 (ill.), 16, 17 (ill.)
Steel, *4:* 812
heat conduction experiment, *3:* 618–22, 620 (ill.), 621 (ill.)
steel wool rust experiment, *4:* 817–20, 818 (ill.)
Stems, *5:* 884, 884 (ill.)
leaf/stem cuttings and auxins experiment, *6:* 1209–16, 1213 (ill.), 1214 (ill.)
plant hormones and growth experiment, *5:* 886–90, 888 (ill.), 889 (ill.)
water storage in, *5:* 899
Stereo speakers, *4:* 673
Stevenson screens, *6:* 1283
Sticky notes, *1:* 22, 22 (ill.), 26–30, 27 (ill.), 28 (ill.), 29 (ill.)
STM (Scanning tunneling microscope), *4:* 748
Stomachs, expandable, *4:* 775
Stomata, *5:* 885, 898, 899
Storm chasers, *6:* 1150 (ill.), 1151
Storms, *6:* **1147–63**
design an experiment for, *6:* 1161–63
formation of, *6:* 1147–48
hail, *6:* 1151–52, 1151 (ill.)
hailstone formation and temperature experiment, *6:* 1158–61, 1159 (ill.), 1160 (ill.), 1161 (ill.), 1162
lightning sparks experiment, *6:* 1152–55, 1154 (ill.)
thunderstorms, *6:* 1147–49, 1149 (ill.)
tornadoes, *6:* 1149 (ill.), .1150 (ill.), 1155 (ill.)
water vortex experiment, *6:* 1155–58, 1157 (ill.)
Stratification, *4:* 772, 775–80, 778 (ill.)
Stratocumulus clouds, *6:* 1273
Stratus clouds, *6:* 1272, 1273
Strawberries, *3:* 454–57, 455 (ill.), 456 (ill.)
Streams, *1:* 1–2, 4, *2:* 271–84
See also Rivers

Strength
of materials, *4:* 687, 687 (ill.)
polymer strength experiment, *5:* 914–19, 917 (ill.), 918 (ill.)
of polymers, *5:* 912
seashell strength experiment, *5:* 1022–25, 1023 (ill.), 1024 (ill.), 1025 (ill.)
tape strength experiment, *4:* 687 (ill.), 688–91, 689 (ill.), 690 (ill.)
of wood, *6:* 1297
String and sound experiments, *5:* 1096–99, 1097 (ill.), 1098 (ill.), 1099–1102, 1100 (ill.), 1101 (ill.)
Structures, *6:* **1165–74**
acid rain damage to, *1:* 3, 12–15, 14 (ill.), 15 (ill.), 16
arches in, *6:* 1166–67, 1167 (ill.), 1173 (ill.)
building properties of wood experiment, *6:* 1302–6, 1304 (ill.), 1305 (ill.)
design an experiment for, *6:* 1172–74
earthquake destruction experiment, *2:* 317–21, 319 (ill.), 320 (ill.), 321 (ill.)
forces acting on, *6:* 1165–66, 1166 (ill.)
rigidity of beams experiment, *6:* 1170–72, 1171 (ill.)
strength of arches *vs.* beams experiment, *6:* 1167–70, 1168 (ill.)
Styrofoam, *4:* 691–94, 693 (ill.), 694 (ill.), *5:* 1102–5, 1104 (ill.)
Subatomic particles, *2:* 257
Subliming, *2:* 216
Subsoil, *5:* 1067, 1067 (ill.)
Substrate, *2:* 360
Sugar
caramelization of, *3:* 463–64
crystal formation experiment, *2:* 246–50, 246 (ill.), 249 (ill.), 254 (ill.)
for food preservation, *3:* 452
in food spoilage, *3:* 478
from photosynthesis, *5:* 884–85
in solutions, *5:* 1032
sugar fruit preservation experiment, *3:* 454–57, 455 (ill.), 456 (ill.)
unknown mixtures experiment, *5:* 1039–43, 1041 (ill.), 1042 (ill.)
Sulfur, *1:* 88, *4:* 761
Sulfur dioxide, *1:* 1, 3, 17 (ill.), 45
Sulfuric acid
in acid rain, *1:* 164
for cave formation, *1:* 129
endothermic *vs.* exothermic reaction experiment, *1:* 157 (ill.), 158–59, 158 (ill.), 159 (ill.)
Sumerians, *2:* 375, 389
Summer season, *5:* 983
Sun and sunlight
food drying experiment, *3:* 458–61, 458 (ill.), 459 (ill.), 460 (ill.)
heat energy from, *3:* 589
heliotropism and plant movement experiment, *6:* 1201–4, 1202 (ill.), 1203 (ill.)
ocean penetration by, *4:* 772
orbits around, *5:* 982
in photosynthesis, *4:* 871–73
solar eclipse, *2:* 325–29, 325 (ill.), 328 (ill.), 329 (ill.)
solar energy from, *5:* 1081–82, 1081 (ill.)
tides and, *5:* 983–84, 993–94
for timekeeping, *6:* 1175, 1176
in weather, *6:* 1271, 1271 (ill.)
Sun prints, *2:* 329–30, 330 (ill.), 331 (ill.)
Sundials, *6:* 1177, 1177 (ill.), 1189
Sunflowers, *6:* 1201–4, 1202 (ill.), 1203 (ill.)
Superglue. *See* Cyanoacrylate glue
Supersaturated solutions, *2:* 246
Supertasters, *1:* 180–86, 184 (ill.)
Surface area
evaporation and surface area experiment, *6:* 1253–56, 1253 (ill.), 1254 (ill.), 1255 (ill.)
nanosize and properties experiment, *4:* 750–53, 752 (ill.)
in nanotechnology, *4:* 748
Surface currents, *4:* 773
Surface tension, *3:* 440 (ill.), 441, 448, *6:* 1261–64, 1261 (ill.), 1263 (ill.)
Suspensions, *4:* 723, 724, 725
suspensions *vs.* solutions experiment, *4:* 725–30, 729 (ill.)
Tyndall effect experiment, *4:* 730–32, 731 (ill.), 732 (ill.)

Sweet taste, *1:* 177, 182–86
Swim bladder, *3:* 402, 403, 403 (ill.)
Synthesis reactions, *1:* 163
Synthetic dyes, *2:* 299–300, 304–7, 306 (ill.), 307 (ill.)
Synthetic fibers, *2:* 301–4, 302 (ill.), 303 (ill.)
Synthetic polymers, *5:* 911–12

T

Tadpoles, *4:* 645–46, 646 (ill.), 647–51, 648 (ill.), 649 (ill.), 650 (ill.)
Taiga biome, *1:* 103–4
Tails (comet), *2:* 216
Tape (adhesive), *1:* 21–22
  environmental effects experiment, *1:* 26–30, 27 (ill.), 28 (ill.), 29 (ill.)
  tape strength experiment, *4:* 688–91, 689 (ill.), 690 (ill.)
Tartaric acid, *3:* 464
Taste
  design an experiment for, *1:* 189
  in fish, *3:* 403–4
  genetics of, *1:* 180
  how color affects taste experiment, *2:* 207–10, 208 (ill.), 209 (ill.)
  how it works, *1:* 177–79, 178 (ill.)
  pedigree for taste experiment, *3:* 559–61, 561 (ill.)
  smell-taste relationship experiment, *1:* 186–89, 187 (ill.)
  supertaster experiment, *1:* 180–86, 184 (ill.)
Taste buds, *1:* 177–79, 178 (ill.), 180–86, 184 (ill.)
Taste cells, *1:* 177–79
Tasters, *1:* 180–86
Tectonic plates. *See* Plate tectonics
Telescopes, *6:* 1110–11, 1111 (ill.)
  combination of lenses experiment, *6:* 1113–17, 1114 (ill.), 1116 (ill.)
  development of, *6:* 1109, 1123
  for space observation, *6:* 1109–10, 1110 (ill.), 1111 (ill.)
Temperate forest biome, *1:* 106–8, 106 (ill.), 107 (ill.), 108 (ill.)
Temperature
  adhesives experiment, *1:* 26–30, 27 (ill.), 28 (ill.), 29 (ill.)
  cloud formation and temperature experiment, *6:* 1277–80, 1280 (ill.)
  cool temperature and crystal growth experiment, *2:* 250–53, 252 (ill.)
  desert biome experiment, *1:* 108–11, 109 (ill.), 110 (ill.), 111 (ill.)
  dewpoint, *6:* 1285 (ill.), 1286–89, 1287 (ill.), 1288 (ill.)
  dissolved oxygen level changes from, *2:* 272, 273 (ill.)
  enzyme action and temperature experiment, *2:* 368–72, 370 (ill.), 371 (ill.)
  evaporation and temperature experiment, *6:* 1248–53, 1250 (ill.), 1251 (ill.)
  in food spoilage, *3:* 478
  for germination, *3:* 565
  germination temperature experiment, *3:* 566–70, 568 (ill.), 569 (ill.)
  greenhouse temperature increase experiment, *3:* 592–96, 593 (ill.), 594 (ill.)
  hailstone formation and temperature experiment, *6:* 1158–61, 1159 (ill.), 1160 (ill.), 1161 (ill.), 1162
  ocean convection currents experiment, *4:* 780–83, 782 (ill.)
  radiometers for, *1:* 43
  salinity and stratification experiment, *4:* 775–80, 778 (ill.)
  spoiled milk and temperature experiment, *3:* 485–88, 487 (ill.)
  tadpoles and temperature experiment, *4:* 647–51, 648 (ill.), 649 (ill.), 650 (ill.)
  temperate forest biome, *1:* 108
  temperature of different colors experiment, *2:* 210–12, 211 (ill.), 212 (ill.), 213
  transpiration rate and environment experiment, *5:* 904–7, 906 (ill.)
  viscosity and temperature experiment, *3:* 441–44, 442 (ill.), 443 (ill.)
  warm air *vs.* cool air experiment, *1:* 36–39, 36 (ill.), 38 (ill.)
  in weather, *6:* 1271, 1284
  See also Cold temperature
Tenderizer. *See* Meat tenderizer
Tendrils, *6:* 1192
Tennis balls, *4:* 749

Tensile strength
of materials, *4:* 687
polymer strength experiment, *5:* 914–19, 917 (ill.), 918 (ill.)
of polymers, *5:* 912
tape strength experiment, *4:* 687 (ill.), 688–91, 689 (ill.), 690 (ill.)
Terraces, soil, *2:* 386
Tetra fish, *3:* 407–9, 409 (ill.), 410
Textiles, *4:* 686, 696
Thales of Miletus, *2:* 325
Theophrastus, *3:* 565, *6:* 1283–84
Theory of special relativity, *6:* 1179, 1180 (ill.)
Thermal energy. *See* Heat
Thermal inversion, *1:* 47, 47 (ill.)
Thermal pollution, *1:* 49
Thermal properties, *4:* 687
Thermometers, *1:* 151
Thiamine, *4:* 760
Thickness, *5:* 1099–1102, 1100 (ill.), 1101 (ill.)
Thigmotropism, *6:* 1192, 1205 (ill.)
Third law of motion, *3:* 492, 492 (ill.), 494, 580
Thomas, Robert Bailey, *6:* 1284
Thorax, *3:* 632
Threads, *5:* 1048–49, 1050 (ill.), 1057–60, 1058 (ill.), 1059 (ill.), 1060 (ill.)
Thunder, *6:* 1148–49
Thunderstorms, *6:* 1147–49, 1149 (ill.), 1150, 1151, 1151 (ill.)
Thyme, *2:* 392–95, 394 (ill.), 395 (ill.)
Thymine, *2:* 286–87
Tides, *3:* 580, *4:* 777 (ill.), 784, *5:* 992 (ill.)
Earth's rotation effect, *5:* 983–84
moon's effect on, *4:* 774, 775 (ill.), *5:* 983–84
Sun's impact on, *5:* 983–84, 993–94
Time, *6:* **1175–89,** 1176 (ill.), 1178 (ill.)
design an experiment for, *6:* 1188–89
devices for measuring, *6:* 1177–78, 1177 (ill.)
history of, *6:* 1175–78
pendulum oscillation time experiment, *6:* 1180–85, 1182 (ill.), 1183 (ill.)
space-time, *6:* 1179–80, 1180 (ill.)
water clock experiment, *6:* 1185–88, 1187 (ill.)
Time zones, *6:* 1178–79, 1179 (ill.)
Titan Arum, *3:* 423, 427
Titration, *4:* 860, 865–68, 865 (ill.), 866 (ill.), 867 (ill.)
Tomatoes, *1:* 164
Tools, *2:* 390–92, 400, *5:* 969
Topsoil, *5:* 1064, 1066–67, 1067 (ill.)
erosion of, *2:* 375, 375 (ill.)
soils for fossil casts experiment, *3:* 526–29, 528 (ill.)
See also Soil
Tornadoes, *6:* 1149–51, 1149 (ill.), 1150 (ill.), 1155 (ill.), 1284 (ill.)
water vortex experiment, *6:* 1155–58, 1157 (ill.)
weather forecasting of, *6:* 1286
Torricelli, Evangelista, *1:* 34, *6:* 1284
Tortoises, *5:* 1019
Toughness of materials, *4:* 687
Toxicity, *1:* 164
Trace fossils, *3:* 524
Trace minerals, *6:* 1226
Traits, genetic, *3:* 554–55, 556–59, 558 (ill.), 559 (ill.), 562
Transfer of energy, *5:* 930, 930 (ill.)
Transformation of energy, *5:* 929
Transforming factor (DNA), *2:* 285–86
Transpiration
transpiration rate and environment experiment, *5:* 904–7, 906 (ill.)
of water, *5:* 885, 890, 892 (ill.), 893 (ill.), 898, 899
Tree resins, *3:* 523–24
Trees
angiosperm, *6:* 1295, 1296 (ill.)
annual growth of, *1:* 71–72, 72 (ill.), 73 (ill.)
coniferous, *1:* 103, 104 (ill.), *6:* 1295
deciduous, *1:* 107–8, 107 (ill.), 192
growth pattern experiment, *1:* 74–79, 78 (ill.)
lichen on, *1:* 79
rainforest, *1:* 105–6
structure of, *6:* 1295–96, 1297 (ill.)
wood from, *6:* 1295
See also Forests
Troglobites, *1:* 130
Troglophiles, *1:* 130–31
Trogloxenes, *1:* 130
Tropical forests, *2:* 376

Tropisms, *6:* **1191–1206**
design an experiment for, *6:* 1204–6
geotropism, *6:* 1191
heliotropism and plant movement experiment, *6:* 1201–4, 1202 (ill.), 1203 (ill.)
phototropism, *6:* 1191–93, 1191 (ill.), 1192 (ill.), 1193 (ill.), 1209
phototropism maze experiment, *6:* 1193–97, 1195 (ill.), 1196 (ill.)
root growth and gravity experiment, *6:* 1197–1201, 1198 (ill.), 1199 (ill.), 1200 (ill.)
thigmotropism, *6:* 1192, 1205 (ill.)
Troposphere, *1:* 33, 35–36, *3:* 600, *6:* 1271
Trough, *4:* 773, 774 (ill.)
Troy (ancient city), *2:* 230–31
Truffles, *3:* 540
Tsunamis, *2:* 322
Tube worms, *4:* 775
Tulley, John, *6:* 1284
Tundra, *1:* 103
Tunnels, trace fossils of, *3:* 524
Turgor pressure
role of, *5:* 899, 899 (ill.), 900 (ill.)
salinity and turgor pressure experiment, *5:* 900–904, 900 (ill.), 902 (ill.), 903 (ill.)
Turtles, *5:* 1019
Twigs, *1:* 72, 72 (ill.), 74–79
Tyndall, John, *3:* 589
Tyndall effect, *4:* 725, 725 (ill.), 730–32, 731 (ill.), 732 (ill.)

U

Ultraviolet rays, *1:* 46, *4:* 661–64, 662 (ill.), 663 (ill.)
Umami, *1:* 177
Unconfined aquifers, *3:* 601, 603 (ill.)
Unicellular organisms, *1:* 141, 144 (ill.)
Unit cells, *2:* 243
Upwelling, *4:* 773

V

Vacuoles, *1:* 142, *5:* 898–99, 899 (ill.)
Vacuum-seal, *3:* 453
Van der Waals' force, *1:* 20, 21 (ill.)
Vanilla, *4:* 797
Variables, *5:* 1007–8
Vega (star), *6:* 1123
Vegetables
color change by cooking, *3:* 465–66
composting, *2:* 230, 236–39, 236 (ill.), 238 (ill.), 239 (ill.)
for scurvy, *4:* 759
Vegetative propagation, *6:* **1207–21,** 1207 (ill.), 1208 (ill.), 1209 (ill.)
design an experiment for, *6:* 1219–20
genetics of, *6:* 1208, 1208 (ill.)
leaf/stem cuttings and auxins experiment, *6:* 1209–16, 1213 (ill.), 1214 (ill.)
potato reproduction experiment, *6:* 1216–19, 1218 (ill.)
Vehicles. *See* Cars
Velcro, *4:* 685, 686 (ill.)
Velocity, *3:* 441, 491–92, 493, *5:* 985, 985 (ill.)
See also Speed
Veneer, *6:* 1297–98
Venomous snakes, *1:* 62
Vibrations
for sound conduction, *3:* 403, *5:* 1095, 1096 (ill.)
string length and sound experiment, *5:* 1096–99, 1097 (ill.), 1098 (ill.)
string thickness and sound experiment, *5:* 1099–1102, 1100 (ill.), 1101 (ill.)
Vinegar
acid-copper reduction experiment, *4:* 813–17, 814 (ill.), 815 (ill.)
baking soda reaction, *1:* 165
bone loss experiment, *1:* 117–20, 119 (ill.)
brine shrimp experiment, *1:* 5–8, 7 (ill.)
chemical titration experiment, *4:* 865–68, 865 (ill.), 866 (ill.), 867 (ill.)
copper patina experiment, *1:* 173–75, 174 (ill.), 175 (ill.)
electrolyte solution experiment, *2:* 335–40, 337 (ill.), 338 (ill.), 339 (ill.)
electrons released by metals experiment, *4:* 838–40, 840 (ill.), 841 (ill.), 842
for food preservation, *3:* 452, 452 (ill.), 479

moldy bread experiment, *3:* 481–85, 481 (ill.), 482 (ill.), 483 (ill.)
molecule size and osmosis experiment, *4:* 806–9, 808 (ill.), 809 (ill.)
mystery powder identification experiment, *5:* 1009–13, 1011 (ill.), 1012 (ill.), 1013 (ill.)
pH of household chemicals experiment, *4:* 861–65, 861 (ill.), 863 (ill.)
rusting experiment, *1:* 152–56, 155 (ill.)
safety for, *1:* 119
soil pH and plant growth experiment, *5:* 1074–77, 1074 (ill.), 1076 (ill.), 1079 (ill.)
structure damage experiment, *1:* 12–15, 14 (ill.), 15 (ill.), 16
unknown mixtures experiment, *5:* 1039–43, 1041 (ill.), 1042 (ill.)
Vines, *6:* 1192, 1205 (ill.)
Violet light
bending, *2:* 204–5
light colors and plant growth experiment, *4:* 873–77, 875 (ill.), 876 (ill.)
temperature of different colors experiment, *2:* 210–12, 211 (ill.), 212 (ill.), 213
wavelength of, *2:* 203
Virchow, Rudolf, *1:* 142
Viscosity, *3:* 439–41, 441–44, 442 (ill.), 443 (ill.)
Visible light, *4:* 659, 660, 787, *6:* 1112
Vision, color, *2:* 205–6, 205 (ill.)
Vitamin A, *6:* 1224
Vitamin B, *6:* 1224
Vitamin C
for food preservation, *3:* 479
moldy bread experiment, *3:* 481–85, 481 (ill.), 482 (ill.), 483 (ill.)
for scurvy, *4:* 759, *6:* 1223
sources of vitamin C experiment, *6:* 1226–31, 1229 (ill.)
Vitamin D, *6:* 1224, 1226
Vitamin K, *6:* 1224
Vitamins, *4:* 760, *6:* **1223–36,** 1224 (ill.), 1225 (ill.), 1226 (ill.), 1234 (ill.), 1235 (ill.)
design an experiment for, *6:* 1234–36
discovery of, *6:* 1223–24
fat-soluble *vs.* water-soluble, *6:* 1224–25, 1224 (ill.)
sources of vitamin C experiment, *6:* 1226–31, 1229 (ill.)
Volatilization, *4:* 847
Volcanoes, *6:* **1237–45,** 1237 (ill.), 1245 (ill.)
build a model volcano experiment, *6:* 1240–42, 1240 (ill.), 1241 (ill.)
design an experiment for, *6:* 1244–45
eruptions of, *5:* 969–70, 970 (ill.), *6:* 1237, 1238–39
formation of, *6:* 1237–38
natural pollutants from, *1:* 48
seismographs for eruptions experiment, *6:* 1242–44, 1242 (ill.), 1243 (ill.), 1244 (ill.)
Volta, Alessandro, *2:* 334, 335 (ill.)
Volta Pile, *2:* 335 (ill.), 344
Voltage, *2:* 334
Voltmeters, *2:* 334, 337 (ill.)
construct a multicell battery experiment, *2:* 340–44, 341 (ill.), 342 (ill.)
electrolyte solution experiment, *2:* 335–40, 337 (ill.)
Volume
in density determination, *2:* 257
of fluids, *3:* 439
nanosize and properties experiment, *4:* 750–53, 752 (ill.)
surface area ratio, *4:* 748, 750–53, 752 (ill.)
Voluntary muscles, *1:* 115
Vortex, *6:* 1150–51, 1150 (ill.), 1155–58, 1157 (ill.)

W

Waals, Johannes Diderik van der, *1:* 20
Walking stick insect, *1:* 62
Warm air
convection current experiment, *1:* 39–42, 41 (ill.)
in storm formation, *6:* 1147–48
thermal inversion, *1:* 47, 47 (ill.)
warm air *vs.* cool air experiment, *1:* 36–39, 38 (ill.)
Warm climate, *5:* 1065

Warm fronts, *1:* 35, *6:* 1285
Washing soda, *4:* 835–38, 835 (ill.), 837 (ill.)
Waste, organic, *2:* 229, 230, 235–39, 236 (ill.), 238 (ill.), 239 (ill.)
Water
  adhesion and weight experiment, *6:* 1264–68, 1265 (ill.), 1266 (ill.)
  adhesion by, *6:* 1259–61
  cave formation, *1:* 127–29, 128 (ill.), 135–39, 137 (ill.)
  cohesion of, *6:* 1259–61, 1268 (ill.)
  comet composition experiment, *2:* 218–21, 220 (ill.)
  dead zones in, *2:* 271, 273
  design an experiment for, *6:* 1268–69
  drinking, *3:* 604, 605–9, 608 (ill.), 609–12, 610 (ill.)
  electricity conduction through, *2:* 333
  electrolyte solution experiment, *2:* 335–40, 337 (ill.), 338 (ill.), 339 (ill.)
  evaporation and surface area experiment, *6:* 1253–56, 1253 (ill.), 1254 (ill.), 1255 (ill.)
  evaporation of, *1:* 20–21, *6:* 1247
  in food spoilage, *3:* 478
  for germination, *3:* 565–66
  hard, *6:* 1226, 1231–34, 1232 (ill.)
  heat capacity experiment, *3:* 625–28, 626 (ill.), 627 (ill.), 628 (ill.)
  heat capacity of, *3:* 617
  heat convection experiment, *3:* 622–25, 623 (ill.), 624 (ill.)
  mineral oil, water and iodine experiment, *1:* 170–73, 170 (ill.), 171 (ill.), 172 (ill.)
  minerals in, *6:* 1225–26
  molecules of, *1:* 20, 21 (ill.), *4:* 747, 748 (ill.), *6:* 1259, 1259 (ill.)
  mystery powder identification experiment, *5:* 1009–13, 1011 (ill.), 1012 (ill.), 1013 (ill.)
  nanosize and properties experiment, *4:* 748, 752 (ill.)
  plant growth experiment, *1:* 9–12, 11 (ill.)
  plant water uptake experiment, *5:* 890–93, 892 (ill.), 893 (ill.)
  properties of, *3:* 440, *6:* 1259–70, 1259 (ill.), 1260 (ill.)
  relative density compared to, *2:* 258
  salt water osmosis experiment, *4:* 803–6, 803 (ill.), 804 (ill.), 805 (ill.)
  sandy, *4:* 723, 723 (ill.)
  from seawater, *4:* 724–25
  in soil, *5:* 1063, 1064 (ill.)
  solar heat storage experiment, *5:* 1090–92, 1092 (ill.), 1093
  solubility in, *5:* 1033
  solubility of elements experiment, *4:* 835–38, 835 (ill.), 837 (ill.)
  specific gravity of, *5:* 997–1000, 998 (ill.), 999 (ill.)
  surface tension cohesion experiment, *6:* 1261–64, 1261 (ill.), 1263 (ill.)
  surface tension of, *3:* 440 (ill.), 441, 448
  transpiration of, *5:* 885, 890, 892 (ill.), 893 (ill.), 898, 899
  tree growth experiment, *1:* 78–79
  van der Waals' force in, *1:* 20, 21 (ill.)
  water absorption by wood experiment, *6:* 1298–1302, 1300 (ill.), 1301 (ill.)
  water vortex experiment, *6:* 1155–58, 1157 (ill.)
  See also Water properties
Water bottle rocket experiment, *3:* 493–501, 495 (ill.), 498 (ill.), 499 (ill.), 500 (ill.)
Water clocks, *6:* 1177, 1177 (ill.), 1185–88, 1187 (ill.)
Water cycle, *5:* 955, *6:* **1247–58,** 1248 (ill.), 1249 (ill.)
  design an experiment for, *6:* 1256–57
  evaporation and surface area experiment, *6:* 1253–56, 1253 (ill.), 1254 (ill.), 1255 (ill.)
  evaporation and temperature experiment, *6:* 1248–53, 1250 (ill.), 1251 (ill.)
Water lilies, *3:* 427
Water plants
  dissolved oxygen levels for, *2:* 271, 273–74, 278–79
  eutrophication, *1:* 49–50, 50 (ill.), 55–58, 57 (ill.)
  photosynthesis by, *4:* 872–73
Water pollution, *1:* **45–60,** 46 (ill.)
  aquifer contamination experiment, *3:* 605–9, 608 (ill.)
  design an experiment for, *1:* 58–59
  dissolved oxygen level changes from, *2:* 272–73

eutrophication experiment, *1:* 55–58, 57 (ill.)
fish effected by, *1:* 50, *3:* 411
of groundwater aquifers, *3:* 604–5, 605 (ill.), 606 (ill.)
from nutrients, *1:* 49–50, 50 (ill.)
from oil, *1:* 48–49, 49 (ill.), 58
from pesticides, *1:* 49, *4:* 846–47, 847 (ill.)
prevention of, *1:* 50
water cleaning experiment, *3:* 609–12, 610 (ill.)
water movement of pesticides experiment, *4:* 851–55, 854 (ill.)
Water pressure, *4:* 772, 773 (ill.), *5:* 948–51, 948 (ill.), 949 (ill.), 950 (ill.)
Water properties, *6:* **1259–70,** 1259 (ill.), 1260 (ill.), 1268 (ill.)
adhesion and weight experiment, *6:* 1264–68, 1265 (ill.), 1266 (ill.)
design an experiment for, *6:* 1268–69
of Newtonian fluids, *3:* 440
surface tension cohesion experiment, *6:* 1261–64, 1261 (ill.), 1263 (ill.)
Water-soluble vitamins, *6:* 1224–25, 1224 (ill.)
Water supply, *3:* 602, 609–12, 610 (ill.), *4:* 771
Water vapor
burning fossil fuels experiment, *3:* 596–98, 596 (ill.), 597 (ill.)
in cloud formation, *6:* 1148, 1272
evaporation and temperature experiment, *6:* 1248–53, 1250 (ill.), 1251 (ill.)
greenhouse effect from, *3:* 590–91
temperature and cloud formation experiment, *6:* 1277–80, 1280 (ill.)
in thunderstorms, *6:* 1147–48
in the water cycle, *5:* 955, *6:* 1247
Water wheels, *5:* 948–51, 948 (ill.), 949 (ill.), 950 (ill.)
Waterfalls, *5:* 956
Watson, James D., *2:* 286–87, 287 (ill.)
Wavelength
electromagnetic waves, *2:* 349 (ill.), 350, 350 (ill.)
of light, *6:* 1112, 1112 (ill.)
ocean waves, *4:* 773, 774 (ill.)
string length and sound experiment, *5:* 1096–99, 1097 (ill.), 1098 (ill.)
Waves
electromagnetic, *2:* 203, 204–5, 204 (ill.), 350, 350 (ill.), *3:* 616–17
ocean, *4:* 773, 774 (ill.), 784
sound, *5:* 1095, 1095 (ill.)
Wax paper, *4:* 666–69, 666 (ill.), 667 (ill.)
Weapons, *2:* 391, 392 (ill.)
Weather, *6:* **1271–81,** 1273 (ill.), 1285 (ill.)
air masses in, *1:* 34–36, 35 (ill.)
air pressure and, *1:* 33–34, *6:* 1271, 1272 (ill.)
causes of, *1:* 33–36, *6:* 1271–72
convection current experiment, *1:* 39–42, 41 (ill.)
design an experiment for, *1:* 42–44, *6:* 1280–81
fronts, *1:* 34–35, *6:* 1285
measuring wind speed experiment, *6:* 1273–77, 1275 (ill.)
sun in, *6:* 1271, 1271 (ill.)
temperature and cloud formation experiment, *6:* 1277–80
thermal inversions in, *1:* 47, 47 (ill.)
warm air *vs.* cool air experiment, *1:* 36–39, 36 (ill.), 38 (ill.)
See also Storms
Weather forecasting, *6:* **1283–93,** 1283 (ill.), 1284 (ill.)
build a barometer experiment, *6:* 1289–92, 1290 (ill.), 1291 (ill.)
computers and, *6:* 1283, 1285
design an experiment for, *6:* 1292–93
dewpoint temperature experiment, *6:* 1286–89, 1287 (ill.), 1288 (ill.)
history of, *6:* 1283–84
Weather maps, *6:* 1285
Weather stations, *6:* 1283
Weather vanes, *6:* 1280 (ill.), 1284
Weathering
glacier erosion trench experiment, *5:* 957–60, 958 (ill.), 959 (ill.)
mountains, *4:* 737
in soil formation, *5:* 1063–65
Weaver ants, *1:* 62
Weaving, *2:* 399

Wedges, *5:* 1048
Wegner, Alfred, *6:* 1237–38, 1238 (ill.)
Weight
  atomic, *4:* 827–28
  crater shape experiment, *2:* 221–25, 224 (ill.)
  tape strength experiment, *4:* 688–91, 689 (ill.), 690 (ill.)
  water adhesion and weight experiment, *6:* 1264–68, 1265 (ill.), 1266 (ill.)
Weissenberg effect, *3:* 444–47, 446 (ill.), 447 (ill.)
Wells, *3:* 601, 604
Went, Fritz W., *6:* 1191–92, 1209
Wetlands, *3:* 604, 606 (ill.)
Whales, *3:* 402
Wheel and axle machines, *5:* 1051–55, 1051 (ill.), 1054 (ill.)
Wheelbarrows, *5:* 1051, 1051 (ill.)
Whirlpools, *6:* 1155
Whirly toys, *3:* 418–21, 418 (ill.), 419 (ill.), 420 (ill.)
White glue, *1:* 20, 22–25, 23 (ill.), 167–70, 168 (ill.), 169 (ill.)
White light, *2:* 203–5, 205 (ill.), *4:* 873–77, 875 (ill.), 876 (ill.)
WHO (World Health Organization), *2:* 390
Widow's peak, *3:* 556–59, 556 (ill.), 559 (ill.)
Wilting plants, *5:* 899, 900 (ill.)
Wind
  air pressure and, *1:* 33–34
  anemometers for, *6:* 1273 (ill.), 1283 (ill.)
  direction of, *6:* 1280 (ill.), 1284
  evaporation and, *6:* 1252–53
  measuring wind speed experiment, *6:* 1273–77, 1275 (ill.)
  for pollination, *3:* 425
  in storm formation, *6:* 1147
  transpiration rate and environment experiment, *5:* 904–7, 906 (ill.)
  in weather, *6:* 1271
Wind energy, *5:* 942, 942 (ill.), 944–48, 945 (ill.), 946 (ill.)
Wind turbines, *5:* 942
Windmills, *5:* 942
Wings
  airplane, *3:* 413, 414, 414 (ill.)
  insect, *3:* 632–33, 633 (ill.)
Winter season, *5:* 983, 984 (ill.)
Wolffia, *3:* 423
Wood, *6:* **1295–1307,** 1296 (ill.), 1297 (ill.)
  building properties experiment, *6:* 1302–6, 1304 (ill.), 1305 (ill.)
  density of, *6:* 1295
  design an experiment for, *6:* 1306–7
  elasticity of, *2:* 321
  glue adherence experiment, *1:* 22–25, 23 (ill.), 24 (ill.)
  grain, *6:* 1297, 1298 (ill.)
  for heat, *5:* 942
  heat conduction experiment, *3:* 618–22, 620 (ill.), 621 (ill.)
  petrifaction of, *3:* 523
  properties of, *6:* 1296–97
  types of, *6:* 1295
  water absorption experiment, *6:* 1298–1302, 1300 (ill.), 1301 (ill.)
  water adhesion and weight experiment, *6:* 1264–68, 1265 (ill.), 1266 (ill.)
Wood finishes, *6:* 1307
Wool, *3:* 509, *6:* 1139–44, 1141 (ill.), 1143 (ill.)
Work, definition of, *5:* 1047
World Health Organization (WHO), *2:* 390
Worms, tube, *4:* 775
Wright, Orville, *3:* 413–15, 415 (ill.)
Wright, Wilbur, *3:* 413–15, 415 (ill.)

X

Xanthophyll, *1:* 192, 201 (ill.), *4:* 872
Xerophytes, *1:* 105
Xylem, *1:* 71–72, *4:* 872, *5:* 884, 898

Y

Years, *6:* 1175, 1176 (ill.)
Yeast
  in bread making, *2:* 359, 360 (ill.), *3:* 464–65, 465 (ill.), 540, 544
  carbon dioxide from, *2:* 359, *3:* 540–41
  in food spoilage, *3:* 477–80, 478 (ill.)
  production of, *2:* 360, 362

reproduction, *1:* 143–44, 147–48, 147 (ill.), 148 (ill.), 149 (ill.), 150
temperature for yeast growth experiment, *3:* 544–49, 547 (ill.), 548 (ill.)
uses for, *3:* 540–41
yeast decomposition experiment, *3:* 541–43, 543 (ill.)
Yellow light, *4:* 873–77, 875 (ill.), 876 (ill.)
Yellowstone National Park, *1:* 88, 88 (ill.)
Yogurt, *1:* 101
Young, Thomas, *4:* 660

Zinc
chemical properties of, *1:* 165
construct a multicell battery experiment, *2:* 340–44, 341 (ill.), 342 (ill.)
electrons released by metals experiment, *4:* 838–40, 840 (ill.), 841 (ill.), 842
for nutrition, *6:* 1226
Zone of inhibition, *1:* 90–91